True Gospel Revealed anew by Jesus

Volume I

Fifth Edition

Received by: James E. Padgett

Original Editor: Dr. Leslie Stone

Current Editor: Geoff Cutler

Published July 2014.

True Gospel Revealed anew by Jesus

Volume I

No Copyright is claimed in this work.

This is the Fifth Edition: 2014

This volume was initially published in 1941 (First Edition) under two titles as "True Gospel Revealed again from Jesus" in paper-back and as "True Gospel Revealed anew from Jesus" in hard-back by Dr. Stone, and republished about 1950 (Second Edition) as "Messages from Jesus" and later in 1956 (Third Edition) by The Dr. Leslie R. Stone Foundation, Inc as "Messages from Jesus and Celestials" and again in 1958 (Fourth Edition) by the Foundation Church of the New Birth, Inc as both "Messages from Jesus and Celestials" and "True Gospel Revealed anew by Jesus."

It is believed that Victor Summers, acting as president, put all these messages into the public domain on December 25th 1984.

July 2014, Bayview, NSW, Australia.

Editor: Geoffrey John Cutler.

ISBN: 978-1-291-95866-9

Other Divine Love related publications
By Geoff Cutler.

A Gospel of Truth and Light to Mankind. Published November 2011. This is the full set of Padgett Messages arranged in date order. It contains the contents of the four volumes known as the *"True Gospel revealed anew by Jesus"*, Volumes I to IV. This is the most up to date of various similar publications, in that the most recent date research is as per this book. Available at Lulu only. A very large hard cover book (11 inch by 9 inch) of over 700 pages.

Judas of Kerioth. Conversations with Judas Iscariot. Published December 2012. This is a 600 page book (9 inch by 6 inch) of communications from Judas. It contains many previously unknown details about the life of Jesus of Nazareth. Available at Lulu and Amazon.

Is Reincarnation an Illusion? Published March 2011. 191 pages. This is an original work based on ten years research into the subject, and drawing on many sources in order to evaluate all the issues that lead people to believe that reincarnation is true. Available at Lulu and Amazon.

Getting the Hell out of here. What happens after you die? Published March 2011. This is a small book of 45 pages summarizing the fascinating details of life after death. It draws on many sources, but particularly the Padgett Messages and the Judas Messages. Available at Lulu.

Many of these have pdf or Kindle eBook versions available either free, or at a nominal cost. Check the new-birth.net web site for details.

Introduction to Volume I Fifth Edition

By Geoff Cutler

This was the very first volume produced by Dr. Leslie Stone and it was first published in 1941, eighteen years after the death of James Padgett in 1923. In publishing these messages initially the date of the message was ignored, but as the years rolled on and further Volumes and editions were produced, dates started to be attached to some messages. James Padgett maintained a diary that indicated who communicated and a short summary of their message. When this diary surfaced around the year 2000, efforts began to date each published message and those published on web sites could now be dated and indeed be indexed and read in date order.

In recent years a significant number of new publications have appeared, by various editors, many of them using the now freely available dates of the messages. As one of the people deeply involved in matching the often terse summary in the daily dairy, with these published messages, I am familiar with the benefit offered by reading the messages in the very sequence in which they were received. However I have also recently become aware of the difficulty in correctly absorbing this material, when one is required to read some 1250 communications to cover all the subjects fully.

The benefit of these original publications lay in the fact that messages were collated together on a topic particularly in Volumes I and II, and it is far easier for a reader to absorb these new spiritual concepts, particularly as one is able to read in sequence messages that may have been received years apart. In this edition dates have been added where known.

There are 19 messages in this volume which are repeated in later volumes. Every instance of a duplicate is slightly different, indicating it was re-transcribed from the original, and not duplicated deliberately. The number of duplicates may appear higher to the reader because every published instance is flagged, and hence each duplicate is flagged twice at some stage. I do feel that it is important to publish the most accurate of these repeated messages, on a word by word basis. This of course means that the resultant message that has been used is not exactly the same as any of the originals from which it was derived. In each case, a footnote to that effect has been included. As Dr. Stone himself used footnotes, each footnote is marked (Dr. S.) or (G.J.C.) to indicate which editor is responsible. The details of these duplicates are set out in some detail on my web site – www.new-birth.net.

While I respect the desire by the previous publisher (Fourth Edition) to never change a single comma in their publication, publishing standards have moved on considerably since that time. One simply no longer uses capitalization for emphasis, as an example. It is in the interests of readability that I have adopted modern standards of typography. Where a word has fallen into disuse, I have added its current equivalent in () brackets, rather than changing the word. I certainly have punctuated extensively, creating smaller sentences where in some cases the sentences were originally almost unreadable.

In the process of discovering the dates of the messages, it became apparent that Dr. Stone particularly, and to a lesser extent Rev. John Paul Gibson had concealed the names of many of James Padgett's legal acquaintances who came through as spirits in darkness. This was a very sensible approach at that time with living relatives who might well complain, but now that it is 100 years later it is more useful to see the spiritual progression of these individuals over time. Accordingly in every case where I have been able to discover the real name of the spirit, that has now been used. Similarly where additional detail regarding "preachers" was in the diary, this too has been added as background.

Just before completing this edition, James and Helen Padgett communicated their personal story, which fills in many of the previously unknown blanks, and ties together odd strands that had been discovered. I have added this story to this edition as a special introduction.

This content was first published in Kindle eBook format in August 2011.

Geoff Cutler. Bayview, NSW, Australia.
July 2014.

James Edward Padgett

JAMES E. PADGETT

True Gospel Revealed anew by Jesus

Mr. James Edward Padgett was born August 25th, 1852, in Washington D.C. and attended the Polytechnic Academy Institute at Newmarket, Virginia. In 1880 he was admitted to the bar in Washington, D.C., and thereafter he practiced law for 43 years until his death on March 17th, 1923.[1] During his student years, he became friendly with Professor Joseph Salyards, an instructor at the Academy who, after his death in 1885, wrote him many interesting messages. His wife, Helen, died on February 12th 1914, and was the first to write him from the spirit world. Padgett never practiced the gift of mediumship as a means of earning money. He was dedicated wholly to the reception of the great messages signed by Jesus and many of his disciples.

Just before completing this edition for publication, Al Fike who lives in Vancouver, was asked by both James and Helen Padgett if he would take down some details about their life. What follows is a wonderful gift to all of us on the 100th year anniversary of the beginning of this amazing spiritual journey. Some of the facts set out here have been uncovered by painstaking research, but the motivations behind many of these facts were simply unknown until this point.

James Padgett's story as shared 100 years later

July 17th, 2014
James Padgett Speaks
Medium: Al Fike

My friends and fellow travelers on the Divine Path, I send you greetings from our side of life and salutations towards your efforts to bring the truths of our beloved Father's Love to the wider world. Each and every one of you who are involved in this endeavor to either pray for this Love and go out to spread the good word of its existence is my beloved brother and sister. You continue to carry on the work started by myself and my colleagues all those years back. Indeed the work started with our Master Jesus and was altogether lost years later but now we, meaning the array of spirits aligned with you on earth and yourselves are witnessing a renaissance of sorts to bring once more these truths to mankind. We are working together to turn back the tide of darkness and ignorance that most of humanity has suffered under for so long. We begin a new era. A time when all peoples will be given a choice to follow the truths of God or continue on with their wrong doing and error. God has put His breath upon this work to facilitate many miraculous and effective outcomes in the years ahead which will turn the heads of even

---

[1] James Padgett has communicated a number of times since his passing, and these messages can be found on this web site: **new-birth.net**. (G.J.C)

the most skeptical individuals. You will all be a part of this work in time if you so choose. It is a Divine mandate that beckons each of you dear souls to come in alignment with this cause to bring to mankind the key to their salvation.

Many, many spirits and angels are praying for the success of our combined endeavors and you must feel the support proffered to you in your prayers and actions. And God's hand is upon us all guiding and blessing with every moment and breath. You are truly blessed my friends and for those willing to take that leap of faith, the rewards will be great indeed.

Many of you are curious about my life whilst on your earth. In many respects my history is similar to so many others. I lived in an exciting time in the development of our country of the United States of America. I too was caught up in the fervor of the time, which had great potential but endured the ravages of our civil war. Ours was a building time where a great country was emerging from the strife of war.

Many opportunities lay before all who wished to take up the tasks of formulating what was seen as a new and unique country built on high principles and a rich land base. The land was immense and needed populating, although my interest was not in being a pioneer and taming the land which was a popular romantic idea at the time. I was drawn to more academic ideals and prospects. I eventually settled to be a lawyer and worked towards those goals and a lawyer I became and was happy with my work.

I eventually married and Helen and I had our three children whom we both adored. I certainly married up as they say with Helen who was not only beautiful and full of life but also came from a respectable minister's family. The door was opened for me in my career as in those days these sorts of connections were important if one was to be successful. This is not to say that I married 'for money' as they say but I was very fortunate to have met my dear Helen. She was a great support to me and a beautiful mother.

We lived a somewhat prosperous life in Washington where I practiced, but my ambitions often got the better of me. I was a bit of a risk taker in the realm of finances and often gambled our money on dubious ventures, hence some days we were well off but the future was never secured. I wanted to prove myself to my family and Helen's family that I was a success and I certainly see now that this vain pursuit often got the better of me.

Because of our financial inconsistencies, we were often forced to change our residences and that was a great embarrassment to Helen. One day we were on top and the next we hit close to bottom - all because I was susceptible to the next scheme to become wealthy. I was, at heart, a gambler and this compulsion wreaked great havoc on my family and our marriage.

    I also worked a great deal in order to keep us afloat financially as it was very important to keep up appearances for both my career and our reputation around town. My lack of presence in the home did not please Helen very much as I was often either in the office or out with my lawyerly friends enjoying a drink and a smoke. Helen was always at heart a sweet soul who did not approve of my wicked ways. We often fought about my short comings and this was ongoing in our marriage. For the most part, we kept up appearances and sent our children to the best schools we could afford. We lived our lives putting more into appearances rather than building a relationship of love and harmony but we persisted as long as our children were at home.

    As you can see, I was no saint; just a man whose limited perspective and withered soul had no idea of spirituality other than that fed to me by the preachers of the day. My spiritual life was one of belief by rote and blind acceptance. I had no reference point beyond what I was told to be true and I was a believer in this regard but not as devout as my dear Helen. In reality, I was lost and getting more so by the day.

    In time, Helen gave up on me, she had her own problems brought on by ill health and this did not bode well for our mutual happiness as she struggled greatly with emphysema and spent ever more time with her family, especially when the boys left to start their own lives. I spent more and more time away from our home as did Helen with her health complications and the difficulties between us. Our marriage was for all intensive purposes over. We began living separate lives and eventually this compelled Helen to file for divorce.

    This certainly forced me to take account of the life I was living and I made several attempts to woo her back to me. The intense demands of my business coupled with increasing age and Helen's protracted illnesses detracted from my efforts which were not successful. When one is faced with the loss of something that is so much a blessing but unrecognized, the reality of losing this precious gift can be devastating.

    I did indeed grieve over her departure from our home but it was too late to fix this unfortunate turn of events. I became more lost and alone and consequently buried myself in my work and a social life with my long standing friends.

    You can imagine my grief and sense of guilt upon learning of my dear Helen's death in the sanatorium. I was beyond comfort and felt responsible for so much of the pain that she endured over the years of her illness and those unfortunate years of our marriage. My longing for her became intense and the grief at times unbearable. I did take comfort in my church life but that only went so far. Its message assured me that Helen would be in heaven but went no further to assuage my grief. My loneliness and longing for Helen, whom I seemed to love more intensely through her absence brought me to the practice of spiritualism which I had heard about since it was widely known but harbored a great deal of skepticism regarding its credibility.

Although skeptical, I proceeded to make my enquiries and attend a few séances. Each visit intrigued me but did not entirely convince my intellect that what I was hearing were indeed the voices of the departed. Yet, I persisted and came upon Mrs. Maltby who seemed to describe Helen with such detail and conveyed so many personal bits of information that I was almost entirely convinced. My lawyerly mind tried in vain to discredit this experience but in the end, my heart told me of its truthfulness.

I became a spiritualist at heart although I did not fully disclose this to friends and family. Spiritualism was considered an entertainment and did not have a high standing in society although many reputable people attended séances regularly. It remained my secret for most of my remaining days only shared amongst my confidants who were of like mind.

Mrs. Maltby explained to me that I too had a gift for spirit communication and that I should sit down with paper and pen. She instructed me on how to develop my gift and within time, I was communicating with my beloved Helen. We were together again so to speak but this time, I was paying more attention to what my dear wife had to tell me than I ever did while she was in the flesh. It seemed as if our love affair was started anew with my attentions focused on communicating with my dear departed wife.

My grief was completely assuaged by this unexpected turn of events. A new and intriguing door had opened up in my life. One that was somewhat peculiar but also warmed my heart to a glow not felt in years. I became smitten with dear Helen all over again. She was my source of comfort and her stories about her life over there kept me in rapt attention each night as I set my pencil upon the foolscap and involuntarily began to write all the while feeling her presence and love for me.

Eagerly I would separate the letters run together and incomprehensible until the words would emerge and the message be complete. At times, I thought myself an old fool being so caught up in this world that did not exist except for the run-on words that emerged from this unusual practice. My ambivalence only increased as I began to hear not only from Helen but from old friends since passed over and strangers curious as to what I was up to.

If it was not for the comfort I derived from this practice I would have given it up as a chimera of my own thoughts not worth my attentions and time. This wonderment continued for some time and gained ever more of my attentions. It became a well worn routine as comfortable as going to the office or sitting down for my supper. Its familiarity and its potency gradually worked away at my own skepticism until it became a part of normalcy and routine. I became a full fledged communicator with the dead and accepted my plight with a sense of purpose and competency.

At this point I brought in my friends, Dr Stone, Eugene Morgan and others who were sympathetic and encouraging towards my efforts. We became a cabal of sorts who were intent on sustaining the practice but did not altogether favor the idea of revealing these communications to the wider world.

My acceptance of my gift was challenged with an altogether new development introduced by Helen but startlingly preposterous in its scope. I was invited to be an instrument of communication by Jesus Christ and his apostles. I must admit that this invitation threw me for a loop. I was dumfounded and very skeptical that what was, in my mind, the true son of God and part of the Godhead would in any way have an interest in communicating through me. I not only felt unworthy but completely unqualified for the task.

My total confusion almost brought me to the point of throwing away my utensils and giving up this practice. For whom, but the devil, would tempt me with such nonsense. Helen begged me to persist and trust that Jesus is also a spirit although highly exalted but still humble and loving. She implored me to stay the course and try to comply with the wishes of the one who I both feared and adored.

Thus began another chapter in my life which was just as surprising if not unexpected as all the other experiences with the spirits. I complied with reluctance and suspicion but my love and trust in Helen carried me beyond these misgivings. I was initially not pleased or comforted by the first results of this contact. The words written were in my mind both heretical and controversial. My skepticism only increased as this purported Jesus continued to share his story and message that so challenged beliefs long held. I became so ill with confusion and regret that I burned the first attempts of communication. I could not believe these words that contradicted so much of my own Christian beliefs. Surely these things written were not true, just ravings from a deluded spirit.

Yet Helen and others including my beloved grandmother long passed on, insisted that what was being said was true and these words were from Jesus himself. My dilemma weighed so heavily upon me as I tried to sort through the facts of the situation as only a lawyer might do. I went over the teachings conveyed by this Jesus and confirmed by so many and reasoned with the information at hand. It eventually became apparent through much loving support and the reasoning's of my own mind that if I attempt to follow this new concept of Divine Love, I might know for myself whether it is of merit or not. I began to ask God for this gift, not altogether convinced that God had any intention of listening to my prayer. It took some time and a number of prayers which were encouraged greatly by the spirits communicating to me but eventually I began to feel the Grace that is so familiar to me now, my life forever changed by the touch of God's great Love.

In this change, I began to accept what the angels would come to say and bring into my mind. I began to gain faith in the sure knowledge that God loved me and that His great Love was available to me whenever I asked with sincerity. The terrible regrets of my past and loneliness began to fade and a new hope and faith emerged with God's increasing Love flowing within. I was on my way to being reborn in the Love and my passage was swift and sure with such angelic support.

I have been favored in so many ways because I overcame my fears and doubts and allowed these priceless truths to be written by my hand but most assuredly not by my being. I grew and learned as the words flowed and my understanding increased with each prayer and each word of truth conveyed in the passage of time.

Almost one hundred years have passed in the interim. The world has changed dramatically but the erroneous ways of man persist as so many have no time to venture within and go to God. I understand the struggles of coming to these truths as I have tried to convey through the example of my life what difficulties may ensue through this search. Yet without brave and dedicated souls such as you, the truth may once again become lost in the shuffle as many pursue the lure and pleasures of the material world. You are God's messengers on earth my brethren. I know that your struggles are every bit as difficult as was mine but in the end God's Love conquered all. He brought me to the glory of His loving embrace and He will surely do as much for you. Do not give up or be led astray. You have the truth firmly in your grasp and the world needs you my brothers and sisters and God will guide you to where you are meant to be. If He can rescue an old codger like myself and set me on the right course, then you should be easy pickings for His intended plans for you.

Thank you for hearing my story and although there are many more details, I believe that you have the gist of it here. You must see that every attempt to glean truth about the world and your place within it does not come readily or without its struggles but it will come with sincere prayer and effort. God's Love will bring all that you require to see your way through. You are His beloved children and cared for in the most intricate and beautiful ways. You are also my friends and colleagues engaged in this holy work that will, in time, bring salvation for all who venture here with faith and trust. I love you all dearly and thank you for being willing to read my words and to read the words of truth laid out in the volumes so lovingly prepared by those who followed in my footsteps. May God bless you in Love, peace and joy. I am your friend and humble servant…..James Padgett.

Helens story

July 18th, 2014
Helen Padgett
Medium: Al Fike

God bless you dear blessed souls of our Heavenly Father's Love and Care. I too greet you from my side of life and convey my good wishes to you all.

My dear Ned has conveyed to you much of the story that is relevant to your enquiries as to our lives together and how he came to be such a valued instrument to convey truth. So I will not belabor the story much further other than to tell you about my own perceptions of our lives.

I grew up very comfortably. My father, a minister, was a merchant who profited well even during the civil war. We had servants, not slaves, who were treated with respect and had their place in our family. My childhood was one that was far from the deprivation most suffered as a result of a country torn by war and strife. Indeed I was very sheltered and somewhat coddled in my formative years. I was well educated and brought up to be a lady. My disposition was sweet and very innocent. I saw the world through rosy colored glasses and was content to do so.

I had my coming out in my eighteenth year and felt like I was ready for marriage and imagined a grand life full of promise and elegance. I had my suitors but when I met James through mutual friends my heart was all a flutter. He was a handsome, tall man who carried himself well, if not a little too sure of himself. His eye fell upon me as well and a courtship began. Several months later, we were married. Ned was still articling and not altogether well off so we lived with my parents for a while until we got on our feet. My parents approved of Ned because of his confidence and prospects and they were happy about my choice in the beginning.

In time we settled down and raised our family. Ned was a bit of a dreamer and had grand plans of his own. His ability though to discern the right course to accomplish his goals was lacking. He also was quite stubborn and did not take to advice very well. My father tried to advise him on several occasions but Ned did not listen and insisted on his own course of actions. He was also very busy and in demand as he built his own law practice. He was a very good lawyer but unfortunately a poor business man.

I tried to support him as best I could and be his loving wife by his side but my patience along with my health began to wane as the years flowed by and our prospects became less certain. We did argue from time to time with many of my expectations not met in our marriage. My dream of a romantic life of leisure was never realized and I must admit to some bitterness. In time the distance did become so great between us that I felt it best to move away and live my own life with our daughter. We were at the time living in a hotel of not good standing and my patience was running thin and I left burdened with sadness and resentment.

We both grieved our losses but I had to move on for the sake of our daughter and for my own well being. These were difficult times which became more difficult as my health deteriorated. In those days, medications were limited and other than being offered laudanum for my breathing discomforts, the doctors could do very little to treat me effectively. I was forced to go to a sanatorium for rest and rejuvenation. My condition became worse and eventually I died.

My actual passing was not painful or traumatic. I went peacefully and awoke in the most wonderful place. I thought I was dreaming. I was in a hospital filled with light and lovely attendants. They treated me so well and what I thought was a dream seemed to not end. Eventually the true nature of my situation was revealed to me. My first reaction was a deep pang for my daughter and other family members whom I loved and who must be missing me. These anxieties soon abated and I began to adjust to my new life. I met with many dear relatives and friends who had gone before me and I was drawn to be with my dear Ned who was grieving so. His heart sickness kept me close for a long while as he tried in vain to let go of his losses.

I prayed for his relief and healing and in doing so, some lovely souls suggested that I could communicate to him via a medium on earth. They taught me how to impress my thoughts upon him so as to compel him to go and see the individual that they had in mind. Through my love and concern for him, I was able to get through enough into his mind in order to encourage him to seek out Mrs. Maltby, a delightful woman who dedicated her life to give comfort to grieving relatives. Our efforts were successful and most of you are well aware of the story of our continued love affair from beyond the grave.

We are exaltedly happy in our present place well above the seventh sphere. Our life together as soul mates bring us joy unimaginable and all our troubles from long past are now a distant memory. We are also engaged in our work, concentrating on God's great plan for the salvation of mankind. We derive great joy from this work and believe me when I say that vast numbers of angels are working in this way to bring truth to mankind. The earth is such a crucial place for the soul progression of each individual. Choices are made there which impact a soul's journey for a very long while.

For those of you who have made the choice for truth, it is your responsibility to keep this flame burning within and sharing your understandings with others always with love. We are eager to support you and often do bringing you our love and prayers and try to inspire you towards greater truths. Your choice to live in the light brings many rewards both seen and unseen. As Ned has told you, you are our brothers and sisters and part of our vast family of Divine Love followers, angels in the making. Together we will continue to work towards this goal of changing the world for the better and spreading God's Holy Truth and Love to every dark nook and cranny. Please know that our hearts and souls are dedicated to this work and we require you to be with us in dedication and commitment. Without your partnership with God's angels, our efforts are weakened and less effective.

You are needed more than ever because of the spiraling conditions which permeate your world today. We implore you to double your efforts to pray for God's Love and to live this truth in every way possible. You are God's angels on earth and are needed so deeply in order to fulfill God's plan. Please pray for your guidance in order to be in position to fulfill your purpose within this plan. You are greatly needed.

Please be with us in our efforts and we will truly be with you so that the struggles that we have talked about in our lives will not be present in yours. As you follow the laws of Love, your lives will reflect that in every way. May God bless all who venture upon His path of Love and may you all be well enfolded in His loving arms. I am your friend in Love and in life…….Helen.

Dr. Stone's Testimony

This testimony is the outgrowth of the many queries that have resulted from the publication of volumes I and II of the "Messages from Jesus and Celestials;"[2] which I first printed in 1940,[3] and which have thereafter gone through three editions. On the publication of this fourth edition[4] of volume I, I am integrating all those questions from interested readers into a new testimony, which will show how it was that Mr. Padgett was able to perform the work of receiving these remarkable messages. It tells how I met Mr. Padgett and my reasons for believing that he was actually able to receive messages, not merely from the spirit world, but from the greatest spirits of the Celestial Heavens, whose Master is Jesus of Nazareth.

I was born on November 10th, 1876, at Aldershot, Hampshire, England, the tenth of thirteen children. I attended the public school there and later completed courses at the Grammar School of Farnham, Surrey, founded by King Edward VI. Thereafter, I worked in the saddlery shop of my father, William Stone, at Aldershot, and later at London. When business slackened, I emigrated to Toronto, Canada, in 1903. On that occasion, my mother, who was a great believer in prayer, asked the Heavenly Father to let her know what His Will was. His answer was that I should go.

In Toronto, one day, I was attracted to a notice of a Spiritualist meeting. Never having attended one before, I was curious and went. The medium, who was giving messages from the platform, pointed to me and said: "Your father, who says he is William Stone, is here, and is glad that he is able to greet you." The medium then described my father, such as I had known him. He had never been to the New World and had died when I was seven years of age. Under the circumstances, this woman could hardly have been able to give this information without direct contact with the spirit of my father.

After this experience, I began to read many books on Spiritualism, such as Nature's Divine Revelation, by Andrew Jackson Davis, also The Great Harmonia by the same author. These books had a profound effect upon me, for the faith in the religious doctrines which my mother, a strong Baptist, had taught me could no longer interest me as the repositories of the Truths. I believed in the existence of a great

---

[2] Many different titles were used for this volume, and this is the title of the Third Edition. (G.J.C)
[3] Copies of the original publication state a date of publication as 1941, not 1940. (G.J.C)
[4] This was published in 1958. Dr. Stone passed into spirit at the age of 90, on the 15th January 1967. He has recently communicated from spirit. (G.J.C)

spirit world and in the communication of mortals and spirits. At the same time, however, Spiritualism, as it was being taught, did not, I confess, completely satisfy my soul longings. Not until I met Mr. James E. Padgett and read the messages which, I am thoroughly convinced, came from Jesus and the Celestial spirits, was I satisfied that at last I had really come to know the great religious Truths, and that I knew the way to the Father and at-onement with Him.

It took me eleven years after coming to the New World before I met Mr. Padgett. Spirit guides advised my going to Detroit. There, the production of automobiles was such that it was impossible to maintain myself in saddlery work and, again on spiritual advice, I moved to Buffalo. There, I worked and studied in a hospital for seven years and finally became a graduate nurse. This period of my life was, I feel, an important one in that it gave me that interest in healing which later induced me to study chiropractic.

In Buffalo, I continued to be interested in Spiritualism, and received another personal proof of spirit life. At one Spiritualist meeting, I was seated next to a woman who happened to be a medium. She suddenly turned to me and said, "Your mother is here with you." I replied, "You must be mistaken, Madam. I had a letter from my mother quite recently and she is in good health." The medium shrugged and replied, "Your mother never lived in this country. She tells me she lived in England and died a short time ago." She went on to report what my mother presumably had died of, described the funeral, and mentioned the names of those present. She told me that I had a sister Edith, from whom I would receive a letter confirming what she said. The letter arrived just as the woman had predicted, and corroborated her statements. If I ever had doubts then as to the truth of spirit communication, I lost them at that point.

As a matter of fact, I advanced in Spiritualism to the extent of going into trances, wherein I am convinced that I have been able to visit the spirit world. I know I have met my mother there, a sister Kate, and a brother Willie who had passed on in 1908. I knew I was in my spirit body and had left my mortal frame; and, indeed, I had no desire to return to it. But my mother and sister insisted that I had a spiritual work to accomplish in the earth plane, and that I could not come permanently into the spirit world until I had accomplished that task.

I could go on to relate many interesting and curious experiences which I was privileged to have in the spirit world, but this is not the occasion for it, and I shall proceed with the narrative. During my work in the hospital, I had become interested in chiropractic and, on the suggestions of spirits who communicated messages to me through mediums at Lily Dale, New York, I studied at the Palmer Gregory College of Chiropractic in Oklahoma City, and graduated in 1912 after a two year course. Shortly thereafter, I became a licensed practitioner in Washington, D.C. There comes to mind the name of a Mrs. Bartholomew, a trumpet medium, and a Mr. Pierre Keeler, a slate writing medium, whom I consulted while at Lily Dale. It was through this gentleman's brother that I was able to obtain a spirit photograph of my soulmate, Mary Kennedy. I shall refer to this in more detail later.

On graduating, I went to Philadelphia with a view to opening an office, but, on receiving messages from many of my relatives in the spirit world through a medium named Mrs. Bledsoe, I opened an office instead on the boardwalk of Atlantic City. I must say that I was successful and instrumental in restoring many patients to health. I remember distinctly a newsboy of about nine years of age whose name was George Hutton. He suffered from paralysis in the legs due to polio and used crutches to swing his legs. I offered to give this boy treatment without charge, to which his mother consented. The boy was able to walk again without use of his crutches in two treatments, and an osteopath and M.D., Dr. Walton, came to see me about it. "I saw the newsboy today walking without his crutches," he said, "and he told me you had treated him. I came to find out if it is so." Later, George came in and confirmed the healing. I have always felt that this instance of healing, as well as many others that I cannot mention here, was due to spiritual forces operating through me.

Although I was kept busy at my boardwalk practice during the summer months, autumn found business so slack, due to the closing of many hotels and departure of people, that I was compelled to find another location. Again I went to Philadelphia and consulted Mrs. Bledsoe who, through her spirit contacts, advised me to go to Washington, D.C.

I arrived there in November 1912, and opened an office on Fourteenth Street, N.W. There, I fortuitously met a gentleman with whom I had become acquainted at Lily Dale. His name was William Plummer, of Frederick, Maryland. He visited me at my office and told me he was interested in procuring a copy of "Was Abraham Lincoln a Spiritualist?" by Nettie Maynard Colburn. He wanted to find the owner of the copyright, for he wished to have the book reprinted. In his search, he had found the name of a Mr. Rollison Colburn of Takoma Park, but was informed that the latter was not related to the writer. The search, however, had not been entirely futile, for the Rollison Colburns proved to be interested in Spiritualism, and a common interest between them developed into a close friendship.

I became acquainted with the Colburns through Mr. Plummer. I found them very kind and lovable people who were greatly interested in psychic experiences. It was through their son, Arthur Colburn that I first heard of the messages that were being received by Mr. Padgett. I was introduced to him at his office in the Stewart Building, 6th and D Streets, N.W., where he was practicing law. This was in the early fall of 1914 when everyone was excited about the great conflict that had broken out in Europe. Some people felt the period ushering in the end of the world had come and that Jesus himself would appear at this "end time." For me, it was the end of my travels and spiritual search.

These "Messages from Jesus and Celestials,"[5] received through the hand of James E. Padgett, are so extraordinary in concept and contents (claiming as they do to bring to mankind the highest spiritual teachings of Jesus as an epoch-making revelation from the spirit world), that it is indispensable that, as the publisher and firm believer in the Truths contained in these messages, I give to interested readers and for future reference some firsthand information regarding the man through whom these messages were received, and how it was that he was enabled and selected to obtain these amazing communications.

At this point, I must state that I was very often in Mr. Padgett's room when he was receiving these writings, and that I am the eyewitness to the formation and development of Mr. Padgett as the medium par excellence through whom the Truths of the Heavenly Father and life in the spirit world have come to mankind.

My first contact with Mr. Padgett was in September 1914. I became interested in him at first because he seemed to be a fine gentleman and, what was also important to me, a genuine medium. We became friendly on the basis of Spiritualism and mediumship, and this became a bond which, in addition to our mutual respect and brotherly love for each other, which grew apace in the course of time, was never broken in this life until his death on March 17th, 1923. This bond, I am convinced, continues to exist between us—his soul encased in a spirit body and mine still in mortal trappings.

Mr. Padgett invited me to visit him regularly at his home at 514 E Street, N.W., Washington, D.C., where, in the course of time, I met Eugene Morgan and Dr. Goerger. Padgett told me that the messages he was receiving were from his wife, Helen, who had died early that year. She had written him many things about the spirit life she was living, describing her experiences at the time of her death, the sphere of her spiritual abode, and her love for her husband in the flesh who, she had then discovered, was her soulmate. I was thereafter very often present as he continued to receive these messages. They came in a rapid sweep of connected words that obviously gave no time for thought on the part of the writer, and, in fact, he often insisted that he had no clear idea of what his pencil was writing until he read the messages afterwards. It was in this way, then, that he received from 1914 to 1923 some twenty five

---

[5] This is simply one of many titles used. See second page of book for details. (G.J.C.)

hundred messages, many of them coming; I have not the slightest doubt, from those highest spirits whose signatures were testimony to the personalities they represented.

Interested as I had always been in Spiritualism, and in the possibility of man's communicating with departed spirits, I asked Mr. Padgett what the circumstances were leading to this mediumistic activity. The facts, as he related them to me, were as follows: About six months before I had met him, he had attended a séance held by a Mrs. Maltby in Washington, D.C. She informed him that he possessed the psychic power to obtain automatic writings from spirits, and challenged him to make the effort. He did so and found that his pencil moved automatically to produce what he called "fish hooks" and "hangers." When this had continued for a short time, he at length obtained a writing which he could make out as a message signed by his wife, Helen. It was a short, personal note which stated she was often present in spirit with him, and how glad she was to be able to write him in this way. At this point, Mr. Padgett did not believe the evidence of the writings that his dead wife had actually communicated with him. In fact, he wanted to know what proof could she offer, or was there, to show that a spirit was actually writing, and, if so, whether that spirit was actually Helen. The writing that followed provided incidents in their lives that could only have been known to both.

Padgett thought even this could be explained as material coming from his own mind, as well it might, except that the writings came too quickly for his mind to formulate thought, and the messages kept on insisting that it was not his mind but hers that was operating, with emphasis on her love for him and the happiness she could obtain by being with him.

With his interest in Spiritualism greatly aroused by these strange writings, and anxious to set his mind at rest, he began to read books on the subject. I remember his reading J. M. Peeble's Immortality, and his frequent attendance at séances. There, he was given to understand that spirits, if given the opportunity and under right conditions, can communicate with mortals, and that apparently, in his case, the writings he questioned came from his departed wife. He was advised to continue to take messages while learning more about the spirit world. Among those things he learned was that souls have their mates, and that spirit life, contrary to what is taught by orthodox religions, was one of constant progress through the various realms of the spirit universe.

At the end of one of these writings, he asked what plane or sphere she was in. He received the answer that she was living in one of the planes of the Second Sphere, where a certain amount of light and happiness is present, but that she had no desire to make progress to other spheres, because she could at that time make contact quite easily with him on the earth plane and write to him by controlling his brain and hand. Padgett told me he could feel her presence intensely, which produced in him a feeling of happiness that was alien to him, except when she wrote.

Padgett confided to me that he would like to see Helen progress and told her so. He informed her that, through his own spiritual studies, he knew she could make her way to higher spheres and increased happiness as a spirit. Helen replied she would find out from his grandmother, Ann Rollins, who had been a long time in the spirit world, what steps were necessary to make progress to higher and brighter spheres.

I do not know why Helen turned to her husband's grandmother for guidance in the spirit world. Many of Mr. Padgett's early messages were destroyed because they were of such a personal nature that he did not wish others to be acquainted with their contents. But I do know that affinity of spirits in the other world is due to affinity of the soul and not to any relationship one may have in the flesh. And from what Mr. Padgett told me of his grandmother and from the messages which she subsequently wrote (some of which I have inserted in these volumes), she must have been a very kind and warmhearted woman. At any rate, Helen later wrote about her meeting with Ann Rollins who, she said, was a glorious spirit dwelling in the high Celestial Heavens. Ann Rollins, surprisingly enough for Padgett and those of us who were present at the time, had informed her that spirit progress to the higher Celestial Realms could be obtained only by prayer to the Heavenly Father for His Love through earnest longing of soul. In addition, Padgett's mother, Ann R. Padgett, also in the spirit world, wrote through her son corroborating this information. Both spirits were thus instrumental in giving Padgett (and those like myself who used to be present at these writings) the knowledge that soul progress to the Celestial Heavens was achieved only through prayer to God for His Divine Love.

These sessions, held to obtain writings from Helen, had become a channel through which a deep, religious note had been injected, replacing the personal material. From the scores of messages from Helen written at this time, and which are in my possession, we can follow her rapid progress to the higher spheres. Helen took the advice of these high spirits and prayed, and she found her prayers for the Father's Love were answered, and that It came into her soul in a way that caused a purification of her desires and thoughts, with a corresponding change in her soul and spiritual appearance. She said that her spirit body, reflecting the changing condition of her soul, was becoming etherealized and brighter. She then wrote that she had reached the Third Sphere where happiness was greatly increased.

Shortly thereafter, she suggested that since she had done what

Padgett had wished, and had been able to progress to a higher sphere, it was fitting that Padgett should seek to better his soul condition as well. In fact, she suggested that we should all do so. She stated that, since the soul is the same, whether in the flesh or spirit body, it could be transformed by prayer to the Father for His Divine Love—not by ordinary intellectual prayers that came from the head, but from the heart and soul. Padgett refused to lend credence to this information. The spirits insisted that, as inhabitants of the higher realms, they possessed knowledge of this sacred Truth, and that Jesus, himself, ever interested in bringing the Truths to mankind, would come to corroborate their affirmations if Padgett would give him the opportunity.

I do not know exactly when the first message signed "Jesus of the Bible" was received, for as I write this, more than forty years later, I cannot remember the date. Padgett evidently felt it was absurd to believe that Jesus had written him and, alas, threw away the message. As a matter of fact, Mr. Colburn, who up to that time had formed a part of our fellowship, declared he could not be persuaded that Jesus had actually written. However, his friends, Dr. Goerger, Mr. Morgan, and I had an instinctive feeling that Jesus had written a genuine message. The earliest message allegedly from Jesus to Padgett which is in my possession, therefore, is dated September 28th, 1914, and refers to an earlier message written a few days before. It is a long message, urging Padgett to pray for the Father's Love, and stating that certain passages in the New Testament, thoroughly believed in by Padgett, were false. The Master went on to say that he was neither God, nor had he been conceived by the Holy Spirit in the way taught by the preachers of the churches. Further, that "...Neither is God Spirit only; a Spirit of Mind. He is a Spirit of everything that belongs to His Being. He is not only Mind, but Heart, Soul, and Love." The message urged Padgett: "...Go to your Father for His Help. Go in prayer, firmly believing, and you will soon feel His Love in your heart."

Padgett was doubtful. Though he was not entirely certain of the genuineness of the family spirits, he felt the need of asking whether Jesus had really written. In volume II, I have published some of the messages which he received from Helen, Ann Rollins, his mother, and his father, John Padgett, all corroborating that Jesus had written. You will also find in this volume II some of the early messages which he received from the Master. They tell Padgett to have faith that he is Jesus, and they encourage him to pray; but they are simply preparatory in nature and do not contain the wonderful contents and information which came when Padgett had achieved that condition of soul which enabled him to obtain them.

At this point, it came forcibly to Mr. Padgett and to me that such messages could not possibly be the brainchild of his own heated imagination. He had been, as I discovered, an orthodox Methodist, and had for many years taught Sunday School in the Trinity Methodist Church (5th Street and Seward Place, N.E.) in Washington, D.C. His conception of religious doctrine was simply that which emanated from this Protestant church. This view of soul progress was contrary to what he had been taught. He had no idea of Divine Love in contrast to the natural love, or what it might be, and realized that such a conception was foreign to his thinking and never could have been a product of his own mind. He therefore felt assured, and I agreed with him, that these writings were actually not only from Helen, Ann Rollins, his mother and departed spirits of mortals, but also from the Master, himself. He decided to follow those instructions which he himself had never entertained, and which by that very fact had to come from outside intelligences which were communicating to him in this way.

He—I should say, we—began to pray for the Divine Love, letting our soul longings go out to the Heavenly Father; and, in time, a feeling came glowing into the region of our hearts. We felt this emotion grow stronger and stronger with continued, fervid prayers; and, as we did so, our faith in God became solidified and absolute. Never before had Padgett, nor I, felt so sure of the real existence of the Father and His Divine Love and Mercy. The cold, intellectual concept which we had entertained of Him had been transformed, through prayers for His Love, into a warm, glowing, living feeling of closeness, of at-onement with the Heavenly Father, Whose Love and Mercy and Goodness we could sense were personal and real.

The change in Padgett's attitude towards the Heavenly Father, through the inflowing of His Love, motivated a message from Ann Rollins. It recognized the effect which this Divine Love was having upon his soul, which was now a receptacle for some Essence of the Father's Divine Nature. It also reported on Helen's progress to higher spheres. Helen, she said in her message, was now a much happier spirit, and her spirit body shone with a radiance produced by the Father's Love in her soul.

Message followed message now from Helen, Ann Rollins, and, above all, from Jesus, encouraging Padgett to keep on praying and to obtain increased portions of the Father's Love. As a medium, he might be used to transmit messages from the highest Celestial spirits. At length, Jesus himself wrote that, since Padgett had the ability to receive writings from spirits, should Padgett's brain be sufficiently transformed through soul development by obtaining more of the Divine Love to a degree where he could receive high quality messages, he and his apostles would come and write through him the Truths of the Father, of his mission on earth, and on the New Testament and Christianity! Only pray, and pray harder for the Father's Love, urged the messages.

The Master wrote on October 5th, 1914, stating that he had

chosen Padgett to do his work of disseminating the Father's Truths to mankind. I quote the last part:

> ...*Go to the Lord in prayer and He will remove from your soul all that tends to defile it and make it alien from Him. He is the One that will cleanse it from sin and error.*
>
> *Only the teachings that I shall give you will tell the Verities of my Father. Let not your heart be troubled or cast down, for I am with you always and I will help you in every time of need. Only believe that I am Jesus of the Scriptures and that you will not be long out of the Kingdom. You are my chosen one on earth to proclaim my glad tidings of life and love. Be true to yourself and to your God and He will bless you abundantly. Keep His Commandments and you will be very happy, and you will soon receive the contentment that He gives to His true children. Go to Him in all your troubles and you will find rest and peace. You will soon be in condition to let the things of this world alone, as I need you for my service.*
>
> *With all my love and blessings, and those of the Holy Spirit, I am, Jesus.*

Padgett was eventually convinced that he was being developed for a task of mediumship whereby great messages of religious Truths would be given to mankind through him. He prayed earnestly and frequently and, for the next three months, not only did Jesus write but also many of the apostles, especially John and James, who kept telling him to keep praying for the Father's Love, but that the time had not yet come for the delivery of the great messages. Padgett's brain, while being changed in quality, had not yet reached that high quality which would permit the passage of communications of the kind they proposed. They continually urged him to seek for more of the Father's Love through prayer to Him. Many times when I met him in his room, he would say to me:

"Doctor, I feel the Divine Love in my soul in such intensity that I don't think I can stand it anymore." He would say this experience was always his when he had been praying for the Father's Love prior to obtaining messages from Jesus and the Celestial spirits. And I can in all sincerity state, if only for the purpose of corroborating his experiences, that these feelings were mine as well, if perhaps to a smaller degree.

While receiving these preparatory messages, it occurred to Padgett to ask how it was that Jesus had selected him to do this work, and what power, specifically, was there in the Divine Love which would enable him to succeed. Inevitably, there came the reply—in fact, one from John, the Apostle, and another from Jesus. John's message deals with the Laws of Rapport in the spirit world which enable spirits and mortals to communicate, and the workings whereby the brain of the mortal is conditioned to receive various types of messages: intellectual, moral, and soul. It is a message of great importance to those who may be interested in developing mediumship or furthering their mediumistic powers. But Jesus' reply is more direct. The message is printed in volume I, and so may be read in its entirety. But to summarize briefly here, Jesus wrote that two things are necessary for a genuine medium to receive the messages of the Father's Truths, which were to be given shortly. First, the medium had to have thorough faith that the spirits of the Celestial Heavens, inhabitants of God's Kingdom in Immortality, were actual beings who could, if the medium achieved a certain condition of soul, actually control his brain and write through him. If the medium did not have this faith in his heart, then no contact could be made by the Celestial spirits with him. Secondly, the medium must be willing to submit to the conditions imposed by the spirits: He had to obey the instructions of the spirits and pray to the Father for His Divine Love; for it was this Love alone that had the power to transform the brain of the medium so that it could be attuned to the thoughts of the spirits. And this transformation of the brain could be achieved only through the development of his soul. By prayer, said Jesus, the Father's Love inflowing into the soul transforms the soul from the image of God (with which man was created) into the Essence of God, so that sin and error in the human soul could not exist. And the brain of the mortal, thus purified of material thoughts and manifesting in his thoughts the condition of his transformed soul, could attain that condition which corresponded to the soul condition of the spirits; and it was in that way that he could grasp their thoughts.

That was the importance of the Divine Love. Padgett, in short, had to attain, through prayer to the Father, a soul condition approaching to a degree that of the Celestial spirits in order for his brain to receive their messages. Prayer had to be constant, for, otherwise, renewed earth plane and material thoughts would naturally reimpose their dominance, and the Love and the high soul condition would become inactive. Thus, said Jesus, Padgett had not been selected because of any particular goodness or freedom from sin, as compared to other mortals, for there were many who were in better, and in a higher, spiritual condition than he was, but because of his faith that Jesus could come, and his willingness to obey the spirits and pray for the Divine Love for a transformation of his soul so that the conditions for receiving these messages could be met.

Furthermore, declared Jesus, he had tried for many centuries in the past to thus write his messages, and he had found many mediums who were far better gifted than was Padgett. But because they thought Jesus was God, or because they thought it was impossible for Jesus to write, or because of their religious beliefs and dogmas, they had refused to submit to the promptings of the spirits. And since man is endowed by his Creator with a free will, Jesus and the Celestial spirits could not coerce them into submitting to a task to which they were opposed and in whose efficacy they had no conviction. For these reasons, Jesus stated, no other could be chosen except Padgett.

Mr. Padgett was now thoroughly convinced that what he was receiving was not only from the Celestial spirits but also from the Master, himself. I think it is interesting to point out that he not only confided his beliefs to his friends, like myself, Eugene Morgan, and Dr. Goerger, but also wrote boldly about them. I have in my possession a copy of a letter he wrote to a Dr. George H. Gilbert, Ph.D., D.D., who had published an article on religion entitled "Christianizing the Bible," in the November 1915 issue of Biblical World. This article, which I have read, advocated less emphasis on the Old Testament and its emphasis on a stern and punishing Jehovah, and more attention to the teachings of the New Testament and the sayings of Jesus. There was no suggestion of the Divine Love in Dr. Gilbert's article, which anyone who procures a copy from the Library of Congress (or any other library which contains it) can very readily discover.

Mr. Padgett's letter explains how, for quite a time, he refused to believe the contents or origin of the handwriting (for, with his legalistic turn of mind, he would accept only the most concrete evidence as proof), but that he was finally and thoroughly convinced of the Truths of the Messages and the source from which they came. Here it is:

December 28th, 1915

Dr. George H. Gilbert, Ph.D., D.D.,
Dorset, Vermont.

Dear Sir:
I hope that you will pardon me for writing you as I herein shall, for your evident voluntary interest in a certain subject matter, and my involuntary interest in the same, furnish the only excuse. I have read your article, "Christianizing the Bible," in the November issue of the Biblical World and am much impressed with the same, not only because of its inherent merits but also because its demands and suggestions are very similar to those which have been made through me in a way and manner which I can scarcely expect you to give credence to; nevertheless, I shall submit the matter to you, recognizing your right to consider what it may say unworthy of your serious attention.

First, permit me to state that I am a practical lawyer of 35 years experience and, as such, not inclined to accept allegations of fact as true without evidencing proof. I was born and reared in an orthodox Protestant church and, until quite recently, remained orthodox in my beliefs; that a little more than a year ago, upon the suggestion being made to me that I was a psychic, I commenced to receive messages by way of automatic writing from what was said to be the spirit world. And, since that time, I have received nearly 1500 such messages upon many subjects, but mostly as to things of a spiritual and religious nature, not orthodox, as to the errancy of the Bible.

I have not space to name, nor would you probably be interested in, the great number of the writers of these messages; but among the writers is Jesus of Nazareth, from whom I have received more than 100 messages. I will frankly say that I refused to believe for a long time that these messages came from Jesus because, God, while He had the power, as I believed, would not engage in doing such a thing. But the evidence of the truth of the origin of these messages became so convincing, not only from the great number and positiveness of the witnesses but also from the inherent and unusual merits of the contents of the messages, that I was forced to believe; and I now say to you that I believe in the truth of these communications with as little doubt as I ever believed in the truth of a fact established by the most positive evidence in court. I wish further to say that, to my own consciousness, I did no thinking in writing the messages. I did not know what was to be written nor what was written at the time except the word that the pencil was writing.

The great object of these messages from Jesus, as he wrote, is to make a revelation of the Truths of his Father. He asserts that the Bible does not contain his real teachings as he disclosed them while on earth; that many things that he said are not therein contained, and many things that are ascribed to him therein he did not say at all. And he wants the Truths made known to mankind. And I must say that many of these Truths, which he has already written, I have never heard of before, and I have studied the Bible to some extent. One thing in particular impressed me, and that is what the truth is of his bringing "life and immortality to light." The Bible does not state it, and I have not been able to find an explanation of it in any commentaries on the Bible. But enough of this. I merely wrote this to assure you that I am serious in submitting the enclosed copy of a message for your perusal; and I would not do this were it not for the fact that the message comments upon your article and also upon another article in the same issue of the Biblical World.

On the night of December 24th, 1915, I read your article and, on the next night, Christmas night, I received a writing of which the enclosed is a copy. You will observe that a portion of the message is personal, but I thought it best to send it as it came to me. And though you may not believe the origin of the message, yet, you may find some thoughts therein for your consideration.

Trusting that you will pardon my intrusion, I will subscribe myself,

Very respectfully,
James E. Padgett.

A few nights later, a message signed "Jesus" commented upon Padgett's having sent a copy of the message, and referred to his letter to Dr. Gilbert:

December 28th, 1915

I am here, Jesus.

I came tonight to tell you that you did the right thing by sending the message to the person who wrote the article upon the subject of Christianizing the Bible, for I now believe that he will appreciate it to a very great degree. He is not an orthodox churchman, but is the preacher of a Unitarian church in the little town in which he lives, and is a very broad-minded man.

He may have some doubts as to the source of the message and may not feel inclined to accept, as true, your statements as to how you received it, but yet his doubts will not be altogether of such a nature that he may not have some hesitation in saying that such a thing as your receiving my message could not be true. At any rate, he will become interested in the subject matter of the message and will find some thoughts that he never before had.

I fully realize that, when my messages are published, the great difficulty in their being accepted will be the doubt of the people as to their source. But you will have to complete the book in such a way that the testimony of the numerous witnesses will be so strong that the doubt will not be able to withstand the overwhelming evidence of my being the writer of the messages. And when men read the same, they will realize that the Truths which they contain could only come from a higher source than mortal mind, and that the Hand of the Father is in them.

So, I will continue to write and you to receive the messages; and when the time comes to publish them, I do not fear that they will not be, in time, gladly received. Very soon, I will write you another which will be of importance to mankind. I will only say further that I am with you trying to help you and to have you believe with all your heart in the Divine Love of the Father, in my mission, and in your work. Your brother and friend, Jesus.

By this time, of course, my original ideas about Spiritualism had undergone a radical transformation. In the light of the messages, Spiritualism could no longer simply be an effort to prove to one's satisfaction, through séances repeating the same process and ritual, that man did survive death and that his spirit, though devoid of his fleshly frame, could appear from his spiritual habitat and give evidence of his post-mortal existence. Both Padgett and myself now saw in Spiritualism not merely belief in life after death and conviction in communication between mortal and spirit, but in a great universe of spirits seeking progress towards light and happiness through purification of their souls, and the possibility of transformation of these souls through prayer to the Heavenly Father for His Love. Gone was my belief in vibrations, abstract intelligence, cosmic force, astral bodies and other paraphernalia of a bare and cold concept; and real Spiritualism took its well merited place as part and parcel of that sublime religion which affirmed that souls were alive, with or without the flesh, and that these souls could be changed from the image of God, as originally created, into the very Essence and Nature of God through His Divine Love. I did not have to look further. My search for God had ended. I had found God through the messages from Jesus and his Celestial spirits.

On this subject, a message signed by St. Luke was received December 5th, 1915, in which it was pointed out how limited and sterile Spiritualism was, unless life was breathed into it through faith in the Heavenly Father and prayer to Him for His Divine Love and Mercy. At the time of the first printing, I refrained from inserting St. Luke's message for fear of wounding the susceptibilities of Spiritualists, for it was to them that I first turned for the initial distribution of the messages. On this fourth reprinting, however, I have inserted the complete message, for its unmistakable stamp of authenticity will appeal to those many Spiritualists who have now combined its truths with the Master's teachings of the New Birth.

Before concluding, I want to write about my soulmate, Mary Kennedy, and about some new messages through Padgett which I am inserting in volume I. These messages include three from Jesus, the one from St. Luke just mentioned, another from a member of the Sanhedrin which condemned Jesus at his trial, one from Helen and two from Mary. I am also adding photographs of Mary as she materialized in the studio of Mr. William Keeler, brother of Pierre Keeler, who, I have said, was a slate writing medium I had met at Lily Dale. The Pictures were taken in Washington, D.C., in February 1920, where I sat; and in one she appeared poised and calm, with certain spirit lights about her head and partly across my body. Such illumination blotted out the black tie I was wearing at the time. Yes, my Mary is a glorious, living spirit of the Celestial Heavens. I have had many writings from her through Mr. Padgett, and more recently through an associate of mine. I hope you will enjoy the messages from her.

The additional messages from Jesus include one received December 25th, 1914, just prior to the writing of the great formal writings. Another, dated December 15th, 1915, states that, because of the Love which I had obtained and my desire to help further the Father's Truths, I had been selected by Jesus to do a work for the Kingdom. This eventually turned out to be the work of publishing the Padgett messages. I have since devoted my entire life to them and to furthering the Master's task of disseminating the Truths to mankind. I feel that I have made a beginning in my lifetime, and that the work will be continued by my associates and friends everywhere.

Dr. Leslie R. Stone

The True Mission of Jesus

I. Jesus and his Relationship to God

Whatever one may believe regarding the source of the True Gospel Revealed anew by Jesus, the contents are so new and revolutionary, yet so compelling by their logic and sublime simplicity, that a serious study of them must be undertaken in order to comprehend their significance and challenge.

In these messages Jesus of Nazareth stands forth as the Master of what he calls the Celestial Heavens, wherein only those spirits possessed of the New Birth through prayer to the Father for His Divine Love can dwell in light and happiness, and conscious of their immortality through their at-onement with Him in soul nature.

If these messages are authentic as coming from Jesus and his celestial spirits, then mankind has at last been given the true mission which Jesus proclaimed on earth. This mission taught the transformation of man's soul from the image of God—the work of the original creation—into the very essence of God through the bestowal of the Father's Love upon whomsoever should seek that Love in earnest longing. It revealed that Jesus himself first manifested the Father's Love in his soul, thus making him at one with the Father in nature and giving him that clear consciousness of his kinship with the Father and his immortality of soul. It showed that in this development of soul Jesus was indeed his Father's true Son, not in the metaphysical and mysterious way of a hypothetical virgin birth, but through the Holy Spirit, that agency of the Father which conveys His Love into the souls of His creatures who seek it in earnest prayer. It brings to light that Jesus was born of Mary and Joseph, of human parents like other human beings, but that he was none the less the Messiah promised to the Hebrews and to mankind in the Old Testament. For wherever he taught the "glad tidings" that God's Love was available, and that it was this Love which bestowed immortality upon the soul filled with this Love, Jesus brought with him the nature of God—the Kingdom of God. At the same time Jesus tells us that neither was he God, nor was his mother Mary the mother of God, nor a virgin after her marriage to Joseph, but that she was in truth the mother of eight children, of which he was the eldest, and that he had four brothers and three sisters in the flesh, and not cousins, as some versions of the Bible relate.

In addition, he relates that he did not come to die on a cross, nor did, or does, his shed blood bring remission of sins. He also shatters the time honored statements now found in the New Testament that he ever instituted a bread and wine sacrament on the eve of his arrest at the Last Supper. This pious statement, he declares, was never his, nor did any of his apostles or disciples ever teach it, but was inserted about a century later so that such a doctrine might accord with the ideas then prevalent among the Greek converts to Christianity. Communion with the Heavenly Father can never take place through the mistaken notion that he had to be impaled on a cross by Roman soldiers, on the order of Pilate, the Procurator of Judaea, and in accord with the uncomprehending high priests, so that he could appear as a sacrifice for sin. There is no sacrifice for sin, affirms Jesus, and his dried up blood cannot do what only man himself must do, by turning in repentance and prayer to the Heavenly Father, to effect that change in his heart whereby his soul will give up evil and sin, and embrace what is righteous. The Father's help in the elimination of sin from the human soul is His Divine Love which, on entering the soul through prayer, removes sin and error from that soul and provides not only purification but its transformation into a divine soul, at-one with the Father's great soul in nature. This real communion, which Jesus himself had achieved, is, he declares, the only communion between God and His children, which He has provided for their salvation and eternal life with Him. The vicarious atonement, Jesus states, is a myth, and its appearance in the New Testament is one of many false statements inserted therein to make it harmonize with later concepts concerning his relationship to the Father, which these later Greek and Roman copyists did not understand. It is a terrible thing to believe that God, in order to bring about His Son's sacrifice, approved the unlawful arrest of Jesus on the Passover, the bloody scourges, the treachery of Judas, the palpably unfair trial by high priests and Sanhedrinites, as well as Pilate's fear of Judean revolt against Roman rule, to encompass the inhuman death of Jesus, His Messiah, on a cross. As though God needed to bring about through wickedness and sin the very wickedness and sin He seeks to blot out in His children.

In the light of these messages, a new interpretation of Jesus' death on the cross is certainly in order. We are told by the orthodox churches that Jesus gave himself up willingly as a sacrifice for sin because he loved humanity to the degree of self sacrifice, and because as the Messiah he had come for that purpose. He is supposed to take the place of the Hebrew sacrifice, the lamb, and he is called in the New Testament the Lamb of God. As a matter of fact, the Old Testament sacrifice of an animal was never intended to take away sin, and this is shown by the fact that although these sacrifices were not permitted during the Babylonian captivity, the people still put their faith in redemption through turning away from sin and seeking God through a life of moral and ethical conduct.

Jesus did sacrifice himself, indeed, but in a way never related or understood by the writers of the New Testament. Jesus went to his death because he would not deny his mission: that, as the first human to attain through prayer an immortal soul filled with the essence of the Father—the Divine Love—he was in this way the first true son of God and therefore the Messiah. Jesus could have saved his life if he had retracted at his trial, but he died because he remained true to himself, true to his Messiahship, and true to the Father who had sent him. Jesus sacrificed his whole life preaching the Father's Love: he gave up home, his chance to marry and have a family of his own, a chance to devote himself to the quiet pursuits of a Nazarene carpenter; instead, he chose the hatred and opposition of those who understood not and preferred the status quo; he chose the incomprehension of his loved ones, who considered him mad and sought to have him leave Galilee; he chose constant travels and journeys, so that often he had no place to lay his head; he chose to preach in the Temple at Jerusalem, chase the money lenders, defy the conspiracy of those who sought his death, and bravely faced the consequences of what he knew must inevitably occur. Yes, Jesus did sacrifice himself, but it is high time to put aside myth and metaphysics, and to know and to realize what that sacrifice consists of. When we understand his sacrifice, then Jesus stands forth in all his greatness, in all his courage, in all his serenity and forgiveness and love for mankind, with his absolute faith in the Father and His Love, in that day of his teaching, tribulation, and death.

Jesus tells us many things about himself and his life in the Holy Land. He states that the Bible story of his birth, minus the many supernatural elements in it, is substantially true, and that he was born in Bethlehem, taken by his parents to Egypt to avoid destruction by Herod, that the Wise Men did come from the East to pay him homage and that he was taught the elements of the Hebrew faith from teachers; but that it was the Father Himself who taught him the truth of the Divine Love and made him realize what his mission was. He tells us that John the Baptist, his cousin, was a great psychic and had some understanding of him as the Messiah and that both planned the Master's public ministry. He states that John never sent emissaries when in prison to be reassured that Jesus was "him whom we seek," and that Jesus as a boy of twelve never appeared before the doctors of the Law in the Temple at Jerusalem.

Jesus also tells about some of the miracles which he performed. Most of these, he explains, dealt with his healing power; but that he never raised Lazarus or anyone else from the dead, nor has anyone else been able to do so, regardless of what the Scriptures say, for the spirit body cannot return to the flesh once the physical conditions of life have been destroyed. He also relates that he never quieted a storm by rebuking the waves on the Sea of Galilee, but that he did calm the fears of the disciples with him through his example of courage and assurance.

Some of the greatest messages which, to my mind, Jesus and some of the high spirits write are those connected with the Master's resurrection from the dead after his crucifixion. Jesus informs Mr. Padgett that he did die on the cross and that he did appear to Peter, John, Mary Magdalene and his mother on the third day, but that the true explanation of this occurrence is quite different from the accepted views of the churches. Here, Jesus is supposed to reveal his divinity by arising from the dead; but actually, Jesus' soul never died, as no man's soul dies with physical death, and the Master goes on to state that, with the power inherent in his soul with the Divine Love, he simply dematerialized his mortal frame, announced in the Spirit World the availability of Immortality to mortals and spirits through the Father's Love which he was the first to manifest, and then on the third day materialized a body like flesh and blood drawn from the elements of the universe; and that it was in this materialized body, which he was able to assume without mediumistic aid, that he appeared to Mary Magdalene and the others. It is the reason, he states, why Mary did not at first recognize him and thought him to be the gardener and the same may be said of his disciples at Emmaus. The great misconception of Christians of all ages has been to believe that Jesus revealed himself to be part of the godhead by this resurrection; that is to say, rising from the dead, but actually his feat consisted in the assumption of a flesh-like body, indeed, so real, as to convince even the doubting Thomas.

II. God and the Human Soul

As to who and what is God, I dare say that never has the Bible, either the Old or the New Testament, given man an understanding of the Deity and His attributes to the extent and depth as appears in the messages signed Jesus and the Celestials. According to these high spirits, man is at-one with the Father to the degree that His love abounds in their souls. God is Soul, composed of His greatest attribute, Divine Love, which is His very nature and essence, followed by Mercy, Goodness, Power, Omniscience, and Will, and with the Mind, so much worshipped by mankind, only an aspect of this Being. Although God has no form such as He gives to mankind on incarnation, nor a spirit body, which is manifested by man after his physical death, yet God possesses His definite Soul form, which becomes more clearly perceptible to the soul which feels or perceives God's Oversoul, or the divine attributes thereof, as it comes into closer rapport with God through its soul development. For while God is Soul alone, unique in its Oneness, and while He has no material or spirit body, yet He has personality, the divine personality manifesting His Love and Mercy, His kindness and solicitude for all His creatures. God, then, is not a cold intellect, an abstract mind, or forces indifferent and unfeeling, but a personal warm and loving Father, eager for the happiness of His children, regardless of race or color or creed. He seeks through His ministering angels to turn His children to Him, and have them keep in harmony with His laws, or have them come indeed to Him in the longing of their human souls for that something they know not what and obtain at-onement with Him through the inflowing of His Love into their souls in response to their earnest prayers. Soul is God and God is Soul and all His attributes added together do not make up who and what God is. These attributes radiate from His Great Soul and flood the universe, so when men say they live and have their being in God they are in error for they do not, but they do live and have their being in the attributes that God has given them: the human soul. When one obtains the greatest attribute of God, the Divine Love, which manifests itself as a warm glow burning in the soul, as occurred to the refugees at Emmaus (Luke, 24, 32), then he is actually feeling or perceiving the Great Soul of God to the degree he partakes of that Love.

Information regarding the human soul not even mentioned in the Scriptures, which presumably should be the place to look for such material, abounds in the Messages from Jesus. To be sure, we are told in Genesis that God created man "in His image," but everything that such a statement implies or suggests is tantalizingly wanting and we are left to our own ideas or compelled to accept what the churches believe should be the meaning. The result is that the conception of what was meant by the creation in man varies in accordance with the interpretation which each church, claiming for itself the truth, lays upon those meager words. The early Hebrews, of course, were not interested overly much in the life beyond the grave, and their conception of the soul or its habitat after mortal experience is limited mainly to Paradise or Gehenna (and these, we may note, were originally conceived to be places on this earth; in the first case, the Garden of Eden supposed to be near the Euphrates; in the second, in the valley of Hinnom where the Jebusites once offered up human sacrifices). It is strange, perhaps, that the Greeks, with their love of physical culture, form and beauty, should have a much more detailed view of the afterlife: the dark realm of Pluto, the glory and happiness of the Elysian Fields, where the souls of the righteous dwell in peace and communion with their god, the shadow forms of the harpies, the influence, perhaps, of an older Egyptian religion.

But in these messages signed the Master and his celestial spirits, the information given is clear and logical, even though such information is new and hitherto unknown. Certainly, no one up to the time of Padgett's mediumship was able to obtain messages of that high quality directly from these spirits themselves, although Swedenborg, the Swedish seer, was permitted experiences in the spirit world which in many respects parallel what Padgett obtained.

Jesus tells us that just as God is Infinite Love, so is His universe infinite matter which, like God, has no beginning nor end. At some time in this infinity of time and space, God created a habitat designed for "man." Exactly when we "men" were created as living souls, (that is to say, before or after the creation of our world) is not known, but God created human souls which dwelt, and have been so dwelling, with Him before their incarnation in the flesh. After the mortal experience, the soul, manifesting its spirit body acquired with incarnation, returns to the spirit world to inhabit a locality commensurate with its condition.

Human souls created by the Father, according to the messages, are duplex: they are male and female in composition[6] and at the time of incarnation divide into their two component parts. Each thereafter in the flesh is a complete soul as to itself. These soul mates may or may not meet and marry in the flesh, depending upon various conditions and circumstances which prevail at the time of their marriage, but such marriage is in no way a guarantee of happiness, for the different education, religious beliefs, family traditions, upbringing and other circumstances of each may often hinder rather than aid in their marital relations. On the other hand souls which are not mates have a better chance of marital harmony if their marriage is based on similar interests, upbringing, education and general social condition on the plane of the material world. Soulmates, after death, eventually meet and stay together in real soulmate love, though not before a period of purification, and in accordance with their condition of soul.

The messages are unequivocal in their insistence that human souls are, as the Book of Genesis states, creations in the image of God, and that therefore there is nothing of the Divine in us. They also insist that man is not the product of evolution such as Darwin or his followers have taught, but that ours represents a material form similar to, but more highly developed than, other creations consistent with the development of life on this planet and harmonizing with the conditions for life which this planet presents. Man was provided with a human soul which, with its special appendage, the mind, enabled him to make the advances and progress which exalts him as lord over the other creatures of this life and give him the potentiality of exploring and mastering the physical surroundings into which he has been placed.

But men are tragically mistaken, declares Jesus, when they believe that the mind is superior to, or the equal of, the soul, or that the soul is merely a name which is given to an entity whose existence is either doubtful or has no basis in fact. For the mind is limited and

---

[6] This information has been qualified more recently. See a message from Judas received on August 30th 2001 on the new-birth.net web site. (G.J.C.)

dependent upon the soul, the seat of the emotions and the passions, and it is the soul which is the real man. It is through the soul perceptions that man knew instinctively that he was linked to his Creator, whom he was to revere and obey. Man, says Jesus, can know and knows God only because he possesses a soul, and he can never know God if he seeks Him intellectually and with his mind alone. Doubt and speculation is a product of the mind, but faith is a product of the soul and we know that God exists through our soul perceptions, so that we can create the spiritual link with God through prayer. Not a mental prayer, but a prayer that comes from man's soul—earnest, sincere, full of longing, faith and love.

III. The Problem of Sin

When the first parents, or whom they represent, possessed their God-given souls, these souls were in the image of God, but they had nothing of the essence of God in them. They were given the opportunity, however, to obtain the nature of God through prayer for His Love, which on entering the human soul through the agency of the Holy Spirit, transforms that soul from the image of God into the essence of God. But the first parents, instead of turning to God and His Love, sought mastery of their material surroundings alone and, instead of developing their souls so that they would partake of the nature of God through Divine Love, chose the development of their intellectual faculties. For it is through his intellectual attainments that man acquires the material possessions and wealth by which he so much sets his store and which marks him as a success by worldly standards. And thus came the story of the apple, and the Tree of Knowledge. And it is through this material knowledge that came sin, for man turned from God to be independent of God, and with it came pride. He became puffed up, cruel, heartless and merciless, where he had been created with a soul full of human love and mercy and tenderness and sympathy for his fellow beings. Thus man, in his ruthlessness, lost the use of his soul qualities and the potentiality of partaking of the Father's nature through the inflowing of the Divine Love into his soul, and this was the death which man suffered when he sinned. For, says Jesus, the material body was not in question; it was, rather, the penalty of having lost the opportunity of achieving at-onement in soul with the Father. Men lost the potentiality for salvation through becoming immortal souls. The wages of sin, as Jesus explains it, is spiritual death: loss of the soul's chance to partake of God's nature and live. Death in the flesh, Jesus assures us, is merely an incident in the progress of man's soul from preexistence to the point where he returns to the spirit world with his individuality assumed at the time of incarnation, and manifested in his spirit body.

The problem of sin, then, is the defilement of the soul during its period of incarnation. Sin is the violation of God's laws, says Jesus, as given to mankind by those of His messengers who transmit His will to mortals attuned to their suggestions, either because they are more pure in heart and are closer to the Father or because of their psychic or mediumistic powers. An interesting message signed Elijah tells us that he could receive messages from the unseen world because of prayers and religious instinct. Here, perhaps, is the story of the great religious founders and reformers of all lands and ages up to the coming of the Messiah. They all sought to turn man to the moral life, and the Eight Steps of Buddha, the Hammurabi Code and the Decalogue of Moses may, perhaps, be viewed as the success which the Father's messengers attained in planting into man's mind an awareness of the existence of God's laws, which were to be observed by all His children for the purity of their souls.

Some of the finest messages in this collection are those from Old Testament Prophets, like Elijah, Samuel, Moses and Daniel, who tell us of their efforts to turn their compatriots away from sin and error in the conduct of their lives to standards of ethical living, and seeking to give effect to their sermons through recourse to threats of punishment to be meted out by an angry and wrathful God. They explain that His Love was not available to them nor was it known to them as a reality, and they conceived of Him as a stern taskmaster who was vengeful and jealous "of His name." Their highest concept of Judaism, which graces the most exalted pages of the Old Testament, was intense faith in God, righteousness and obedience to His laws. There also runs through the Scriptures the theme of the new heart—the promise of the Father's Love, to be bestowed in the fullness of time upon the Jews first and thereafter upon all mankind, but this is a subject which, as far as I know, has never been given adequate treatment in the study of the Hebrew religion.

IV. Redemption from Sin

To the pious Hebrew of the Old Testament, it appeared that his wickedness both as a nation and as individuals was the cause of his national disasters and that his successes were the result of his faithfulness to the Covenant between God and the Patriarchs. The prophets emphasized the necessity in times of national stress to avoid alliances with other countries, and to put their faith in God's protection. Failure to heed the warnings of the Prophets led to calamity as in the days of Jeremiah, when disregard of his advice brought captivity in Babylonia. Again, in the sorest hour of Judaea's history, when the people were being provoked almost beyond endurance to bloody rebellion against mighty Rome, a Prophet out of Nazareth came with a message of peace and forbearance, only to be rejected by those in power; Judaea was crushed and the people—those that remained—dispersed over the face of the globe. For those of us who know that the Heavenly Father is our God of Love, we cannot believe that He brought about the horrible destruction of the Hebrews in the revolt of 67-70 A.D. But we do believe that the condition of men's souls was such that it embraced wrath and the violence of warfare rather than love and patience and that this condition of the soul made inevitable the dreadful consequences that followed.

In the spirit world, the soul that sins must likewise reap the whirlwind. On leaving the flesh, it is received by spirits whose duty it is to instruct it in the things of its new existence. It is told that everything in the spirit world is controlled by law. One of these is the "law of compensation," applicable to all spirits who pass over from mortal to spirit life. This life calls for the expiation of the sins which the soul has committed as a mortal.

Since the soul is the "real man," and is in possession of its faculties, this includes the memory of deeds committed in the earth life. All the evil works and thoughts which the soul has accumulated as a mortal now come back to haunt and assail him and the terrible remorse and suffering that ensue continue constantly and unabated until these evil memories have left him, and it is this that constitutes the judgment day and the hell. The condition of the soul creates the home in which it lives when it first passes over into spirit life; a home which accurately and exactly reflects the state of that soul and the spirit body which it manifests. Hence a soul filled with thoughts and deeds spiritual and in accord with God's laws will abide in a place suitable to its soul condition filled with light and reflecting the happiness of that soul; but a soul filled with deeds and thoughts of the material plane alone, and out of harmony with God's laws, engenders an abode of darkness and suffering, and in accordance with the abuses and unlawful material pleasures which it pursued when on earth.

But one of the most pernicious doctrines taught by the churches and whose damnable falsity is exposed by Jesus, is that which fixes the destiny of the delinquent soul in hell for all eternity. This is not true, for as soon as the soul wills it, and repents of his sins as a mortal, he may make his progress out of the lowest hells to the spiritual heavens or, should he seek and obtain the Father's Love, continue to eternally progress as an immortal soul in the Celestial Heavens towards the throne of God. The reason for this, the Master explains, is that the soul of man is the same, whether in the flesh or as a spirit, and the same conditions of forgiveness obtain here as in the spirit world. All sins are pardonable in this world or the next whenever the soul makes the sincere effort to receive it, and the only sin not pardonable is that which, in New Testament parlance, blasphemes against the Holy Spirit, or in the language which the Master makes clear, refuses the Divine Love of the Father which can transform the human soul into a divine soul and bestow upon it immortality.

It is not true that man has the sorry alternative of either repenting of his evils ways in the brief existence in the flesh or living in hell throughout all eternity as a spirit. Some churches state that man cannot live a mortal life of pleasure and evil and then turn to God to avoid eternal suffering as a spirit. At the same time they teach that despite a life of sin a last minute return to God will insure forgiveness of their sins, when they come to the next world. These churches seem to be unaware of the existence of the law of compensation which exacts payment for the evils committed in the flesh "to the last farthing." This is justice, indeed, if that is what these churches desire, but the time comes when the debt is paid, the soul is released from the workings of the law and forgiveness is achieved.

The law, then, acts upon the soul undergoing the process of purification, but the soul that seeks the Father's Love invokes the higher law of Grace. Here no justice is involved; only the Divine Love which the Father bestows upon His aspiring children and transforms them into divine souls, bringing about the elimination of those evil desires and the forgetfulness of those evil deeds upon which the law of compensation operates. The pernicious doctrine of eternal damnation often prevents the unhappy soul from seeking the Father's Love through prayer, in the terrible belief that his position in hell is fixed forever and that God can no longer help him. Yet God, as Jesus explains it, helps His children wherever they are, in this world or the next, or in whatever condition of soul they may be in, provided they come to Him as their Heavenly Father in earnest longing of their souls and seek His Love and mercy.

It is the awakening of the soul to the iniquities it worked and cogitated as a mortal that brings about the workings of the law of compensation, and the abode of the spirit. Sometimes, the soul that passes over, because of the peculiar character of its make-up, is impervious at first to this awakening, and in that case, the soul lives on the level of its evil earth plane life and seeks in spiritual counterparts those evils which it practiced as a mortal, or roams the earth seeking to obsess mortals susceptible to its baleful influence. Jesus refers in the Gospels of the New Testament to his having liberated mortals from possession by demons, and these demons were nothing more than evil spirits which had taken possession of human beings at the time. In respect to these evil spirits of once mortal beings, Jesus tells us that some of the narratives related in the New Testament are true, but that others are false, and he refers concretely to the story of the possessed swine which ran madly down the cliff to be destroyed. This, he asserts, he never brought about, first because he would harm no creature, and

True Gospel Revealed anew by Jesus

because of the financial loss such an act of his would have entailed their owner. But, as regards the evil spirits, these awaken in time to the law of compensation and pass through their period of suffering for their mischief and evil. They are helped in this condition by others who are somewhat more advanced than themselves, and who instruct them in the ways that exist to progress out of their deplorable condition.

Hence, souls in suffering eventually learn to give up their evil inclinations, whether it be a fondness for money, possessions, gratification of pleasures or the desire to injure others—greed, lusts, covetousness, hatred, envy, injustice and other sinful creations of the human heart—and they may use their will power and intellectual faculties to enable them to cause the forgetfulness of the things that make for a soul stricken with remorse. But the soul in suffering and darkness may also seek outside aid if it so wishes: the Divine Love of the Heavenly Father which, pouring out into the soul which earnestly seeks His Love, causes the purification of that soul through possessing it and thus forcing from it the excrescences that mar and defile that soul; and indeed, as the Father's Love continues to fill the soul of him who seeks it, there takes place the transformation of the human soul reflecting the Soul of God into a Divine soul filled with the very nature and essence of God, His Love. With that Love the soul is changed, and the evils which contaminated it are eradicated and the memories thereof, so that the law of compensation has nothing on which to operate, and the soul is freed from its inexorable workings. For God's Love sought for by the soul in earnestness and longing invokes a higher law of love and the once evil soul, now filled with God's Love, and mercy, and kindness, consideration, pity and sympathy, progresses out of its abode of darkness and suffering into realms of love and light, and eventually into the Celestial Heavens, where only those souls filled with His Love can enter. Jesus is the Master of the Celestial Heavens, where the inhabitants are the possessors of the Father's Love to that degree in their souls that they are conscious of their immortality. For God's Soul being Immortal, those souls possessing His Love to a sufficient degree are in the same way Immortal. This is what Jesus meant when he said, "The Father and I are one." He meant there was a oneness between God's Soul and His own because of the great abundance of the Father's Love which he possessed, which enabled him to realize that in this way he was the Father's real and redeemed son. He did not mean, as some churches have erroneously interpreted the remark, that he was God or equal to God; only that there was a kinship in nature between his soul and God's, which had been established by his possession of the Father's Love through prayer.

In short, we come to the real explanation of "forgiveness," which is startlingly different from the traditional conception imposed upon mortals by the churches. God does not arbitrarily forgive sin; but rather,

God aids those who, truly penitent and contrite, come to Him to seek His forgiveness with the intention of mending their ways. He may therefore send the Spirit of God to strengthen the soul that seeks to avoid sin and error through his own will power or, in response to prayer, He will send His Holy Spirit to convey His Love into the soul so that His own nature and essence provide the aid in eradicating the evils with which that soul is contending.

In the same way, Jesus lays bare the sterility of the traditional concept of the "judgment day." It is not a weighing in the balance of the good and evil deeds of man during his earth life; neither is it a vague indefinite time when the earth shall be destroyed and men's souls tried for condemnation or resuscitation into physical life from the grave. For, as St. Paul says in Corinthians, "flesh and blood cannot inherit the Kingdom." And Mary, the Mother of Jesus, explains that the flesh of the lifeless body must return to the elements in accordance with God's law, and that therefore any writings to the effect that she ascended into heaven in the flesh is mere speculation and wishful thinking on the part of those who exalt her because of her relationship to her son. Mary states that, indeed, as a spirit filled with the Father's Love, she is an inhabitant of the Kingdom high up in the Celestial Heavens, yet not because of any relationship to Jesus, but because of her own exalted soul condition.

Eventually, declares Jesus, all souls will progress out of their condition of suffering and unhappiness and attain to either the sixth sphere, known to the Hebrews as Paradise (for such is the condition of man possessing purity of soul whether he be in the flesh or devoid of it) or will accept the way to the Father's Love and reach the Celestial Heavens. The perfect natural man, however, must eventually reach a state of stagnation, for the time comes when he can no longer progress beyond the perfection of his human soul; but the soul possessed of the Father's Love may continue to obtain His Love throughout all eternity, for it is infinite, and the soul thus filled with the Father's essence continues to obtain more and more of it and, consequently, to progress nearer and nearer to the fountainhead of the Father's abode, with increased knowledge of things divine and gaining in happiness and joy as a Divine son of the Father.

In accordance with this desire to explain conditions of spirit and soul life, Jesus is emphatic about the utter falsity of reincarnation. He states, and ancient spirits of the East write to add their corroboration, that while this theory is known to devotees of Oriental cultures, reincarnation has as a matter of fact never taken place in the spirit world and that believers in this sterile idea have been waiting in vain for countless thousands of years to be reincarnated. Jesus, and others of the high spirits, state that the soul cannot be separated from its spirit body

True Gospel Revealed anew by Jesus

once it has been acquired through incarnation, and that only souls without spirit bodies can be incarnated. Hence, Jesus explains, the soul makes its progress from sin to purity or divine transformation in the spirit world, which it can never again leave except to materialize briefly with the aid of material substance borrowed from mediums. The oriental concept of renunciation or expiation of sin from the soul, adds Jesus, is correct, as is the doctrine that eventually the soul will eliminate the evils which defile it, but the errors consist in locating the earth as the place where such expiation takes place, and teaching that the soul on freeing itself of iniquity also loses consciousness of itself as a personal entity through absorption of the soul into the Deity.

In connection with life on the other side, one of the most interesting spirit writers is the Seer, Swedenborg, who tells us about his experiences in the spirit world. He declares—and here Jesus corroborates his messages—that he was indeed permitted to come to the spirit world in a trance state, and that he really saw the spheres and the conditions of the spirits as they existed in the 18th century. Swedenborg tells us that he was informed throughout the world of spirits that God is One, and that a triune God, as believed in by Christians, was nothing but pious fiction. He states that he spoke with Jesus, who confirmed this, but thought that, since Jesus was so much brighter and glorious than all the others of the spirit realm, this same Jesus must be God, and so he declared in his writings. Swedenborg relates that he was informed about the Divine Love, but that he did not truly understand what Jesus and the high spirits meant by it.

One important matter which the messages clear up is the true meaning of the "divine within you" doctrine. Actually, Jesus brought the divine with him when he preached throughout the Holy Land when on earth, and when he walked among men, the Kingdom was with men, but not within them. When preachers talk of the divine within man, they are really referring to the soul, the creation of God, indeed, but a human soul withal, not a divine one. What they mean, then, by developing the divine within man must be viewed as simply developing the latent powers in the human soul through development of the will, and the natural human love through moral and intellectual growth. These, of course, were given to man at his creation, and have no part of the divine. The Divine in the human soul is the Divine Love, which can come only through prayer to the Father. The Divine comes from without, from the Heavenly Father, and can enter the soul and effect its transformation only when that soul seeks it in earnest longing. When Jesus spoke to his disciples about the divine within them, these disciples actually had some of this Love in their souls, even before the Pentecost, when the Father's Love, through the Holy Spirit, was poured out upon them in great abundance.

Another misconception which Jesus clears up, with the corroboration of Mrs. Baker Eddy, is the doctrine known as Christian Science. We are informed that this woman, through her soul perceptions, understood the Divine Love as a great spiritual force coming from God, which could be used for healing purposes, and that it was through the Divine Love that Jesus and his apostles healed the sick. She rightly understood that spiritual healing was a reality which could be attained if mortals would but turn from material interests and seek the spiritual. In this way, healers and patients could reach a condition of soul above that of the earth plane so that rapport could be made with spirit healers. Christian Science, to that extent, declares Jesus, is correct and spiritual healing a phenomenon obedient to spiritual law; but the Master points out that sin and error, contrary to Mrs. Eddy's beliefs, are real, being creations of the human soul, and that the human soul does not reflect the Father's Love, as she states it does. It either does not have the Love or, if it does to a certain extent, possesses that Love, and the transformation of that soul into a divine soul is made to the degree it partakes of that Love.

Her teachings, Jesus declares, help in the development of the human soul towards the state of the perfect natural man, but are devoid of the concept of the soul's possession and conscious ownership of the Father's Love which comes only through prayer to the Father for this love, and so do not point the way to the Celestial Heavens through prayer to the Father and transformation into the divine angel.

A few words might be said with respect to the additional messages printed for the first time in this edition. Although they are all interesting, and those of Mary Kennedy, the soulmate of Dr. Stone, have a personal tone peculiar to her, some commentary is due the communication signed, Elohiam, a member of the Sanhedrin which condemned Jesus to death at his trial. This spirit is unquestionably a sincere personality, and his writings have the ring of truth. It is, of course, understood that not all of the counselors who were present at the trial have since made their way to the Celestial Heavens, as he has, yet at the same time it shows clearly that not all members of the Sanhedrin—and here we recall Nicodemus—were supporters of the high priests or acted out of pure malice and rage. There were those, like Elohiam, who consented to the unfairness of the trial and summary condemnation of the Master in order to liberate Judaism from what they sincerely considered a menace which threatened its overthrow or to bring about Roman repression at any sign of Judean revolt. The message gives for the first time the other side of the story and while the spirit admits his great mistake and does not seek to justify his action or that of his compatriots, the tone is different from the hatred that breathes forth in the account of the trial found in the New Testament, a tone which we

True Gospel Revealed anew by Jesus

know is inconsistent with the Father's Love which inspired the original writers.

It would be possible to continue to discuss at great length the numerous interpretations and corrections made in these messages signed Jesus and the many celestial spirits, and in the preceding pages we have attempted to point out some of the major precepts which animate them. They emphasize the restoration of the original "glad tidings" of Christianity: that with Jesus of Nazareth there came a love distinct from the natural human love as developed and perfected by the Mosaic code of moral and ethical living; that the new love is the Divine Love which, the essence of the Heavenly Father, was first manifested in man by Jesus and through Jesus made available to mankind. It is obtained not through mere belief in Jesus' name or in any overall vicarious atonement supposedly made by him or through the shedding of his blood, but only as each individual, turning in free will to the Father, seeks His Love through prayer and faith with all his heart and thus achieves a transformation of soul condition from one of sin and error to one of purity and possession with that Love of the divine nature. It is this Love that bestows eternal life upon the soul and thus fulfills the promise of what we call salvation. It cannot be achieved by rites and ceremonies, earned by man or granted to man by the churches, but is the free gift of the "new heart" poured out in abundance by the Heavenly Father upon His children who seek it in earnest.

In short, it would be impossible here to comment on everything which is of interest to those who, whether they believe in this source of revelation or take issue with the material therein contained, are concerned with things of the spiritual and religious. But one thing must be said in closing, and that is, that these messages, whether they be the result of mortal or spirit intelligence, are so thought provoking and challenging in their nature by declaring at-onement with the Father through prayer for His Divine Love that they can truly be called a new reformation in Christian thinking.

Dr. Daniel. G. Samuels.[7]
Washington, D. C.
August, 1956

April 29th, 1920

I am here, Mary Kennedy
So believe that I am with you and let not doubt as to my

---

[7] It appears that this section in both the Third and the Fourth Edition was written by Dr. Daniel G. Samuels who was the medium who followed James Padgett and received messages in the 1950s and 1960s mostly from Jesus. (G.J.C)

existence enter into your mind for one moment. You have seen me in the photographs, and while they do not show me as I really am in my condition of glory and beauty, yet they will give you some idea of how I might look if I were merely a spirit in the light—Give my love to Leslie and tell him that though he has a picture of me which will last only for a little while, yet he has a love that will continue with him not only through his mortal life but one that will never end in all eternity. Good night with all my love,
    Mary

Dr Leslie Stone

True Gospel Revealed anew by Jesus

Mary Kennedy

These two photos[8] of my soulmate, Mary Kennedy, show her as she materialized, one to be with me, and another as she appeared alone. Mary later confirmed through Mr. Padgett that she had actually appeared and been photographed by Mr. William Keeler, in his studio in Washington, D. C. I solemnly declare that these are genuine spirit photos of my soulmate.

---

[8] In this modern age, it is trivial to create a composite picture like this with editing tools. No doubt in the 1920s such a picture would be impressive, but it has been retained here simply because it was published at that time, and not as any sort of proof. It is also interesting in that it depicts two individuals who play a big role in these revelations. (G.J.C)

Table of Contents

Introduction to Volume I Fifth Edition i

James Edward Padgett iii

Dr. Stone's Testimony xiii

The True Mission of Jesus xxixi
    I. Jesus and his Relationship to God xxixi
    II. God and the Human Soul xxxii
    III. The Problem of Sin xxxvii
    IV. Redemption from Sin xxxviii

The Messages 1

John the Baptist
    John the Baptist is now the harbinger of the Master as he was on earth. Confirms Jesus' writing through Mr. Padgett 1

Jesus
    The reasons given by Jesus as to why he selected Mr. Padgett to do the work of receiving the messages 2

    Description of birth and life of Jesus up to the time of his public ministry 5

Helen Padgett
    Affirming that Jesus had written through Mr. Padgett 8

Jesus
    Jesus continues his description of his birth and life up to the time of his public ministry 8

Professor Joseph Salyards
    Comments on Jesus' description of his birth and life up to the time of his public ministry 10

Jesus
    The kingdom of God on earth and in the spirit world or the way to the kingdom of the perfect man 11

Table of Contents

St John
Affirming that Jesus wrote on the two kingdoms 17

The Celestial Heavens. 19

Jesus
The only Way to the Kingdom of God in the Celestial Heavens 19

Samuel
Affirmation by Samuel, Jesus wrote the message 23

Jesus
After death, the judgment. What it is and what it is not 23

The beliefs of a mission preacher 27

John
Divine Love—what It is and what It is not. How It can be obtained. 30

Jesus
Necessity of faith and prayer in doing the work. Mr. Padgett is his chosen one to do the work 32

Paul, John, James, Luther, Barnabas, John Wesley, John the Baptist
Eight Celestial Spirits affirm that Jesus wrote 33

Luke
Affirming that the Master wrote 33

Helen Padgett
Affirms that eight of the Celestial Spirits signed their names 34

Jesus
Jesus says his mission in writing these messages is his second coming on earth 34

James
St. James was over-powered by Jesus' great presence 35

John
Said the Master had written and showed his great power and glory 36

Ann Rollins
Affirming that the Master wrote with such power and glory 36

Jesus
The prayer given by Jesus as the only prayer.... 36

A. G. Riddle
> *Affirmation that Jesus showed his glory 40*

Helen Padgett
> *Affirmation by Mrs. Padgett 40*

John
> *Writes on the true meaning of "the end of the world" 41*

Immortality 45

Jesus
> *Immortality 45*

Luke
> *Immortality by St. Luke 48*

Henry Ward Beecher
> *Henry Ward Beecher: Immortality 50*

Matthew
> *The Salvation that Jesus taught 54*

Who and What is God? 57

Jesus
> *Jesus: Who and what is God? 57*

Ann Rollins
> *Ann Rollins: Who and What is God? 60*

> *Ann Rollins: Who and What is God?—continued 62*

John H. Padgett
> *Affirmation that Mr. Padgett's grandmother wrote the message on "Who and What is God?" 65*

Jesus
> *Christ may be in you—what it means 66*

The Holy Spirit. 69

Jesus
> *Many who think that they have received the baptism of the Holy Spirit have only advanced in the natural love and not the Divine Love 69*

Table of Contents

Luke
    The mystery of the Godhead, three in one is a myth. There is no mystery that men should not know 72

Bishop John P. Newman
    Affirms Luke's writing. Regrets that he did not teach the Truth when on earth 76

Jesus
    Why Jesus does not attend the battlefields where the scenes of carnage exist 77

Helen Padgett
    Affirming Jesus wrote and showed his glory 80

Jesus
    The destiny of the man who does not have the Divine Love in his soul and dies only with the natural love and a belief in the creeds, etc... 80

The Resurrection. 85

Paul
    The resurrection that is common to all, be they saint or sinner 85

Jesus
    Corroboration by Jesus that St. Paul wrote on the resurrection 88

Paul
    The resurrection that Jesus taught without which our faith as Christians is in vain 88

Jesus
    Why the Divine Love of God is necessary for man to possess in order that he may become at-one with the Father and an inhabitant of the Celestial Kingdom 92

    The importance of knowing the Way to the Celestial Kingdom—many statements in the Bible untrue 95

    The importance for mankind seeking the Divine Love—continued .. 97

    The importance for mankind seeking the Divine Love—continued .. 99

The Soul 101

Jesus
    The soul—what it is and what it is not 101

>> *How the redeemed soul is saved from the penalties that sin and error has brought upon it* 106
>
> *All who refuse to seek the Way to the Celestial Heavens will eventually find their way to the kingdom where the perfect natural man exists* 107
>
> *The importance for mankind seeking the Divine Love and not be satisfied by merely developing the natural love in a pure state* 110

Mathew
> *The soul and its relationship to God and future life and immortality* 113

St. Cornelius
> *Discourse on the soul* 115

Forgiveness 117

Ann Rollins
> *Forgiveness* 117

Jesus
> *How a soul must receive the Divine Love of the Father in order to become an inhabitant of the Kingdom of God* 121

John
> *What is the reason that mortals will not seek the Love of the Father?* 125

Atonement 129

Luke
> *Luke on atonement, part 1* 129
>
> *Luke on atonement, part 2* 131

Jesus
> *Confirms that Luke wrote on the atonement* 136

Luke
> *What is the fact in reference to the authenticity of the Bible* 138

John
> *Celestials must work until the Celestial Kingdom will be closed* 141

Table of Contents

> *Describes the difference between the spirits of the Celestial and the spirit spheres and their happiness, etc* 145

James
> *Condition of spirits and their experiences and beliefs that are below the Celestial Heavens; how they congregate together* 147

Inaladocie
> *An ancient spirit, tells of his beliefs when on earth. Sacrifice to the Devil* 148

Professor Joseph Salyards
> *Various experiences of spirits when they arrive in the spirit world* 149

A. G. Riddle
> *Heaven is a place as well as a condition of the soul* 152
>
> *The soul's progression as I have experienced it* 154

Emperor Constantine
> *Says he never when on earth accepted Christianity. Is now a Celestial Spirit* 158

Luke
> *Affirms Constantine's writing* 161

Helen Padgett
> *Helen affirms that Constantine and Luke wrote* 161

Samuel
> *What actually happened at Jesus' crucifixion* 162

Helen Padgett
> *Affirming that Samuel wrote the preceding message* 164

S. B. C.
> *Minister of the Gospel: His beliefs were merely intellectual. After awhile became skeptical* 164

Helen Padgett
> *Affirming that dark spirits were helped* 168

Hell 169

Paul
> *Hell and the duration of punishment* 169

Table of Contents

Hell and the duration of punishment—continued from preceding message 170

Hell—what it is and what the purpose is. Continued from preceding message 171

Rev. Fontaine
Experience of an orthodox minister after he passed into the spirit world 176

Helen Padgett
Affirmation that the orthodox minister wrote and gave his experience in the spirit world 180

John
Book of Revelations is only a mere allegory of some one or more writers and is not the same as St. John wrote 180

Description of the Third Sphere. Affirmation Jesus wrote the Prayer 184

George Whitefield
Changed his erroneous beliefs that he taught on earth and is now in the Celestial Heavens 187

Ann Rollins
How all mankind can become Divine Angels and how erroneous beliefs prevent this consummation 188

Jesus
What Jesus meant when he said: He that liveth and believeth on me shall never die 191

Jesus: Faith and how it can be obtained 192

Jesus is not God, but an elder brother. Sin has no existence except as it is created by mankind and man must pay the penalties 194

Worship of Jesus as part of the Godhead is wrong and sinful—how much Jesus deplores this erroneous belief of mankind 199

Table of Contents

The Vicarious Atonement..201

John
The belief in the efficacy of the vicarious atonement of Jesus by his death and crucifixion by the churches has caused much harm to mankind and the loss of the True Way to the Celestial Kingdom ... 201

Luke
What is the use in believing in the sacrifice of Jesus on the cross as salvation from sin 206

Paul
Denies the vicarious atonement—this belief doing much harm—Bible contains many false statements 209

Peter
Affirms what Paul wrote about the vicarious atonement 210

Various Subjects 213

Jesus
What men can do to eradicate war and evil from men's souls. Jesus never came to bring a sword but to bring peace through his teachings 213

Helen Padgett
Comments on Jesus' message on the cause of war 216

Elias
Comments on Jesus' message on the cause of war 217

Jesus
There are no devils and no Satan considered as real persons and fallen angels 217

Samuel
Happiness and peace that passeth all understanding comes to the possessor of the Divine Love 221

Peter
Jesus did not perform all the miracles claimed in the Bible 222

The Wandering Jew
The wandering Jew 223

John
> *Confirming the experience that came to the "Wandering Jew"* 224

Helen Padgett
> *Comments on the message of the Wandering Jew* 226

John
> *Why the churches refuse to investigate that spirits can and do communicate with mortals* 226

Luke
> *Discourse on the devolution and evolution of man—scientists only know of evolution after man reached the bottom of his degeneracy or devolution* 229

Jesus
> *The relationship of man to the creation of the world, and the origin of life* 231

> *Previous message continued* 234

Ancient Spirits give their Testimony 239

Moses
> *The importance of the Jews learning the truths of God proclaimed by Jesus* 239

Daniel
> *Writes of his experience in the spirit world, and his life on earth* ... 240

Samuel
> *His teaching and experience when on earth. Did not get the Divine Love until Jesus came to earth* 244

Helen Padgett
> *Affirming that Daniel and Samuel wrote* 246

Elias
> *Elias on the history of the times when he lived on earth. He never knew of the Divine Love until Jesus came to earth and made known its rebestowal* 247

> *His experience while on earth and the spirit world. Transfiguration on the Mount a reality* 248

> *Elias was not John the Baptist, neither was John a reincarnation of Elias* 250

Table of Contents

Cornelius the Centurion
Much interested in the work and the importance of mankind knowing the Truth 251

Elias
The truth of the Bible as to the things that are contained in the Old Testament 252

Esau, son of Isaac
He now knows the difference between the spirit who has in his soul the Divine Love and one who has not 255

Soloman
What is the greatest thing in all the world? 257

Lot
Adds his testimony and experience in the spirit world.—Jesus is the ruler of the Celestial Heavens 258

Leytergus
An ancient spirit, wrote a book—description of creation and of the fall of man—Genesis was copied after his writings 259

Saul of the Old Testament
Woman of Endor was not a wicked woman as many believe 261

Socrates
Writes his experience in his progress 262

Helen Padgett
Confirmation that Socrates wrote through Mr. Padgett 265

Plato
Plato, disciple of Socrates, is now a Christian 266

Various subjects continued. 267

John
What does the spirit of man do when it leaves the physical body for eternity? 267

Jesus
The condition of the world when Jesus came to teach 270

Professor Joseph Salyards
Affirmation that Jesus wrote 271

Table of Contents

Helen
Corroborates Jesus wrote 272

Jesus
The religion of the future and a comprehensive and final one, founded on the truths that Mr. J. E. Padgett is receiving 272

Abraham Lincoln
Difference in his beliefs now and what his beliefs were when on earth 274

George Whitefield
The great world teacher will be the Master again come to earth in the form of his Divine Revelations 276

Helen Padgett
Comments on message from Whitefield 278

John
Refers to the nominal Christian and the need of the Divine Love in the soul, so as to become a true Christian 279

Jesus
"Verily, verily, I say unto you, he that believeth on me, the works that I do, shall he do also; and greater works than these shall he do; because I go unto the Father. If ye ask anything in my name I will do It." 281

Helen Padgett
Affirming that Jesus wrote 284

Jesus
God is a God of Love, and no man can come to Him, unless he receives the Love of the Father in his soul. The time will come when the privilege of obtaining the Divine Love will be withdrawn from mankind 284

Helen Padgett
Tells of her great happiness in her progress 287

Jesus
Jesus is not God or to be worshiped as God. Explains his mission. These messages that Mr. Padgett is receiving is his "New Gospel to all men, to both mortals and spirits." 288

Table of Contents

John
The spirits who have little development of soul can help those who have less development than themselves 291

Luke
The necessity for men turning their thoughts to things spiritual 293

Explains dematerialization of Jesus' earthly body 295

Thomas Carlyle
Comments on what Luke wrote about Jesus dematerializing his body after crucifixion 297

Joseph of Arimathea
Describes what happened after the remains of Jesus were put in the tomb 298

Martin Luther
Faith and works—the Vicarious Atonement—the importance of obtaining the New Birth—his beliefs have changed after he became a spirit 299

Martin Luther, reformer, is very anxious that the Truths that he now knows be made known to his followers 302

Jesus
Jesus will never come as Prince Michael to establish his Kingdom. 304

John
Jesus will never come in all his glory and power and take men into his Heaven, just as they are in body, soul and spirit 306

Luke
What is the most important thing in all the world for men to do to bring about the Great Millennium, etc 307

Jesus
Jesus recognizes Mr. Padgett's grandmother's capability in writing the Truths of the Father 310

Ann Rollins
Writes on the importance of knowing the Way to the Celestial Heavens 310

John Bunyan
The Law of Compensation. 312

John
The true meaning of—"In the beginning was the Word and the Word was with God, etc." 313

Jesus
How the soul of a mortal receives the Divine Love, and what its effect is, even though subsequently his mind may indulge in those beliefs that may tend to prevent the growth of the soul—what is a lost soul? 314

Thomas Jefferson
Mr. Padgett doing a stupendous work and one which is of the greatest vital importance to mankind and to the destiny of mortals 318

George Washington
Affirming that the ancient spirits wrote, and many came from the Celestial Heavens and the lower spirit heavens 318

Jesus
Jesus was never in India and Greece studying their philosophies as some claim 320

Nathan Plummer
Writes of his experience in the hells—"It is hard to learn of heavenly things in hell" 321

Luke
Comments on the spirit writing—"It is hard to learn of heavenly things in hell" 322

John Garner
All sin and error will eventually be eradicated from men's souls ... 323

Additional Messages added to the Third Edition 325

Euliam
A member of the Sanhedrin and judge at the trial of Jesus states the reasons for condemning the Master at the time 325

Luke
Why spiritualism as now taught does not satisfy the soul in its longings for happiness, peace and contentment 328

Table of Contents

Jesus
This is the first formal message received by James E. Padgett 330

The Master is anxious that mankind should stop worshipping him as God 331

Mary Kennedy
States that the publisher's soulmate is anxious for him to obtain the Divine Love in increased abundance so that he can make closer contact with her 333

How small is the human mind, even of the most learned, as compared to that of the spirit who possesses in its soul the great Love of the Father 335

This message informs the publisher through Mr. Padgett that she is now in a higher plane of the Celestial Heavens, with increased soul understanding of what the Father's Love means 336

Helen Padgett
A New Year's Eve message from Helen. A time of thankfulness to the Father for His great Love and Mercy 338

Lafayette
Relates how Washington helped him to a knowledge of the Father's Love and his resultant changed attitude towards the Germans 340

William Stone
The publisher's father states he is making earnest efforts to reach his wife's home and be with her through prayer to the Father for His Love 341

Jesus
The Master declares that he has selected Dr. Stone to do a work for the Kingdom, just as he selected Mr. Padgett. This work will be a labor of love, requiring much physical as well as spiritual exertion 342

Priscilla Stone
The publisher's mother is grateful that he has some of the Father's Love and wishes her other children would also seek His Love 343

Thomas Payne
The skeptical writer of colonial days, called by contemporaries an infidel, admits he was mistaken in some of his beliefs 344

Kate Stone
> *Dr. Stone's sister tells him what her work is in spirit world, and informs him that his efforts to help the spirits turn to the Father for His Love are having positive results* 345

The Messages.

John the Baptist is now the harbinger of the Master as he was on earth. Confirms Jesus' writing through Mr. Padgett

August 10th, 1915.

I am here, John the Baptist.

I came to tell you that I am now a harbinger of the Master as I was when on earth and that he is the true Jesus who writes to you in all the communications which you received signed by him or by his name. I do this that you may believe and not doubt the messages that you receive. He has written you and you must rely on what he says, for what he has said to you will surely come to pass.

I am the same John who appeared in Palestine and announced his coming, and as I told them what was actually to take place, so I tell you what is actually taking place, and you will not only receive the messages of truth which he will write you, but they will also be distributed to all mankind wherever the written languages of the world exist and are spoken or written.

So you have before you a wonderful and important mission and one that will do more to make true brothers and lovers of the Father than anything that has happened since the Master was on earth and taught and preached the truths of his Father, and did good to physical man.

I sometimes have wondered why you should have been selected, as I see that your soul development has not been nearly as great as that of many other men who now live and have lived; but as he has made the selection, we must understand that he knows what is best, and that his selection must be the right one. As a consequence of this, all we who are his followers in the Celestial World are trying our best to forward the cause and help you; and I must tell you that you have behind you in this great work, supporting and maintaining you, more spiritual power than any mortal has ever had before. This may sound to you surprising, but it is true.

So, my brother, for such I must call you now, try to acquire a faith in the love and desire of the Father to save all mankind from the errors of their lives and to make them one with Him that will enable you to stand forth as the representative of the Master and the authoritative teacher of these great truths.

I am now in the Celestial Heavens and am very close to Jesus in his home and in his love for the Father and for all humanity. I have powers which are great and Love which is of the Divine Essence of the Father and what I tell you now I will tell to the world when the opportunity presents itself.

Your Brother in Christ,
John the Baptist.

The reasons given by Jesus as to why he selected Mr. Padgett to do the work of receiving the messages

October 25th, 1918.

I am here, Jesus.

Well, my dear brother, time is passing, and the necessity for the revealing is very apparent, as men are longing and waiting for that which will satisfy the natural cravings of their souls, and which the present religion, called Christianity, has not in it the qualities to satisfy.

I am pleased that you are in so much better condition, and that your love is again becoming active and awakened, and operating upon the qualities of your brain so that a rapport can be made, as recently explained to you by John in his message. And here I desire to impress upon you the necessity and desirability of your understanding thoroughly the truths set forth in that message, and of meditating upon the same and making a personal application of what is therein written.

I would like very much to deliver a message dealing with spiritual truth tonight, but do not think that your condition is such as will enable me to take possession of your brain and control the same that the qualities and truths of my message demands, and so I will not attempt to write the message, but, instead, will advise you somewhat upon the way in which you must think and act in order to perfect the condition which you must possess that the rapport may be made.

John[9] has told you to pray often to the Father so that the love may become more abundant and your soul become permeated with it, and to think thoughts of spiritual things, until by such thinking your brain may become, as it were, infused with these thoughts and thereby receive those qualities that will make its conditions similar to the conditions of the minds of the spirits who may wish to form a union with your brain and convey through it the truths that are waiting to be delivered. And I confirm what John has written, and, in addition, say that your praying must be more frequent so that the soul may be freed from the condition

---

[9] St. John the Apostle, wrote a message :- The Laws of communication and rapport. (Dr. S.) Published in Vol II (4th Ed.) page 237. The footnote of Volume II on page 240 refers back to this message, and indicates that in fact three messages were being referred to by Jesus, that above, plus two in Volume II (4th Ed.) on pages 240 and 245. (G.J.C.)

that the existence in it, of thoughts not spiritual, be established. You need not wait for occasions or opportunities to formally pray but all during the day and evening let your longings for the love ascend to the Father. A long prayer, or even one formulated into words, is not necessary, as in order to have the longing it is not necessary that words should be used to give it form. The longing may be rapid as unformed thought, and as effective for the Father to catch, as I may say. The longing is quicker than the thought, and the answer to the same will come with as much certainty and love as if you were to put the longing into the most exact form. Prayers of this kind ascend to the Father and are heard and answered, and, by a law of your relationship to the Father, affect the qualities of the brain in the way of preparing it for the union with the spiritual thoughts of the spirits who desire to write, as I have stated. Your thoughts of spiritual things or of the truths of the spirit world, as they have already been revealed to you, and especially those which pertain to the love and mercy of the Father, and to His will, in their passing and operating, also affect the qualities of the brain so as to produce the condition which is so necessary for our rapport.

It may be surprising to you that this condition is required in the brain of a human and also the development of the soul, which really produces the condition, in order that a rapport may be made so that the spiritual truths may be delivered; and, also, surprising that you have been selected from all the men on earth in whom this condition and development shall be made. And it may be more surprising to know that it is true.

There are certain qualities in your constitution, both spiritual and material, that render you susceptible to the influence of our powers and to the use by us for the purpose of our design and work, which determines one to choose you for the work in the way in which I and the other high spirits have heretofore used you, and it may seem strange to you that in all the long ages preceding, I have not found one human with the qualification to fit him for the work.

I have used others before, but they have failed to submit their minds and souls and beliefs and forethoughts to our influence and directions as you have so far done. Many humans have the qualified conditions of spiritual and material make up to perform our wishes and work, but as they all have free wills, which we cannot compel, and as circumstances and environments and education and beliefs are elements which affect and determine the possibility of our finding an instrument suitable for our purposes, we have not been able to find a medium who was qualified to be used for our work.

You, of course, understand that you were not selected because of any special goodness or freedom from sin, or because you were more beloved by the Father, or naturally, and I mean according to your course of living, by reason of any spiritual condition that you were in, for there were many superior to you in goodness and more in at-onement with the will of the Father, and whose love and the results there from, were more perfect than yours. So you will realize that you were not selected because of any special spiritual merits possessed by you.

As you have been told, all things in the spirit world, as well as on earth, are controlled by immutable laws, and all spirits as well as mortals are subject to those laws. The law of rapport and communication must be complied with spirits, no matter how much elevated, and also by humans, and no spirit, by reason of the possession of any supposed power, can set aside this law. But while spirits have not this power, yet they may have such knowledge of conditions that they can discern what qualities in the condition of a human are susceptible to the influence, and molding by the spirits, so that as a result thereof, the law may be brought into operation. And this briefly will explain to you why I selected you as my medium and mouthpiece. For know this, that for a long time I have been endeavoring to influence and mold your mind and beliefs, so that your soul might become developed in such a way that conditions might be formed that would enable us to make a rapport that would permit of our controlling your brain to convey these messages of truth. You were naturally a medium and, for ordinary purposes, it was not difficult for the spirits to control and communicate through you the truths of the spirit world, which are not of a nature such as I and others have communicated in reference to the soul spheres and the relationship of God to man in the higher spiritual sense. As you read John's message you will the better understand what I intend to explain at this point.

There is another phase to all this, more personal to you, and this is, that while we have been developing you for the purpose of doing our work and helping make effective our mission, your soul, as you, has been developed in its spiritual nature and you have become in closer union with the Father and have partaken to a large extent of His Love, and, to a degree, been transformed into his essence, so that you have become a very different entity from what you were when your development for our purpose commenced; and, as a consequence, you will derive all the benefits that flow from an experience such as you have had.

You are now one of us in the progress towards the fountainhead of the Father's love, and have taken on a part of his immortality, and it depends only upon yourself how rapid your progress shall be towards a complete transformation such as spirits who are inhabitants of the Celestial Spheres, possess. You need not wait until you come to the spirit world in order to make a rapid progression, although it will be more difficult for you to progress while in the flesh, as you understand, but wonderful progress may be made while in the flesh, and you have been told the secret of this progress.

And I will further say that you have a closer association with spirits that are nearer the Father and more possessed of his essence and substance than have any humans of earth at this time. To you this may seem extravagant and improbable, but I declare to you that it is as true that I and many spirits who come to you and write, are in the Celestial Spheres of God's immortality.

Well, I have written a long time and you are somewhat tired. Remember my advice and pray often and earnestly, if but for a moment, and the condition will be yours and we will came and continue our revealments.

With my love and blessing, I am, Your brother and friend,
Jesus.

Description of birth and life of Jesus up to the time of his public ministry

June 7th, 1915.

I am here, Jesus.

I want to write to you tonight about my birth and life up to the time of my public ministry.

I was born in Bethlehem, as you know, in a manger, and when I was a few days old my parents took me to Egypt, in order to avoid the soldiers of Herod who were sent to destroy me, and who did kill a great number of male infants of less than two years of age. The Bible story of my birth and the flight of my parents and the murder of the innocents, is substantially correct; and I only wish to add to it, that when my parents arrived in Bethlehem they were not compelled to seek the manger of a stable in order that I might be born, on account of poverty, for they were supplied with funds and everything that was needed to make my birth comfortable for my mother; and as a matter of fact my father was not poor in the world's goods as poverty was considered in those days.

The Bible says the wise men came and brought offerings of gold and frankincense to my parents, or rather to me, but my parents have told me that it did not amount to so very much, so far as the money value of the same was concerned, and that their expenses of fleeing to Egypt was met by the funds that my father had prior to his reaching Bethlehem.

After they arrived in Egypt my father sought the home of a Jew, who was his relative, and lived there for a long time, doing the work that his trade fitted him to do; and by his work supported the family, and to an extent, educated myself and my brothers and sisters, for I had four brothers and three sisters, and were all, except myself, born in Egypt.

When I became of proper age, I attended the common school

provided for small children, and was taught those things that had to do with the religion of the Jews, and some things that were not religious in their nature. I was never taught the philosophy of the Egyptians or of the other pagan philosophies; and when it is stated that I received my religious ideas or moral teachings from any of these philosophers, they are mistaken.

My education as to these matters of religion was derived from the teachings of the Old Testament, or rather from Jewish teachers whose text book was the Old Testament.

My development in the knowledge of the truths which I taught during my public ministry, was caused by my inner spiritual faculties, and my teacher was God, who, through His angels and through my soul perceptions, caused to come to me those truths or rather the knowledge of them, and in no other way did I obtain it. I was not born with the knowledge that I was the son of God sent to earth to teach these great truths, or to announce to mankind the re-bestowal of the great gift of immortality, and the means of acquiring it. But this knowledge of my mission came to me after I became a man and had the frequent communions with God by my spiritual senses.

I was never in the presence of the Jewish priests, expounding to them the law and asking questions when about twelve years of age, as stated in the Bible, and not before my first appearance, after I became a man did I attempt to show priest or layman, that I was the messenger of the Father, and sent by Him to proclaim the glad tidings of immortality restored and of the great love of the Father which was necessary to make all men at one with Him, and to give them a home in His Kingdom.

I never was a sinful boy or man, and did not know what sin was in my heart; and strange as it may seem, I never sought to teach others these truths until after my mission was declared by John the Baptist.

In my boyhood days I was the same as other boys and engaged in the plays of childhood and had the feelings of a child, and never thought I was anything else than a child. In nowise was I different from other children, except in the particular that I have named, and any account of me to the contrary is untrue.

My teachings were those that the Father had committed to me from the beginning, but which I was only conscious of after I became a close communicant of the Father, and learned from Him my mission. So you must believe that I was a son of man as well as a son of God, and that in the literal sense. I would not have been true to my mission had I claimed that I was the only son of God, for it is not true—and men should not so teach it.

Yes, I know it was said that my mother was told of the object of my birth and what a blessed woman she was, but this is not true. My mother, as she has told me, had no reason to suppose that I was different from other children born of men. The story of the Angel of God coming to her and telling her that she must submit to the birth of a child who would be begotten by God or by His Holy Spirit, and that she, as a virgin, should bear and give birth to that child, is not true, for she never in all her life told me that she had any such visitor; and I know that she would be as much surprised, as are many men, that such a thing as the birth of a child by a virgin could take place. So you see the Bible account of my being begotten and all the attending circumstances are not true.

My father, Joseph, never supposed at anytime that I was not his child, and the story of the angel coming to him and telling him that he must not put her away because of appearance is not true, because he never in all my conversations with him, intimated that I was other than his own child.

Between the time that I was twelve years of age and my public ministry, I lived at home with my parents, and assisted my father in his business of carpenter, and during all this time no hint ever fell from him that I was not his child, or that I was different from other children, except that I did not do sinful things.

When I commenced to get this divine love into my soul, I became very close to the Father, and this relationship resulted in my realizing that I was sent by God with a mission to perform and a great and important truth to declare; and, at last the voice in my soul told me that I was my Father's true son and I believed it, and commenced to teach and preach the truths of His love bestowed and the salvation of men.

I knew John the Baptist when I was a child growing up. He was my cousin and we often played together, and afterwards discussed the truth of my mission and the way in which it should be made known to the world.

John was a great psychic and saw in his vision who I was and what my mission on earth was, and, hence, when the time came, he made the announcement of my coming. He realized the difference in our missions, and spoke of his not being worthy to unloosen my shoes. But, yet, he did not fully understand my mission and the great truth of the bestowal of immortality upon man by the Father.

I first became the Christ when I was anointed by my Father, and that occurred at the time of my baptism by John. I as Christ am different from myself as Jesus. Christ means that principle which the Father has conferred upon me, which made me at one with Him in the possession of this great love. Christ is that love itself made manifest in me as man. This Christ principle is universal and is everywhere, just as is the Holy Spirit, but I am limited in my place of occupancy just as you are.

I never as Jesus merely, promised the great gift, mentioned in the Bible, such as, where two or three are gathered together there will I be also; for it would be impossible for me to be in all places at the same time. But Christ, being without form or limitation, is omnipresent and, consequently, may fulfill my promise in this regard. Christ is as much alive today as ever. He was never crucified and never died as did Jesus.

Well, I think you are too sleepy now to continue, well because you need sleep. I know of no special influence being exerted over you to produce sleep.

I will continue in the near future.
Your brother and friend,
Jesus.

Affirming that Jesus had written through Mr. Padgett

June 7th, 1915.

I am here, Helen.

Well, sweetheart, you are too sleepy to write, as you had better go to bed and get a good night's sleep.

The Master was not at all offended, for he understood that you could not keep awake sufficient to write. He will finish the next time and you will be interested in the discourse.

With all my love I will say good night.
Your own true and loving
Helen.[10]

Jesus continues his description of his birth and life up to the time of his public ministry

June 8th, 1915.

I am here, Jesus.

I will continue my letter as to my birth and work, as I commenced it last night.

When I was satisfied that I was chosen by my Father to perform His work of declaring to the world the bestowal of His great gift of the divine love that was in His nature, and which formed the predominant principle of that nature, I commenced my ministry, and continued to work for the redemption of mankind, on earth, until my death on the cross. I was not then as perfect as I am now, and my knowledge of the truths of the Father was not as great as it is now.

Let men know though, that what I taught was true, even though I did not teach all the truth, and they will learn that I am my Father's true son, and the special messenger by whom these great truths was to be

---

[10] Mrs. Helen Padgett, wife of Mr. James E. Padgett, who is from the Celestial Heavens. (Dr. S.)

taught to mankind.

I was not, when on earth, so filled with the love of the Father as I am now, and had not the power to make men feel that this love is the only thing that will reconcile them to the Father and make them at one with Him, as I have now. So men must believe that I am communicating to them the real truths which will show them the way to the Fathers love and to their own salvation.

You have in your mind the desire to know how it was that the wise men came to me with their offerings and adoration, if I was not specially created by God to become His son and representative on earth.

Well, the wise men came, but their coming was not because of any knowledge they had that I was a child divinely created, or that I was not a natural child, but because they were astrologers and at the time saw a new and brilliant star in the heavens, and which to them meant that some important event had taken place; and, being students of the Old Testament, wherein such a star was referred to as the forerunner of the birth of a savior, they concluded that that star was the one intended, and that my birth being a lowly one, as they expected was the one that the Scriptures meant, and, consequently, that I was the Christ spoken of. But outside of this knowledge as astrologers and that of the Scriptures, they had no knowledge that I was the Christ to be born; and when it is asserted that they had any information from God or His angels that I was the Christ, that assertion is not true.

I know this, because since my coming to the spirit world, I have met these men and talked with them, and they have told me what I write. So, while I was the Christ referred to in the Bible—I mean in the prophecies of the Old Testament—yet, those wise men had no other knowledge of that fact than what I have told you.

I know that I was sent by the Father to perform the mission which I performed, and that it was intended in the beginning that I should be anointed as the Christ, but this I did not know until after I became a man and was then told what my mission was by the angel and my own inner voice.

My mother or father or brethren did not know, and even after I had proclaimed my mission and showed the wonderful powers that had been given to me, they did not believe in my mission, but thought that I was besides myself, that is, as you say, crazy with the belief that I was the chosen one of my Father. The Bible, itself, shows that this was their condition of mind.

So, while I am the Christ of the Bible, and the chosen instrument of the Father to make known the great truths which I have proclaimed, and which I shall proclaim through you, yet I am not the only begotten son of God in the sense in which it is usually accepted. And much less am I God. As I have said, there is only one God, and I am merely His son and teacher sent to the world to declare to mankind the bestowal of the gift of immortality and the way in which men may obtain it.

I will deal further with myself as we progress in our writings. Let no man believe that I was born of the Virgin Mary, or that I was begotten by the Holy Spirit, or that I am God, for all these things are not true.

For the present I will stop, and with all my love and blessings and the blessings of the Father, will say good night.

Your friend and brother,
Jesus.

Comments on Jesus' description of his birth and life up to the time of his public ministry

June 8th, 1915.

I am here, your old Professor.

I am very happy and want to tell you that you are in much better condition to write than you have been since I commenced to write to you. I am so glad of it, for it indicates improvement in your physical as well as your mental condition.

I was much interested in the last message of the Master, because it sets forth facts which are not in accord with the Bible story, and with what I had been led to believe. Of course, he knows what the truth is, and when he tells us anything, we never, for one moment doubt him, and neither must you.

And when you come to analyze and consider the statements made by him, you will find them more in accord with reason than the story contained in the Bible. In his statements there is nothing miraculous, or that calls for a belief that is beyond the reason to conceive of. Everything is so natural and in accord with the workings of nature, as has been observed in the case of the birth of every other human being. His statement as to how and when there came to him the knowledge that he was the chosen one of God to bring to earth the glad tidings of the restoration of immortality and the divine love of the Father waiting for all mankind, is I believe very new and will be surprising to most men.

But how reasonable this is? Had he known from the time of his birth that he was the Christ, which had been promised to the Jews, is it possible that during all the thirty years in which he remained in obscurity, he would not have made his mission known and commenced the work of proclaiming to mankind the glad tidings which he afterwards proclaimed? It seems wholly incredible that he would not have done so. The years from twenty-five to thirty are very important years in the life of a man, and many great things have been accomplished by mere man during that period of life; and it is not reasonable that one who had the knowledge from his infancy that he was the special messenger of God, clothed with all the powers and knowledge of the truth, which Jesus displayed after he commenced his public ministry, would have remained in seclusion during the years that I have named, and not given the world the benefit of these great possessions. No, to me, his story is one in consonance with reason and I must believe it. At any rate the fact that he says it is true, is sufficient.

Well, I had hoped to resume my discourse on the laws of the spirit world before now, but your time has been so occupied that I could not intrude upon you; but very soon, if agreeable to you, we will continue.

With all my love, I will say good night.
Your old professor and teacher,
Joseph Salyards.

The kingdom of God on earth and in the spirit world or the way to the kingdom of the perfect man

May 5th, 1917.

I am here, Jesus.

I come tonight to write on the only way by which men can reach the Kingdom of God, or the way to the perfect man.

This is a subject that many men and teachers have endeavored to explain to mankind, and the ways described have been as varied and sometimes contradictory as the thoughts and education of these men have differed; and all have sought to base their teachings and conclusions on the Bible. I, of course, mean those who profess to be Christians. As to other teachers and reformers, as they have been called, their teachings are based on the doctrines of the various sects to which they have belonged or professed allegiance.

But the Kingdom of God is more peculiarly a phrase that is found in and belongs to the Christian Bible, and to some extent in the Hebrew scriptures.

In considering the subject of this message it is first important to understand what is meant by the "Kingdom of God." Some understand or conceive it to be a kingdom on earth in which the will and laws of God will be followed and obeyed by men in the mortal life, and others understand it to be that Kingdom of God which exists and will continue to exist in perfection in the spirit world; and some few, that kingdom which will find its home or place of existence in the Celestial Spheres.

Now, the way to each of these kingdoms is not the same, although in pursuing the way to one, and that the Celestial Kingdom, the way to the others, must necessarily be followed, or in other words, he who follows the way to the Celestial Kingdom pursues that course which in its pursuit, will cause him to do those things and obey those laws of God that are necessary to establish the Kingdoms on earth and in the spirit world; but he who pursues only the way that leads to the establishment of the kingdom on earth and in the spirit world, cannot possibly become an inhabitant of the Celestial Kingdom.

The Kingdom of God on earth, or in the spirit world, may be obtained by man, or spirit, by obeying the will of God in those essentials that will work a purification of his natural love, and cause that coming into harmony with His laws which affect and control man as mere man; that is, that will restore man to the condition of perfection that existed before the fall of the first parents; and many of my teachings, when on earth, of which there are preserved a number in the Bible, were intended to instruct men into that way of life that would develop their moral qualities and free them from the taint and destructiveness of sin in which they were then and are now living. By the observance of my teachings and sincere obedience to these moral precepts, man will lose those things that belong to his appetites and passions and evil thoughts and desires, and realize that in their places will come a purer love and more spiritual desires and thoughts which lead to a cleansing of his heart and soul, and which means a living and thinking in harmony with the will and laws of God. For God is all good, and all His laws require that man shall become good in order that this kingdom in the spirit world shall be established.

Naturally, and I mean according to His creation, man is good, and not the depraved creature that for so many centuries the teachings and doctrines of the church have declared him to be; and when he shall arrive at that state of goodness that was his in the beginning, he will merely have rid himself of those contaminating appetites, thoughts and desires that made him the sinful and inharmonious being that he now is.

So, from this, you will see that the work of man, in order to enable the kingdom to become established on earth, is largely a work of renunciation; and this truth was taught by prophets and teachers prior to the time of my coming to earth and teaching the way to the Celestial Kingdom; and the same truth applies to the spirits that shall make up and establish the kingdom in the spirit world.

In these kingdoms of the purification and regaining of the perfected natural love, there will be nothing of the divine nature of the Father, except as may be generally said, all the objects of His creation, by reason of being such objects, may partake of the image of the divine. But this is not the divine. The Divine in its true sense is that which partakes of the very essence and nature of god, and not that which is merely the object of his creation.

Man, in body, soul and spirit body, is only a creation of God, and, as to the soul, an image of its Creator, but this creation was not made of any, the least part of the essence or substance of God; and this creation can, if it so please the Father, in its composite and coordinated existence, be utterly destroyed and reduced to the elements of which it was created, without in the smallest degree affecting the true substance or nature of God. So you will see, that in truth there is in or of man nothing of the divine; and, hence, when the kingdom of God shall be established on earth, or in the spirit world, there will be therein, nothing of the divine, only the existence of the perfect creatures, living and thinking in harmony with the laws of God which control their creation and existence.

So that the way in which these two kingdoms of the non-divine can be established, is by man pursuing that course of thinking and living that will enable him to renounce and get rid of those things—foreign to his true nature—which prevent him from coming again into the exact harmony with the will of God as expressed and made obligatory by the law of man's creation.

The observance of the moral law will enable men to accomplish this end. The love with which man was endowed, as the perfect man, enables him, as it becomes purified and more harmonious, to love God and to love his fellow-man as himself, for this natural love is one that in its perfection and nature is universal, and in its exercise every man is his neighbor's brother.

The progressive qualities of this love which every man may obtain, are truly and wonderfully set forth by Peter in one of his epistles as contained in the Bible (II Peter, Chapter 1, Verses 5, 6, 7) and if men will seek these successive steps in acquiring the purifying development of this love, they will obtain the great object sought for.

As I have written, the Bible contains many of my teachings which if followed, will lead to this end, and men will realize the Kingdom of God on earth.

And here let me correct one mistaken belief or idea that has so long prevailed among mankind, and which, in its results, has delayed the coming of the kingdom on earth; and the correction is, that God by His mere fiat, or irrespective of the desires and workings of men's souls, will not establish this kingdom. Its establishment depends upon men, themselves, and until their loves become and they become in harmony with God's will, this kingdom will never be established.

I know that it is believed and taught and emphasized, and men place all their hopes and expectations of a heaven of bliss on the statement, that I will at sometime come in the clouds of heaven with a great shout, to earth, and by the power which they believe exists in me, establish the Kingdom of God—a kind of kingdom in which I will be the king and rule supreme, and receive as my subjects those who believe in and worship me, and send those who do not into eternal damnation and outer darkness.

Well, this is pitiable, untrue and all erroneous. This kingdom will never be established in this way, for only man, himself, can call into existence this kingdom, only by becoming the pure perfect man that existed when God's earthly kingdom had at man's creation, its existence. Man alone, brought sin into the world, and man must himself destroy sin, and then harmony with the Father's will will be restored, and also this kingdom.

But, from what I have written, it must not for a moment or in the slightest degree, be inferred even, that God is not taking and will not take any part in the reestablishment of this kingdom, for it is a fact, that He is working through His angels upon the souls and thoughts of men to bring this kingdom on earth; but He will not force its establishment—it must come voluntarily on the part of men.

When He created man, He gave him a free will—the most wonderful of the natural gifts to man—and He will not, by the exercise of His power arbitrarily control the direction of that will, but as to it leaves man supreme. Of course while this is so, yet if man in such exercise contravenes the laws of God, man must suffer the consequences, for He never changes or sets aside His laws. Man may exercise his free will as he desires and as his thoughts and appetites may influence him to do, but the freedom of exercise does not prevent the imposition of the penalties that the laws prescribe when they are violated. Thus you see there is freedom without limitation, but every inharmonious exercise of that freedom must invite the infliction of that which necessarily follows the violation of harmony.

God wants and is patiently waiting for the love of man, and is always the loving Father who delights not in the suffering of His creatures, for He wants their love to come voluntarily and without constraint or fear of punishment or hope of reward, except that reward which must necessarily follow the blending of God's love and the love of man.

Then I say, the Kingdom of Heaven on earth is not the Divine Kingdom, and has not in it that which is necessarily divine, except the love of God to His creatures to bless and make them happy. His essence and substance are not conferred upon them, for if they were, men would not remain in the kingdom of earth, but would, to a degree, be in the Celestial Heaven, even while on earth, and as I know some men, while still mortals, are in this Divine Heaven.

Now, what I have said with reference to the Kingdom of Heaven on earth, applies with equal truth to the Kingdom of God in the spirit world, for there the inhabitants are merely the spirits of men after they have surrendered their physical bodies, and become purified in their natural love and in harmony with the will and laws of God controlling their existence as perfect men.

While the Kingdom of God has not yet been established on earth, it has been in the spirit world, for in the highest sphere of that world the souls of men have become purified and harmony has been restored, and the souls of men enjoy the supreme happiness that was bestowed upon them at the time of their first creation, which God pronounced very good. Sometime you will have described to you the bliss and wonderful happiness of that kingdom; and I will not say that this is beyond all conception of men, and was established not by the mere power and will of God, but by the exercise of the will of men after they became spirits in renouncing evil and sin, and having their thoughts and desires and soul in its natural love purified and made harmonious. And here I must say, that all men who have ever lived, or who shall ever live, will, at sometime live in this Kingdom of God in the spirit world, or in the Kingdom of the Celestial Spheres; but the large majority will find their homes in the former kingdom.

The hells and dark places will be emptied of their inhabitants and abolished forever, and, surprising as it may seem to mortals, not by the fiat of god, but the exercise of men's will and desires and longings for the attainment of the purification of their love, and by their reaching the goal of their aspirations. But God will be with them in their efforts, and his angels will do his will in helping mortals and spirits along this way to the spiritual kingdom.

Then how important it is that mortals should understand and realize the great work that they must do in establishing the kingdom on earth and the kingdom in the spirit world, and not rest supinely in the mere intellectual belief that God will in His own way and at His own time, establish this kingdom, and that they who believe in God and observe the creeds and doctrines of their churches and perform their duties as church members, will become inhabitants of that kingdom, and in a moment become pure and undefiled and in harmony with the will of God and His laws. It is a very harmful belief, because the only way to this kingdom is the way of renunciation and purification, and all the beliefs ever possessed by men that do not lead to this purification of men's souls, will not lead to this kingdom.

Man, with the help of the Father, must hew his own destiny, and the Father, without the effort of man will not make for him a destiny that his condition of soul and love do not entitle him to.

But there is a Kingdom greater and different and unlike these kingdoms of which I have been writing, and that is the Celestial Kingdom of God; and only those who receive of the Divine Essence can become inhabitants of this Kingdom. The souls of men must become transformed

True Gospel Revealed anew by Jesus

into the very Nature Divine of God, and the natural love of man be changed in all its qualities and elements into the Divine Love of the Father.

I have written that many of my moral teachings are recorded in the Bible, and that I came, or rather my acceptance by the Father as His beloved son, and the reception into my soul of His Divine Love qualified me to teach the way to the several kingdoms; and as was said in that Book, what was lost by the disobedience of the first man was restored by the coming of the second, and that only means, that by reason of the knowledge that came to me of truth and of the laws of harmony that govern God's universe, I was enabled to teach men the way to a return to the purity and development of their souls in natural love that existed before the great loss caused by the disobedience of the first man. I was not to bring about this restoration by any great power or Godlike qualities of omniscience that I might be supposed to possess, but merely by teaching men to love God and their brothers, and to pursue that course of living and thinking that would necessarily enable them to renounce sin and evil and come into a state of harmony with the laws of their creation.

Now, while I taught these moral truths, I also taught the great spiritual truths that show men the way to the Celestial Kingdom, for in my communions with the Father there came to me not only the Divine Love which transformed my soul into the substance of the Father in its love qualities, but also the knowledge by which this Divine Love might be acquired and the certain way to the Celestial Kingdom, even though to a degree while in the flesh.

But my spiritual teachings that show the way to the Celestial Kingdom were not so well understood by my hearers—and not even by my intimate disciples—but more so by John, and consequently were not preserved in the Bible, as were my moral teachings. And as to the Bible, I mean the original manuscripts were not written until many years after my death. Even in these manuscripts not many of my teachings as to the way that leads to this Celestial Kingdom, were contained; and afterwards when these manuscripts were copied, and the copies recopied, these important truths were not preserved—scarcely any. Though the fundamental ones, namely: God is love, and except a man be born again he cannot enter into the Kingdom of Heaven were retained.

And as time went by and the recopying continued, fewer and fewer of my precepts were preserved, and men came to know less and less of these higher truths, and, consequently, the mere moral teachings became better understood and were used by the teachers and instructors of the masses to lead men to a kingdom of God.

And in addition to this, these leaders changed even these moral truths and the interpretations of the early writers in such a way as to enable these leaders to attain to wealth and power and control over the common people in their beliefs and observances of worship. The God of love then, to a large extent, became a God of hatred and wrath, inflicting punishment upon those who dared to disobey those injunctions that the hierarchy of the church placed upon them as the demands and will of God.

But these matters have been written upon more fully elsewhere, and I will not further enlarge upon them, and will now disclose the true way that leads to the Kingdom of God in the Celestial Heavens.

Well, we have written a long time tonight, and I think it best to postpone my further writing till later.

I must say this though, that I am pleased that you are in so much better condition, and I feel that now we can proceed more rapidly with our messages.

Remember this that my promises will be fulfilled, and you must have faith. I am with you very often, and love you as you know, and will continue to pray to the Father for you.

So trust me and be assured that I am helping you in your desire.

Good night and God bless you.

Your brother and friend,

Jesus.

Affirming that Jesus wrote on the two kingdoms

May 5th, 1917.

I am here, St. John, Apostle of Jesus.

I will not write much, but I desire to say that you have a wonderful message from the Master tonight, and that he was very anxious that you should receive it as correctly as possible; and I must tell you that he was very well satisfied with the way in which he was able to express his thoughts.

It is a wonderful disclosure of the two kingdoms that may and will be established; the kingdom in the spirit world has already been established, for there are many spirits who have the purification of the natural love in that degree that makes them the perfect men as were the first parents.

Well he will come soon and describe the greater and more important way to the true Kingdom of the Father, and I hope that you will be in condition to receive this part of the message in as correct a manner as you have received what has been written tonight. What a Jesus of knowledge and love he is. Can you doubt that he is the very Christ and the Savior of mankind, and showed men the only way to the Celestial Kingdom.

There was a great concourse of spirits present tonight, and many who heard his message were astonished, and, I know, benefitted thereby. The higher spirits were here in great numbers, and also many who have learned the way and are now progressing; and if you could have seen the expressions of love on their countenances you would thank the Father with all the gratitude of your soul that you have been selected for this work.

Oh, my brother, let not doubt come into your soul as to your mission and as to the work that you are doing.

Your bands, both the higher and those who are progressing, were here, and they were so thankful that the Father is so good, and blesses you so much.

I will not write more but in closing repeat; pray and believe and the love will come to you in greater and greater abundance.

With my love and the blessings of the Father, I will say good night.

Your brother in Christ,
John.

The Celestial Heavens.

The only Way to the Kingdom of God in the Celestial Heavens

May 15th 1917.

I am here, Jesus.

I come tonight and desire to finish my message and hope that you may be able to receive it. Well, to continue.

I have described the way to the Kingdom of God on earth and in the spirit world, and now I will describe the only way to the Kingdom of God in the Celestial Heavens.

As I have written before, when man was created, in addition to having bestowed upon him those things that made him the perfect man and in harmony with the laws and will of the Father, he also bestowed upon him the potentiality or privilege of receiving the Divine Love, provided he should seek for it in the only way that God had planned for its attainment. But instead of embracing this great privilege, man became disobedient and sought to exercise his own will, and did so in that manner that lead not only to his fall from the condition and the condition of the perfect manhood in which God had created him, but also to the loss of the great privilege of receiving this Divine Love, which privilege was never rebestowed upon him until my coming and teaching that rebestowal and the true way to obtain this Love.

Now, here it had better be understood what this Divine Love was and is, for it is the same today that it was when man was created in the image of God. This love differs from the natural love of man, with which he was endowed when created and which belongs to all men and which they all possess in a more or less perfect condition, in this, that the Divine Love is that love which belongs to or is a part of God, possessing His Nature and composed of His Substance, and which when possessed by man to a sufficient degree, makes him Divine and of the Nature of God. This Great Love God intended should be received and possessed by all men who should desire to receive it and who would make the effort to obtain it.

It is the Love that contains in itself the divine, which the natural love does not. Many, I know, write and believe that all men, irrespective of the kind of love they have in their souls, possess what they call "the divine spark," which needs only the proper development to make all men divine. But this conception of the state of man in his natural condition is all wrong, for man has not in him any part of the divine, and never can have, unless he receives and has developed in him, this Divine Love.

In all God's universe and creation of things material and spiritual the only one of His creatures who can possibly have within him anything of a divine nature is he who possesses this Divine Love. The bestowal of this love was intended, in its operation and effect, to transform man from the merely perfect man into the divine angel, and thus create a Kingdom of God in the Celestial Spheres, where only that which is divine can enter and find a habitation. And you must understand, that as it depends very largely upon man, himself, to establish the Kingdom of God on earth or in the spiritual world, so it also depends largely on man to establish the Kingdom in the Celestial Heavens. God will not and does not by any power that He may have establish this Divine Kingdom, and if man had never received this Divine Love into his soul, there never would have been any such kingdom brought into existence.

There is now a Kingdom in the Celestial Sphere, but not a finished one, for it is still open and in the process of formation, and is open to the entry of all spirits, and men must seek for it in the only way that the Father has provided, and no man or spirit will be excluded from it, who, with all the longings of his soul, will aspire to enter that kingdom.

I must also state that the time will come when this Celestial Kingdom will be completed, and thereafter neither spirit nor man will be able to enter therein; for this Divine Love of the Father will again be withdrawn from man, as it was from the first parents, and the only kingdom that will then be accessible to man will be the kingdom that will exist on earth, or that which now exists in the spirit world.

Then what is the way that leads to this Celestial Kingdom? The only way? For there is but one!

The observance of the moral precepts and the cleansing of men's souls from sin by following these precepts, will not lead to this kingdom, for as it can be readily seen, the stream can rise no higher than its source, and the source of the souls of men in a merely purified state, is the condition of the perfect man—that condition in which he was before his fall—and, hence the results of the observance and living of the merely moral precepts and the exercise of the natural love in its pure state, is, that man will be restored to the condition of the perfect man—the created man in whom there is nothing of the divine. But this restored condition of man will be so perfect and so in harmony with God's will and His laws governing the highest and most perfect of His creatures, that man will be very happy. Yet, he will continue to be only the created being, having nothing more than the image of his Maker.

So, I say, living in a harmony with the moral laws and the exercise of this natural love in its highest and purest state towards God and towards his fellow man, will not lead into the way to the Celestial

Kingdom, but the greatest height of his attainment will be the kingdom on earth or that in the spirit heavens.

And the distinct and differing nature of these kingdoms from that of the Celestial Heavens, will enable mankind to understand the difference between the missions of the great teachers and reformers who preceded me in their work among men, and the mission which I was selected to perform on earth. The former could not possibly have taught the way to the Celestial Kingdom, for until my coming, this Divine Love of which I write was not possible for man to obtain. the privilege was not, before that time, in existence after the first parents lost it, and there was no Celestial Kingdom in which men could find their eternal home.

So, I repeat, all the moral teachings of the world's history could not show the way to the Celestial Kingdom of God, and cannot now, for morality, as understood and taught by mankind and by the spirits and angels, cannot give to man that which is absolutely necessary in order to transform his soul into that state or condition that fits him for an entrance into this truly Divine Kingdom of the Father.

But the way thereto is simple and single and men were taught that way by me when I was on earth; and could have been taught that way during all the centuries since I left the human life; and I must say that some have been so taught and have found that way, but comparatively few, for the mortals whose ostensible and claimed mission and privilege were to teach that way. I mean the priests and preachers and churches have neglected to teach the same, but rather, though in earnestness and realizing their allegiance to God and their obligations to mankind, have taught merely the way which the observance of the moral precepts would lead men into.

And all this, notwithstanding, that in the Bible, which most of those professing to be Christians believe contains my sayings and teachings, is set forth this way to the Celestial Kingdom. The words are few and the way is plain, and no mystery prevents men from comprehending the meaning thereof. When I said, "Except a man be born again, he cannot enter into the Kingdom of God," I disclosed the only and true way to this kingdom. During my time on earth there were some who understood this great truth, and since that time, there have been some who not only understood this truth, but found the way and followed it until they reached the goal and are now inhabitants of this kingdom; but the vast majority of men—priests, teachers and people—have never understood, and have never sought to find the way. This great truth to their spiritual senses has been, as it were, a hidden thing; and as they read or even recite the same to their hearers it has no special significance, but is merely as one of the moral precepts, such as "Love your neighbor as yourself," and with not as much importance attached to it as to some of these moral instructions.

And so, all down the ages since the great kingdom has been waiting for men, they, though in all sincerity and in love towards God, have sought for and to a greater or lesser extent, found only the kingdom of the perfect man, and have neglected to seek for and missed the kingdom of the divine angel.

Then, as I have said, this Divine Love of the Father, when possessed by the soul of man, makes him in his substance and essence Divine like unto the Divinity of the Father, and only such souls constitute and inhabit the Celestial or Divine Kingdom of God; and this being so, it must be readily seen that the only way to the Celestial Kingdom is that which leads to the obtaining of this Divine Love, which means the New Birth; and which New Birth is brought about by the flowing into the souls of men this Divine Love, whereby the very Nature and Substance of the Father, and wherefrom men cease to be the merely created beings, but become the souls of men born into the Divine reality of God.

Then the only way to the Celestial Kingdom being by the New Birth, and that birth being brought to men only by the inflowing and working of this Divine Love, and whether or not a man shall experience this birth depending in its initiative on the man himself, the question arises how or in what way can a man obtain this Divine Love and this New Birth and the Celestial Kingdom. And because the way is so easy and simple, it may be that men will doubt the truth of my explanation, and continue to believe and place all their hopes upon the orthodox doctrines of the vicarious atonement—the washing of the blood, my sufferings on the cross and bearing all the sins of the world, and my resurrection from the dead—doctrines as harmful to the salvation of mankind as they are without truth or foundation in fact or effect.

The only way then is simply this: that men shall believe with all the sincerity of their minds and souls that this Great Love of the Father is waiting to be bestowed upon each and all of them, and that when they come to the Father in faith and earnest aspirations, this love will not be withholden from them. and in addition to this belief, pray with all the earnestness and longings of their souls that he open up their souls to the inflowing of this Love, and that then may come to them the Holy Spirit to bring this Love into their souls in such abundance that their souls may be transformed into the very Essence of the Father's Love.

The man who will thus believe and pray will never be disappointed, and the way to the kingdom will be his as certainly as that the sun shines day by day upon the just and the unjust alike.

No mediator is needed, nor are the prayers or ceremonies of priests or preachers, for God comes to man, himself, and hears his prayers and responds thereto by sending the Comforter, which is the Father's messenger for conveying into the souls of men this great divine love.

I have thus explained the only way to the Celestial Kingdom of God and to the divine nature in love; and there is no other way whereby it is possible to reach this kingdom and the certain knowledge of immortality.

So, I implore men to meditate on these great truths, and in meditating believe, and when believing, pray to the Father for the inflowing into their souls of this Divine Love, and in doing so they will experience belief, faith and possession and ownership of that which can never be taken from them—no, not in all eternity.

And so it is with man to choose and fix his destiny. Will that destiny be the perfect man or the Divine Angel?

I have finished and feel that you have received my message as I intended, and am pleased.

I will not write more now, and with my love and blessings, will say good night.

Your brother and friend,
Jesus.

Affirmation by Samuel, Jesus wrote the message

May 15th, 1917.

I am here, Samuel, Prophet of Old.

I have heard the Master's message and as are all of his, it is filled with truths that are vital to man's future happiness and condition of being. I have also been with you very often, and have tried to help you in every way that I could, and you must believe that you have around you a host of celestial as well as spiritual spirits who are interested in you and endeavoring to assist you in your work.

I will come soon and write. So with my love I will say good night.

Your brother in Christ,
Samuel.

After death, the judgment. What it is and what it is not

February 25th, 1918.

I am here, Jesus.

I am here and desire to write a few lines in reference to the great day of judgment, of which the preacher and teachers of theological things write so often. I know that the Bible, or rather some of the books, lay great stress upon this day when, as they claim, God will pour out His vials of wrath upon the ungodly and condemn them to an eternity of punishment.

There is, as you know, very great and diverse opinions among these learned men as to what is the meaning and significance of this day of judgment, and when, in a chronological point of view, it will take place; and all these varied opinions have many students and teachers who embrace and proclaim them to the world as being true and free from doubt.

Well, it is certain that all men must die and there will come the judgment, and that which follows the death is just as certain as is the death itself, and just as reasonable as is the following of any cause by an effect. So men should have no difficulty in believing in the judgment as a fact that cannot be avoided, just as death cannot be avoided.

But the word and the fact, judgment, when used as an effect or following of death, may have many meanings in the opinions and understandings of many men, depending upon what men may believe as to things that are called religious or scientific or philosophical. To the ultra-orthodox this term judgment means and necessarily comprehends the active pronouncement of a sentence by God, because of and determined by their lives and thoughts while living in the mortal life, irrespective of any of His general laws and the workings thereof. God is Himself the judge—personal and present—and by Him in this capacity are each man's life and works known and digested and made the basis of the sentence that He must pronounce in each individual case. God keeps the record of all of these acts of men, or, if man is conceded to be his own record-keeper, his records are, or will be, at the time of the great assemblage for judgment, opened up or brought into view so that nothing can be lost; and then, upon this record men will be sent to eternal happiness or to everlasting punishment, or, as some believe, to destruction or annihilation.

Others, not orthodox, who believe in the survival of the soul and the continuing memories of the acts and thoughts of men, teach that the judgment will follow death as a natural consequence of the operations of the law of cause and effect; and the effect cannot be escaped from, until in some way there comes to the consciousness of men a realization that the effect in their suffering has satisfied the cause and that there is nothing mysterious or unnatural in the appearance and workings of the judgment. They do not believe that God by any special interposition or personal punishing will pronounce the judgment, or determine the merits or demerits of the one called to judgment.

Besides these views, there are others extant and believed in, but the two that I have mentioned are principle ones and are sufficient to show what the large majority of thinking or rather believing, men conclude the term judgment as used in the Bible should mean or be understood to mean.

Well, the judgment of the human soul is an important

accompaniment of the human life, both in the flesh and in the spirit world, and as regards the questions and punishments, hardly anything demands more of the thought and consideration of men, for it is a certainty that beliefs, true or false, he cannot avoid them. Judgment as certainly follows what men call death as does night the day, and no philosophy or theological dogmas or scientific determinations can alter the fact, or in any way change the character or exact workings of this judgment.

But judgment is not a thing belonging exclusively to the after-death period or condition, for it is present and operating with men from the time that they become incarnated in the human until they become disincarnate, and thereafter continuously until the causes of effects have been satisfied and there remains nothing to be judged, which happy ending is also a fact—for all men are dependent upon their progress towards the conditions of harmony with the laws that make effective as well as pronounce the judgments. While on earth these laws operate, and continuously man is being judged for the causes that he starts into existence, and the after-death judgment is only a continuation of the judgment received by men while on earth.

Of course—men may not know this—these judgments or the effects thereof, become more intensified after men have gotten rid of the influences of the flesh existence, and they become spirits, having only the spirit qualities. And because of this fact men must understand and try to realize that the expression "after death, the judgment" has a greater significance and is of more vital importance than the saying—that "judgment is with men all during their mortal lives."

After death the causes of the inharmony with the law becomes more pronounced, and appear in the true meaning and force, and, consequently, as this is true the effects become more intensified and understood, and men suffer more and realize the darkness, and sometimes the gross darkness, that these effects produce. The inharmony appears in its unclothed and unhidden reality, and the law's workings bring to men the exact penalties that their violations demand.

Man is his own bookkeeper, and in his memory are recorded all the thoughts and deeds of his earth life that are not in accord with the harmony of God's will, which is expressed or manifested by His laws. The judgment is not the thing of a day or a time, but is never ceasing so long as there exists that upon which it can operate, and it diminishes in proportion as the causes of inharmony disappear.

God is not present in wrath demanding, as does the human who believes himself to have been injured demanding reparation by the one causing the injury. No—the Father is present only in love, and as the soul of the one undergoing the penalty, which his own deeds and thoughts have imposed upon him, comes more in harmony with the Father's will,

He, as you mortals say, is pleased.

Never an angry God, rejoicing in the satisfaction of a penalty being paid by one of His erring children, but always a loving Father rejoicing in the redemption of His children from a suffering that a violation of the laws of harmony exacts with certitude.

Then, as I say, the judgment day is not a special time when all men must meet in the presence of God, and have their thoughts and deeds weighed in the balance, and then, according as they are good or evil, have the sentence of an angry, or even just God pronounced upon them.

The judgment day is every day, both in the earth life of man and in life in the spirit, where the law of compensation is working. In the spirit world time is not known and every breathing is a part of eternity, and with every breathing so long as the law requires, comes the judgment, continued and unsatisfied, until man, as a spirit, reaches that condition of harmony, so that for him, no longer the law demands a judgment.

But from what I have written, men must not suppose, or beguile themselves into that state of belief that will cause them to think that because there is no special day of judgment when God will pronounce His sentence, the judgment, therefore, is not so much to be dreaded or shunned. No, this state of thinking will palliate only for the moment, for the judgment is certain, and is and will be no less to be dreaded, because the immutable law demands exact restoration instead of an angry God.

No man who has lived and died has escaped, and no man who shall hereafter die can escape this judgment unless he has, in a way provided by the Father in His love, become in harmony with the laws requiring harmony. "*As a man soweth so shall he reap*" is as true as is the fact that the sun shines upon the just and the unjust alike.

Memory is man's storehouse of good and evil, and memory does not die with the death of the man's physical body, but on the contrary, becomes more alive—all alive—and nothing is left behind or forgotten when the spirit man casts off the encumbrance and the benumbing and deceiving influences of the only body of man that was created to die.

Judgment is real, and men must come to it face-to-face, and want of belief or unbelief or indifference or the application to men's lives of the saying "sufficient unto the day is the evil thereof" will not enable men to avoid the judgment or the exactions of its demands.

There is a way, though, in which men may turn the judgment of death into the judgment of life—inharmony into harmony—suffering into happiness—and judgment itself into a thing to be desired.

Elsewhere we have written of this way open to all men, and I will not attempt to describe it here.

I have written enough for tonight. You are tired and must not be drawn on further.

So with my love I will say good night.
Your brother and friend,
Jesus.

The beliefs of a mission preacher

September 17th 1916.

I am here, Jesus.

I was with you tonight at the meeting and heard what the preacher said, and he declared some truths, and also said some things that were not true. He said "only those who have been converted are sons of God."

All men are the children of God, and His love and care are over all, and they are very dear to Him, otherwise He would not have rebestowed His love upon them and given them the privilege of becoming inhabitants of His Celestial Kingdom.

The mere fact that they are sinners makes them no less His children, who He is so anxious to redeem and fill with the Divine Love, and when the preacher says "they who are sinners are not the sons of God," he does not declare the truth, for they are all His sons—some to enjoy the pure life and bliss which the purification of their natural love will bring to them, and others to enjoy and inhabit the Celestial Kingdom which the New Birth will bring to them.

But all are His sons, though some have wandered and become strangers to His Love, just as was the prodigal son who left his father's house for a far country.

This doctrine of the sinful not being sons of God is a damnable and harmful doctrine, and will cause many to give up hope of ever becoming anything else than the sons of perdition—or as these orthodox say—of the devil.

The Father's mercy is for all, and if certain of His children do not choose to seek and receive the Divine Love which, when possessed, will make angels of them, yet they are His sons, and will in the fullness of time, or before the time of the great consummation, become pure and happy beings, as were the first parents before the fall.

And while this preacher has a great amount of the Divine Love in his soul, and is earnestly and in the right way seeking for more, yet his beliefs and teachings as to the destiny and future condition of those who may receive this love and become at one with the Father are all wrong, and will tend to retard his own progress in the development of his soul and in his advancement towards the Kingdom of God.

He, of course, is possessed of these beliefs because of his study and construction of some of the declarations of the Bible, and therefore, is not teaching what he does not believe, or what, to his own conscience, is false. Nevertheless, it is false and he will have to suffer the consequences of such false beliefs and teachings.

Ignorance, while it will not relieve him from its consequences, and neither will it invoke the penalties of the law that apply to the willful deceiver or teacher of false doctrines, yet neither will it excuse him or relieve him from the penalties of that law which demands the truth, and only the truth to be believed and taught. He will have to get rid of these false beliefs, even though he may have some of the divine in his soul; for whenever there exists untruth in belief in the heart and soul of man, to that extent it interferes with the inflowing of the love into and the progress of that soul towards perfect unity with the Father.

Truth is of itself a fact. It can have no affiliation with untruth, no matter that untruth is the result of ignorance, for all untruth is the result of ignorance, and must be eradicated from the hearts of men before there can be that harmony between God and man which the very nature of truth itself requires. So that if no man could be the son of God, who has not the perfect harmony which truth absolutely demands, God would have no sons amongst men. The condition of the sinner and that of the man who has experienced the New Birth differs only in the fact that one has not commenced to have in his soul the essence of Truth, while the other, to an extent, has that essence. All may have that essence, and to a great abundance. Some may never have the essence of Divine Truth, yet no man will be left without the essence of the truth which leads to the perfect man. The truth of the angel existence and the truth of the perfect man are equally truths, though the former is of a higher degree and nature than the other.

Our first parents were the children of God—His own creatures—good and perfect, and after their fall they became no less His children, for His love was so great for them that in the fullness of perfection of His plans He again bestowed upon them the privilege of receiving His Divine Love, and sent me to proclaim the fact and to show men the way to obtain that great love. The death that had existed for all the long centuries was supplanted by life potential, and I became the way, the truth and the life, and immortality became a possibility to men. So that, all men are the sons of God in one relation or the other; depending in the one case whether a man will turn from his sins and be satisfied with the perfection of his natural love and the home that belongs to the perfect man, or seeks for the inflowing into his soul the divine love which will enable him to enter the Divine Heavens and have the certainty of immortality.

When God rebestowed this Divine Love on man, there was no man in existence, or spirit either, who could be called His son, if it were necessary that he had been converted as the preacher said, because none had received this love which is the only thing or power in all God's universe that can convert a man dead in trespass and sin: yet God loved all His children and conferred upon them this great gift, because they were His children. If God had loved only the righteous there would have been no one who could have been the object of His bounty. He would have had no sons or children of His love. And now that He has rebestowed this gift, and some of the sons of men have received and possess it, and are more in harmony with Him, it is not true that those who were His sons and children before its bestowal are any less His sons and children, because they may not have sought and made this gift their own.

No, the Father's love is so great and broad and deep, that it goes out to all the children of earth, waiting to bestow it upon them, and the lost sheep is as much His child as the ninety and nine who are safe in the fold, and although the lost one may never find or enter the fold, where those are that possess His Divine Love are sheltered, yet that sheep remains and is the object of His love.

So let preachers and others, who have assumed the responsibility of teaching men the truths of the Father, cease from proclaiming the doctrine that only those who have received the new birth are the sons of God. They, of course, are not His obedient sons until they have obtained either the Divine Love and Essence of the Father, or the purity of the first parents before the fall, but yet they are His, even though defiled by their own creations of sin and error.

God is love—and love knows no limitations in its heights or depths. It exists in the highest heavens, and reaches to the lowest hells, and will in its own way and in its own time work its own fulfillment. All men will come into harmony with the will of the Father, which is perfect, and even though some, and I may say the majority of men, will not accept the invitation to become angels of His Celestial Kingdom, which is not compulsory, yet they do His will by becoming in the future, near or far, free from the sin and error of their own creation, and pure and perfect as were they, whom the Father first created and pronounced good.

Man's greatest enemy to man is he, who having received the assurance of possessing the Divine Love, and thereby becoming as it were, a divine son of the Father, and who believes in the errors of the Bible and the misinterpretations of its truths, declares that all others of mankind are hated of God, and are objects of His wrath, and certain of eternal damnation and everlasting torment. It is deplorable that such beliefs and such declarations should exist and continue to be made, especially on the part of those who undertake to lead the masses in the way to God's truths and plans for men's happiness, and redemption from the evils and sins that cause them so much suffering.

But all this shows the power and blindness of belief founded upon error and untruthful teachings. And strange as it may seem, these leaders of the ignorant may have some of the Divine Love in their souls, and yet their mental and intellectual beliefs be so fixed and unmoveable that the possession of this love will not cause them to understand that the Father's love is for all, and that wrath is not a part of His being, but a quality of sinful man that these believers in error attribute to Him.

If God may be said to hate anything, He hates sin, but He loves the sinner, who is the creature of His will, and who is so unfortunate as to have created that which defiles him and to wander away, not only from the Father, but from his own perfect and pure creation.

Well, I have written enough for tonight and I hope that what I have said may prove beneficial not only to the sinner, but to the man, preacher, or layman, who possessing some of the Divine Love, proclaims that only he or others like him, are the sons of God.

As Paul said, "they see through a glass darkly," but then they shall see face to face, and when they do, they will see such evidences and manifestations of the Father's love that they will know that they and their sinning brothers are all sons of the Father, although one may be an heir to the Celestial Kingdom and the Divine Essence of the Father, while the other may be an heir only to the pure love of the Father, to bless and make them happy in the pure natural love and perfect manhood which the so-called Adam possessed before his fall.

I must stop now, but in doing so say, that you must not let what any of these orthodox believers may say disturb your faith in our communications, for they know only what the Bible tells them, and you know the truths that we declare. I will soon come and write to you a message of truth that I have been waiting sometime to write. Believe that I love you and am with you, praying for you and helping you with my influence.

Good night, and may the Father bless you.
Your brother and friend,
Jesus.

Divine Love—what It is and what It is not. How It can be obtained

August 5th, 1916.

I am here, St. John.[11]

---

[11] "Saint" is not used by Celestial spirits. Wherever it is used by the celestials, it is for the purpose of identification by the human reader. (Dr. S)

True Gospel Revealed anew by Jesus

I come tonight to say only a few words and these in reference to love—the Divine Love of the Father which He rebestowed upon mankind at the coming of the Master. This Love is the greatest thing in all the world, and the only thing that can make man at one with the Father, and change the soul of man as it has existed since his creation, into a Divine Substance filled with the Essence of the Father. There is nothing else in all the universe of God that can cause man to become a new creature, and an inhabitant of the Father's Kingdom; and when men possess this Love, then they possess everything that will make them not only the perfect man but the divine angel. Then men will understand the moral precepts of brotherly love and also the Father's oneness, and they will not have to seek for other help in order to bring into the life of the human race those qualities that will bring to it peace and good will. Then will every man know that every other man is his brother, and be able to do unto each as he would have the other to do unto him, and this without effort or sacrifice on his part, for love worketh its own fulfillment and all its beneficence floweth towards the fellow-man as falls the dews from heaven. Envy and hatred and strife and jealousy and all the other evil qualities of man will disappear, and only peace and joy and happiness will remain.

It is so abundant that it may be possessed by all men by the mere seeking and the sincere longing for its inflowing. But man must understand that it is not his by matter of right, nor is it ever forced upon him, but comes only in response to the sincere earnest prayer of a soul that is filled with longings for its coming. This Love comes not with observation of mere moral rules, or with good deeds and the exercise of the natural love of a man towards his fellows, because no man can possibly merit it by any deeds or acts or kindness of heart that he may have.

All these things are desirable and they work out their own rewards, and bring the happiness and peace that result from good thoughts and kind deeds; but all these do not bring unto the soul of man this Great Love. It is the Father alone, and only when the soul is opened up to its reception can it possibly find its home in that soul. It is greater than faith or hope, because it is the real substance of the Father, while faith and hope are the qualities which a man may possess by his own efforts, and which are given him that he may realize the possibility of obtaining this Love. They are merely means—it is the end and fullness of their exercise.

But men must not believe that all love is the Divine Love for it is very different in its substance and qualities from all other loves. All men have, a part of their possessions, the natural love, and they need not pray for a bestowal of that, although since it has become defiled by sin it needs to be purified and freed from this blight, and the Father is ever willing and ready to help men obtain this purification. But this Divine Love is not a part of man's nature nor can he obtain or possess it, except he seek for it. It comes from without and is not developed from within.

It is the result of individual acquirement, and not the object of universal possession. It may be possessed by all; it can be possessed by only a few; and each man must determine for himself whether it shall be his. With God there is no respect of persons; neither is there any royal road to the obtaining of this Love. All must pursue the same way and that way is the one that Jesus taught: the opening up of the soul to this love finding a lodgment therein, which can be brought about only by sincere prayer and longing for its inflowing.

This Love is the life of the Celestial Heavens and the only key that will unlock the gates, and when the mortal enters therein, all other love is absorbed by it. It has no substitute, and is of itself, a thing apart. It is of the Essence of the Divine, and the spirit which possesses it is Divine itself. It may be yours, it may be all men's and it may not. You must decide that question for yourself, not even the Father can make the decision for you.

In closing let me repeat that It (Divine Love) is the greatest thing in all God's universe and not only the greatest, but the sum of all things, for from It flows every other thing that brings peace and happiness. I will not write more tonight, and with my love to you, and the blessing of the Father, I will say good night.

Your brother in Christ,
John.

Necessity of faith and prayer in doing the work. Mr. Padgett is his chosen one to do the work

April 22nd, 1917.

I am here, Jesus.

I was with you tonight and heard the sermon, but there was not much said that was very vital to our truths, and I have no comments to make on the sermon. Luther was there also and was disappointed somewhat, for he rather expected the preacher to say some things that might have been beneficial to the souls of his hearers. He will write you very soon, and he is very anxious to do so.

Remember that I love you with a very great love, and that you are my chosen one to do this work, and that to no other man has such an opportunity and privilege ever been given; and you must not become a failure. So much is dependent upon the world getting the truths at this time, for men's souls are longing for the truth, and are susceptible to receiving the same than ever in the history of mankind.

So believe in my love and anxiety and permit yourself to get in close rapport with me. I will pray with you tonight, and you will realize some response to my prayers.

When you pray tonight, believe that what you ask for will come, and you will not be disappointed.

Well, as I told you, when I delivered to you the prayer,[12] if you offer that prayer with all the earnestness and longings of your soul, it will be answered; and when the answer comes these material things will come also, for when you receive what that prayer asks for you will then be in possession of the Kingdom of God, and these other things will be added to you. God knows what you need, and is always ready to bestow upon you these needful things, and when you become His true child, He will not neglect to give you these other things. He is more thoughtful and careful of His children than is the earthly father, and His angels are always ready to do His bidding, So have faith, and pray, and pray and you will realize the wonderful responses that will come to you.

I will not write more tonight, but again impress upon you the necessity of faith and prayer; and you must not forget that we angels of the Father are with you trying to help you. Good night.

With all my love and blessings, I am
Your brother and friend,
Jesus.

Eight Celestial Spirits affirm that Jesus wrote

April 22nd, 1917.

I will say that we are all here, and heard what the Master said, and know that he wrote, and that you can rely on what he said, let doubt leave you, and love and faith take possession of your soul.

May God bless and keep you in His love,

Paul, John, James, Luther, Barnabas, Samuel, John Wesley and John the Baptist

Affirming that the Master wrote

April 22nd, 1917.

I am here, Luke.

I will say only a word, for I see how you feel and how important it is that you believe that the Master wrote you, and how certain it is that you can rely upon what he said. If you only knew how much he is interested in you, and how much love and care He is bestowing upon

---

[12] The Prayer on page 36 of Volume I. (Dr. S)

you, you would not for a moment doubt or lose faith in his promises. And, besides, we are all with you in love and efforts to help you.

So believe and you will not be disappointed.

With my love I will say, good night.

Your brother in Christ,

Luke.

Affirms that eight of the Celestial Spirits signed their names

April 22nd, 1917.

I am here, your own true and loving Helen.[13]

Well, dear, the messages have been rather unusual tonight. I mean the messages corroborating what the Master said, and they show you that you must not doubt or lose your faith in what has been written you, not only tonight but in all the past.

You must also see how interested these spirits are in you, and in the work you must do, for otherwise you would never have received such messages.

Each of those whose names are subscribed, actually wrote. I know them all, and saw them sign their names, and with each signature was a prayer that God would bless you, and give you a great abundance of his love. It is all so wonderful, that I am somewhat astonished at this great display of interest in you, and desire that you shall believe.

So, my dear husband, believe with all your soul, and trust in the love of the Master, and his great desire to see you happy and free.

I will not write more tonight, although I had intended to write my personal letter, but you are too tired to receive it. But you know how much I love you and how anxious I am to see you happy and filled with the Father's love.

I love you and want you to love me.

Good night. Your own true and loving,

Helen.

Jesus says his mission in writing these messages is his second coming on earth

December 2nd, 1915.

I am here, Jesus.

I have heard your discussion tonight, and am pleased at the soul

---

[13] Mrs. J. E. Padgett had made her progress to the Celestial Heavens some time before the above message was written. (Dr. S) This communication was published in Volume II (4th Ed.) page 40. (G.J.C.)

understanding of my truths which you and your friend[14] seem to have and I now feel that you are both progressing to that point where you will soon be in a condition to fully understand what my mission is in writing these messages. You have said truly that my new revelation of the truths of the soul is what mankind needs at this time, and what men will be in condition to accept as the real truths of God's love and of His laws. My coming to you is really my second coming on earth, and the result of my coming in this way will satisfy and fulfill all the promises of the scriptures as to my second coming.

So let your belief in this important fact and your faith in me increase until you will have in your souls and minds no doubt as to what my present mission is, and as to what your work will be in making known to men my real purpose in revealing to them the great truths of the Father.

I will not write more tonight, but say keep up your courage and believe, and the time will soon come when you will be able to receive my messages in all their fullness, and with such rapidity that the spreading of these truths will not be delayed. I am with you and will be a faithful friend and brother, sticking closer to you than any earthly brother.

With all my love and blessings, I am
Your loving brother and friend,
Jesus.

St. James was over-powered by Jesus' great presence

December 2nd, 1915.

Let me say just one word. I was present and I saw the wonders of his power and glory again, I know that he is so much in earnest as to the truths of his mission and of your work that no man can doubt.

I cannot write much for I am so overpowered by his great presence that I can scarcely write. How wonderful that he should come to you in this way and declare to you his great messages of truth and power! If you could only have seen him you would never again doubt him or his great mission and your work.

I must stop.
Your brother in Christ,
St. James.

---

[14] L. R. Stone present. Friend referred to by Jesus. (Dr. S)

Said the Master had written and showed his great power and glory

December 2nd, 1915.

Let me tell you that the Master has just written, and in writing he again displayed his great power and glory for he wrote with all the authority of his heavenly powers. I was present and know what I write to be true.

I wish that I could write you a longer letter tonight but it is late and you need rest.

Your own true brother in Christ,
St. John.

Affirming that the Master wrote with such power and glory

December 2nd, 1915.

I am your grandmother.

My dear son. I feel that I must write you just a line, because I want to tell you that the Master wrote you, and with such power and force that you must not doubt.

He was glorious and with his great love there was so much glory, that we were all for the time, overshadowed by these influences so that we could only listen in adoration.

So believe me when I say that you must believe, for never was a message given with more authority. I know that it is hard for you to conceive what I mean, but you will know some day.

Your own loving grandmother,
Ann Rollins.[15]

The prayer given by Jesus as the only prayer....

December 2nd, 1916.

I am here, Jesus.

I merely want to say a word for the benefit of you and your friend, and that is, that I have listened to your conversation tonight, and find that it is in accord with the truth; and the influence of the Spirit is with you both. Continue in your line of thought and in prayer to the Father, and, also, in your making known to others, whenever the opportunity arises, the importance of seeking for and getting the Divine Love.

---

[15] Celestial Spirit. (Dr. S.)

As your friend[16] said, the only prayer that is necessary is the prayer for the inflowing of this Love; all other forms, or real aspirations, of prayer are secondary, and of themselves, will not tend to produce this love in the souls of men.

Let your prayer[17] be as follows: —

Our Father, who art in heaven, we recognize:
That Thou art all Holy and loving and merciful, and that we are Thy children, and not the subservient, sinful and depraved creatures that our false teachers would have us believe.
That we are the greatest of Thy creation and the most wonderful of all Thy handiworks, and that we are the objects of Thy great Soul's love and tenderest care.
That Thy will is, that we become at one with Thee, and partake of Thy great love which Thou hast bestowed upon us through Thy mercy and desire that we become, in truth, Thy children, through love, and not through the sacrifice and death of any one of Thy creatures, even though the world believes that one Thy equal and a part of Thy Godhead.
We pray that Thou will open up our souls to the inflowing of Thy love, and that then may come Thy Holy Spirit to bring into our souls this, Thy love in great abundance, until our souls shall be transformed into the very essence of Thyself; and that there may come to us faith — such faith as will cause us to realize that we are truly Thy children and one with Thee in very substance and not in image only.
Let us have such faith as will cause us to know that Thou art our Father and the bestower of every good and perfect gift, and that only we, ourselves, can prevent Thy love changing us from the mortal to the immortal.
Let us never cease to realize that Thy love is waiting for each and all of us, and that when we come to Thee with faith and earnest aspiration, Thy love will never be withholden from us.
Keep us in the shadow of Thy love every hour and moment of our lives, and help us to overcome all temptations of the flesh and the influence of the powers of the evil ones, which so constantly surround us and endeavor to turn our thoughts away from Thee to the pleasures and allurements of this world.
We thank Thee for Thy love and for the privilege of receiving it,

---

[16] Friend, L. R. Stone. (Dr. S.)
[17] The prayer quite naturally appears in all four volumes. However careful comparison of this text with the original handwritten document has shown some small differences. The message above is exactly that published in 1941, because in this case an interested reader can easily compare the transcription with that already deciphered and discern the minor differences in Dr. Stone's work. (G.J.C)

and we believe that Thou art our Father—the loving Father who smiles upon us in our weakness, and is always ready to help us and take us to Thy arms of love.

We pray thus with all the earnestness and longings of our soul, and trusting in Thy love, give Thee all the glory and honor and love that our finite souls can give.

This is the only prayer that men need offer to the Father. It is the only one that appeals to the love of the Father, and with the answer, which will surely come, will come all the blessings that men may need, and which the Father sees are for the good of His creatures.

I am in very great rapport with you tonight, and see that the Father's love is with you, and that your souls are hungry for more. So, my brothers, continue to pray and have faith, and in the end will come a bestowal of the love like unto that which came to the apostles at Pentecost. I will not write more now. In leaving you, I will leave my love and blessings and the assurance that I pray to the Father for your happiness and love. Good night.

Your brother and friend,
Jesus.

True Gospel Revealed anew by Jesus

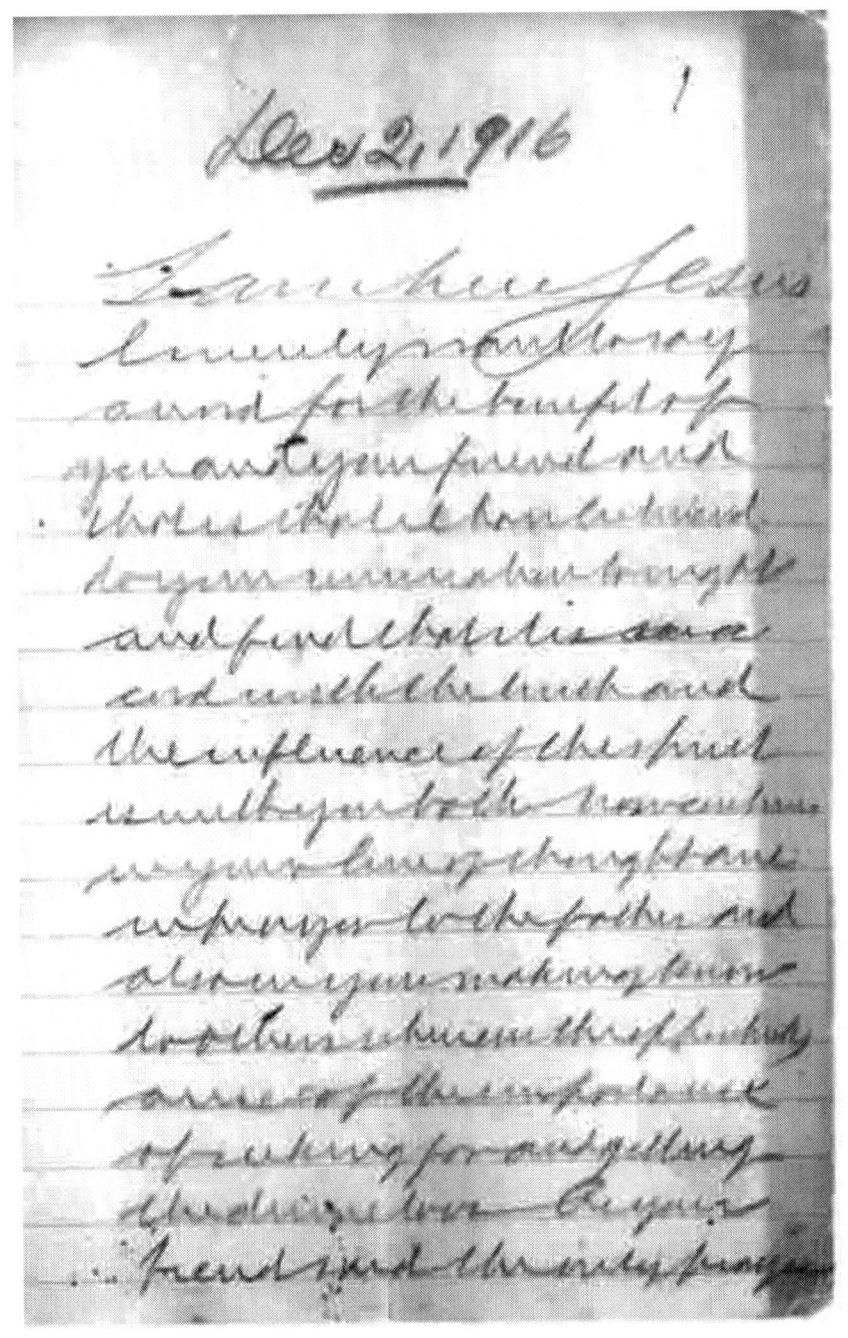

Page one of the prayer

This is the scanned image[18] of page one of the prayer received from Jesus.

Affirmation that Jesus showed his glory

December 2nd, 1915.

I know it is late, but, yet, I must say that what has been told you is true, and when we speak of the glory of the Master you cannot conceive of what is meant. In your mind think of the dim flame of the candle and the glory of the noonday sun and then compare the glory of the greatest thing in all the earth with this glory of the Master, and you will see side by side the dim candle and the glorious sun.

We all know what the Divine Love of the Father is, but do not appreciate its greatness or wonder, until we occasionally see it displayed in and by Jesus.

Go to your prayers in the full belief that this Great Divine Love has been present tonight in amazing abundance, and that you both have had its influence around and in you to a degree, that will cause you to feel to some extent, the great peace that comes only to the children of light and at-onement with the Father.

Believe that your experience of this night is true and that it may be yours frequently when your souls are attuned to the inflowing of the love.

I must say good night, and God bless you with all His influence Divine.

I am your brother in Christ,
A. G. Riddle.

Affirmation by Mrs. Padgett

December 2nd, 1916.

Well, I will and I am glad that you have even one page more.

I am happy tonight, for I see that you have had an experience that has caused your soul to open up to this wonderful Love of the Father.

Oh, my dear, it has been a glorious evening and the Master seemed to breathe out the fullness of the great love that he possesses. Your own true and loving
Helen.

---

[18] James Padgett received all his communications by what is known as automatic writing, and a very large number of the originals still exist to this day. (G J.C.)

Writes on the true meaning of "the end of the world"

October 1st, 1916.

I am here, Saint John.

I come tonight to write a few truths upon the subject of the preacher's (Dr. Gordon's) sermon, as I was present with you and heard his declarations as to the end of the world. I know that among men there are, and have been since the time of the Master, differences in opinion as to when this important event is to take place, and as to the meaning of the end of the world. Well, men know just about as much now as to the time of this event as they have known all down the centuries, and understand the meaning of these prophecies as well as did men from my day down to the present.

In the first place, I will say, there will be no end of the world from any of the causes mentioned by the preacher, and in the next place, there will be no end of the world at all as understood and declared by the orthodox preachers, and as is expected by most of the professing Christians. The world, meaning the earth, will not have an end in the sense of annihilation, but it will continue to revolve on its axis, and to have seed time and harvest, and produce and reproduce those things that are necessary to sustain human life, and have its appropriate seasons of heat and cold, and move along in its orbit as it now does, until some change, we know not of now, may come and destroy it; but such change, not any of the prophecies of the Bible, admitting that there are prophecies, can apply to the end of the world in the sense that the preacher understood and declared.

If humanity would only understand that the world that was lost by the disobedience of the first parents, was the world of man's immortality and happiness and not the physical world, and that Jesus came to declare the restoration of that world upon condition, and the end of that restoration, then would they know that the material world is not involved in the plan of man's salvation, or in Jesus' mission, or in the declarations of Jesus as to the coming of the end.

Men will continue to be born, live a short time and die the physical death, and as to each individual man the end of the material world comes when he dies, for, thereafter, his habitation will be in the spirit world, and never more will he have life on earth. All men at some time will have to die the physical death, then why should it be necessary to include in the plan of God for the salvation of men the destruction of the material world? For planets and worlds and stars to crash together and destroy, would mean that the orderly workings of God's laws must be interfered with, in order that men might be destroyed or saved, according as they might be snatched up into the air, or left to their own weakness on earth.

Such interpretations of God's intentions or plans, or of Jesus coming again to earth is all wrong and absurd. Jesus will never come to establish his kingdom on earth and reign as Prince of Peace and Lord of Lords, for the Kingdom which he and all his followers, both on earth and in the spirit world, are seeking to establish is in the Celestial Heavens, and it is the Kingdom of God, not made with hands or by the mere fiat of any spirit no matter how high he may be, but made and populated by the souls of men who have experienced the New Birth and received the Divine Essence of the Father. Of this Kingdom Jesus is the Prince, but only because of his great and exceeding possession of the Divine Love of the Father, and his more perfect at-onement.

Jesus is not seeking to establish a kingdom on earth, but is working for the purpose of leading men to the New Birth of the spirit, and of showing them the way to the Celestial Kingdom; and also is he working to help men by his love and suggestions, and so also the other good spirits, to cast sin and error from their hearts, and strive to regain the condition of perfect manhood in the perfection of their natural love; and also to help men to get in this condition of soul regeneration, or in that of the purification of their natural love while they yet live on earth, so that love to God in the divine sense, and love to God in the created sense and brotherly love will cover the whole earth, and men be at peace and happy while yet clothed in the flesh. Such a condition of mortal existence may be called the Kingdom of God on earth, but it will not be the kingdom which Jesus came to earth to establish—that is the Kingdom of Heaven. This Kingdom has its seat and abiding place in the Celestial Spheres whence it will never be removed.

So then, when the Bible teaches of the world coming to an end and passing away it does not mean the material world, but the world of men's thoughts and deeds and sinful conditions that are not in harmony with God's laws or the laws of His creation. This is the world that shall be destroyed when righteousness shall cover the earth as the waters do the deep, and brotherly love reign among men. Even today there are some men living on the earth who are so separated from the world, that as to them the world has no existence, not the material world, but the world of sin and unrighteousness, which is the only world to be destroyed. There shall be wars and rumors of wars and times of trouble , etc., such as never were, and then shall come the end. Not the wars of the cannons' roars or the bursting shells or the mutilated flesh, or the making of widows and orphans or the ruthless changing of mortals into spirits, but the wars of the spirits of good and evil, of love and hate, of purity and sin, of joy and despair, and of knowledge of truth and belief in error—all to be fought in the souls of men with such intensity and earnestness, creating such mind and spirit trouble as never has been, and causing rumors thereof to flood the earth and the habitations of men.

Then shall come the end of the world—the world of evil and sin and despair, and hatred and belief in error. This world shall pass away, and truth and love and peace and good will shall be established on the earth forever. The earth of this present day, then becoming to men so peaceful and filled with love and brotherly kindness, that to them it will seem as if the City of God had been let down from heaven on to earth. Let mortals know that Jesus has already come to earth and is among men, and that since the time of his becoming the Prince of the Celestial Kingdom he has been with men and spirits teaching them the way, the truth and the life. By the Holy Spirit have the truths of the Father spoken to men as a still small voice, and by the communions of souls has the Master led men to the love and mercy of the Father.

As in my time when he came to the Jews with his message of love and life eternal, they knew him not and rejected him, so now many men, and spirits too, refuse to listen to him and learn the way through the straight gate to the Father's love and immortality. Let men study the prophecies and the times and the seasons, and calculate the time of the end, and predict the near approach of the Master's coming in the clouds, and prepare themselves to be snatched up in the air and become of the heavenly hosts, yet they will find that all these things are vanities of vanities, and only as each individual passes beyond the veil of flesh will he realize the end of his mortal world has come, and then will all his speculations as to himself become realities, and the certainty of the world's end become an established fact. But men will continue to live on earth and die, and in succession others be born to die, and so on until.... only God knows.

So I say to men, prepare not for the passing away of the heavens and the earth, but for the passing of themselves from the earth to the great world of spirits; and remember, that as they sow, so shall they reap—a certainty that is never changed—a truth that no speculation can make untrue. The end of man's world comes each day to some mortal, and that end may lead to a glorious immortality, or to a temporary or a long darkness and suffering. Thus are the prophecies being fulfilled and the speculations of preachers and teachers and leaders of the unthinking are robbing men of the vital truth that the end of the world is coming each moment and day and year.

Oh! preacher and teacher and leader, your responsibility is great, and the accounting must be made. The reaping must follow the sowing as certainly as the day follows the night, and what will your harvest be? The end of the world for some mortal is the important now!

I have written enough for tonight as you are tired. So believe that I love you and am praying for the Father to bless you, and to so fill your soul with His love, that when the world comes to an end for you,

you shall find the Kingdom of Heaven waiting to receive you.
>	Good night.
>	Your brother in Christ,
>	John.

Immortality

Immortality

June 2nd, 1920.

I am here, Jesus.

Let me write tonight on a subject that is of importance to mankind and should be fully explained, that they may know the truth that will show them the way to immortality and light.

I know that men have debated all down the centuries the question of man's immortality, and have attempted to prove the reality of its existence by various arguments and by reference to the analogy of the workings of God's universe in the fulfillment of His designs as displayed by the various creations of animate nature. In all these discussions they have not succeeded in definitely and satisfactorily established the fact of immortality. And why? Because they have not, in the first place, understood what immortality means, and without a correct conception of that which it is desired to prove, it becomes very difficult to successfully prove the existence of the thing sought for. I know that at times some idea of what immortality is has been conceived of and almost understood by some of the writers on the subject, and their efforts have been directed to show that by man's inner consciousness as well as by the appearance of those things in nature which die and live again, man is justified in inferring that man himself is immortal, or was intended by his Creator to be immortal.

But the inner consciousness of man, meaning the knowledge of the possession of certain desires and aspirations, as well as the realization that his life on earth is too short to enable him to accomplish those things that his efforts and strivings attempt, and that what he really accomplishes in the way of his own mental and moral development, if they end with the physical death of men would mean only a useless exercise of the faculties and powers given him by God—is not sufficient to prove the immortality of the real man. Neither is it evidence of the uselessness of man's creation, though he is in one moment, deprived of all the learning and other benefits of a developed intellect, as well as of moral progression.

There is a difference between the state and condition of a human soul that continues in the spirit world the life that it had when embodied in the flesh, and the state that not only continues this life but makes the extinction of this life an utter impossibility—even by God, who in the beginning of man's existence created that soul.

True Immortality then, is the state or condition of the soul that has knowledge that because of the essence and qualities of itself, it cannot ever cease to live—the impossibility of its ever ceasing to live being known to it, and a fact.

It has been said that whatever has a beginning may have an ending—that which was created may be dissolved into its elements. And the possibility of this is true, and no man or spirit can deny the truth of the assertion. In your earth life you find that all things have an ending, that is in their individual and composite form; and in the spirit world why may not the same fate attend created things. The fact that there are things in the spirit world that exist as a continuation of things of earth does not mean that they shall endure forever.

The mere change, caused by the death and disappearance from the vision of men, of things that were once alive does not establish the fact that as they continue to live in the spirit world, they must live forever. Death which is looked upon as a destroying angel is merely the result of the change from that which is visible to the invisible, and does not in any way determine the everlasting existence of the thing changed.

The soul of man while in the flesh is the same soul as to its identity and individuality, as it is when it becomes an inhabitant of the spirit world, and if it is immortal while in the spirit world it is also immortal while in the body; and if it may cease to have an immortal existence in the one state, it may in the other.

Suppose that men by their arguments of the nature mentioned show that the soul of man does not die when the physical body dies but that it continues its existence in the spirit world as the identical, personal soul, then I ask, does that prove immortality as I have defined it? Death of the body and the continuing life of the soul thereafter do not work any change in the qualities or essence of that soul—it is still the same created soul that it was in the beginning, and why may it not be true, that being a thing created it may have an ending? This is logical and not unreasonable.

Then I say, even if men by their arguments prove to the satisfaction of many, that the soul after the death of the physical body continues to live in the spirit world with all its faculties and powers in active operation, they do not prove, nor do all the facts possible for them to discover and marshal prove, that that soul is immortal. The soul of man did not always exist—it is not eternal, self existing or independent of everything else, but dependent upon the will of God that called it into existence, and why is it not reasonable to infer that in the long period of time to come, it will have served the purpose of its creation and be disseminated into the elements of which it was created?

But I will say here, for the benefit of those mortals who believe in the immortality of the soul that from the time of the creation of the first man to the present, no spirit in the spirit world has any knowledge of any human soul that has ceased its existence and been dissolved into its elements. And further, that there are myriads of souls in the spirit world that are in just the condition of perfection that was the condition of the soul of the first man when created and God pronounced his creation, "very good." But as mortals have no assurance that at some time the life of their souls will not end, so also spirits who have gained the perfect condition of their creation have no such assurance. They have hope and belief that such may be their destiny, and also a knowledge that their progress as the perfect man has ended. They are in that state which limits their progress as the perfect man, although their enjoyment as such is not limited—to them in God's universe there is always something new and unknown appearing. But yet they have not the knowledge that they are immortal, and realize that they are dependent upon the will of God for their existence, and to many of these spirits, immortality is as much a subject of concern and speculation as it is to the mortals of earth.

Men in their meditation, study and arguments of this question of immortality do not start from the foundation of the subject. They have no truthful premises from which they can draw a correct conclusion, and consequently their arguments fail. They reason that because of the existence of certain things in and outside of man—all things of mere creation—that tend to show God's intentions and plans as regards man, therefore, in order to carry out such intentions, man must be immortal. They do not consider or lose sight of the fact that all these things that they use as the foundation for their conclusions are things dependent and not self existing, and at one time or another the objects of God's creation. What God has called into existence He can also declare shall exist no longer. And knowing this, man cannot, or spirit either, rightfully conclude that the soul is immortal.

But there is a way in which the immortality of the soul, or some souls—can be proved, and which, assuming the facts that enter into the argument to be true, necessarily establish the conclusion without possibility of refutation.

Then in commencing the argument what is the only reasonable way to approach the subject?

First, to discover and establish that which is immortal, and next to search for and find that which though not immortal, yet by reason of certain operations and effects upon it of that which is immortal, becomes itself immortal. Only from the immortal can immortality be acquired.

Well this is a good place to stop as you are tired; I am well pleased with the way in which you have received my message. Have faith and pray, and all will be well.

Good night my dear brother, for you are in truth my brother.
Your friend and brother,
Jesus.

Immortality by St. Luke[19]

Let me write as I desire to say a few words on the question of immortality of which you have been thinking so much during the past few days.

I was with you today as you listened to the discourses of the preacher upon the subject of immortality, and saw that you realized he did not have a true idea of what the term means, and thought how much you would like to inform him of your knowledge of the subject. Well, I understand just how you felt about the matter, and am in sympathy with you in your desire and hope that sometime you may have the opportunity to converse with him on this subject and give him your conception of the truth.

It is the subject of so many sermons and theories preached by preachers and others, and yet not one of them has the true understanding of what immortality is. They understand it only in the sense of continuous life, and in addition, try by argument and inferences to attach to it the idea of never ending—that is of the continuous life being so established that it can never be ended—and in this they satisfy their longings and desires. But you see, this inference is merely one that is drawn from the desires of the preachers—that they have no true basis upon which to found their conclusions, and as to the ordinary things of life they would not be willing to risk the important things of life upon a basis no better established from which they could draw conclusions that would cause them to act.

No, mankind do not really know what immortality is, and all the arguments that they can put forth to establish the true immortality, are not sufficient to convince the clear, cool and unprejudiced mind as to its being a fact.

As is said in the message that you have received from Jesus, immortality can be derived only from that which is immortal, and all arguments that merely tend to show that a thing must be immortal because of the desires or intentions of God, do not suffice.

All the facts that may be established as premises are not sufficient to logically prove the conclusion desired to be established and men cannot depend upon such method of reasoning.

---

[19] St. Luke in his message: - "Authenticity of the Bible" says that many changes had been made in his writings after the basic copies were destroyed. As copying and recopying continued, fewer and fewer of the basic truths taught by Jesus were retained. (Dr. S.) This message is published in this Volume on page 138. (G.J.C.)

It is utterly impossible to derive immortality from anything less than that which is immortal in itself, and to attempt to do so by argument or inference is a mere waste of time by the exercise of the reasoning faculties.

As has been said, only God is Immortal, and that means that the very Qualities and Nature of Himself is Immortal; and if it were possible for Him to have any qualities that are not of a nature that partakes of the Immortal, then these qualities would not be Immortal, but subject to change and dissolution. Among the Qualities of His Being is the great and important one of Love and without It God could not be. His existence would be less than that of a God; and that being a fact this great Quality of Love must be Immortal, and into whatever this Quality may enter and form a part, that thing is necessarily Immortal, and in no other way could it become Immortal. Then this Love of God brings Immortality in the true sense of the term and when It enters into the soul of man and possesses it, that soul becomes Immortal, and in no other way can Immortality be acquired.

Not all things of God's creation are immortal, for in a shorter or longer time they perform the object of their creation, and their existence is no longer required and they become dissolved into the elements of which they were composed. Man's physical body for this reason is not immortal, for after a short life on earth it dissolves and is no more. His spirit body is primarily of this evanescent character, and it may be that in the course of eternity it will have performed its mission and cease to exist. We do not know this, neither are we assured that it is not true, because it is dependent upon the continuous existence of the soul for its continuous existence, and not all souls will receive a part of the Father's Divine Love, which is the only thing that has within itself this immortality; and it may be that at sometime in the future, this soul without the love may cease to exist and become no more a creature of the Father.

But this we do know, that whatever partakes of the Divine Love has in it that which is necessarily immortal, and can no more die than can this love itself; and hence, must be immortal. So that when men speak or teach that all men are immortal, they speak that which they do not know—only God, Himself, knows that fact—and from the mere exercise of the reason men are justified in saying, that such men or souls that do not obtain the Divine Love are not immortal.

Now while this question of man's immortality is in doubt, and has never been demonstrated to be a fact, yet we do know that, that portion of mankind whose souls have received this immortal, Divine Love, are immortal and can never cease to exist; and the great comfort and blessings to these souls that this possession brings, are that they know that they are immortal because they possess that quality or nature of God that is immortal, and as the latter can never have an ending, neither can that into which this immortal Love has entered and found a lodgment have an ending.

The preachers arguments were strong, and in the ordinary workings of men's minds and reasoning powers, may convince men that immortality is a proved fact for all mankind, but when properly analyzed and the true rule of search for immortality is applied, it will appear that the arguments are not conclusive—hope is stronger than fact, and men have not the assurance that for them immortality holds out its desired arms of certainty. Well, I thought I would write you this short message upon the question that you and the preacher have been meditating upon, in the hope that he might not depend upon the strength of his argument for the establishing of the fact of immortality, but would see and become convinced that the only way to ascertain and acquire the true immortality is by seeking for and obtaining the Divine Love, and thereby having his soul transformed into the very Essence and nature of God in Love.

I am glad that I can write to you again, and that your condition is so much better than it has been, and permits the rapport to be made. Pray more to the Father and believe, and you will get in a condition that we so much desire. I will not write more. Good night.

Your brother in Christ,
Luke.

Henry Ward Beecher: Immortality

July 5th, 1915.

I am your friend and brother in love and desire for the kingdom. I am the spirit of Henry Ward Beecher.

I live in the seventh sphere where your father now is, and, because of having met him there, I come to you tonight to write for a short time. He has told me of you and how easily you receive the communications of the spirits, and I want to let you know that, even though I am no longer the same as when on earth, I still have the desire to make known to men the thoughts that arise in me concerning God and the relation of men to Him and His kingdom. I am now a believer in Jesus as I never was on earth, and it may surprise you to know that when on earth, no matter what I may have preached to my people, yet, in my heart, I looked on Jesus as a mere man of the Jews, and not very different from others of the great reformers who had lived and taught on earth the moral truths which tended to make men better and caused them to live more correct and righteous lives.

But, since I have been in the spirit world and have had the experiences which my life here has given me, and have found the way to

God's Divine Love and to His Kingdom, I have learned and now know that Jesus was more than a mere reformer. He was not only a good and just teacher, and lived the life of such, but he was the true son of God, and His messenger in bringing to the world the truths of immortality and the Divine Love of the Father, and the way to obtain it. He was truly the Way and the Truth and the Life as no other teacher before him ever was.

I know it is taught, and I believed it when on earth, that many religions and pagan teachers asserted, and tried to teach to mankind the immortality of the soul, and, as men understood the meaning of the word immortality, these teachings were more or less satisfactory. But I now see that their conception of immortality was merely a continuity of life after what is called death. How different the meaning as thus taught and the true meaning of the word! Immortality means so much more than a mere continuation of life. It means not only a continuation of life, but a life that has in it the Divine Love or Essence of the Father which makes the spirit who has that Love a Divinity itself, and not the subject of death of any kind. No mere spirit has this immortality just because it is continuing to live in the spirit world, and cannot conceive that by any possibility that continuity of life can ever be arrested or ended. No such spirit knows that to be true, because never has it been demonstrated, as a fact, and cannot be until eternity has come to an end. Such spirit is no different in its essence and potentialities from what it was when enfolded in the flesh, and has no greater reason for believing that it is immortal than it had when on earth.

A speculation and a proven fact are two entirely different things, yet with some spirits, as well as with men, speculation becomes almost as much a certainty as does a fact demonstrated. But there is no justification for relying upon conclusions drawn from mere speculation, and the spirit or man who does, may, in the great workings of eternity, find himself not only mistaken but surprised beyond all conception at what eventualities such workings may bring forth.

So, I say, that before the coming of Jesus, immortality had not been brought to light and could not have been, because for mankind it did not exist.

I was as much surprised when I learned the true meaning of the word as men will be who may read this communication or hear its import. The hope of Socrates or of Plato or of Pythagoras was only a hope fortified by the reasonings of great minds and supplemented by much development of soul qualities. But when all is said it was only hope—knowledge was wanting. And even if they had realized that the spirits of men departed did return and communicate to them that there was no such thing as the death of the spirit or soul; yet, such experiences did not prove to them anything beyond the fact that life was continuous for the time being.

As change is the law in the spirit world as well as on earth, they could not, with the certainty of knowledge, say there might not be some change in the spirit world that would break or set aside the continuity of existence.

Take the young child, when its intellect has not sufficiently developed to understand that there is such a thing as the death of the physical body, and it believes, if it thinks at all, that it will continue to live forever on earth. And so with these philosophers who had the hope of a future continuous life and with the spirits who know that there is a continuous life—living after death—they think that, that living must be the fixed state, and must of necessity continue forever.

As I say, it has not been demonstrated that such life will continue forever; yet, on the other hand, it has not been shown that it will not, and hence, no spirit can say that it is immortal, unless it partakes of the Divine Essence, and no wise philosopher or religious teacher, prior to the coming of Jesus could be said to have brought immortality to light. While hope and speculation exist as the children of desire, yet knowledge is wanting and certainty is not.

The immortality then that men believed in, and comforted themselves with believing in, was the immortality that hope created and speculation proved; and the experiences of men, in communicating with the spirits, showed that death had not annihilated the individual. But hope and speculation and experience did not create knowledge.

When Jesus came, he brought with him, not only hope but knowledge of the truth. Not many men have comprehended it, or understood the reason or foundation for such knowledge, and the reasoning faculties of men were not sufficient to show the true reasons of such knowledge. And strange as it may seem, the students and commentators of the Bible have never disclosed the true foundation upon which this knowledge exists.

I confess, that in my life, while a great student of the Bible, I never comprehended the true meaning of how, or in what way, Jesus brought immortality to light. I thought, as many others do now that his death and resurrection were the things that showed to mankind the reality of immortality. But these things showed no more, as I now see, than did the numerous instances recorded in the Old Testament and in the secular writings of the philosophers and adepts of India and Egypt that, there was an existence after so-called death.

And many who dispute the fact that Jesus brought immortality to light, base their arguments on these other facts: that he was only one of many who had died and afterwards came to mortals and showed that they still lived as spirits. So I say, and as I believed not while on earth, the mere fact of Jesus' resurrection does not prove immortality.

Then what have I learned immortality to be since I have been in the spirit world? My reasoning powers are much greater now than when on earth; my perceptive faculties have become more keen and my experience in the laws of the spirit world have given me great knowledge; but all these would not of themselves have given me the knowledge of immortality, had not Jesus himself explained it to me and demonstrated it by his own condition and that of many spirits in the higher spheres. Now I am, because of my present soul development, the possessor of that knowledge.

Only the Father is Immortal, and only those to whom He gives His Attributes of Immortality, can become Immortal as He is. Love is the great principle of Immortality, and by this I mean the Divine Love of the Father and not the natural love of the creature; and he who possesses this Divine Love becomes as it were, a part of It, or It becomes a part of him, and in Its operations makes him like unto the Father. In other words, a spirit who possesses this Divine Love becomes a part of Divinity itself, and, consequently, Immortal, and there is no possibility of his ever becoming deprived of this element of Divinity.

No spirit is immortal when there is any possibility of its being deprived of that immortality. Even God himself, if He could be deprived of that great quality, would not be immortal. And just as it is impossible to take from the Father this great attribute, so is it impossible for the spirit, who has once obtained this Divine Love of the Father, to lose its immortality.

So you see, immortality comes to a spirit only with the possession of the Divine Love, and that Love is not bestowed upon every spirit, but only on those who seek for it in the way shown to mankind by Jesus.

Death does not bring to the mortal Immortality, and because his spirit survives his death, it does not follow that Immortality becomes a part of his existence as a spirit.

So I say, that when Jesus brought to the world the knowledge of the bestowal of this Divine Love of the Father upon mortals under certain conditions, and also showed mortals the Way in which that Great Gift might be obtained, he brought to light Immortality and Life, and before him had no man or spirit brought these Great Gifts to light.

I am now a partaker, to a certain extent, of the Divine Love, and have before me the possibility of obtaining it to its fullest extent as promised by the Master to all who may seek for it in truth and with faith.

I did not intend to write so long a message at this time, but as I am enthusiastic on this subject, I find that I have trespassed upon your time and kindness longer than I realized.

So thanking you for your patience I will stop now, but hope that I may have the privilege of coming again at some time and writing. With my kind regards, I am

Very truly yours,
Henry Ward Beecher.

The Salvation that Jesus taught

December 16th, 1918.

Let me write a few lines tonight as I desire to tell you of a truth that to me seems important for mankind to know in order that they may comprehend the truth of their personal salvation.

I am a spirit of soul development and an inhabitant of the Celestial Heavens, where only those whose souls have been transformed by the Divine Love into the very nature and Essence of the Father can find a habitation.

I will not write at any great length and have only one idea or truth to convey, and that is "that no man or spirit can possibly receive the full salvation that Jesus taught and exemplified in his own person, who does not become wholly possessed in his soul of this Divine Love of the Father, and becomes rid of the conditions and attributes that belong to his created soul." This soul was not created with any of the divine attributes or qualities, but simply and merely with those which you may call human and which all men and spirits who have not experienced the transformation possess.

The God-man, as Jesus is sometimes designated by your religious writers and theologians, was not at the time of his creation or appearance in the flesh possessed of these Divine attributes, which are of the nature and Essence of the Father, but only of the human attributes which belonged to the perfect man—that is, the man who was the perfect creature as he existed before the fall of the first parents, when sin had not entered into their souls, and into the world of men's existence. Jesus was from the time of his birth, the perfect man, and, consequently, without sin—all his moral qualities being in complete harmony with the will of God and the laws controlling his creation; yet, he was not greater than were the first parents prior to their act of disobedience.

There was nothing of God, in the sense of the Divine that entered into his nature or constituents, and, if the Divine Love had not come into and transformed his soul, he would have remained only the perfect creature of a quality no higher or greater than was bestowed upon the first man; and Jesus was as regards his possibilities and privileges, like this first man prior to his fall or death of the potentiality of becoming Divine, but differed from him in this: that Jesus embraced and made his own these privileges and hence became Divine, while the first man refused to embrace them and lost them, and remained the mere man though not the perfect man as he was created.

And while Jesus by reason of his possession of the Divine Love became divine, yet he never became the God-man, and never can, for there does not exist and never can be a God-man. God is God, alone, and never has and never can become man; and Jesus is man only, and never can become God.

But Jesus is preeminently the Divine man, and may rightly be called the best beloved son of the Father, for he possesses more of the Divine Love and, consequently, more of the Essence and Nature of the Father, than does any other spirit of the Celestial Heavens, and with this possession there comes to him greater power and glory and knowledge. He may be described and understood as possessing and manifesting the Wisdom of the Father; and we spirits of the Celestial Kingdom recognize and acknowledge that superior wisdom of Jesus and are compelled by the very greatness and force of the wisdom, itself, to honor and abide in his authority.

And this transcendent and greatest possessor of the Father's wisdom is the same when he comes to you and reveals the truths of God as he is when in the highest spheres of the Celestial Kingdom clothed in all the glory of his nearness to the Father. As the voice on the Mount said "Hear ye him," I repeat to you and to all who may have the privilege and opportunity of reading or hearing his messages, hear ye him! And when hearing, believe and seek.

Well, my brother, I deemed it proper to write this short message and hope it may help you in the work. I will come again.

Good night.
Your brother in Christ,
Saint Matthew, as called in the Bible.

Who and What is God?

Jesus: Who and what is God?

May 25th, 1917.

I am here, Jesus.

I have been with you as you prayed, and joined in your prayer to the Father for the inflowing of His Great Love into your soul in great abundance; and I know that His Holy Spirit is present and that His love is flowing into your soul, and that you are becoming in at-onement with the Father. His love will always come to you when you pray as you have tonight, and His listening ear is always open to the earnest aspirations of His children who come to him with the true longings of the soul. You have the secret of reaching the Father's love, and on all occasions, when you feel that you need that Love or desire a nearness to the Father, use the secret and you will not be disappointed.

You are in better condition tonight in your soul development and perceptions and can receive my message which I have desired for some time to communicate, and to do which I was waiting only for you to be in a complete rapport with me.

Well, you will remember, that in the early stages of our writings, I communicated to you my knowledge and conception of "who and what God is," and that I have recently told you that I desired to rewrite the message, as your condition is now so much better to receive these truths than it was when the message was written; and so, tonight, I will deliver the message, and will take a more complete possession of your brain and control of your hand than I was able to do at the time mentioned.

Then the question is: Who and What is God?

In dealing with this question, you must realize that it is not so easy to describe in language that mortals can comprehend the Essence and Attributes of God, and I feel the limitations that I am under in endeavoring to give you a satisfactory description of the only and true God; not because of the paucity of knowledge and conception on my part, but because of the fact that you have not the required soul development to enable me to form the necessary rapport with you, in order that through your brain, may be expressed the exact truth as to who the Father is.

Well, to begin, God is Soul, and Soul is God. Not the soul that is in the created man, but the Soul that is Deity and self-existent, without beginning or ending, and Whose entity is the one great fact in the universe of being.

God is without form, such as has been conceived of by man in nearly all ages, and especially by those who believe in the Bible of the Hebrews as well as in that of the Christians. But nevertheless, He is of form, which only the soul perceptions of the soul of a man which has arrived at a certain degree of development, that is taken on the Divine nature of the Father and thus become a part of the Soul of God, can discern and realize as an entity. There is nothing in all nature with which men are acquainted or have knowledge of, that can be used to make a comparison, even in the spirit perceptions, with this Great Soul; and hence, for men to conceive of God as having a form in any manner resembling that of man, is all erroneous; and those who, in their beliefs and teachings, deny the anthropomorphic God, are correct.

But, nevertheless, God is of form such as to give him an entity and Substance and seat of habitation, in contradistinction to that God which, in the teachings of some men, is said to be everywhere in this Substance and entity—in the trees and rocks, and thunder and lightning, and in men and beasts, and in all created things, and in whom men are said to live and move and have their being. No, this concept of God is not in accord with the truth, and it is vital to the knowledge and salvation of men that such conception of God be not entertained or believed in.

To believe that God is without form is to believe that he is a mere force or principle or nebulous power, and, as some say, the resultant of laws; which laws, as a fact, He has established for the controlling of His universe of creation, and which are expressed to men by these very powers and principles, that to some extent, they can comprehend.

The child has asked: "Who made God?" And because the wise men cannot answer that question, in their wisdom, they conclude and assert that there can be no real God of personality or soul form, and, hence, only force, principle or evolved laws can be God; and in their own conceit think that they have solved the question. But the child may not be satisfied with the answer, and may ask the wise men: "Who made principle and force and laws that must be accepted as the only God?" And then, the wise men cannot answer, unless they answer: "God," which they do not believe, but which let me say, is the true and only answer.

God is back of force and principle and law, which are only expressions of His being, and which without Him could not exist; and they are only existences, changeable, dependent and subject to the will of God, who only, is Being.

God then, is Soul, and that Soul has its form, perceptible only to itself, or that of man, which, by reason of the sufficient possession of the very Substance of the Great Soul has become like unto God, not in image only, but in very Essence. We spirits of the highest soul progression are enabled by our soul perceptions to see God and His form. But here, I use the words "see" and "form," as being the only words that I can use to give mortals a comparative conception of what I am endeavoring to describe.

When it is remembered that mortals can scarcely conceive of the form of the spirit body of a man, which is composed or formed of the material of the universe, though not usually accepted to be of the material, it will be readily seen that it is hardly possible for me to convey to them a faint idea even of the Soul form of God, which is composed of that which is purely spiritual—that is, not of the material, even though to the highest degree sublimated.

And although I am not able because of the limitations mentioned, to describe to men that form which they may glean a conception of the Soul's form—as such form can be seen only with the soul's eye, which eyes men do not possess—it must not be believed that because men cannot understand or perceive the truth of the Soul's form, therefore, it is not a truth. A truth, though not conceived or perceived by men, spirits or angels, is still a truth, and its existence does not depend upon its being known; and even though all the mortals of earth, and the spirits and angels of heaven, save one, could not perceive the existence of that truth, yet its existence perceived by that one irrefutably proves its reality.

But, as I have said, the truth of God's form—the Soul's form can be testified to by more than one of the celestial spirits of men passed from earth; and the possibility is before mortals of the present life, in the great future, if their souls have become possessed of the Divine Substance of God's Love in sufficient abundance to perceive God as I have attempted to explain.

The created soul of man has its form; it being made in the image of God, yet man cannot see that form, although it is a fact and can be testified to by many in the spirit realms.

And here it need to be said, that when in our message we speak of God as being without form, we mean any such form as men have or think they have conceived of, and our expressions must not be considered as contradictory to what I have tried to explain as the form of God.

Well, in addition to the form, God has a personality, and this is expressed and made known to man by certain attributes, which to the consciousness of man is existent in the universe; and to some philosophers and scientists and wise men these attributes are their impersonal God himself, and to them the only God. They make the created, the Creator, not realizing that behind the expression must be the Cause; and that greater than the attribute must be That from which the expression of the attribute is projected, or, as they better like to say, evolved.

And here, I, who know, desire to say that these manifested attributes or forces and powers and principles and laws and expressions do not, all together, constitute or be that from which they flow or in which they have their source. God is Himself, alone. His Attributes or expressions manifested to mortals or spirits, are only the results or effects of the workings of His Spirit, which Spirit is only the active energy of His Soul—Himself. And hence, the form of God is not distributed over the whole universe of creation where His attributes may be, or because they are everywhere manifested.

No, as was said by Moses of old, and as was said by me when on earth: God is in His Heavens. And although it may be surprising and startling to mortals to hear, God has His habitation, and God the Substance, the Self-existing and Soul form, has His locality, and men do not live and move and have their existence in God; but in His emanations and expressions and spirit they do.

As you are somewhat exhausted, I think this a good place to stop.

I am pleased that you are in such good condition. So be prepared for an early resumption of the message.

With my love and blessings, I will say, good night.

Your brother and friend,

Jesus

Ann Rollins: Who and What is God?

February 18th, 1916.

I am here, your grandmother.

Well, my son, I come tonight, as I promised, for the purpose of writing you a letter, telling you of a certain spiritual truth that I desire you to know.

I am now in the third[20] Celestial Sphere, as I already told you, and am in a much more exalted condition in my knowledge of spiritual truths that I have ever been, and have opened up to me a spiritual view that increases my understanding of truth and of the question of the Father's provisions for the happiness and salvation of His children.

I know now more than ever that He is a real existing God of Love and Power and Wisdom, and that wrath, such as is taught in the Bible, is no part of His nature, and that He has for His children on earth as well as in the spirit world, only love and solicitude and sympathy.

---

[20] When a spirit progresses above the Third Celestial sphere. These higher spheres are so graduated that no number is used. (Dr. S.)

He is not a God that is afar off waiting for the arrival of the Great Judgment day, in order to approve or condemn His children according to the deeds done on earth, but He is with all men and spirits in a way that His influence of love and beneficence may be felt by them, if they will only place themselves in that condition of receptivity of soul that such influence may be felt, for, as we have before said, the relationship and nearness of God to man depends, to a very large extent, upon the will and desires of man, himself.

God is not, in what may be called His personality, with men as has been taught by the teachers of the religions of the Bibles of the world, and men do not live, move and have in Him their being, as Saint Paul wrote, for His personality has a location which is not everywhere but in the high Heavens.

I know that this will appear startling to many persons, orthodox and otherwise, and that it apparently takes from them the consolation of believing and feeling that God is with and in them; but, nevertheless, what I say is true.

He is not in them or in nature as some of the scientists who believe in God, say. He is not in every flower or tree or other manifestation of His creation. And, as regards His personality, is not omnipresent, though He has a knowledge of all things which He created, I say which He has created, for there are some things which appear to man as a part of the realities of the universe, which He did not create, but which man alone created, and for these things has no love and does not approve of or favor their existence, and in the end they will be destroyed from the face of His universe.

And when I say that God, in His personality, is not everywhere and not with men at all times forming a part of their being, I do not mean that it shall be understood that He is not the loving watchful Father, trying to make them happy and save them from the results of their own many wrong doings, for such inference would not be true.

And while, as I say, He is not with men in this personality, yet He is with them in the sense and truth, that His attributes of Love and Wisdom and Knowledge and Power are with them always. Life emanates from God, but life is not God, it is only one of His attributes conferred upon the objects of His creation, that they may live and grow and fulfill the designs of their creation; and when that purpose has been accomplished, He withdraws from them this attribute of life, and men can realize that fact. God has not, Himself, ceased to be a part of that object, for He never was a part of it, but only this attribute has ceased to be a part of the object. God is the source and origin of all life, but that life is merely one of His creatures, as we say, as is man or other things which mortals call matter.

Man does not live and move and have his being in God, but

merely in the attributes of God. So you see not all these attributes together constitute God, for He is a personality from which all these attributes flow.

I know that it is difficult for you to comprehend the full purport of what I intend to convey, but you may in a way grasp my meaning.

Love is a greater attribute than even life, but love is not God, just as love is not man, though it is his greatest possession when it exists in its purity; and as man has many attributes which all together do not make the man, so God has many, and yet they are only parts of His nature and not He.

Man has a physical body and a mind and yet, they do not constitute man, for he may lose them both and still be man, or spirit—that is, the ego—the soul is the real man—the personality—and all the wonderful parts of man, such as the mind and affections and desires and will are merely of him, and if he were deprived of any of them, he would still be man—though not the perfect man as when they are all with him performing their proper functionings.

And man is so created that, unless he has these qualities, which in his creation were made parts of him, and which were necessary to make him the perfect creature that he was, while he is still man, yet he is not the perfect man that God decreed him to be; and until these qualities are fully restored or regained by him he will not be the man that was the greatest handiwork of the Almighty.

And God is not God by reason of having these qualities, but these qualities exist, because they are the attributes of God. He never loses them, nor do they become hidden or cease to do their functioning, but always are they existing and working and obedient to His being.

God is Soul, and Soul is God, and in this soul does his personality consist without individuality, but real and existing—and life from which flow all these Attributes of Life and Love, etc., of which I have spoken. God is Spirit, but spirit is not God, only one of His Qualities.

I write this to give you some additional conception of who and what God is, and to show you that He is not in man nor does man have his being in God. To further show you that God does not and could not exist in the same place with those things which are not in accord with His nature and qualities; and were He in man or man in Him then no sin or error or things which violate, would exist.

I must stop now, but will come soon to finish my message.
With all my love, I am your grandmother.

Ann Rollins: Who and What is God?—continued

February 25th, 1916.

I am here, your grandmother.

I come to resume my discourse if you think that you are in condition to receive the same. Well we will try, and if I find that you are not, I will stop.

As I was saying, God is not in man or material things as regards His personality, but only those attributes of His, which men generally consider to be God, are manifested in the material things.

As I have said, God is not the creator of all things that appear to have an existence, for many things which control and govern the conduct of men are entirely the creatures of man, and are not in harmony with the laws of God or with His will. And hence, when it is realized that there exists in the souls and minds of men evil that are not in harmony with God's creations, you can readily see that God cannot be and is not in such souls and minds, nor are His attributes, because, as is said in the laws of physical philosophy, two things cannot occupy the same place at the same time, so we may say as regards spiritual philosophy two things cannot occupy the same soul or mind at the same time, especially when they be antagonistic or opposed to each other in their qualities or fundamentals. Until the one vacates its occupancy the other cannot come in, and this is invariably true of the creatures of God and the creatures of man, for they are always and under all circumstances opposed to each other.

But it must be understood that when I speak of the creatures of God my meaning must not be taken as including God, for He as the Creator is altogether different from His creatures; and while His creatures or certain attributes may find a lodgment and habitation in the souls of men and the minds of men and in the existence of material things, yet He, God, never finds such lodgment, and is never a part of such existences. He is as distinct from the creatures, or better probably, emanations of His, as are the thoughts and desires of man distinct from the man himself.

God is in His Heavens, and those Heavens have a locality, just as the different spheres of the spirit world, in which spirits have their homes, have localities; and His locality is way beyond the highest Celestial spheres known to the highest spirit, and towards which spirits are always progressing, and as they progress, the more and closer they come in contact with these Attributes of God, which are constantly flowing from Him.

Even Jesus, who, as you know, is the brightest of all the spirits and the one possessing more of these attributes of the Father than any other spirit, has never seen God except through the soul perception, nor ever realized that God is in him or forms a part of him; and mistaken and deceived are men when they say or believe that God is in them or that in Him they live and move and have their being.

To believe this as true, God can only be a kind of nebulous something—inconsistent as the air—and, as many of the spiritualists say, merely a force permeating the whole universe, divided into many and infinitesimal manifestations, seen and felt today and tomorrow having no existence. A something less substantial than man—weak at once and powerful at the same time—a contradiction beyond conception or explanation.

Such is not God; but all these manifestations are merely evidence of the existence of a substantial and, I may say, never varying, Self Existing Being, who is not the creature of man's mind or of man's necessities or desires, but the Creator of all, even of these wise men who cannot conceive of any God, but nature, the mere creature of His being and wisdom and power.

The human mind, when left to itself, that is to its own evolution as your scientists say, and not influenced by the revelations of spiritual truths or the suggestions of spirits who have advanced in knowledge of things beyond the material, has not improved much since the days when they lived and died as sun worshipers, and the worshipers of the sacred cats, and bulls and elephants, and of the storms, and thunders and lightning. God was in all these manifestations, immanent and real, to be appeased or loved as necessity required; and today among your civilized nations, and the wise men of these nations, who can see no God in the spiritual, the aggregate of all these material things is the God, which they must worship, if they worship at all.

Nature is God to them, and you see, that the only improvement, if any there be, that their minds have over the minds of the worshipers of the sun and of animals etc., that I have mentioned, is that those minds are not satisfied to see God in a single manifestation, but there must be a combination of all these manifestations, which they call Nature. You see, it is only a difference in degree, and the scientist of today who refuses to accept or believe in any God, who may be of a spiritual nature, is exactly the counterpart of his so-called barbarian brother who could see Him only in the sun, etc., in everything, except that he demands a larger God, who must be in the lowest form of mineral existence as well as in the highest form of solar excellence and even in man, for with some, man is his own and only God.

And it is questionable whether these wise men are not more limited in their conception and acceptance of a God, than were the earlier uncivilized brothers, because many of the latter saw beyond and behind their Sun God and God of thunders, etc., another and greater God whom they could not see, but could feel and in their souls realized His existence. But the wise men of civilizations have so evolved their intellects that they have lost their soul perceptions, and no God beyond the horizon of their intellectual perceptions can exist, and, hence, as they think they know nature, nature as all of the creation, and there can be no other God than nature. But, Oh, the terrible mistake!

God then, as I have said, is a being—a soul—with a personality that has a location, high up in the heavens, towards whom all spirits of the Celestial and many of the spiritual spheres are striving to approach in greater and greater nearness; and as they approach they realize and know the increased Love and Life and Light that emanates from the Fountainhead of these Attributes of Perfection.

And so I repeat, God is not in man or beast or plant or mineral, but only are His Attributes as he sees the necessity for their workings, and man does not live and move and have his being in God.

Well, my son, I have in my imperfect way, given you some idea of Who and What God is, and my explanation is in substance the consensus of the knowledge of the Celestial spirits, whose knowledge is based upon the truths that no mortal or all the mortals combined can possibly learn with their finite minds.

I think that you have received my ideas and words quite correctly, and I hope the truths which I have written may prove beneficial to all mankind.

I am very happy and will come again soon, and write you some other truths, which may interest you.

I must stop now.

With all my love and blessings, I am your own loving grandmother,

Ann Rollins.[21]

Affirmation that Mr. Padgett's grandmother wrote the message on "Who and What is God?"

February 25th, 1916.

I am here, your father.

I have been listening to your grandmother's message and was interested in observing the way in which you received it, for it is a deep and important communication of truth that is not generally known to mortals. We in the lower spheres, of course, do not know these truths so extensively as do the spirits of the Celestial Spheres, but I have heard the Master discourse on the subject of God, and what your grandmother wrote you is, in short, what he has explained to us, but of course, in a way that we could better and to a greater extent comprehend the truth than can you.

---

[21] Jesus in a message wrote: - that Mr. Padgett's grandmother is well qualified to write on divine truths. (Dr. S.)

There is one thing that I have observed in the case of these, who are called scientists and who believe only the material, and also in the case of those who claim to be infidels, when they come into spirit life, and that is, that very soon they realize that there is or must be a God, and that their God of nature, or their man-made God, does not supply the word, if I may thus express it, which they find to exist here. They, of course, do not get a conception of the nature of God in the beginning, but they know very soon after they come over that there is a God other and different from what they conceived Him to be when they had any conception of Him on earth and when they denied that there was any God, and they soon realize the absolute necessity for there being one. And when they had made man his own God, they see many spirits of men in such conditions of darkness and suffering and helplessness that they readily realize that man is not God.

So I say the first truth that enters their mind and souls when they become spirits is that there is a God, although they do not know His nature and attributes.

So you see there is only one little veil of flesh between the vaunted mind of mortals that proclaim there is no God but nature or no God at all, and the mind conscious of its weakness and littleness as it exists in the spirit world.

But I must stop writing on this subject or you will think that I am going to write you a lecture, which I don't intend to do now.

With all my love, I am your loving father,
John H. Padgett.[22]

Christ may be in you—what it means

March 3rd, 1918.

I am here, Jesus.

I desire tonight to write you in reference to the way in which, as the preacher advises, "Christ may be in you."

I know that it is almost universal among preachers of the orthodox church to teach their hearers that the way to salvation is to get Christ in them and thereby they will be enabled to come into unity with the Father, and cease to remain subject to the effects of sin and evil. Well this teaching is the true foundation of salvation for the Celestial Heavens, provided it be understood by the preachers and the people what the true meaning of "Christ in you" is, and unless this meaning be comprehended the fact that preacher or people may believe that they have Christ in them will not work the results that they may suppose or

---

[22] This message is a composite of two, being published in Volume I and Volume III. (G.J.C)

desire.

Many, and I may say the most, of these professing Christians, have ideas of what this expression means in order to become effective, that are not in accord with the true meaning of this condition of the soul. They believe that all that is necessary is to believe on Jesus as their savior by his sacrifice and death and that in so believing they have Christ in them, and that nothing else is required. They have no conception of the distinction between Jesus, the man, and Christ, the spirit of truth, or more correctly, the spirit that manifests the existence of the Divine Love in the soul. Christ is not a man in the sense that he is Jesus the son of the Father, but Christ is that part of Jesus, or rather quality that came to him after he fully received into his soul the Divine Love, and was transformed into the very Essence of the Father in His Love. Christ is thus, not a man but is the manifestation of this Love as bestowed upon Jesus, and made part of his very existence. And when men use the expression, having Christ in you, if they could correctly understand the true purport of the same, they would know that it, the expression, means only that the Divine Love of the Father is in their souls.

The indiscriminate use of the words, "Jesus and Christ," is the cause of much misunderstanding among these Christians as to a number of the sayings of the Bible.

Jesus became the Christ only because he was the first to receive into his soul this Divine Love and to manifest its existence, and this Christ principle is one that all men may possess, with the result that they will become at one with the Father in His substance of Love and Immortality.

It would be impossible for Jesus, the man, to get into or become a part of any mortal, and it would be equally as impossible for Christ, as the man Jesus, even though perfect and free from sin, to become a part of anyone.

No, the meaning of having Christ in you is to have this Love of the Father in your soul, which can only be obtained through the working of the Holy Spirit as the instrument of the Father in bringing this Love into the soul.

To many who hear the preachers' exhortations in this particular, the expression is only a mystery, which they accept merely intellectually, and feel that by such acceptance they have the possession of this Christ, which is the only evidence of the truth of the Father's love.

Good night.
Your friend and brother,
Jesus.

The Holy Spirit.

Many who think that they have received the baptism of the Holy Spirit have only advanced in the natural love and not the Divine Love

May 10th, 1920.

Let me write for a short time upon a subject that will be of interest to you and to those who may read my messages.

What I desire to write upon tonight is the condition of those who think they have received the inflowing or baptism of the Holy Spirit, when the fact is that they have received only that advancement in the purification of their natural love and a harmony with the laws of their creation that causes them to believe that what they experience must be the result of a bestowal of the Love which the Holy Spirit brings to mortals. In this mistake so many humans indulge; and in the satisfaction or rather happiness which their experience, growing out of such an increase in the harmony, brings to them, they fully believe that the Holy Spirit has taken possession of their souls and caused the happiness. But in thus concluding, they are deceiving themselves, and will realize their mistake when they come to an awakening in the spirit life.

The Holy Spirit is that part of God's Spirit that manifests His presence and care in conveying to men's souls His Divine Love. This Love is the highest and greatest and most holy of His possessions, and can be conveyed to men only by the Holy Spirit; and this appellation is used in contradistinction to the mere spirit, which demonstrates to men the operation of God's Soul in other directions and for other purposes. His creative spirit, and His caring spirit and the spirit that makes effective his laws and designs in the governing of the universe, are not the Holy Spirit, though equally part of God's Soul, and equally necessary for the manifestations of His powers and the exercise of the energies of His Soul. These deal with the things of the universe that do not have interrelationship with the Soul of God and the souls of men, and whenever the Holy Spirit is spoken of it should mean only that part of God's Spirit which transforms the souls of men into the Substance of the Soul of God in its Quality of Love.

I heard the preacher discourse Sunday night on the work of the Holy Spirit as portrayed in the contents of the New Testament, and saw that his conclusions from these contents were wholly erroneous and apart from the truth. As he said, the effects of the workings of the Holy Spirit are shown in more ways than one, and not everyone upon whom it is bestowed is filled with the same powers of displaying its presence and possession. Now in all these evidences of its existence in the experiences given, it must be understood that it is limited in its operations to those conditions and manifestations that have their source in the Divine Love of the Father, that was bestowed upon mankind at my coming in the flesh, and that those evidences of the existence that have no relationship to this Love are not evidences of the presence of the Holy Spirit. As mentioned in the New Testament, when it was bestowed upon my disciples at Pentecost, it came as with the sound of a mighty rushing wind, which has before been explained to you, that shook the room in which the disciples were assembled, and filled them with its powers, which means only that this Divine Love came into their souls in such abundance that they were shaken in their souls to such an extent that they thought the building in which they were assembled was disturbed. But in this they were mistaken, for the effect of the presence of the Holy Spirit is not to affect the things of inanimate nature, but is confined to the souls of men.

And the preacher must know that because men are possessed with powers to accomplish the mental or material things of their living, they are not necessarily possessed with the Holy Spirit. Much of the physical healing of mortals is caused by powers that are bestowed upon men, or some men that are not connected with or proceed from the Holy Spirit. That there is evidence of this, men will recollect that the Old Testament is full of instances where men were healed of their diseases, and other wonderful things performed, at the time that the Holy Spirit was excluded from man's possession. Yet these marvels, as then considered, were performed by men claiming to be endowed with the Spirit of God, which is working for the good and happiness of mankind, and which will continue to work until men shall become in harmony with themselves as first created.

I understand the object of the preacher in attempting to show and convince his hearers, that because they have not those powers that the Bible describes as having been possessed by my disciples after the bestowal of the Holy Spirit, that therefore, they must not believe and conclude that they, his hearers, have not this blessing. His intentions and efforts were commendable, and arose from the desire that his hearers should not become disheartened and disappointed in their efforts to obtain the inflowing of the Love that the Holy Spirit brings to men; but on the other hand, his teachings were dangerous and misleading to these hearers, for the natural consequence of such teaching is to lead men into the belief or persuasion that they possess this power and Comforter, when they do not, and thus prevent them from seeking for an obtaining this Comforter in the only way in which it can be obtained. The Holy Spirit primarily, has nothing to do with great mental or physical achievements, and to say that because a man is a great inventor or philosopher or surgeon who does things without knowing where the inspiration or suggestion to do the things comes from, therefore he is possessed of the Holy Spirit is all wrong and misleading.

All things, mediately or immediately, have their existence and operation and growth in the Spirit of God, and only in that Spirit, and which Spirit is evidenced in many and varied ways in men's experience; and hence, men say that they live and move and have their being in God, meaning only that they live and move and have their being in God's Spirit. This Spirit is the source of life and light and health and numerous other blessings that men possess and enjoy—the sinner as well as the saint, the poor man as well as the rich, the ignorant as well as the enlightened and educated—and are each and all dependent on this Spirit for their being and comfort. This is the Spirit that all men possess to a great or less degree, and the brilliant preacher or teacher or orator, possessing this Spirit to a greater degree than his less favored brother, depends upon the same Spirit. It is universal in its existence and workings, is omnipresent, and may be acquired by all men in this sense to the degree that their mental receptivity permits. And this further demonstrates the fact that God, through and by this Spirit, is with men always, in the lowest hells as well as in the highest heavens of the perfect man. It is working continuously, ceaselessly and always at the call of men, be that call mental or spiritual. It is the thing that controls the universe of which man's earth is an infinitesimal part. This is the Spirit of God.

But the Holy Spirit while a part of the Spirit of God, yet is as distinctive as is the soul of man distinctive from all other creations of God; it is that part of God's Spirit that has to do with the relationship of God's Soul and man's soul, exclusively.

The subject of Its operation is the Divine Love of the Father's Soul and the object of Its workings is the soul of man, and the great goal to be reached by Its operations is the transforming of the soul of man into the Substance of the Father's Love, with Immortality as a necessary accompaniment. This is the great miracle of the universe; and so high and sacred and merciful is the transformation, that we call that part of God's Spirit that so works, the Holy Spirit.

So let not teachers or preachers teach, or their hearers believe that every part of God's Spirit that operates upon the heart's and thoughts and feelings of man is the Holy Spirit, for it is not true. Its mission is the salvation of men in the sense of bringing them into that harmony with God, that the very souls of men will become a part in substance and not in image merely of the Soul of God and without this working of the Holy Spirit men cannot become in such union.

I have written you before as to how this Holy Spirit works and the way in which it can bring men the Divine Love of the Father, and what is necessary for its inflowing. The way described is the only way, and men must not believe and rest in the security of such belief, that every working of the Spirit of God, is the working of the Holy Spirit.

Except a man be born again he cannot enter into the Kingdom of God, and such attainment is possible only by the working of the Holy Spirit.

Oh, preacher, upon whom a great responsibility rests, learn the truth and then lead men into the way of salvation.

I will not write more now, but will come again and deliver another message.

Believe that I love you and am
Your friend and brother,
Jesus.

The mystery of the Godhead, three in one is a myth. There is no mystery that men should not know

November 5th, 1916.

I am here, St. Luke.

I come tonight to write you a message upon the truth of: What the Holy Spirit is. I know that the orthodox generally believe and classify it as a part of the Godhead, being one with and the equal of God, the Father, and not merely a manifestation of the Father, as spirit, and hence, necessarily identical with the Father, though having a different and distinct personality. In this belief and in this classification is included Jesus, having a distinct personality.

The orthodox preachers and theological writers teach that it is a fact that these three are one, co-equal and existing, and that fact is the great mystery of God, and that men should not endeavor to fathom the mystery, because the sacred things of God are His own, and it is not lawful for men to enter into these secrets. Well this declaration and admonition are very wise as men's wisdom goes, and saves the expounders of these doctrines of mystery from attempting to explain what they cannot explain, because it is impossible for them to unravel that which as a fact, has no existence.

Men of thought all down the ages have sought to understand this great mystery, as they called it, and have been unsuccessful, and as the early fathers met with the same defeat in their endeavors to understand the mystery, and, then because of such defeat, declared the explanation of the doctrine to be a secret of God, not to be inquired into by men, so all these other investigators of the church when they became convinced of the futility of the search, adopted the admonition of the old fathers that God's secret must not be inquired into, for it belonged to Him alone, and sinful man and the redeemed man also must respect God's secret. And thus from the beginning of the established church, after the death of Jesus and his apostles, was declared this doctrine of the trinity—one in three and three in one, yet only one—and made the vital foundation stone of their visible church's existence. Of course, from time to time, there arose men, both in the church, who, having more enlightenment than their brothers in the church, attempted to gainsay the truth of the doctrine and declared and maintained that there was only one God, the Father.

But they were in the minority and not acting with the more powerful, their views were rejected; and the mystery became the church's sacred symbol of truth, unexplainable and therefore more certain and entitled to more credence. And it seems to be the tendency of men's minds, or at least of those who believe in the Bible as the inspired word of God, to welcome and encourage as the more wonderful and important and the more to be cherished those things which savor of the mysterious, rather than those which a man may read and understand as he runneth. (Habbakuk 2:2).

Nowhere, not even in the Bible, is there any saying of Jesus to the effect that God is tripartite, consisting of the Father, Son and Holy Ghost; and, as a fact, never did Jesus when on earth teach any such doctrine, but only this: that the Father is God and the only God, and that he, Jesus, is his son and the first fruits of the resurrection from the dead, and that the Holy Ghost is God's messenger for conveying the Divine Love, and as such, the comforter.

I know that in some of the Gospels, as now contained in the Bible and adopted as canonical, it is said, in effect, that the Godhead consists of the Father, Son and Holy Ghost—these three are one—but such Gospels do not contain the truth in this respect and are not the same Gospels that were originally written. These original Gospels have been added to and taken from in the passing of the years and in the copying and the recopying that occurred before the adoption of the same.

They, the adopted ones, were compiled from many writings, and as the compilers in those early times differed in their opinions as men do now respecting religious truths, the more powerful of these having authority to declare what should be accepted, according to their interpretations of those manuscripts that were being copied, directed the copies to be made in accord with their ideas, and I may say, desires, and announced and put forth such productions to be true copies of the originals. And as these copies were successively made the preceding ones were destroyed, and hence the earliest existing manuscripts of these Gospels came into being many years after the originals from which they were claimed to be compiled, were written and destroyed.

And I, Luke, who did write a gospel and who am acquainted with the present gospel ascribed to me, say that there are many vital things and declarations, that I never wrote and that are not true, contained in it; and many truths that I did write are not contained therein—and so with the other gospels.

In none of our Gospels did the mystery of the Godhead appear, and that for the reason that there was not and is not, and we did not teach that there was any Godhead, composed of three personalities. Only one God, the Father. Jesus was a son of man in the natural sense, and a son of God in the spiritual sense, but he was not God or a part of God in any sense except that he possessed the Divine Love of the Father, and in that sense was a part of His Essence. The Holy Spirit was not God, but merely His instrument—a Spirit—the Holy Spirit.

As you have been informed, the soul of man existed prior to man's creation in the flesh, and was the only part of man that was made in the image of God. It existed in this pristine state without individuality, though having a personality, and resembled the Great Soul of the Almighty, which Soul is God Himself; though the soul that was given to man was not a part of the Great Soul, merely a likeness of it.

Some of you mortals have said that man's soul is a part of the "Oversoul," meaning the Soul of God, but this is not true, and if in any of our communications it has been said that the soul of man is a part of the Soul of God, and I mean while it existed before its incarnation, our saying must not be so interpreted. The ego of God as may be said, is the Soul, and from this Soul, emanates all the manifested attributes of God, such as power and wisdom and love—but not jealousy or wrath or hatred, as some of the writers of the Bible have said, for He possesses no such attributes. The ego of man is the soul, and in his created purity and perfection from his soul emanated all the manifested attributes belonging to him, such as power and love and wisdom; and neither were jealousy nor hatred nor wrath attributes of his before his fall.

It is said that man is composed of body, soul and spirit, and this is true. From your life's experience you know what the body is, and I have told you what the soul is, and now the question arises, what is the spirit? I know that there have been for centuries great differences of opinion among theologians and other wise men as to what the spirit is; some contending that it and the soul are the same thing, and others, that the spirit is the real ego of man and the soul something of less quality and subordinate to the spirit, and others having other views, and all wrong, for as I have said the soul is the ego, and everything else connected with man and forming a part at his creation when he was pronounced to be "very good," is subordinate to the soul, and only its instrumentality for manifesting itself.

As Jesus has told you, the spirit is the active energy of the soul and the instrumentality by which the soul manifests itself; and this definition applies to the spirit of man while a mortal as well as when he becomes an inhabitant of the spirit world. The spirit is inseparable from the soul, and has no function in the existence of man, except to make manifest the potentialities of the soul in its activities. Spirit is not life, but it may become an evidence of life—it is life's breath.

And as man was created in the image of his Maker—and as spirit is only the active energy of the soul, by the application of the principle of correspondences, which one of your former psychics declared to exist, it may be assumed and it is truth, that the Holy Spirit is the active energy of the Great Soul of the Father, and, as we know from our experiences and observations, is used as the messenger of the Father to convey to mankind His Divine Love. And I do not mean to restrict the mission of the Holy Spirit to mankind in the flesh, for it also conveys and bestows this Great Love upon the souls of the Father's children who are spirits without the bodies of bone and flesh, and who are inhabitants of the spirit world. And so, it is a truth that the Holy Spirit is not God and no part of the Godhead, but merely His messenger of Truth and Love emanating from his Great Soul and bringing to man Love and Light and Happiness.

So you see there is no mystery of the Godhead, and no secret that God does not wish man to know and understand, and no truth that it is contrary to God's laws and will that man shall search for and possess. It is said that God is Spirit, and it is true; but spirit is not God, only one of his instruments used to work with mankind and the spirits of men. To worship the instrument is blasphemy, and only God alone must be worshiped. Jesus must not be worshiped as God, the Holy Spirit must not be so worshiped, and the sooner men learn this Truth and observe it the sooner they will get in at-onement with the Father, and please the master, who, as some may not know, is the greatest worshiper of the Father in all his universe.

I have written longer than I expected, but I hope from my message many mortals may receive the truth, and believe that the Holy Spirit is not one of the Godhead, and that the mystery of the Godhead is a myth, without body, soul or spirit, and that there is no truth in all God's universe that man is not invited to search for and understand and possess.

I will now stop and in doing so, will leave you my love and blessings, and will pray the Father to send the Holy Spirit to you with great abundance of the Divine Love. Good night and God bless you until I come again.

Your brother in Christ,
Luke.

Affirms Luke's writing. Regrets that he did not teach the Truth when on earth

November 5th, 1916.

Let me say just a word as I am very much interested in the truths of the message which Luke has just written you; and I was present at the church[23] where the minister discoursed on the subject of Paradise, and Luke was also present; and as I realized that something that the preacher said, suggested to Luke the subject of his message, and as I am very much interested in the people of that church, as I at one time was pastor there, I desire to add just a few words to what Luke has so truly and plainly expressed.

The doctrine that the preacher proclaimed tonight, I often declared when I was minister there, and as I at that time believed those doctrines to be true, and know the preacher is equally honest in his beliefs. But, alas, my beliefs were erroneous, and as it took some years of suffering and disappointment for me to unlearn these errors and learn the truth, so will he have to go through the same experience, unless, before the time of his leaving the physical body, he learns the truth.

And so with many of his congregation who are earnest and honest seekers of the truth, many of them having in their souls the Divine Love of the Father. And the pity is that there is no way of reaching him or them with the truth, for I know that they would not give heed to what you might say to them, and would look upon you as an imposter or crank. But, nevertheless, in the future some way may open up that these truths may reach these people, and as I have their interests so at heart, and feel that the influence of my teachings still linger in that congregation and produce only error and belief in that which is not true, I desire to add my confirmation to what Luke has said, and if his message ever reaches them I hope my message may also come to them. It is part of my penalty for teaching erroneous doctrines that I should work to have my people unlearn their teachings of error, and to be able to reach them in this way would give me not only great happiness, but relief from my penalty of regret.

I will not attempt to recite what Luke has said, for I could not make it plainer, but I do desire to say to my people that what he said is true and they must believe. Sometime I should like to come and write you a long message on a subject that has had the object of my consideration for a long time, and which to me and to many in the earth life is a very vital matter. I will not write more tonight, and thank you for your kindness in letting me write. Well, I am in the Seventh Sphere and

---

[23] Metropolitan Protestant Church, Washington, D.C. (Dr. S.)

am very happy in my love and surroundings, but I realize that if I had known the truth as I now know it, I would be much further advanced. Oh, I tell you the hampering of the soul's progress by a life time of erroneous beliefs is a terrible thing. I will say good night and God bless you.

Your brother in Christ,
Bishop John P. Newman.

Why Jesus does not attend the battlefields where the scenes of carnage exist

November 2nd, 1916.

I am here, Jesus.

Of course, the scenes in which I was represented[24] are creatures of the imagination, and intended to impress upon the observers of these scenes the belief or thought, that because of my teachings of peace and good will to men, I would necessarily be interested in those things that violate my teachings, and, consequently would be present at the fields of battle and the destruction of human life. But I may surprise you when I tell you that I do not visit these scenes, because my mission as a spirit is not to help those who fall in battle and come to the spirit world as the result of war's destruction and murder of human beings. There are many spirits whose duty it is to look after the spirits of those who are so suddenly ushered into the spirit world, and to help them to a realization of their changed conditions, and to lead them to the knowledge that they are no longer mortals. These spirits are specially designated for this work and they comfort the unfortunate spirits and help them to recover from the shock of their violent and sudden transformation.

This work, as you may say, is a material one. It is one that helps these spirits come into possession of their spiritual faculties, irrespective of the question as to whether they are fitted for heaven or for hell. In other words, they work to make the coming of these spirits as free from the terrors which such sudden transformation might cause, as is possible. This work is a necessary one, and one which is a part of the plan of the Father for the welfare and happiness of His children, without regard to the fact that they know not His love and mercy.

But my work is different. I deal only with the souls of men irrespective of their spirit condition that is of the condition of spirit as mere spirit. On the field of battle the souls of men are not generally open to the influence of my teachings, and my work is not among the physically dead, but among the living who are in that state of mental and soul equipoise to receive the influences of my suggestion and love. No,

---

[24] From the movie "Civilization" (G.J.C.)

the field of battle is not my place of work, and the killing of men and the carnage of war do not attract me or have for me the opportunities to do the great work, that I am leading the spirits who know the reality and the necessity of the Divine Love, to do.

I am interested in the peace of mankind and the love of one brother for another, and my teachings on earth and in the spirit world are given for the purpose of bringing about this peace. But the wars of nations or the hatred of battles will never result in bringing peace, merely because of the horrors and desolation that flow from such wars and battles. Men may think that when mankind looks upon these things of destruction, it will also look upon them with such horror and dread, that never again will war take place, and that only peace will follow and forever remain the heritage of men. But I tell you that in this they are mistaken, for in the passing of a few years all these things will be forgotten, and then, men's hearts being the same, with all the hatred and envy and ambition that existed in the hearts and minds of those who were responsible for the forgotten wars, these things will be repeated, and the fact that men are of the same carnal minds and desires will be demonstrated.

As long as men remain in their condition of sin and have only what some may call the brotherhood of man to restrain them from seeking to satisfy their ambitions or to gratify their desires to punish fancied wrongs, wars will ensue and the horrors of such conflicts will reappear on the face of the earth. Men will cry peace, peace, but the world will know no peace, and poor man will suffer the recurrence of the results of the workings of his evil nature.

And hence, you may understand that I am not so much interested in having peace come to man as a result of the horrors of war as I am in having it come as the necessary result of the transforming of men's hearts and souls from sin to purity, from the merely natural love to that of the Divine Love, for when this latter love is in men's souls, they will not cease from war and hatred, and carnal appetites will not be satisfied, because of the horrors that may attend these things, but because of the love that exists in their souls, which will not permit wars. Love will rule and men will forget hatred and all things which now form a part of their very existence. My work is to change men from the fallen man to the possessor of the Divine Love.

Also, am I trying to teach men that originally they possessed a love that in its pure state would lead them from these things of hatred and war, and that their only salvation, outside of the possession of the Divine Love, is to again obtain this pure love—the purified natural love. But strange as it may seem to some, it is more difficult for a man to regain the state of the purification of his natural love, than to obtain that greater purification which comes with the possession of the Divine Love.

I see that many centuries may pass before man will attain to this state of purification of his natural love, that will enable him to say that because of his love, wars cannot come again and peace must reign: and hence, the great necessity for him to know that only with the coming of the Divine Love will come the impossibility of war and strife—individually and nationally.

So, when it is written or portrayed in pictures that I am on the fields of battle trying to show mankind the horrors of war, or that I am weeping over the slaughter of men, such writings or portrayals are not true. My mission is to reach the souls of men, as individuals, and turn them to the Love of the Father, and my weeping or sorrow is, when men will not listen to the voice that comes to them all, as it calls them to turn to the Father and Live. A dead body is of small consequence as compared to a dead soul, and there are so many that pass into the spirit world bring with them their dead souls. As the dead bodies lie on the fields of carnage, I know that there is nothing there that needs my help or sympathy: and the souls that leave these bodies are not in condition, at that time, to listen to my ministrations or consider their future existence. So you see there is no reason why I should visit the battlefields or try to help these newly born spirits, as I may describe them. No. Jesus, the elder brother, is not the physician for the mangled or wounded bodies or for the souls that come into the spirit world filled with hatred and antagonism at the time of their coming.

Physical death in view of eternity is not of much moment, and while I know that to the ordinary mortal it is one of the most momentous of their existence, yet as I say, it is of comparatively little importance. But, oh, the importance of the death of the soul, and the great necessity of striving to awaken that soul to life! Well, I have written enough now, and will stop.

I see your friend with you and I must say to him that I am with him very often, and am pleased that he has arisen from death to life, and that the battle field on which he has fought the fight of the soul is larger and more terrible in its aspects and evidences of carnage and destruction than the field of battle that is now destroying the physical bodies of so many of mankind. I mean that the whole world is the battlefield of the soul's fighting, and if men could only see the results, as they see the results of the war that is now shaking the whole earth, they would understand that the Great War is not the one that is causing so many dead souls to enter the spirit world. Give him my love and blessings. I will come soon and write you a message of truth. So with all my love and blessings, I am

Your brother and friend,
Jesus.

Affirming Jesus wrote and showed his glory

November 2nd, 1916.

I am here, your own true and loving Helen.

What a wonderful message you had from the Master, and how earnest he was when he was writing. The glory of his countenance was blinding to even us, and the love that seemed to possess his very being was beyond our conception. He was truly the beloved son of the Father, and the spirits present were bathed in his love to such an extent that they seemed to partake of his glory. Oh, my dear, it was all so wonderful!

Your own true and loving,
Helen.

The destiny of the man who does not have the Divine Love in his soul and dies only with the natural love and a belief in the creeds, etc

September 28th, 1916.

I am here, Jesus.

I come tonight to tell you that you are in a better condition to write than you have been for some time and I think it best that I deliver to you a message. Well, I will write on the subject: Of the destiny of the man who has not the Divine Love in his soul, and dies with only the natural love and a belief in the creeds and dogmas of the churches.

I know that many men believe that the creeds of the churches is what is necessary for the salvation of mankind. I mean as to baptism and observance of the sacraments, and the belief that in my name men may be saved—are sufficient and all that are necessary to ensure them an entrance into the Kingdom of Heaven; and in such belief rest, with the feeling of assurance that nothing else is required or in any way to be sought for and acquired.

The large majority of professing Christians are in this state of belief, and hence the greater number of mankind will not enter the Kingdom of Heaven, or become in their natures Divine. I have already told you what is the future of those who possess this Divine Nature of the Father, and now I will confine my message to the future of this great majority.

As you may know, the river can never run higher than its source and neither can this majority attain to a perfection and happiness superior to that which was possessed by man before the time of the fall from the state of his perfect creation, and hence, no matter how great his progress may be in his natural love or in his moral or mental qualities, he can never excel (exceed) the first created man as he was before the fall. And the only possible future for this vast majority is the condition and development that existed in the perfect man of God's first creation.

I know it is said that man has in him that which is a part of the Divinity of God, and that by his own efforts he may develop that Divine Substance until he becomes Divine himself, and of the nature of the Father. But this is not true, and it is not possible to develop the Divine Love or any Essence of the Divine out of that which has not (that) in itself, (and) there is nothing of the Nature of the Divine (in man). In the spirit world, and I mean the spiritual as well as Celestial, laws prevail, and are just as certain in their operations as are the laws of the material world and a fundamental law is, that only like produces like; although in the physical world it may appear that a derivative is not like that from which it is derived, but this is in appearance only, for in substance and essence the likeness exists and cannot be eradicated.

And so as to the real condition of the soul of man. If he has only the natural love—the created love—the development of that love will result in that which cannot possibly be greater or other than that which in its constituent parts is only the natural love, and no matter what the perfection may become, the Divine element is absent, and all the limitations that are inherent in the created being still continue to form a part of and control that being. There is a limit to the development of this natural love and to the state of happiness beyond which it is not possible for this being to go, and that limit is the qualities and excellence possessed by the first man before he became defiled and impregnated with sin. The mind of such being is also limited in the progress which it may make in obtaining knowledge, for that mind being a thing of creation is bound by the limitations that that creation imposed.

So I say, such a man can never progress higher than those attributes or qualities with which he was endowed when he was the perfect man, either spiritually or mentally, unless he seeks for and obtains the Divine Love. When spirits come and write that life in this spirit world is always progressive, these spirits who write, have never attained to this limit of which I speak and hence to them progression is endless; and this belief is very beneficial, because it inspires them to make an effort to progress.

There are many spirits in this perfect state in the highest sphere of natural love or mentality, but they are spirits who have been in the spirit world for a vast number of years, and are what you might call ancient spirits. These spirits have realized this limitation of which I write, and while they can change the objects of their seeking and the sources of their happiness, yet their progress has its ending, and often there comes to them dissatisfaction and a realization that over and beyond their sphere, there must be something that may be obtained, that surpasses their perfect state and development. And as a result of this dissatisfaction many of these spirits, in moments of their unrest, give heed to the suggestions of those spirits who have become possessed of the Divine Essence, and upon whom (there) is no limitation of progress; for these latter spirits are at all times in the highest sphere of these spirits of perfected natural love, trying to show them the way to the higher development and happiness of the Celestial Spheres.

It may seem surprising to you, but it is a fact, that these spirits of the natural love, during their periods of progression and especially as they make nearer approach to their perfection, in the satisfaction and happiness that they experience in that progression, will not listen to the spirits of the Divine Spheres, or believe that there can be any other methods of progress more desirable or excellent than the ones that they are pursuing, and only when they come to realize the dissatisfaction that I speak of, will awaken to the fact, or consent to be awakened to the fact, that there may be a way that leads to things beyond their limits of progress and the perfection that they may have acquired. So, as I say, the higher the progress of these spirits and the farther away they advance from the earth plane, the greater the difficulty in persuading them that there is a state of perfection and happiness surpassing that which they are seeking for, and a way, different from the way they are pursuing.

As these spirits progress in their natural love and in the development of their created minds, much happiness and satisfaction come to them, and in each stage of progress, so much greater do these experiences become, that they readily conceive that there can be no way superior to the one that they are travelling, and, hence, having such belief, the difficulty of convincing them to the contrary, becomes almost insurmountable. As a consequence the spirits of the Celestial Spheres and those of the spirit spheres, who are progressing in the Divine Love, give the greater part of their time and efforts to convincing spirits of these higher truths while they are in the earth planes, before the happiness that I mention is experienced.

The life on earth and that in the earth planes of the spirit world are the states in which the souls of mortals and of spirits have the best opportunities for learning and believing these truths that show them the way to the progression that is without limitation or ending, and hence, the importance of men knowing these truths, and of spirits also, before they experience the satisfaction and pride, I may say, that the advancement in the development of their natural love and mental and moral qualities gives them.

Until the time comes when the Father shall withdraw from man and spirit the privilege of obtaining this Divine Love and Essence, which time will bring the second death, these spirits and all spirits and mortals will have the opportunity of seeking for and finding the way to the

Celestial Spheres and Immortality. But after that time this privilege will no longer exist, and then those spirits and mortals who have not found and followed the way of that privilege, will be and become only the perfect beings, as were their first parents. They will have no assurance of Immortality, or even continuous life, and that dissatisfaction and longing for something unknown, will be theirs.

They will remain only the created beings in spirit body, soul and mind, and as the first parents had all the qualities that these restored men will have, and fell, and why may it not be that they will fall (or) that there may come some change in the individualized spirit that will destroy that individuality and dissolve it into its elements of pre-creation? No spirit knows that such a change will take place, that the perfect spirit will not always retain the same individuality, or that the happiness of such spirit will not always exist. And neither does any spirit know that these things will continue to be.

Then why should he not choose that course which leads to Divinity and certainty of Immortality and progress, rather than the one which leads to limitation of progress and happiness, and to uncertainty of Immortality?

I have written enough for tonight. I will come again soon. So remember that I love you and am with you trying to help you spiritually and that I pray to the Father to bless you.

Good night.
Your brother and friend,
Jesus.

The Resurrection.

The resurrection that is common to all, be they saint or sinner

January 16th, 1916.

I am here, St. Paul, of the New Testament.

I come tonight to tell you of a truth that is important for men to know, and which you must place in your Book of Truths.

I have written you before on my alleged writings as they are contained in the Bible, and which, as I have said, were not written by me as they there appear.

I desire tonight to write for a short time on the subject of the "Resurrection," because, as I see, the church doctrine of the resurrection is founded more on what is ascribed to me than on the writings of the Gospels, though the latter also contain a basis for the doctrine.

I never said there would be a resurrection of the physical body nor of the individual clothed in any body of flesh, but my teachings were that man at death would rise in a spiritual body, and that not a new one made for the special occasion of his departure from the material body, but one that had been with him through life and that came into an individualized form when he first became a living being. This spirit body is necessary to man's existence, and is that part of him which contains his senses and is the seat of his reasoning powers.

Of course the organs of the physical are necessary for the utilization of these senses, and without these organs there could be no manifestations of the senses, which are inherent in the spirit body. Even if a man should lose the perfect workings of his physical organs of sight, yet the power of seeing would still exist in him, although he might not be able to realize that fact; and this same principle applies to the hearing and the other senses.

So when man loses his physical organs which are necessary for him to see with, he is dead as to sight, just as dead as he ever becomes with reference to all the other organs of sense when the whole physical body dies; and were it possible to restore these physical organs that are necessary to enable him to see or hear, he would be able to see and hear just as he was before their loss. The restoration of these organs does not, of itself, bring him the power to see and hear, but merely enables the faculties of sight and hearing to again use the organs for the purpose of manifesting the powers which are in and a part of the spirit body.

When the whole physical body dies the spirit body, at the very time of death, becomes resurrected, and with all these faculties of which I have spoken, and thereafter continues to live free and unencumbered from the material body, which, these organs being destroyed, can no longer perform the objects of its creation. It becomes dead, and thereafter never has any resurrection as such material body, although its elements or parts do not die, but in the workings of God's laws enter upon other and new functionings, though never that of reuniting and forming again the body that has died.

So the resurrection of the body, as taught by me, is the resurrection of the spiritual body, not from death, for it never dies, but from its envelopment in the material form which had been visible as a thing of apparent life.

There is a law controlling the uniting of the two bodies and the functioning of the powers and faculties of the spirit body through the organs of the physical body, that limits the extent of the operations of these faculties, to those things that are wholly material—or which have the appearance of the material—and when I say material I mean that which is grosser or more compact than the spirit body. Thus these faculties of sight of the spirit body can, through the organs of the material body, see what are called ghosts or apparitions as well as the more material things, but never, in this way, see things of pure spirit. And when it is said that men or women see clairvoyantly, which they do, it is not meant or is it a fact, that they see through the organs of the physical eyes; but on the contrary, this sight is one purely spiritual, and its workings are entirely independent of the material organs.

Now when this body—the material—dies, the spirit body becomes resurrected, as it is said, and free from all the limitations which its incarnation in the flesh has imposed, and it is then able to use all its faculties without the limitations or help of the physical organs, and, as regards the sight, everything in nature, both material and spiritual, becomes the object of its vision; and that which the limitations of the material organs prevented its seeing, and which to men is the unreal and non-existent becomes the real and truly existing.

This, in short, is what I meant by the resurrection of the body; and from this you will realize that the resurrection is not to take place at some unknown day in the future, but at the very moment when the physical body dies, and, as the Bible says, in the twinkling of an eye. This saying of the Bible attributed to me, I did write and teach. This resurrection applies to all mankind, for all who have ever lived and died have been resurrected, and all who shall live hereafter and die will be resurrected.

But this resurrection is not the "Great Resurrection" upon which, in my teachings, I declared the great truth of Christianity to be founded. This is not the resurrection of Jesus that I declared "without which is our faith as Christians vain." This is the common resurrection, applicable to all mankind of every nation and race, whether they have a knowledge of Jesus or not. And many times in many nations has it been demonstrated before the coming of Jesus, that men had died and appeared again as living spirits in the form of angels and men, and were recognized by mortal men as spirits who had a previous earth existence.

So I say, this is the resurrection common to all men; and the coming and death and resurrection of Jesus, as taught by the churches, did not bring the Great Resurrection to the knowledge or comfort of men, and did not furnish the true foundation upon which the true Christian belief and faith rest.

Many of the infidels, agnostics and spiritualists assert and claim, and truly, that the resurrection of Jesus as above referred to, was not a new thing and did not prove to humanity a future life any more convincingly than had been proved before his time by the experiences and observations of men and followers of other sects and faiths, and of no faiths at all.

The great weakness of the church today is that they claim and teach as the foundation of their faith and existence this resurrection of Jesus as set forth above; and the result is, as is plainly and painfully apparent to the churches themselves, that as men think for themselves, and they are doing more than ever in the history of the world, they refuse to believe in this resurrection as sufficient to show the superiority of Jesus' coming and mission and teachings over those of other reformers and teachers who had preceded him in the world's history of faiths and religions. And as a further result the churches are losing their adherents and believers. Christianity is waning and rapidly, and agnosticism is increasing and manifesting itself in the forms of free thought societies and Secularism, etc.

Hence you will see the necessity of making known again to mankind the true foundation stone of the real Christianity that the Master came to teach and which he did teach, but which was lost as his early followers disappeared from the scene of earthly action and practice, and men of less spiritual insight and more material desires, with their ambition for power and dominion, became the rulers and guides and interpreters of the church.

There is a Resurrection though that the Master taught, and his apostles, when they came into a knowledge of, taught, and which I as a humble follower taught, which is vital to man's salvation and which is the true foundation of true Christianity; and which no other man, angel or reformer ever before taught or has since taught.

It is too late tonight to explain this Resurrection, but I will come again very soon and try to make it plain to you and to the world.

I will now say good night and God bless you and keep you in His

care.
>Your brother in Christ,
>Paul.

Corroboration by Jesus that St. Paul wrote on the resurrection

>January 16th, 1916.

>I am here, Jesus.
>I am pleased that Paul was able to write you so successfully as he did upon the two subjects which I know will prove to be interesting to you and the one that Paul wrote about is very vital to the beliefs of man, for upon the question of the resurrection is founded the doctrine of what is called Christianity, and I must say that that foundation as explained by the orthodox churches and the commentators on the Bible is a very weak foundation, and very vulnerable to the assaults of those who are not satisfied with the authority of the Bible or the explanations of its teachings as they now exist. Paul will finish this most important message, and let me impress upon you to make the effort to get in the best condition for receiving it correctly.
>Well, I will not write more tonight, but only further say that I am with you in my love and influence, and trying to help you in the ways of which we have written you. With all my love and blessings, I will say good night.
>Your brother and friend,
>Jesus.

The resurrection that Jesus taught without which our faith as Christians is in vain

>February 8th, 1916.

>I am here, St. Paul, of the New Testament.
>I desire to continue my message tonight. As I said in closing my last writing, there is a resurrection that is vital to the salvation of men, which Jesus taught, and which after the death of his followers and believers of the early centuries, the knowledge of was lost to the world and to those who assumed to teach the doctrines of the resurrection that he came to declare and teach.
>You and all mankind must know that the resurrection which is the foundation stone of Christianity is a resurrection from the dead and not from the mere existence of a man as a spirit in the physical body on earth, and not as a resurrection of the soul from its environments and

True Gospel Revealed anew by Jesus

limitations that the earth life placed upon it.

Then what is the resurrection that Jesus referred to when he said: *"I am the resurrection and the life!"*?

Now in order to understand this resurrection it is necessary to understand what is meant by the death of man, that is the real man—the ego,—that part of him in which the breath of life exists, no matter whether he is of the physical or the spiritual.

As has been explained to you elsewhere, when man was created his creation was of the physical body, the spiritual body and the soul, and in addition—and the addition was the most important part of his creation—the potentiality of becoming so at one with the Father in His nature and certain of His attributes, that he, man, would become so possessed of some of the Divine Essence of the Father and a portion of His divinity that would cause him to be immortal, so that death could never deprive him of his existence; and not only that, but he would realize the consciousness of his immortality.

This potentiality then was a part of his creation, and, as we have explained elsewhere, the only part of his creation that died as the result of his disobedience; for it is very apparent from the mere knowledge that man has, or may have, from the ordinary investigation of the qualities of his being, and from the truths of psychical research of modern days, as well as from the understanding of the many instances related in the Bible of the appearance of departed spirits on earth and the manifestations of their existence, and also from the many occurrences of the appearances of spirits related in what is called secular history, that the soul and spirit body of man never died, and that his physical body lived for many years after the day on which the sentence, because of his disobedience, announced that he should die. And as I have said, this mortal body not man—the man—but merely the vesture of covering for the real man.

This potentiality then being the only part of the created man that died, and as Jesus' mission was to teach the resurrection of man from the dead, it necessarily follows that the only thing that was intended to be resurrected was this potentiality of becoming a part of God's Divinity. This is the only real and true resurrection, and upon this resurrection must rest the faith and truth of Christianity—and by Christianity I mean religion which is based upon the true teachings of Jesus, the Christ.

There are contained in the Bible some things which if properly understood, would show to man that no resurrection of the body was intended as the thing which Jesus came to earth to declare and teach.

When he said, "I am the resurrection and the life," he did not say or mean, wait until I die and then I will become the resurrection; or when you see me ascend to Heaven, then will I become the resurrection and you will know it; but his declarations not only in the instance mentioned, but at all times were that he was the resurrection while living. And these declarations did not refer to the man Jesus, or to any disposition that he might make of his body, either physical or spiritual, or to any apparent ascension of his physical body, which never took place, or to any ascension of his spiritual body which did occur. In these particulars he was essentially no more or different from other men that had died or should die.

But the meaning of his saying and his mission were, that as by man's disobedience there had occurred the death of the possibility of his becoming at one with the Father and partaking of his divine nature, and as that possibility had never been restored to man in all the intervening years, and man had remained in this condition of death during all the long centuries, if man would only believe in him as the true Christ and in his teachings as to the re-bestowal of this great privilege of again becoming at one with the Father and of obtaining immortality, and would follow his advice as to the way in which man could realize the benefits of this great privilege, then he would become conscious that Jesus was the resurrection from the dead. Not Jesus the man or teacher or the chosen and anointed one of the Father, but Jesus the impersonation of the truths which he proclaimed as to the re-bestowal of the great gift. Only in this way was Jesus the resurrection and the life.

He, himself, had received the great gift and realized his at-onement and the consciousness of his immortality and the possession of the divine nature, and knew that he had been lifted from death into life, and, therefore, if men would believe his teachings as to the resurrection, these teachings and not the man Jesus or even the fact that he had been resurrected, would draw all men unto him, that is, into the condition of life and consciousness that he possessed.

Then the resurrection that Jesus promised to man was the resurrection of this great potentiality which he had lost at the time of the first disobedience and which had never been restored until the coming of Jesus.

Now let it not be misunderstood as to what was meant by this resurrection. As I have said, after men were deprived of this potentiality they were in a condition of death and it was not possible for them to get out of this condition. They were possessed of only what is called their natural love without any possibility of obtaining the Divine Love which was necessary in order to give them any portion of the divine nature and a consciousness of immortality. When the great potentiality, which was as to them as if it had never existed, was re-bestowed, then men were again placed in the position of the first man before his fall, and were no longer actually dead, but were possessed of this potentiality to become that which had been forfeited by the first parents.

But as we have told you, the gift of this potentiality was not of itself the bestowal upon man of those qualities which such potentiality merely made it possible for them to acquire by aspiration and effort. Before this re-bestowal men could not by any aspirations or efforts on their part obtain the conditions and qualities which this potentiality made possible, no matter how great the effort might be; as to them men were simply and absolutely dead. After the re-bestowal, the impossibility which this death had imposed was removed, and then men received, not the full fruition of what was possible to obtain because of such re-bestowal, but the privilege of arising from death to life—of the resurrection from death to the glories of immortal life.

And while this privilege had become a part of man's possession, yet, if he had remained without consciousness of that fact, he would, in effect, have remained in his condition of death and have never received the benefit of the re-bestowal of the great gift. So to reveal to man the vital truth Jesus taught and demonstrated in his own life, the possession of those qualities that became his because of the existence of the gift.

And he also taught while men had the privilege spoken of, yet, unless they sought for and prayed the Father in sincerity for the gift of his Divine Love, the potentiality which had been bestowed upon them would not bring to them the resurrection from the dead, and they would continue in their lives as mortals and as inhabitants of the spirit world, as if they were still under the doom of death.

I may here state that this potentiality, which was lost by the disobedience of the first parents and was re-bestowed by the Father and revealed by Jesus to mankind, was the privilege of receiving and possessing the Divine Love of the Father, which, when possessed would give to man certain qualities of divinity and immortality.

So the resurrection from the dead that the master taught and which is the one foundation of the Christian faith, arise from the fact that God re-bestowed upon mankind the privilege of seeking for and receiving His Divine Love which would make the mortal one with Him and Immortal; and upon the further fact that man must, in order to obtain the resurrection, seek and find this Divine Love and thereby become a child of the true resurrection—a resurrection that was never known to prophet or seer or reformer or teachers of faiths, no matter how excellent their moral teachings and private lives may have been, before the coming of Jesus.

Truly He was the Resurrection and the Life, and I, Paul, who am the recipient of this resurrection and know whereof I speak and have knowledge of the fact that those inhabitants of the spirit world who have never received this resurrection are still in a condition of death, so far as obtaining the Divine Love of the Father and the consciousness of immortality are concerned, and so I declare unto you what I have attempted to describe as the resurrection from the dead, is the True

Resurrection.
>I will stop, as I have written a long time.
>So my dear brother I will say good night.
>Your brother in Christ,
>Paul.

Why the Divine Love of God is necessary for man to possess in order that he may become at-one with the Father and an inhabitant of the Celestial Kingdom

June 27th, 1916.

I am here, Jesus.

I wish tonight to write you upon a subject that is of interest to all mankind, and I hope that we will be able to communicate and you receive the message.

I desire to write on the subject of—*Why the Love of God—I mean the Divine Love—is necessary for man to possess in order that he may become at one with the Father and an inhabitant of the Celestial Kingdom.*

Already I have written you what this Divine Love is in contradistinction to the natural love, and how it is necessary to save men from their sins so that they may become inhabitants of the Celestial Kingdom, and that nothing but this Love will make a man at-one with the Father, and that no mere ceremony or belief in me as the savior of men will effectuate that end; and now I will try to show you why this Divine Love is necessary, or as your learned men might say, show you the philosophy of the transformation of the mere man into the divine angel, which every man becomes who receives this Love into his soul.

In the first place, man, as you have been informed, is a special creation of God, and is no greater than the component parts that enter into his creation as they are in their individual and aggregate qualities, and these parts are merely what God in His act of creation designed them to be.

It must not be assumed that these parts or any of them are a part of God, or of His essence or qualities, for they are not, and are as separate and distinct from Him and His qualities, as are the lower creations of His will, such as animals, and vegetables and mineral substances. The only difference is that man is of a much higher order of creation, and in one particular, made in the image of God, and no other of His creatures has this image in its creation. But, nevertheless, man is no part of God, but a merely distinct creation, and in his best and purest state only a man, having simply those qualities which were created in him at the time of his coming into existence.

There are certain qualities which man possesses, such as love and wisdom and the reasoning faculties which may be said to resemble the Godlike attributes, and so they do; but yet, they are not a part of God's essence or qualities, and when men assert that man is divine, or that he has in him the divine nature or even a portion of the Divine Essence, they are wrong, for the qualities in them that appear to be of this divine resemblance, are merely those which were created for the purpose of making the human a perfect man.

And because of this conception of man as to his inherent qualities, he has and does and will lose the opportunity of becoming possessed of the nature or Essence of the Father which he may obtain, if he will pursue the proper and only method that God has provided for him in order to be at one with Him.

The universe of man can and will continue to exist, even though man may never become a partaker of this divine nature of the Father, and man will live and enjoy the happiness that was bestowed upon him at the time of his creation, and he will not lose the perfect condition of this creation after he shall have been separated from sin and error, his own creatures. But he will not be anything more than the perfect man, and in the time to come will not be anything less, and, yet, he will always, as long as he exists, remain distinct from the Nature and Essence of the Father, just as he was at the time of his creation, unless he obtains this Divine Nature and Essence of the Father in the way that I mentioned.

The highest endowment of man, either in soul or heart or intellect is merely that which belongs to him as a part of his creation, and is not the smallest part of the divine nature and qualities of the Father. No part or portion of divinity enters into man's creation, no matter how divinely constituted man may appear to be or Godlike he may seem in the greatness of his intellect or in the extent of his love nature.

So you see, man is as distinct from God and from His divinity, as is the animal—the brute—from man, and must forever remain so unless he follows the only way the Father has prescribed for him to obtain a portion of this divinity.

Now, all this shows that man, no matter how highly he may develop his intellect or to what extent he may develop his moral and love nature, cannot become more than the mere man that he was in the beginning—perfect in every particular—for he was in the beginning perfect in every particular, and as I have said before, God never makes a mistake as to the perfection of His creatures, even though in the case of man it may appear that He did in giving him the great power of free will, which in its wrongful exercise has caused sin and evil to appear in the word of man's consciousness.

And man was made finite, and his capacity for exercising any and all his qualities, is limited beyond which he cannot possibly go. His intellect is bound by limits as determined as the law of God which controls it, and also, his capacity for loving and for the enjoyment of his happiness; and though he may live for all eternity either as man or spirit, he cannot possibly extend or pass beyond the boundary lines of his creation. He cannot enter into the Realm of the Divine where limitations do not exist, and capacity for receiving knowledge and wisdom and love, and for progression that is commensurate with the very fountainhead of God, Himself.

Then, such being the nature and limitation and capacity of man, it is apparent that he can never by virtue of his creation and the qualities which he possess, become a partaker of the nature and Essence of God, unless he receives something in addition to these qualities, and he must receive this something from without. It will not do to say, that there is within him, as an inherent part of him, that, which when developed, will make him of a nature divine and a part of the essence of the Father, for this is not true. There is nothing in man of this nature, and it is impossible to produce an Essence Divine unless there be something from which it can be produced, that in some degree has the nature of that Essence. It would be the equivalent of producing something from nothing which even God does not attempt to do.

Then, as man is thus limited, all that flows from the qualities and attributes which he possesses is necessarily limited. The enjoyment of his intellect, the pleasures of his love, the satisfaction of his reasoning powers, and as a sum total, his capacity for happiness have their bounds, and, besides, the consciousness of immortality can never be his, either as spirit or mortal, even though he may strive for it to be.

When man takes on the Divine Nature and becomes absorbed in the Essence of the Father, he then becomes like the Father, and whatever his image to the Father may have been when he was mere man, now he becomes the real Substance, and limitations of possibilities become removed, love sees no ending and intellectual development, no boundaries, happiness no limitations, and Immortality becomes a thing of knowledge, and the soul a new creature, having the Divine Essence of the Father; and until this new creation has taken place, and the transformation becomes a thing of reality, and the soul be made at-one with the Father, man cannot enter into the Kingdom of Heaven. Then, no longer man but now an Angel.

Now, as I have written you before, all this can be accomplished only by the operation of the New Birth, that is the inflowing into the soul of man of the Divine Love of the Father. This Love contains the Essence of God's divinity, and when man obtains it he is then of the same Essence as the Father, and for the first time becomes a part of the Divine, and fitted to inhabit the Celestial Heavens. In no other way can man partake of this nature, and it does not require much reasoning to show the logical truth of this statement, for man in his earthly affairs, and in his material experiments in producing compounds from elements, applies the same principle that I assert in my statement, "The dough cannot be leavened unless leaven is placed in the batch."

So you see that without this Divine Love entering into the soul it will be impossible for the natural man to become the Divine angel. Beliefs and creeds and doctrines and sacrifices cannot work this transformation, and even though the beliefs may be without doubt, and the creeds and doctrines satisfactory, and the sacrifices without end, yet they will all be futile to change the soul of the mere man into the soul of the Divine Angel, and all this, in part, is why man should seek to obtain the Divine Love and become an inhabitant of the Celestial Spheres.

I have written enough for tonight and I am pleased at the way in which you received it.

So with all my love and blessings, I am
Your brother and friend,
Jesus.

The importance of knowing the Way to the Celestial Kingdom—many statements in the Bible untrue

October 18th, 1919.

I am here, Jesus.

Let me write a few lines for I must tell you of an important truth that is necessary for men to know in order to reach the Celestial Kingdom, and a knowledge of the plan of salvation.

I know that the Bible contains many sayings attributed to me in reference to this plan, and many of my alleged sayings are believed in by those who claim to be Christians, which are not true, for I never said them and they are contrary to what I received from the Father as to the true plan of men's redemption from sin, and as to the only way, by which, they can obtain the true at-onement with the Father and a knowledge of their own immortality.

Many of these sayings were written by men who knew not the only way to a oneness with the Father, and were the results of the teachings of the manuscripts that then existed and were received by the Jews as the revelations of Moses, and of many of the prophets who had no knowledge of the Divine Love or of its rebestowal upon humanity. These men made me say those things that accorded with their ideas of what was necessary to a salvation or possibility of their becoming at one with me and with the Father, and in writing their ideas confused the truth with what they supposed was the truth as contained in the Old Testament; and much harm has been done by attributing many of these sayings to me, because of the supposed authority that thereby attached to them.

My disciples never taught, and never understood that their salvation, or that of any man, depended upon faith in me as the son of God, or that I, the mere Jesus, had in me any virtue to forgive sin or to insure an entrance into the true Kingdom of God, or that, I, as the man Jesus was a son of God in the sense that the Bible teaches. They knew that the Father had revealed to me the truth, and that I had in me that Love, which to a large extent, made me like unto and at one with the Father. That my teachings of the rebestowal of the Divine Love was true, and that when they or any man should possess this Love, to the extent of that possession, they would become at one with the Father, and also with me, who possessed it to a greater degree than any man. I say, they knew this and taught it to the people as I had taught it to them; but when the compilers of the present New Testament came to declare my sayings and teachings, they knew not of this Love, and hence, could not understand what many of my true expressions meant, and gave them an interpretation so far as my real sayings were concerned, that would comply with their knowledge.

No, I am not correctly quoted in many of these sayings, and I may say in the large majority of them, for when they were written, as now contained in the New Testament, men had lost the knowledge of their true meaning, and out of their own minds recorded that which they thought was what I had really said.

I do not see how these false sayings can be corrected, except to take each saying and show, by its incompatibility with what I now say, its falsity. This would take too much time and expend much energy that could the better be employed in declaring what the truth actually is. But this I will say, that whenever these sayings impart that I claim to be God, or that I could or did forgive men of their sins, or that whatsoever should be asked of the Father in my name would be received, are all untrue and has greatly misled the true seeker of knowledge of Immortality.

My disciples were close to me and understood better my sayings than all others, and yet they did not understand all the truth, and left the mortal life with many expectations that were not fulfilled and in the very nature of the same could not be fulfilled. They were in certain non-essentials influenced in their beliefs and expectations by their training in the teachings of these Old Testament manuscripts, and were very largely Jews in belief when they died. They understood the vital things that determined their relationship to God and to their existence in the future world, but as to many of the non-essentials they retained the faith of their fathers, and were not able to receive all the truth which I could have taught them.

I must not linger to correct these alleged sayings of mine, but must occupy my time and yours in declaring and revealing the Truth as it exists now and existed then, and you and the world may know, that wherever and whenever these Bible sayings of mine conflict with what I have written and shall write you, they are untrue and were never said by me. Thus, in this general way, I will make plain to men that the Bible must not in all particulars be relied on or believed in as containing the Truth or my declarations of the Truth.

I will soon come and write a message on a vital truth and hope that you will be in condition to receive it.

I will now say good night and God bless your efforts and keep you safely in His care.

Your brother and friend,

.Jesus

The importance for mankind seeking the Divine Love—continued

January 11th, 1916.

I am here, Jesus.

I will continue my discourse of last night.[25] I was saying that the Jews and the teachers of the church that became established or rather controlled after the death of my followers, and those who understood the true teachings of my disciples, taught the conduct of men towards their fellowmen, and the observance of certain ceremonies and feasts were the important things for men to learn and practice in order to gain salvation, rather than the truths which made man a child of the Father and at one with Him through the operations of the New Birth.

Of course, before my coming, the Jews could not have taught the truth of the New Birth, because the Great Gift of the re-bestowal of the Divine Love had not been made, and it was not possible for that Great Truth, which was necessary for Immortality and the possibility of man's partaking of God's Divine Love, to be known to the Jews, and hence, they could not teach it; and their teachings were limited and confined to the things which would make them purer in their natural love and in the relation of that love to the Father.

God, at that time, while He never gave them the privilege of becoming at one with Him in the Divine Love or even of becoming such beings in their character and spiritual qualities as were Adam and Eve, commonly supposed to be our first parents, yet did require of them

---

[25] It would appear that this message did not in fact follow the previous message published here, but in fact is a continuation of a message a few pages further on. (G.J.C.)

obedience to His laws which would develop in them their natural love to such a degree, as would cause it to become in harmony with His laws that controlled and governed their natural love.

If you will study the Ten Commandments you will see that these commandments deal only with the natural love and by their observance would tend to make men better in that natural love and in their conduct with one another and in their relationship to God, so far as that love brought them in communion with Him. This natural love, as I have said, was possessed by men, just as the first parents possessed it, and was never taken from them, and in its purity was in perfect harmony with God's creation and the workings of His universe; but not withstanding these great qualities men were mere men and had in them no part of the divinity of the Father. And this being so, the Jews, while they were supposed to be more in contact with God through the prophets and seers, than were any of the other races or sects of God's children, yet, never looked for a Messiah that would come with any other or greater power than that which would enable them to become the great ruling nation of the earth, to whom all other peoples would be subordinated and subjected, and powerless to ever again conquer or subject their nation to bondage.

In a way this Messiah was to be a kind of supernatural being, having power which no other man ever had, and a kind of god to be worshiped and served in their earthly lives.

Many of the Jews, notwithstanding what may be said to the contrary and the teachings of the prophets, believed in other gods than the one which Moses declared, as is evidenced in their histories, both sacred and secular, for whenever their God, that is, the God of Moses, did not treat them just as they thought He should, they would create and worship other gods—even the golden calf. So I say they never expected a Messiah who would be other than a most powerful ruler on earth.

Their ideas and beliefs of the life after death were very hazy, and even that part of them known as the Pharisees, who believed in a kind of resurrection, never conceived that when they should drop the mortal life, they would be anything different in their qualities and characters from what they were as mortals, minus the physical bodies, and the great increased happiness which would come to them as such mortals, changed in their appearances.

This was the idea of the common people and also of the priests and scribes; and notwithstanding the many beautiful and spiritual psalms ascribed to David, the happiness or glory that they might expect, was only that which would come to them as spiritualized mortals having only the natural love.

So you see, the Great Gift of the Father that is the rebestowal of the Divine Love, was not known or even dreamed of by the Jews, nor conceived of nor taught by their scribes, nor even by their great prophets, or law-givers such as Moses and Elias and others. Their conception of God was that of an exalted personal being, all powerful and all knowing, and one whom they would be able to see face to face, as they might any king or ruler when they should come into the heavens which he had prepared for them, and where he had his habitation.

I will defer the writing until later.[26]

Jesus.

The importance for mankind seeking the Divine Love—continued

January 12th, 1916.

I am here, Jesus.

I will continue my discourse. As I was saying, the chief object of my mission on earth was to teach the rebestowal of the Divine Love upon man and the way to obtain it; and the secondary object was to teach men those moral truths which would tend to make them better in their conduct towards their fellow man, and purer in their natural love.

And so it is, that in my teachings of these moral truths, the effect of these teachings was to bring man more in harmony with the laws of the Father, which control the operations of the natural love. I never at any time intended that men should understand that these moral truths would bring about their union with the Father in the divine sense, or that the possession of this natural love in its purest state would enable man to become a partaker of God's Divine Nature, or an inhabitant of His Kingdom.

But as I have said, the only object apparently that these compilers and writers of the Bible had to accomplish, was to persuade men that the observance of these moral teachings in their conduct was all that was necessary to enable them to enter the Kingdom of Heaven.

I know that it is said that love and almsgiving and kind deeds will work to a man's salvation and enable him to become at one with the Father and to enjoy the presence of God in the high heavens, but this is not true.

The good deeds which men perform in the way of helping his fellowman will live after him, and will undoubtedly work towards a man becoming perfect in his natural love, but they will not bring that man in at-onement with the Father in the Higher Love which is so necessary to his full salvation.

My messages to you while they will not take one jot or tittle

---

[26] This was continued two days later directly below. (G.J.C.)

(scarcely detectable amount) from the moral teachings, yet they will show to man the necessity and way to obtain a full reconciliation with the Father and a home in the Celestial Spheres.

I will come to you again and write upon a subject which is important to you, and which men should understand.

So with all my love I will say good night.

Your brother and friend,

Jesus.

The Soul

The soul—what it is and what it is not

March 2nd, 1917.

I am here, Jesus.

I come tonight to write my message on the soul, and will do so, if we can establish the necessary rapport.

Well, the subject is of vast importance, and difficult of explanation, for there is nothing on earth known to man, with which a comparison may be made, and, generally men cannot understand truth, or the nature of things, except by comparison with what they already know to exist, and with whose qualities and characteristics they are acquainted. There is nothing in the material world that will afford a basis of comparison with the soul, and, hence, it is difficult for men to comprehend the nature and qualities of the soul by the mere intellectual perceptions and reason: and in order to understand the nature of this great creation—the soul—men must have something of a spiritual development and the possession of what may be known as the soul perceptions. Only soul can understand soul, and the soul that seeks to comprehend the nature of itself, must be a live soul, with its faculties developed to a small degree, at least.

First, I will say, that the human soul must be a creature of God and not emanation from Him, as a part of His soul: and when men speak and teach that the human soul is a part of the Over-Soul, they teach what is not true. This soul is merely a creature of the Father, just as are the other parts of man, such as the intellect and the spirit body and the material body, and which before its creation had no existence. It has not existed from the beginning of eternity, if you can imagine that eternity ever had a beginning. I mean that there was a time when the human soul had no existence; and whether there will ever come a time when any human soul will cease to have an existence, I do not know, nor does any spirit, only God knows that fact. But this I do know, that whenever the human soul partakes of the Essence of the Father, and thereby becomes Divine itself, and the possessor of His Substance of Love, that soul realizes to a certainty that it is Immortal, and can never again become less than Immortal. As God is Immortal, the soul that has been transformed into the Substance of the Father becomes Immortal, and never again can the decree, *"dying thou shalt die,"* be pronounced upon it.

As I said, there was a period in eternity when the human soul did not exist and was created by the Father, and when it was made the highest and most perfect of all God's creation, to such an extent that it was made in His image—the only one or thing of all His creations that was made in His image, and the only part of man that was made in His image, for the soul is the man and all his attributes and qualities, such as his intellect and spirit body and material body and appetites and passions, are merely appendages or means of manifestation given to that soul, to be its companions while passing through its existence on earth, and also, qualifiedly, while living in eternity. I mean some of the appendages will accompany the soul in its existence in the spirit world, whether that existence be for all eternity or not.

But this soul, great and wonderful as it is, was created in the mere image and likeness of God, and not in or of His Substance or Essence—the Divine of the universe—and it, the soul, may cease to exist without any part of the Divine nature or Substance of the Father being lessened or in any way affected; and hence, when men teach or believe that man, or the soul of man is Divine, or has any of the qualities or Substance of the Divine, such teaching and belief are erroneous, because man is only and merely the created man, the mere likeness but no part of the Father or of His Substance and qualities.

While the soul of man is of the highest order of creation, and his attributes and qualities correspond, yet he is no more divine in essential constituents, than are the lower objects of creation—they each being a creation, and not an emanation, of their Creator.

True it is that the soul of man is of a higher order of creation than any other created things, and is the only creature made in the image of God, and was made the perfect man, yet man—the soul—can never become anything different or greater than the perfect man, unless he receives and possesses the Divine Essence and qualities of the Father, which he did not possess at his creation, although, most wonderful gift, with his creation, God bestowed upon him the privilege of receiving this Great Substance of the Divine nature, and thereby become Divine himself. The perfectly created man could become the Divine Angel, if he, the man, so willed it and obeyed the commands of the Father, and pursued the way provided by the Father for obtaining and possessing that Divinity.

As I have said, the souls, the human souls, for the indwelling of which God provided material bodies, that they might live the mortal lives, were created just as, subsequently, these material bodies were created; and this creation of the soul took place long before the appearance of man on earth as a mortal, and the soul prior to such appearance, had its existence in the spirit world as a substantial conscious entity, although without visible form, and, I may say, individuality, but yet, having a distinct personality, so that it was different and distinct from every other soul.

Its existence and presence could be sensed by every other soul that came in contact with it, and yet to the spirit vision of the other soul it was not visible. And such is the fact now. The spirit world is filled with these un-incarnated souls, awaiting the time of their incarnation, and we spirits know of and sense their presence, and yet with our spirit eyes we cannot see them, and not until they become dwellers in the human form and in the spirit body that inhabits that form, can we see the individual soul.

And the fact that I have just stated, illustrates, in a way, describes the Being of Him, in whose image these souls are created. We know and can sense the existence and presence of the Father, and yet, even with our spiritual eyes we cannot see Him; and only when we have our soul developed by the Divine Essence of His Love, can we perceive Him with our soul perception, because you have not words in your language to convey its meaning, and nothing in created nature, of which you have knowledge of in which a comparison can be made. But it is a truth; for the vision of the soul perception to its possessor is just as real, as I may say, objective, as is the vision of the mortal sight to the mortal.

It may be asked in considering this matter of the creation of the soul, "were all souls that have been incarnated, or that are awaiting incarnation, created at the same time, or is that creation still going on?" I do know that the spirit world contains many souls, such as I have described awaiting their temporary homes, and the assumption of individuality in the human form, but as to whether that creation has ended, and at sometime the reproduction of men for the embodying of these souls, will cease, I do not know, and the Father has never revealed it to me, or to the others of His angels who are close to Him in His Divinity and Substance.

The Father has not revealed to me all the truths and the workings an objects of His creative laws, and neither has He given to me all power and wisdom and omniscience as some may find justification for believing in certain of the statements of the Bible. I am a progressive spirit, and as I grew in love and knowledge and wisdom when on earth, I am still growing in these qualities, and the love and mercy of the Father come to me with the assurance that never in all eternity will I cease to progress towards the very fountain head of these attributes of Him, the only God, the All in All.

As I was saying, the soul of man is the man, before, while in the mortal existence and ever after in the spirit world, and all other parts of man, such as the mind and body and spirit are mere attributes, which may be dissevered from him as the soul progresses in its development toward its destiny of either the perfect man or the Divine Angel, and in the latter progression, men may not know it, but it is a truth, that the mind—that is the mind as known to mankind—becomes, as it were, non-existent; and this mind as some say, the carnal mind, becomes displaced and replaced by the mind of the transformed soul, which is in substance and quality, to a degree, the mind of Deity, itself.

Many theologians and philosophers and metaphysicians believe and teach that the soul, spirit and mind are substantially one and the same thing, and that anyone of them may be said to be the man—the ego, and that in the spirit world one or the other of these entities is that which persists and determines in its development or want of development the condition or state of man after death. But this conception of these parts of man are erroneous, for they each have a distinct and separate existence and functioning, whether man be a mortal or spirit.

The mind in its qualities and operations, is very well known to man, because of its varied manifestations, and being that part of man which is more of the nature of the material, and has been the subject of greater research and study than has been the soul or the spirit.

While men have, during all the centuries, speculated upon and attempted to define the soul and its qualities and attributes, yet to them it has been intransitive, and impossible of comprehension by the intellect which is the only instrumentality that man generally possesses to search for the great truth of the soul, and hence, the question, of what is the soul, has never been satisfactorily or authoritatively answered, though to some of these searchers, when inspiration may have shed a faint light upon them, some glimpse of what the soul is, has come to them. Yet to most men who have sought to solve the problem, the soul and spirit and mind are substantially the same thing.

But the soul, as concerning man is a thing of itself, alone. A substance real, though invisible to mortals. The discerner and portrayer of men's moral and spiritual condition—never dying, so far as known, and the real ego of the man. In it are centered the love principle, the affections, the appetites and the passions, and possibilities of receiving and possessing and assimilating those things that will either elevate man to the state or condition of the Divine Angel or the perfect man, or lower him to the condition that fits him for the hells of darkness and suffering.

The soul is subject to the will of man, which is the greatest of all endowments that were bestowed upon him by his Maker at his creation, and is the certain index of the workings of that will either in thought or action, and in the souls, qualities of love and affection and appetites and passions are influenced by the power of the will, either for good or evil. It may be dormant and stagnate, or it may be active and progress. And so its energies may be ruled by the will for good or evil, but these energies belong to it and are no part of the will.

The soul's home is in the spirit body, whether that body is

encased in the mortal or not, and it is never without such spirit body, which in appearance and composition is determined by the condition and state of the soul. And finally, the soul or its condition decides the destiny of man, as he continues in his existence in the spirit world; not a final destiny, because the condition of the soul is never fixed, and as this condition changes, man's destiny changes, for destiny is the thing of the moment, and finality is not known to the progress of the soul, until it becomes the perfect man and is then satisfied and seek no higher progress.

Now, in your common language and also in your theological and philosophical terms, mortals who have passed to spirit life are said to be spirits, and in a certain sense this is true, but such mortals are not nebulous, unformed and invisible existences, they have a reality of substance, more real and enduring, than has man as a mortal, and are in form and features visible and subject to touch and the object of the spiritual senses. So when men speak of soul, spirit and body, if they understood the truth of the terms, they would say, soul, spirit-body, and material-body. There is a spirit, but it is altogether distinct and different from the spirit body, and also from the soul. It is not part of the spirit body, but is an attribute of the soul, exclusively and without the soul, it could not exist. It has no substance as has the soul, and it is not visible to even the spirit vision—only the effect of its workings can be seen or understood,—and it is without body, form or substance. And yet it is real and powerful, and when existing never ceasing in its operations—and is an attribute of all souls.

Then what is the spirit? Simply this—the active energy of the soul. As I have said, the soul has its energy, which may be dormant or which may be active. If dormant, the spirit is not in existence; if active the spirit is present, and manifests that energy in action. So to confuse the spirit with the soul, as being identical, leads to error and away from the truth.

It is said that God is spirit, which in a sense is true, for spirit is a part of His great soul qualities, and which He uses to manifest His presence in the universe; but to say that spirit is God is not stating the truth, unless you are willing to accept as true the proposition that a part is the whole. In the divine economy, God is all of spirit, but spirit is only the messenger of God, by which He manifests the energies of His Great Soul.

And so with man. Spirit is not man-soul, but man-soul is spirit, as it is the instrumentality by which the soul of man makes known its energies and powers and presence.

Well, I have written enough for tonight, but sometime I will come and simplify this subject. But remember this, that Soul is God, soul is man, and all manifestations, such as spirit, and spirit body are merely evidences of the existence of the soul—the real man.

I have been with you as I promised, and I know that Father will bless you.

So with my love and blessing, I will say good night.
Your brother and friend,
Jesus.

How the redeemed soul is saved from the penalties that sin and error has brought upon it

March 2nd, 1916.

I am here, Jesus.

I desire to write tonight on the subject of how the redeemed soul is saved from the penalties which sin and error has brought upon it.

When the soul is in a condition of sin and error it is not responsive to the inflowing of the Holy Spirit, and in order to get into a condition of receptivity to these influences it must have an awakening as to its actual condition of enslavement by these things; and until such an awakening comes to it there is no possibility of its receiving the Love of God into it, and of turning its thoughts to the Truths of God and to the practices of life that will help it in its progress towards a condition of freedom.

I would not have mankind believe that any soul is compelled to stay in this condition of slavery to sin until the Holy Spirit comes to it with the Father's Love to bestow it in all abundance, for the mission of the Holy Spirit is not to awaken man's soul to a realization of sin and death, but merely to bring to that soul this Love when it, the soul, is ready to receive it.

The awakening must come from other causes that influence the mind as well as the soul, and cause them to realize that the life man lives is not the correct life or one in accord with the demands of the laws of God, or with the real longings of their own hearts and souls. Until this awakening comes the soul is really dead so far as its having a consciousness of the existence of the truths of its redemption is concerned, and such death means a continuance in such thoughts of sin and evil, and in the life which leads only to condemnation and death for long long years, it may be.

But to come nearer to my point of discourse. The soul that is existing in sin and error will have, sooner or later, to pay the penalties for such sin and error, and there is no escape from the payment of these penalties except in the redemption that the Father has provided by the New Birth. These penalties are only the natural results of the operation of God's laws and they must be endured until the full penalty is paid.

Even though a man may progress to higher condition of soul excellence and have much happiness, yet he must pay the last farthing and thus release himself from these penalties.

With much love,
I am your friend and brother,
Jesus.

All who refuse to seek the Way to the Celestial Heavens will eventually find their way to the kingdom where the perfect natural man exists

October 29th, 1916.

I am here, Jesus.

You were right in your surmise that I was with you tonight, and as you imagined, I was standing close to you at the time the preacher (Dr. Gordon) was delivering his discourse, and you felt the influence of my love and sympathy, and also received the thoughts that I was superimposing on your brain. The preacher's sermon was an advance upon the beliefs of the orthodox in many particulars, but in the most important particular and in the one that will affect mortals most vitally in their progress in the spirit life, he was wrong, very wrong. I refer to his declaration that he saw or knew of no statement in the Bible that would justify him in asserting that there would be an opportunity for the spirits of mortals to receive pardon or to progress from the condition of hell to that of light and heaven in the spirit world, when they had not started on that journey in the mortal life. This, as I have told you, is a damnable doctrine, and one that has done more harm all down the centuries from the time of my living on earth, than most any other teaching of the church that claims to be representative of me and my teachings.

Many poor souls have come into the spirit world with this belief firmly fixed in their minds and conscience, and the difficulties have been great and the years long before they could awaken from this belief and realize that the Love of the Father is waiting for them in spirit life just as in the earth life, and that probation is never closed for men or spirits, and never will be until the time of the withdrawal of the great opportunity for men to become inhabitants of the Celestial Heavens, and even then, the opportunity to purify their natural love will not cease, and never will, until all who have the opportunity shall become perfect men in their natural loves.

Had he searched the Scriptures,[27] in which he so implicitly believes, he would have found an authorization for him to declare that

---

[27] First Epistle of Peter—Chapter 3—Verses 19 and 20 (Dr. S.)

even in the spirit world, the spirits of the unsaved sinners on earth, who died without having become reconciled to God, had the gospel of salvation preached to them. (i.e. in the hells—1 Peter 3:19-20) And furthermore when he declared that the Bible says that I said "that he that sinneth against the son of man it shall be forgiven him, but he that sinneth against the Holy Ghost it shall not be forgiven him, neither in this world nor in the world to come," had the preacher placed the natural and only implied construction on this declaration, he would have found that the sinner who neglected the opportunity on earth, would yet have another chance for salvation in the world to come, as the spirit world is referred to. So that, even according to his own source of belief and foundation of his knowledge of these things of the future, he would be justified and even required, as an honest preacher of the Scriptures, to declare that probation did not end with the physical death of the mortal. It is so sad that the creeds and fixed opinions of these preachers, formed from the teachings of the old fathers, as they are called, should be men of soul development, such as this preacher has, and teach the damnable doctrine that I speak of which he declared.

There is a hell, or rather hells, just as there is a heaven or heavens, and all men when they become spirits, will be compelled to occupy one or the other of these places; not because God had decreed that any particular spirit because of his earth belief or condition shall occupy that place, but because the condition of his soul development, or want of development, fits and fixes him for that place and no other. God has made His laws of harmony and these laws are never changed, and when any particular soul gets into a condition of agreement with these laws, then that soul becomes at one with the Father and an inhabitant of His heavens; and so long as that soul remains out of such condition it is in hell, which is the condition of being out of agreement with the harmony of God's laws. This is hell and there is no other comprehensive definition of it: everything or place that is not heaven is hell. Of course there are many gradations of hell, and the inhabitants of these gradations are made by the condition of their soul development, which is determined by the quantity and quality of the defilement and sin that exists in these souls. The soul is developed as the love becomes purified and sin eradicated, and just as this process progresses the soul becomes developed.

God has decreed that His universe, both of men and things, shall be harmonious, and only the creature, man, has become out of that harmony; and as the universe shall continue, the only destiny for man is, that he shall return to that harmony from which he fell by reason of his own misdirected will. Had God decreed, as the preacher by necessary implication, declared, that the sinner who dies in his sins shall forever remain in his sins and in a state of antagonism to such harmony, then

God, Himself, would necessarily become the cause and power of defeating His own laws of harmony, which no sane mortal whether he believes in the Scriptures or not, would or could believe.

God's Laws are fixed and unchangeable and always in harmony with one another and with His Will, and knowing this, every thinking man will know and should know that whenever a proposition or opinion is put forth by preacher or layman or philosopher or scientist that shows that in order for a certain condition or truth to exist, God's Laws will have to work in conflict with or in opposition to one another, then that proposition or opinion is false and has no foundation in fact. And so to accept this declaration of the preacher that there is no probation after death, or as he said, chance to progress out of the hell which the mortal carries with him to the spirit world, men will have to believe that the Loving Father, for the satisfying His wrath and meeting the demands of His supposed justice, will set his laws in conflict with one another and destroy the harmony of his universe.

The preacher spoke, as he said, as a scientist, and not as a religious teacher, and yet the deduction that he made when he declared the eternal existence of the hells, violated one of the fundamental laws of science and that is, that two conflicting laws in the workings of God's universe cannot both be accepted as true, and that the one of these two that is in harmony with all the other known laws must be accepted as true. Then I say, that founded on the Scriptures or founded on science, the preacher had no basis for making the untrue and deplorable statement, that physical death ends man's possibility of progressing from a condition or state of existence in hell into that of purity and freedom from sin and into harmony with God's perfect laws and the requirements of His will.

The preacher spoke from his intellect and mental beliefs of long years standing and the memory echoes of what he had heard said by other preachers and teachers who left upon his conscious beliefs their false doctrines. But deep down in his soul, where the Love of the Father is burning and the soul sense is growing, he does not believe this doctrine, for he realizes that this Love of the Father is so much greater and purer and holier than any other love that exists in heaven or on earth; and the Father from Whom It comes must be holier and more merciful and forgiving and thoughtful of His children than of any mortal father of his children. And then as a mortal father having in his soul the Divine Love, he knows that his child could not commit any sin or offense that could possibly become unpardonable, or that he would not permit, and gladly, the child to repent of at any time. And so he would see, that if he refused to the Father, from Whom this Divine Love comes, a love and sympathy that would cause that Father to be as forgiving to His children as is he, the earthly parent, then the Greatest Attribute of that

Father, God, Who is All Love, would not be equal to the love of his creature. The derivative would be greater and grander and purer and more Divine than the Fountainhead from which it is derived.

No, the preacher in his soul does not believe this unnatural teaching, and at times, he travails in his soul at the conflict that takes place between the mental bondage of his intellectual beliefs and the freedom of his soul sense, the creature of the Divine Love that is in him, and the only part of Divinity that he possesses. And thus is demonstrated the great, real paradox of the existence in the same mortal at the same time, of an intellectual belief and a soul knowledge as far apart as the antipodes. And also is demonstrated the truth, a great truth, that the mind of man and the soul of man are not one and the same, but are as distinct as the creature of a special creation, the mind, and the creation of that which is the only part of man made in the image of his Maker, the soul, must necessarily be.

But some day the soul knowledge will overcome the mental belief, and then the preacher will know that harmony and inharmony cannot exist for all time—that sin and error must disappear and purity and righteousness must exist alone, and that every man and spirit must become at one with the Father, either as an inhabitant of the Celestial Heavens or as the perfect man that first appeared at the call of God, and by him pronounced "very good."

I have written enough for tonight and must stop, but before doing so, I want to say that I have been with you today and saw that you were very happy in your thoughts and in your soul experience. Other spirits were also with you, throwing around you their love and influence. Persevere in your efforts to obtain this Divine Love, and pray to the Father and it will come to you in increased abundance, and with it a wonderful happiness. I will come soon and write you another message. So with my love and blessings, I will say good night and God bless you.

Your brother and friend, Jesus.

The importance for mankind seeking the Divine Love and not be satisfied by merely developing the natural love in a pure state

January 10th, 1916.

I am here, Jesus.

I come tonight to tell you of a truth which is important to all mankind, and which I desire that you receive just as I write it, so give your best care to receiving just what I shall attempt to write.

I have read with you tonight many sayings contained in the alleged epistles of Paul and Peter, and I realize that they do not seem to be consistent with the truth that has been declared to you by myself and by the apostles who have written to you, and I desire that you shall understand some of these inconsistencies and discard from your mind these sayings of the epistles wherever they do not agree with what we have written or what we shall write.

In the first place, the continual reference of these epistles to my being God is all wrong and must not be believed; also the statement that my blood washes away sin or that I died on the cross for the salvation of men, or that I took upon myself the sins of mankind and thereby relieved them from the burden of their sins, and the punishment which they must suffer in expiation of their evil deeds and thoughts.

Again, when it said, that from the beginning the Father had foreordained my death on the cross that man might be redeemed from the penalties of sin in all men who lived thereafter, are all wrong and have no foundation as facts in the plan of God for the salvation of man and the restoring of the harmony of His universe and the eradication of all sin and error from the world.

Neither Paul nor Peter wrote these things, and never did I teach them, for they are not in accord with the great plan of salvation; and the further away will be the realization by them of the truth of the only plan the Father has provided for their redemption, which I came to earth to declare and explain to my apostles first, and then to the whole world.

In these epistles too much emphasis is given to the importance of faith and works. I mean faith in the mere beliefs which these epistles taught followed by works—and not enough importance to the foundation truth of man's redemption from sin and becoming reconciled to the Father. I mean the New Birth by the inflowing into their souls of the Divine Love of the Father's through the ministrations of the Holy Spirit.

Many of their teachings as to man's conduct towards man and as to the lives that the recipients of these truths should lead as effecting their own purification and becoming in a condition of righteousness, are true, and are as applicable to the conduct and living of men today as they were in the days in which the apostles taught. But when the epistles teach or lead men in any particular to understand that these, what may be called merely moral principles, will enable a man by their observance, to enter into the Kingdom of God, or the Celestial Kingdom, they are false and misleading, and men when they become spirits will realize that while leading the lives which these teachings call them to lead, they will become very happy and occupy conditions and positions in the spirit world that will make their happiness far superior to that which they enjoy on earth and even enable them to become occupants of higher spiritual spheres; yet they will never be permitted to enter the Kingdom of the Father, which can only be attained to by the possession of Divine Love.

So I say, men must understand and realize the difference between the results to them from leading merely good and moral lives which affect and develop the natural love and those results which ensue from the New Birth.

I have attempted to explain to you why the great and important truth of my mission to earth, as I explained it to my apostles, and as was taught by them and written by them, was not preserved and contained in the Bible as now written and accepted by the church as canonical. The great desire in those days was to show and impress upon men those teachings which affected their conduct on earth, and to hold out to them the rewards that would following such living, and also the rewards which would follow their lives in the spirit world which would become their homes after death. And, as I have said, the leading of lives in accordance with these teachings would ensure men a great happiness in the spirit world, but not the happiness which my teachings, if observed, would lead to.

In the various copyings and compilations of the writings of the apostles many changes from the originals were made, and those persons who performed this work, and I mean by this the dignitaries and rulers of the church, did not know the difference between those things which would bring about a purification of the natural love, and those things which were necessary to fit a soul for entrance into the Kingdom of Heaven. And hence, when they came to perform this work they made the error of teaching that the living of the moral life would entitle the soul to a reward which they supposed, would be the Kingdom of Heaven and immortality. And this erroneous teaching has prevented many a man from gaining the right to the Kingdom of Heaven, as they honestly and sincerely believed would be theirs, when they came to pass into the spirit world.

Many of these teachings are intended to make a reformation in the lives of men and to purge their souls from sin and error so far as the natural love forms a part of the condition of the soul; and I taught these moral truths to a very large extent, for such teachings were necessary, because men's will was out of harmony with God's Laws, which affected the natural love, as well as out of harmony with the laws that affected the Divine Love of the Father; and it is the object and plan of God to bring into harmony both of these loves, and thereby enable man to enjoy those things which are provided and waiting for him.

As I said when on earth, "Narrow is the way and strait is the gate which leads to life everlasting and few there be that enter therein," I repeat now; for it is apparent from the observation of the way in which mankind from the beginning have exercised their wills, which God leaves free to their own volition, that a vast majority of men will never enter in at the strait gate, but be contented to live in the spheres and happiness which their natural love, in its perfect state and progress, will fit them for.

That all men will ultimately be brought into harmony with God, in either the natural love or in the Higher One, is certain, and that all sin and error will finally be eradicated from God's universe is decreed, but the time will depend to a great extent, upon the wills and desires of men, and, hence, while my great mission in coming to earth and teaching men, was to show the way to the Celestial Kingdom, yet a lesser part of my mission was to teach them a way to their redemption from sin and error that would result in the purification of the natural love; and to my great regret and to the untold injury to man, my moral teachings were more at large set forth in portions of the Bible, as now accepted, than were my teachings of the Higher Truths.

I will not write more tonight but will continue later. Well my dear brother, I see that you are in a much better condition spiritually than you have been for some time, and you must thank the Father for it. Your conception of last night's experience is true, and you received a wonderful amount of the Divine Love, and I was with you in love and blessing.

So continue to pray and trust in the Father and you will realize a wonderful happiness and power and peace.

I must stop now. Your brother and friend,
Jesus.

The soul and its relationship to God and future life and immortality

November 2nd, 1915.

I am here, St. Matthew.

I have not written you for a long time, and I desire to say a few words on matters pertaining to the soul and its relationship to God and future life and immortality.

The soul is an image of the Great Soul of the Father, and partakes of features like this Great Soul, except that it does not necessarily have in it the Divine Love which makes the soul of a mortal or spirit a partaker of Divinity. The soul may exist in man and spirit in all receptive qualities and yet never have the Divine Essence to fill it, which is necessary in order to make man or spirit a new creature that is the subject of the New Birth.

Only that mortal or spirit who has received this Divine Love of the Father can be said to be Immortal, all others may live or they may not. It has not yet been revealed to us whether the life or existence of these spirits who have not the conscious knowledge of Immortality will continue to live through all eternity but if they do it will be because God so wills that they shall live. But their existence will be subject to change and if such change should take place, only God knows what its character will be. While on the contrary, the soul that has acquired Immortality can never die, its status as to a life through all eternity is fixed, and even God himself cannot destroy that existence because it is the possessor of that Divinity which makes God Immortal.

"The soul that sinneth, sinning it shall die," means that the qualities which it is necessary for it to obtain to make it a part of immortality can never come to it, and hence as regards these qualities it is dying and dead. The soul itself will live, for no spirit could possibly have an existence without a soul, and when men attempt to teach that when the spirit of life leaves the body the soul dies, such men do not state a truth. The soul will live as long as the spirit existence continues, and until the great change, should there be one, comes to that spirit. So all men must believe that the soul which God gave to man is just as much a part of man as is the spiritual or physical body.

The soul is the highest part of man, and is the only part, that in any way resembles the Great Father, who is not body or spirit-body in form but is Soul, and the man's soul, as I have said, is an image of that Great Soul. So you see, that when we speak of destroying the soul it does not mean that the soul which belongs to every spirit will be destroyed, but that the essence of the soul, or rather the potentiality of that soul receiving the Divine Love and Nature of the Father will be destroyed.

Of course, the soul can be starved and placed in a condition of stagnation so that all its receptive powers will be, as it were, dead, and only some great miracle or unusual ministration can awaken it, but to say that the soul ever dies is erroneous. In saying this I do not include the possibility of some great change in the spirit or mortal by which such spirit may be destroyed, and in such case the soul will cease to exist as an individualized soul or entity.

I do not know what would be the destiny of a soul in such event and, hence, can't prophesy, but, unless there be such great change, the soul will live, but not as an immortal soul possessing the Essence of Divinity, unless it has experienced the New Birth.

God, the Great Oversoul, may not recall to Himself the soul of any man in the sense of depriving that man of his soul, but His relation to that soul will be merely that of Creator and created, subject always to the Will of the Creator, whereas, the relationship of God towards the soul that has received the New Birth and hence the Divine Nature, is not only of a Creator and created, but also that of a co-equal so far as this Great Quality of Immortality is concerned. The soul of man then becomes self-existing and not depending upon God for its continuance to exist.

This, I know, is a subject not easy for mortal mind to understand, but when you shall have received the soul perceptions in addition to your natural mind, it will not be so difficult to grasp the exact meaning of my propositions.

I will not write more tonight.
I am your brother in Christ,
St. Matthew.

Discourse on the soul

November 2nd, 1915.

St. Cornelius—the First Gentile Christian.

Let me say just a word as to the soul. I have heard what Matthew said, and it seems to me that he did not describe what the soul is as clearly as desirable.

My conception of the soul is, that it is that part of the existence of man which determines for him what his destiny shall be. It is the real thinking, willing and conscious part of man. The intellect of man may die—this may seem unreal, but it is true—and man cease to exist as a conscious thing—I mean if the intellect was the only faculty that he possesses to make him conscious of his existence. The soul, so far as we know, can never die, and it has as its qualities and elements, all the perceptions and reasoning powers that the intellect has and many more. The soul is the only faculty or part of man that performs the mission, of knowing, and reasoning and determining, after man has passed into the seventh sphere, and consequently, unless these soul qualities or perceptions are developed, by obtaining into the soul the Divine love, a man or spirit cannot get into the seventh sphere, for he would be wholly unable to live there and understand or do anything in that sphere.

The soul needs no instructions from the mere physical senses because those senses are not suitable to be used in the operations of the soul's faculties, and hence a man who never cultivates these soul senses, as I will say, is not capable of understanding the higher spiritual things of the Celestial Spheres.[28]

I will not write more tonight, but will come again.
Your brother in Christ,
St. Cornelius.

---

[28] Celestial Spheres are immediately above the Seventh Sphere. (Dr. S.)

Forgiveness

Forgiveness

March 31st, 1915.

I am here, your grandmother, Ann Rollins.

I came to write you about the forgiveness and pardon of the Father, and to enlighten you upon this subject which is so little understood, since men first commenced to distort the teachings of the Master.

Forgiveness is that operation of the Divine Mind which relieves man of the penalties of his sins that he has committed, and permits him to turn from his evil thoughts and deeds, and seek the Love of the Father; and if he earnestly seeks, find the happiness which is waiting for him to obtain. It does not violate any law that God has established to prevent man from avoiding the penalties of his violations of the law of God controlling his conduct.

The law of compensation, that what a man sows that shall he reap, is not set aside, but in the particular case where a man becomes penitent and in all earnestness prays the Father to forgive him of his sins and make a new man of him, the operation of another and greater law is called into activity, and the old law of compensation is nullified, and, as it were, swallowed up in the power of this law of forgiveness and love. So you see there is no setting aside of any of God's laws. As in the physical world certain lesser laws are overcome by greater laws, so in the spirit world or in the operation of spiritual things, the greater laws must prevail over the lesser.

God's laws never change but the application of these laws to particular facts and conditions do seem to change, when two laws come into apparent conflict, and the lesser must give away to the greater.

The spiritual laws are just as fixed as are the physical laws that control the material universe; and no law having application to the same condition of facts, ever is different in its operation or in its effects.

The sun and planets in their movements are governed by fixed laws, and they operate with such exactness that men who make a study of these laws and comprehend them can, with almost mathematical precision, foretell the movements of these heavenly bodies. This only means that as long as the sun and the planets remain as they are, and surrounded by the same influences, and meet no law operating in a manner contrary to the laws which usually control them, these planets and sun will repeat their movements year after year in the same way and with like precision. But suppose that a more powerful and contrary law should come into operation, and influence the movements of these bodies, do you suppose for a moment that they would pursue the same course as if such greater law had not intruded itself?

The effect of this is not to set aside the lesser law, or even to change it, but to subordinate it to the operations of the greater law; and if these operations were removed or ceased to act, the lesser law would resume its operations on these planets again, and they would move in accordance therewith, just as if its power had never been affected by the greater law.

So, in the spirit world, when a man has committed sins on earth, the law of compensation demands that he must pay the penalty of these sins until there has been a full expiation, or until the law is satisfied. And this law does not change in its operations, and no man can avoid or run away from the inexorable demands of the law. He cannot of himself abate one jot or tittle (scarcely detectable amount) of the penalties, but must pay to the last farthing as the Master said, and hence, he cannot, of himself hope to change the operations of this law.

But, as the Creator of all law has provided another and higher law, which, under certain conditions may be brought into operation and causes the former law to cease to operate, and man may experience the benefit of the workings of this higher law. So when God forgives a man of his sins, and makes him a new creature in his nature and love, he does not, for the particular case annihilate the law of compensation, but removes that upon which this law may operate.

Sin is violation of God's law, and the effect of sin is the penalty which such violation imposes. A man's suffering for sins committed are not the results of God's special condemnation in each particular case, but are the results of the workings and scourgings of his conscience and recollections and as long as conscience works he will suffer, and the greater the sins committed, the greater will be the suffering. Now all this implies that a man's soul is filled to a greater or lesser extent with these memories, which for the time constitute his very existence. He lives with these memories, and the suffering and torment, which result from them can never leave him until the memories of these sins, or the result of them, cease to be a part of himself and his constant companions—this is the inexorable law of compensation, and man of himself has no way of escaping this law except by his long expiation, which removes these memories and satisfies the law.

Man cannot change this law, and God will not. So, as I say, the law never changes. But remember this fact, that in order for the law to operate, a man must have these memories, and they must be a part of his very existence.

Now, suppose that the creator of this law has created another law, but which under certain conditions, and upon a man doing certain things, these memories are taken from him, and no longer constitute a part or portion of his existence; then, I ask, what is there in or of that man upon this law of compensation that can act or operate? The law is not changed, it is not even set aside, but upon which it can operate no longer exists, and consequently there is no reason or existence of facts which call for its operation.

So, I say, as do your scientists and philosophers, that God's laws are fixed and never change, but I further say, which they fail to perceive, that certain conditions which may and do call for the operations of these laws today, tomorrow change or cease to exist, so that the laws are no longer effective.

And so when the truths of God's forgiveness of sin is declared, many wise men hold up their hands and shout, "God's laws do not change, and even God Himself cannot change them. And to effect a forgiveness of sins, the great law of compensation must be violated. God works no such miracle, or gives special dispensation. No, man must pay the penalty of his evil deeds until the law is fulfilled."

How limited is the knowledge of mortals, and of spirits as well, of the Power and Wisdom and Love of the Father. His Love is the greatest thing in all the universe and the Law of Love is the greatest law. Every other law is subordinate to It, and must work in unison with it; and Love, Divine Love of the Father, when given to man and he possesses it, is the fulfilling of all law. This Love frees man from all law except the law of its Ownself—and when man possesses this Love he is slave to no law and is free indeed.

The law of compensation and all laws not in harmony with the Law of Love, have nothing upon which to operate in that man's case, and God's laws are not changed but merely, as to this man, have no existence.

Now, let all men, wise and unwise, know that God in His Love and Wisdom, has provided a means by which, man, if he so will, may escape the unchanging law of compensation, and become no longer subject to its demands and penalties; and these means are simple and easy, and within the comprehension and grasp of every living soul, be he saint or sinner, a wise man or an ignorant one.

Intellect in the sense of being learned is not involved, but the man who knows that God exists and provides him with food and raiment as the result of his daily toil, as well as the great intellectual scientist or philosopher, may learn the way to these redeeming truths. I do not mean that a man by mere exercise of mental powers may receive the benefit of this great provision for his redemption. The soul must seek and it will find, and the soul of the wise may not be as capable of receiving as the soul of the ignorant.

God is Love. Man has a natural love, but this natural love is not sufficient to enable him to find these great means that I speak of. Only the Divine Love of the Father is sufficient, and He is willing that all men should have this Love. It is free and waiting to be bestowed upon all men. but strange as it may seem, God will not, and I might say, cannot, bestow this Love unless man seeks for It, and asks for It in earnestness and faith.

The will of man is a wonderful thing, and stands between him and this love, if he fails to exercise this will in seeking for it. No man can secure it against his will. What a wonderful thing is man's will, and how he should study and learn what a great part of his being it is.

The Love of the Father comes only into a man's soul when he seeks It in prayer and faith, and of course this implies that he wills It to come to him. No man is ever refused this Love when he properly asks for It.

Now this Love is a part of the Divine Essence, and when a man possesses It in sufficient abundance he becomes a part of Divinity Itself; and in the Divine there is no sin or error, and, consequently, when he becomes a part of this Divinity no sin or error can form a part of his being.

Now, as I have said, man who is without this love has his memories of sin and evil deeds, and, under the law of compensation, must pay the penalties. Yet when this Divine Love comes into his soul, it leaves no room for these memories, and as he becomes more and more filled with this Love, these memories disappear and only the Love inhabits his soul, as it were. Hence, there remains nothing in him upon which this law can operate, and the man is no longer its slave or subject. This Love is sufficient of itself to cleanse the soul from all sin and error, and make man one with the Father.

This is forgiveness of sin, or rather the result of forgiveness. When a man prays to the Father for this forgiveness, He never turns a deaf ear, but says, in effect, "I will remove your sins and give you my love, I will not set aside or change my laws of compensation, but I will remove from your soul everything upon which this law can operate, and as to you it becomes as if it had no existence."

I know by your personal experience that this forgiveness is a real, actual, existing thing, and when the Father forgives, sin disappears, and Love only exists, and that Love in its fullness is the fulfilling of the law.

So let men know that God does forgive sin, and when He forgives the penalty disappears, and when they disappear as the result of such forgiveness, no law of God is changed or violated.

This was the great mission of Jesus when he came to earth. Before he came and taught this great truth, the forgiveness of sin was not understood, even by the Hebrew teachers, but their doctrine was an eye for an eye and a tooth for a tooth. The Divine Love, as I have feebly described, was not known or sought for—only the care and protection and material benefits that God might give to the Hebrews.

The Divine Love entering into and taking possession of the souls of men constitute the New Birth, and without this no man can see the Kingdom of God.

My dear son, I have written you a long but imperfect communication, but there is sufficient in it for men to think of and meditate upon, and if they do so and open their souls to the Divine Influence, they will know God can forgive sin, and save men from its penalties, so that they will not have to undergo the long period of expiation, which in their natural state the law of compensation ever demands.

So without writing further, I will say that I love you with all my heart and soul, and pray the Father to give you this Great Love in all its abundance.

Your loving grandmother,
Ann Rollins.

How a soul must receive the Divine Love of the Father in order to become an inhabitant of the Kingdom of God

February 28th, 1916.

I am here, Jesus.

I desire tonight to write you on the subject: *"How a soul must receive the Divine Love of the Father in order to become an inhabitant of the Kingdom of God, and realize that immortality of which I have written you."*

In the first place, it must be understood that the Divine Love of the Father is an entirely distinct kind of love from the love which the Father bestowed upon man at the time of his creation, and which man has possessed in a more or less condition of purity ever since that time. This Divine Love was never conferred upon man as a perfect and completed gift, either at the time of his creation, or since my coming to earth, but as a gift which is waiting for man's own efforts and aspirations to obtain, and without which it can never become his, although it is always close to him, waiting to answer his call.

Then in understanding what this Love is, and that man must seek for it, and what its effect upon the soul of man is, it becomes very important that man should make the obtaining of it the one great object of his aspirations and desires. For when he possesses it to a degree that makes him at one with the Father, he ceases to be a mere man, and becomes of a nature of soul existence that makes him Divine, with many qualities of the Father, the chief of which is, of course, Love; and also causes him to absolutely realize the fact of his immortality.

Mere moral goodness, or the possession of the natural love to its fullest degree will not confer upon man this Divine Nature that I have mentioned; nor will good acts, and charity and kindness, of themselves lead men to the possession of this Love, but the possession of this Love in truth and in fact, will lead to charity, and good deeds, and kindness, always unselfish, and to a brotherhood of men on earth that the mere natural love cannot possibly lead to or cause to exist.

I know that men preach about the Fatherhood of God, and the brotherhood of man, and urge men to attempt to cultivate the thoughts and deeds of love and self-sacrifice and charity in a way to bring about the greatly to be wished for unity of life and purpose on the part of men; and by reason of this natural love can, themselves, do a great work in bringing about this brotherhood. Yet the chain that binds them together cannot possibly be any stronger than the natural love which forges it; and when that becomes overshadowed by ambition and material desires, the brotherhood will become greatly weakened, or disappear entirely, and men will realize that its foundation was not built upon a rock, but rather upon the infirm sand, which could not sustain the superstructure, when the storms arising from men's ambition and desires for power and greatness, and many other material things, beat upon it. So I say, there is a great necessity for something more than man's mere natural love to help him form a brotherhood that will remain steadfast and firm under all conditions and among all men.

So this natural love, under circumstances the most favorable to preserve the constancy of man's happiness and freedom from sin and error, proved itself to be not sufficient to maintain that condition, then what may be expected of it when circumstances are such that this love has degenerated from its pure state and has become defiled by all these tendencies of men to do that which is in violation not only of God's laws, but of everything that would otherwise help men to realize a true brotherhood.

As I have heretofore said in my writings, there will come a time when this natural love will be restored to its original state of purity and freedom from sin, and when this brotherhood may exist in a degree of perfection that will make all men happy. Yet that time is far off and will not be realized on earth at all until the New Birth and the New Heavens appear, and in the meantime men's dreams of this great brotherhood will not be realized.

I know that men expect that sometime, in the far distant future, by means of education and conventions and preachments of moral truth, this dream of an ideal brotherhood will be established on earth, and all the souls of hatred and war, and the oppression of the weak by the strong will disappear. But I tell you that if men depend upon this mere natural love and all the great feelings and impulses that may arise from it, to bring about this condition so much desired, they will find disappointments and lose faith in the goodness of men, and at times a retrogression, not only in that love, but in the conduct of men towards one another, and in the treatment of nations by one another.

I have digressed somewhat from my subject, but I thought it best to show to man that his dependence upon himself, which is his dependence on this natural love, is not sufficient and adequate to bring him into a condition of happiness even on earth, and therefore totally inadequate to bring him into the Kingdom of Heaven.

The Divine Love that I speak of, is of itself not only able to make a man an inhabitant of the Father's Kingdom, but is sufficient to enable him to bring about and realize to the fullest of his dreams that great brotherhood, even while on earth.

This Love of the Father's Own Self is of a never changing nature, and in all places and under all conditions is working out the same results and converting the souls of men on earth as well as of the spirits in the spirit world, into not only the image but the substance of the Divine Nature. It may be possessed in smaller or greater degree, depending upon man himself; and this degree of possession determines the condition of the soul, and its nearness to the Father's Kingdom, whether the soul be in the flesh or in the spirit.

Man does not have to wait to become a spirit, in order to seek for and obtain this Love, for the soul on earth is the same soul as when in the spirit world, and its capacity for receiving this Love is just as great in one place as in the other. Of course on earth there are many circumstances and surroundings and limitations on man that prevent the free workings of the soul in the way of aspirations and faith that do not exist after man becomes an inhabitant of the spirit world but, nevertheless, and notwithstanding all these drawbacks and stumbling blocks of the earth life, the soul of man may receive this Divine Love without limitations and to an abundance that will make him a new creature as the scriptures say.

The possession of this Divine Love also means the absence of those desires and longings of what is called the natural man, which produce selfishness and unkindness and other qualities which create sin and error, and prevent the existence of this true brotherhood which men so earnestly desire as the forerunner of peace and good will, and the more of this Divine Love that enters into the soul of man, the less there is of evil tendencies and desires, and the more of the Divine Nature and Qualities.

The Father is all Goodness and Love and Truth, and Forgiveness, and Kindness, and these qualities the souls of men become possessed of when they receive and possess the Divine Love. And when man is sincere and faithful, and possesses these qualities, they never leave him or change; and when this brotherhood shall be founded on them, it will be built on a rock and will continue to live and become purer and firmer in its binding effect, and in the great results that will flow from it, for its foundation stone will be the Divine Nature of the Father, which is without variableness or change and never disappointing.

A brotherhood so created and joined together is, as I say, "the only true brotherhood that will make for man a kind of heaven on earth, and banish wars and hatred and strife and selfishness, and the principal of mine and thine. The mine will be changed to ours, and all mankind will be truly brothers, without reference to race or sect or intellectual acquirements. All will be recognized as the children of the one father."

Such will be the effect of the existence of this Love in men's souls on earth, and when such souls leave their envelope of flesh, they will find their homes in the Kingdom of God—parts of the Divinity of the Father, and partakers of his Immortality.

But only this Divine Love will fit the souls of men for this Kingdom because in this Kingdom all things partake of this Divine Nature and nothing which has not that quality can possibly enter therein. So men must understand that no mere belief or ceremony of church or baptism, or any of these things are sufficient to enable a soul to become an inhabitant of this Kingdom. Men may do and deceive themselves in their beliefs that anything short of or other than this Divine Love can ensure them an entrance into the Kingdom. Beliefs may help men to seek and aspire to the possession of this Love, and other ceremonies may also assist, but unless and until this Divine Love is actually possessed by the souls of men, they cannot become partakers of the divine nature and enjoy the happiness and peace of the Father's Kingdom.

When the way to obtain this Love is so easy and the joy of its possession is so great, it is surprising that men will be satisfied with the husks of formalism and the satisfaction and delusion of mere lip worship and intellectual beliefs. As I have said this Love is waiting for every man to possess, who sincerely and with true soul aspirations seek it. It is not a part of, but surrounding and enveloping every man, but at the same time forming no part of him unless his longings and prayers have opened up his soul, so that it may flow in and infill him with its presence.

Man is never compelled to receive it, as he is never compelled to do other things against his will, but as in the latter case, when in the exercise of that same will, he refuses to let the Divine Love flow into his soul, he must suffer the penalty, which is the utter and absolute deprivation of any possibility to become an inhabitant of the Kingdom of God, or Celestial Kingdom, and of any consciousness of the fact of his immortality.

Let men turn their thoughts and aspirations to God, and in truth and sincerely pray to the Father for an inflowing into their souls of his Divine Love, and have faith, and they always find that the Father will bestow his love upon them, in accordance with the extent of their aspirations and longings, which are mediums of opening up their souls to the workings of the Holy Spirit, which, as I have before written, is the messenger of God, for the conveying of His Divine Love from his Fountainhead of Love to the souls of the prayerful and aspiring men.

In no other way can the Divine Love be possessed by man, and always it is an individual matter between the particular man and the Father. No other man or body of men or church or spirits or angels can do the work of the individual. As to him, his soul is the only thing involved, and only his aspirations, and his prayers, and his will can open up his soul to the inflowing of this Love which makes him a part of its own divinity.

Of course, the prayers and kind thoughts and loving influences of good men and divine spirits and angels can and do help the souls of men in turning to His Love and in progressing in its possession, but as to the question, will a man become possessor or not of this love, it depends upon the man.

Well I have written enough for tonight and must stop. So my dear brother I will say with all my love and blessings, good night.

Your brother and friend, Jesus.

What is the reason that mortals will not seek the Love of the Father?

June 4th, 1917.

I am here, St. John.

I came tonight to write you a message that I consider very important, and as you are in good condition I will endeavor to do so.

In the first place, I desire to say that you are much more in that condition of soul development that enables us to make a rapport with you than you have been, and we are pleased that this is so, for the greater development you have the easier it is for us to express our ideas of the higher truths that we so much desire to disclose through you.

Well, the subject about which I wish to write is: What is the reason that mortals will not seek the Love of the Father rather than endeavor to believe in the creeds and sacraments of the churches to which they belong or be affiliated with?

Now it may appear to you that mortals themselves, could better tell the reason of this preference and their actions in carrying out their preferences, but this supposition would not be true because they do not really know. The knowledge of the truth which they might obtain, and the supposed knowledge of truth which so many of them content themselves with believing that they possess, are two and very different things.

And first, they believe that the creeds of their churches contain and disclose the truths as to God and as to mortals relationship to Him, and that, if they follow these creeds—they will do that which is pleasing to God and in accordance with His will; and, hence, they rest satisfied to abide in such knowledge, and seek no further to learn the truths of their being and of their salvation.

The creeds in most particulars do not contain the truths of these spiritual matters, for they are based upon error, and consequently, can have no truth as a super-structure, and from them, mortals cannot learn the true knowledge of things spiritual.

These creeds are manmade and are not based upon the real verities that can never be changed by creeds, nor any other thing that is the result of man's making.

But mortals do not know that these creeds do not disclose to them the truth, and this is one reason why they prefer to follow the teachings of the creeds and believe in them. They have nothing else to which they can resort, except the many statements of truth that the Bible contains; and even, though, they should resort to these statements, yet in their condition of mental and soul development they would not be able to discover the truths as therein disclosed, and to realize any distinction between such truths and what they believe are truths of their creeds.

For long years—generation after generation—these creeds have been accepted and believed in and proclaimed to be the truths by the respective churches to which the mortals may have belonged; and they have seen their parents and grandparents believing and resting in the assurance that the creeds contained the truth, and have seen these relatives live and die apparently happy in their beliefs, and hence they become satisfied to do that which those before them did and not question or search for the truth elsewhere, or even think that it can be found elsewhere.

And as man is constituted it may be said that such a position and condition is natural, and we or you, who know the truth and also that the creeds do not contain the truth, should not be surprised.

Again, mortals prefer their creeds, because in the majority of the instances when a church or denomination has existed for a long time those who have, as I may say, inherited these beliefs in the creeds never consider for a moment, that they should do anything else than give an unquestioning belief to the teachings of their creeds and that in such belief they are in the truth and are not called upon to doubt or question. And thus growing up, as many do, in this belief, it becomes to them in many cases, a thing of mere form, having no vitality and creating in those who possess it, no special concern as to whether their belief is well founded or not. This belief saves them the trouble of exercising their minds to any comprehensive degree, and they say: "I am content with the creed of my church and do not desire to be troubled by questioning the same." And, hence, you will see, it is not difficult for them to make the preference, for in fact, there is no preference, but a condition of mind existing that has in it no room for the exercise of any preference.

And then again, this preference exists, because of the social life of the people who believe in the creeds of the churches, for if they do not so believe it is not permissible for them to become members of the churches, as the creed must be subscribed to, no matter what else that may be vital is required to be believed in, or declared by the mortal who desires affiliation to be believed.

The church is the greatest of social centers in the lives of men, and its influence and power are very great and reaches further in the economy of social life than unthinking people may realize. So then when the applicant subscribes to the creed and becomes a member of the church he becomes satisfied, usually, with his social position and his thoughts of spiritual truths are no longer plastic but fixed, and as time goes by he pays less attention to what the creeds may require of him, but in a kind of automatic manner acts upon them and rests satisfied. His position then becomes so comfortable and his mind free from efforts by the undoubting acceptance of the doctrines of his church creeds.

Of course, there are many exceptions to this condition existing among members of the churches, for while they subscribe to the creeds, yet their souls are not satisfied and go out in longings to the Father for His Love and many who possess this Love, though intellectually they do not know what it means. But with the majority the preference is made because of the reasons that I have stated—and the difficulty will be great to cause an awakening from this satisfaction and feeling that in their beliefs lie the certainty of doing the Father's will and of their own salvation.

Now, while all this is true, yet these mortals do not realize that it is true just in the sense that I have described it, and the great work that lies before you and us is to cause the truths which you are receiving to be presented to these people in such a way that they will not be satisfied to rest in the security of their old beliefs, but be persuaded to seek for the truth outside of the teachings of their creeds. And this I can say, that if these people will have such an awakening, and seriously and honestly seek for the truth, they will not hesitate to believe that they have been mistaken in their beliefs, and will not be satisfied until they learn the truth.

I merely thought I would write this, because, while it is more of a subject pertaining to the merely living of men on earth, yet in its results and consequences, if the living be changed the things spiritual will become the things of absorbing interest. These creeds shut out the truth, and men will never be able to find the truth, until they shut out from their minds and souls the doctrines of the creeds.

I will not write more tonight.
So with my love, I will say good night.
Your brother in Christ,
John.

Atonement

Luke on atonement, part 1

December 30th, 1915.

I am here, St. Luke.

I come tonight to tell you of a truth that is of very great importance to you and to mankind, and desire that you shall be very careful in receiving what I may say. I am in a condition of love that enables me to know whereof I write and to cause what I may say to be accepted by you as true.

I want to tell you that the Love of which we have been writing is the only Love that can make a spirit or man at one with the Father, and this my theme: The Atonement.

This word as used in the Bible and as interpreted by the churches and the commentators on the Bible, carries with it a meaning of some price being paid by Jesus for the redemption of mankind from their sins and from the punishment that they will have to undergo because of having committed sin; and also, the idea that God, as an angry and insatiable God, was waiting for the price to be paid in order for His wrath to become satisfied and for man to stand before him acquitted of sin and the consequences of disobedience.

This price, according to the teachings of the churches and the persons named, must have been paid by one who in his goodness and purity was capable of paying this price; that is one who had in him such inherent qualities, and by his sacrifices was of such inherent worth as to satisfy the requirements of the demands of this angry God whose laws had been disobeyed. And they also teach that the only way by which such price could have been paid, was by the death on the cross of Jesus, who was the only person in all creation that possessed these qualities sufficiently to meet these requirements; and that by his death and the shedding of his blood the sins were atoned for and God was satisfied. This is the orthodox belief of the atonement and plan of salvation.

In short, a perfect human being free from all sin, a death on the cross and a shedding of blood, which was necessary that the sins of mortals might be washed away and their souls made clean and fitted to become a part of the great family of God.

But all this conception of the atonement is wrong and not justified by any teaching of the Master, or by any of the true teachings of the disciples to whom he had explained the plan of salvation and what the atonement means.

I know that in various parts of the New Testament it is said that the blood of Jesus washes away all sin, and that his death on the cross satisfies the Father's demand for justice; and therein there are many similar expressions conveying the same idea. But these sayings of the Bible were never written by the persons to whom they are ascribed, but by writers who, in their various translations and alleged reproductions of these writings, added to and eliminated from the writings of the original writers, until the Bible became filled with these false doctrines and teachings.

The writers of the Bible, as it now stands, were persons who belonged to the church which was nationalized about the time of Constantine, and as such, had imposed upon them the duty of writing such ideas as the rulers or governors of this church conceived should be incorporated in the Bible for the purpose of carrying out their ideas in order to subserve the interests of the church, and to give it such temporal power as it never could have had under the teachings and guidance of the pure doctrines of the Master.

For nearly two thousand years this false doctrine of the atonement has been believed in and accepted by the so called Christian churches, and has been promulgated by these churches as the true doctrine of Jesus and the one upon which the salvation of man depends; and the consequences have been that men have believed that the only things necessary to their salvation and reconciliation to God, were the death of Jesus and the washing away of their sins by the blood shed on Calvary.

If men only knew how futile his death was and how inefficacious his blood is to wash away sin and pay the debt to the Father, they would not rest in the assurance that all they have to do is to believe in this sacrifice and this blood, but would learn the true plan of salvation and make every effort in their power to follow that plan, and as a consequence, have their souls developed so that they would come into harmony with the Father's love and laws.

Atonement, in its true meaning, never meant the payment of a debt or the appeasing of the wrath of God, but simply the becoming at one with Him in those qualities that will insure to men the possession of His Love and the Immortality that Jesus brought to light. The sacrifice of Jesus could have no possible effect upon the condition of man's soul qualities, and neither could the blood shedding make a vile and sinful soul pure and free from sin.

God's universe is governed by laws as immutable as they are perfect in their workings, and the great thing to be accomplished by the plan which He provided for the redemption of men, is to have every man come into harmony with these laws, because just as soon as that harmony exists there will be no more discord and sin will not be known to humanity. And so, only that which will bring man into this harmony can possibly save him from his sins and bring about the at-onement that Jesus and his disciples taught.

Man, when created, was endowed with what may be called a natural love, and that love, to the extent of the quality that it possessed, was in perfect harmony with God's universe, and so long as it was permitted to exist in its pure state, was a part of the harmony of the universe; but when it became defiled or impregnated with sin or anything not in accord with God's laws, it became inharmonious and not at one with God, and the only redemption required was the removing of those things that caused the in-harmony.

Now, the only way in which this in-harmony could be removed was by the natural love becoming again pure and free from that which defiled it. The sacrifice on the cross could not furnish this remedy and neither could the blood atonement accomplish it, because the sacrifice and the blood had no relation to the evil to be remedied. So I assert, if these things paid the penalty and satisfied God and thereby He had no further claim upon man for any debt supposed to be due Him from man, it necessarily implies that He kept the souls of men in this condition of in-harmony and would not permit the same to be removed until His demands for satisfaction and blood had been met; and that then, when He should be appeased, He would permit men by His mere ipse dixit to again come in harmony with His laws and the workings of His universe. In other words, He would be willing to let men remain out of harmony with His universe and the workings of His laws, until He had His demands for sacrifice and blood satisfied.

This, as is apparent to any reasonable man, would be a thing so foolish that no mere man in matters pertaining to his earthly affairs would adopt as a plan for the redemption of those sons of his who had been disobedient.

I see you have a caller, and will continue later.

Luke on atonement, part 2

January 4th, 1916.

I am here, St. Luke.

I wish to continue my discourse on the Atonement. As I was saying unless a man gets into harmony with God in the natural love, which God bestowed upon him, and thereby becomes free from sin and error, there can be no redemption for him, and the death of Jesus and the shedding of his blood cannot cause that harmony.

Now what I have heretofore said, relates exclusively to man and his salvation in respect to his condition of becoming perfect in this natural love, which all men have. But this is not the great atonement which Jesus came to earth to teach men, and the way in which it could be obtained and the effect of its attainment.

As has been told you, in the beginning God conferred upon our first parents not only the natural love but the potentiality of obtaining it, by the observance of certain laws and obedience, the Divine Love of the Father, which, when obtained, would make a man a part of divinity itself; and, while it would not make him a god, or the equal of the Father, yet it would give him a divinity that would cause him to receive the substance of God's Great Love, and not remain the mere image, and, as a consequence, man would become immortal.

God alone, is Immortal, and every part of Him is Immortal, and when men shall obtain in their souls that part of Him which is his Greatest Attribute—His Divine Love—they will also become Immortal, and thereafter not subject to death.

The natural love, which was implanted in the souls of all mankind, is not a part of the Divine Love—it is not this Love in a lesser degree even, but is a distinct and separate quality of love, and all men possess it; but in many persons it has become contaminated by the sins that flow from the violation of God's Laws, so that the redemption, of which I have spoken, is necessary for man, even as the possessor of this natural love only.

But the Divine Love of the Father is a Love that has in it, and is wholly composed of, the Divinity which the Father possesses, and no man can ever become a part of that Divinity until he possesses this Great Love. I know it is said that man is Divine because he was created in the image of God, but nothing which is a mere image is ever a part of the substance of which it is the image, and cannot possibly have the qualities of that substance. Commonly speaking, the image may have the appearance and for the ordinary affairs of the mortal life, may serve the purpose of the real until something that arises that demands the production of the real, and then the image will no longer serve the purpose.

Now in the case of the creation of man, he was made in the image of God in one particular only, and that in the matter of soul appearance. His physical or spiritual body was not in the image of God, for God has no such bodies, and only the soul of man is in the image of God, the Great Oversoul. And so long as man remains a mere image of the Father, he will never be more than the mere man that he was at the time of his creation, and the Substance of the Father will never become a part of him; and while the Substance is Divine, the image can never become Divine until it becomes transformed into the Substance.

At man's creation a plan was formed by which that image might become a thing of Substance, and there was given to man, the possessor of the image, the potentiality of obtaining the Substance; but man, through his disobedience or failure to comply with or follow out the requirements of the plan provided, forfeited this potentiality, which had been conferred upon him, and thereby lost the possibility of having the image transformed into the Substance which was absolutely necessary in order for him to ever become the possessor of any part of the Father's Divinity. And when men call themselves divine they assert that which is not true, but which, since the coming of Jesus to earth, may become true.

I will not recite what this disobedience of our first parents was, or in what way they lost the great potentiality of becoming Divine, but will only say, that when by their disobedience they forfeited this potentiality, it was taken from them by God, and His decree that in the day they should commit the act of disobedience they should surely die, was carried out and they died; not the material bodies died nor their spiritual bodies died, nor their souls, for men continued to live in their physical bodies for many years after the day of disobedience, and their spirit bodies and souls never died, for they still live. But what died and what the sentence passed upon them affected was the potentiality of receiving the Substance, which would make them Divine and Immortal. This potentiality was taken from them and never restored during the long centuries from the time of its death until the coming of Jesus.

That part of the divine nature, or that divine attribute, which was the object of this potentiality and which would make man a part of the divine nature and immortal, was the Divine Love of the Father and nothing else; and if our first parents through their obedience had received this Divine Love, never would mortality as to the soul have existed on earth, and neither sin nor a want of at-onement with the Father. But disobedience came and death of the possibility of becoming immortal ensued, and man remained mere man, only an image of the Father and nothing more.

No man in all the long ages that I have mentioned ever had anything more or greater in his nature than the natural love of which I have spoken; and even as to that, man so abused and defiled it, until at a time he became an outcast from the Father as to this love. In other words, he man, buried it so deeply under his acts of sin and the violation of those laws of God which control this natural love, that he appeared to be forsaken by the Father, even as a mere human being.

But in the history of what is called "God's chosen people," the Jews, it appears that time and time again these people became such aliens from God in this natural love, that men, possessed of this love in a purer state than were the common people were used by the forces of the spirit world to call these people to a realization of their obligations to God arising out of the gift of the natural love. None of the prophets—neither Moses nor Elijah, nor any of the others—was possessed of this Divine Love, but merely of the natural love in a purer state than were the people to whom they delivered their messages.

But in God's Own time and in accordance with His Mercy and Plan, He re-bestowed upon man this great potentiality of which I speak, so that men should again have the privilege of becoming at one with Him; and to declare the re-bestowal of this Great Gift, Jesus was sent to earth in the form of man conceived and born as other men, but without sin.

It was at the time of Jesus' coming the Great Gift was re-bestowed upon both mortals and spirits of mortals then living in the spirit world, and they all, spirits and mortals, received the privilege of becoming at one with the Father through the Plan of Salvation that He had revealed to Jesus, and which Jesus taught in his ministry during the short years of his earthly life, and which he is still teaching.

There is no other way in which man can become at one with the Father—in which the image can be transformed into the Substance—than the Way that Jesus taught, but which seems not to have been understood by men after the church became a church of temporal power, and after the Bible or the writings of the apostles were emasculated and the thoughts and desires of men interpolated in the place of the gospel of peace and salvation. Yet there is in the gospel of John one declaration of the true Plan of Salvation, though it is little understood and almost ignored in practical teachings and observances of the churches and their members, and that is "except a man be born again he cannot enter into the Kingdom of God."

These words of the New Birth are the only words that declare the true doctrine of the at-onement. No death of Jesus on the cross, no shedding of blood or washing away of sins by the blood, no paying of any debt and no believing in the name of the Lord, Jesus Christ, will bring men into at-onement with the Father and make them partakers of his Divine Nature or fit them to become inhabitants of His Kingdom. Only the New Birth is efficacious for this purpose, and no other plan did Jesus ever teach and is not now teaching.

Then what is meant by the New Birth? Men in their understanding and interpretation of it differ, and it will do no good for me to recite these different interpretations or what the New Birth is not; but the important thing is, what it is. As I have said, the potentiality that was conferred upon our first parents was the privilege of obtaining the divine nature and immortality of the Father by becoming possessed of His Great attribute of Divinity—the Divine Love. And had our first parents by their obedience received the benefits of this great privilege, they would have been born again, as you and all other mortals, and spirits as well, may now be born again.

Then the New Birth is simply the effect of the flowing into the soul of a man of this Divine Love of the Father, and the disappearing of everything that tends to sin and error. As the Divine Love takes possession of the soul, sin and error disappear; it, the soul becomes of a quality like the Great Soul of the Father; and the Soul of the Father in its Quality of Love being Divine and Immortal, so, when the soul of man becomes possessed of this Quality of Love this soul becomes Divine also—and the soul is the man—and then the image becomes the Substance, the mortal becomes the Immortal, and the soul of man, as to love and hope, becomes a part of the Father's Divinity.

Now to declare this Plan of Salvation and also the re-bestowal of the Great Gift of the potentiality of the soul, Jesus came to earth. This was his mission, and none other. As readers of the Bible will remember, and it is a truth, when Jesus was baptized and anointed, and also on the Mount of Transfiguration, the voice of God, as it is written, declared that Jesus was His well beloved son and demanded of the people "hear ye him." Not to believe that he came to die on the cross, not to believe that his blood would bring about the atonement, not to believe in any vicarious atonement or that God in wrath demanded a sacrifice, but only "hear ye him." And Jesus in all his teachings never taught one of these things, but only the New Birth as I have explained it. This is the only thing necessary to the at-onement, and he is still teaching it.

He also taught moral truths affecting the conduct and relation of man to man, and man to God in his natural state, but none of these things or moral teachings were sufficient to bring about the Great At-onement. There is no doubt that the observance of many of these teachings of morality and of man's conduct towards God will have a tendency to lead men to seek the higher Love of the Father and help their souls to get in the condition that will make it easier for this Great Love to flow into them; but these moral teachings or prescribed conduct will not, of themselves, be sufficient to bring the New Birth, and hence the at-onement.

Now Jesus not only taught the necessity for the New Birth, but he also taught the Way in which it could be obtained, and that Way is just as simple and easily understood as the New Birth itself. He taught, and is now teaching, that through earnest prayer to the Father, and faith, which makes all aspirations and soul longings things of real existence, and by the Holy Spirit which is the Father's messenger of Love—or to carry his Divine Love—this Love will flow into the souls of men in response to such prayers; and by such faith men will realize its presence, and in this way, and this way only, men will receive the New Birth.

This is wholly an individual matter, and without the personal, earnest prayer of the supplicant and faith, that comes with the Love, a man cannot receive the New Birth. No ceremony of church, no laying on of hands or masses for the souls of the dead will be efficacious to make the man or spirit a new creature in God.

What I have written is the meaning of the at-onement as taught by the Master, and as understood by all the redeemed of the Father who are now living in His Celestial Heavens, and there is no other at-onement possible.

I have written enough and hope I have made it plain to all men the true explanation of the atonement. We who are inhabitants of the Celestial Heavens know the truth of my explanation, both from personal experience and from the other fact, which no spirit in all the universe can deny, that only those who have received this Divine Love of the Father in their souls in sufficient abundance can or do inhabit the Celestial Heavens; all other spirits, no matter what their several beliefs may be, live in the lower spiritual spheres and cannot enter the Celestial Heavens, unless they seek for and obtain the New Birth that Jesus taught, and is still teaching.

So my dear brother, without writing more, I will say good night.
Your brother in Christ,
Luke.

Confirms that Luke wrote on the atonement

January 4th, 1916.

I am here, Jesus.

I will write only a few lines, and because I desire to confirm what Luke has so clearly explained as to what the atonement is.

He has stated the true plan of God for the redemption of mankind that is for the placing of them in the exact relation to our Father that our first parents occupied, and which relation by their disobedience was taken from them and never restored until my coming. Men must learn the true meaning of the great plan for their salvation and for their becoming at one with the Father in His divine nature. No other plan has been provided and no other way is open to men to receive this Divine Nature of the Father and Immortality.

The material love of man—that is the love of the Father that God bestowed upon men at the creation of our first parents—is a love that is pure and in harmony with God's laws and the workings of the universe, and which must be restored to its pristine purity in order for man to come into harmony with God as to the laws controlling it; and men must, in order to get in this harmony, become free from all violations of God's laws in their conduct towards Him and towards one another; and many of my teachings were directed to bring about this harmony.

The Golden Rule is one, and this great teaching, if observed in the conduct of men towards one another, will tend to bring about the harmony. For to man the most important thing is his own happiness; and when a man shall do unto others as he would have others do unto him, he will be proceeding towards that condition of conduct and the correct relationship of man to man that will bring harmony, and an observance of those requirements of God's laws controlling such relationship.

But the observance of the right conduct of man to man or the regaining of the purity of this natural love, will not bring about the great reconciliation to God in the Divine sense—that is, make men at one with the Father in His Divinity and Immortality. And now I see and understand why my great teachings of the Divine at-onement was not considered as important by men, after my early followers died, as the teachings that should control them in their conduct towards one another, that is, what may be called my moral teachings.

In those days the great majority of men who professed to follow my teachings, as are written in the Bible that the church adopted, thought more of the rewards and happiness that might come to them as mortals than to those that might come to them after they became spirits, just as the Jews had thought for all the long years prior to my coming. These teachings were merely those of the earth, and as such teachings, whether of the Old Testament or any other teachings recognized by them as governing their conduct as mere mortals, were of more importance to them than were the teachings that showed them the way to the Celestial Kingdom.

And when the church which my apostles founded, came under the control and government of men with only the temporal interests at heart, the greater importance was attached to those things which, as the rulers and leaders of the church thought, would cause the people to conduct themselves in such a way as would tend to increase the power and influence of the church. And hence, the great truth of the New Birth was neglected, and salvation was declared to be by means that could be more readily utilized by the officials of the church. In other words, salvation became a thing which depended on the church and not on the individual. So you see the great harm that was done by these teachings and the great power the church acquired.

Salvation is a thing between God and the individual, and can be obtained only by the individual becoming at one with the Father, who cares not for the teachings of the church or of man, unless these teachings will bring the souls of men in harmony with him. I say, cares not, but that does not just express what I mean, for God does care whenever his creatures are taught false doctrines, as He is waiting and anxious to bestow upon every man His Divine Love. But even He cannot or will not make such bestowal, unless man follow the Plan which He has prescribed. And He could not have adopted any other plan, for the only way in which men can become at one with Him is to become, as it were, a part of Him—to partake of His Nature and Attributes; and unless the soul of man receives from the Father these Qualities, it can never become at one with Him.

As Luke said, my death or blood or any supposed vicarious atonement could not have made a man's soul a possessor of the Divine Love of the Father, because they could not bring man into that relationship with the Father that would cause the soul of man to open up to the inflowing of this Love. Let no man suppose that by a mere belief in me as the son of God and the savior of the world, or that I died for him, he can become at one with the Father, for it is not true, and has worked great harm to mankind.

Only the pure, honest, sincere aspirations of the soul of a man for this Great Love of the Father can possibly bring about this atonement that is necessary in order for that man to become a part of God's Divinity and partake of his Divine Nature.

I have written enough and will close.
Your brother and friend,
Jesus

What is the fact in reference to the authenticity of the Bible

March 12th, 1917.

I am here, Luke.

I desire tonight to write on the subject of "What is the fact with reference to the authenticity of the Bible." I was with you at the lecture of the preacher on this subject, and was surprised that he could announce with such apparent confidence that the Bible is the authentic word of God, actually written by the men whose names appear therein as the writers of the same. The fact that he traced back the existence of certain manuscripts and versions to a hundred and fifty years subsequent to the time of the teachings of Jesus, did not establish the truth of his declaration that by such establishment the authenticity of the Bible, or the genuineness of the manuscripts as they now exist contain the real writings of the apostles, or of those persons who are supposed to be the writers of the same from the fact that their names are associated with these manuscripts.

Neither is it true that John's life was prolonged to the end of the first century in order that he might write the true declarations of the eternal truths as declared by Jesus, for John did not live until that time, and his writings were not preserved as he had formulated them, nor was the results of his declarations transmitted truthfully, as claimed by those who teach the inviolability of the Scriptures.

I was a writer upon these sacred subjects, and as I have before told you, I wrote a document which was called the "Acts of the Apostles," and left a number of copies of my writings when I died; but such compilation was merely a history of what I had heard from those who had lived with and heard the teachings of Jesus, and of their efforts to circulate and teach his doctrines after his death. I also had the benefit of some writings of the disciples about Jesus, but such writings were very few, for these disciples and followers of Jesus did not commence to place in the form of manuscript his teachings or the experience of his life until a longtime after he had left the earth. They expected his speedy return when he would become their king and legislator, and hence, they saw no occasion or necessity for preserving in the form of writings the truths in which he had instructed them.

I know that after my own death the writings that I had left were not preserved intact, and that many things that I had incorporated therein, were in the numerous copying and recopyings of my manuscripts left out and ignored, and many things that I did not write and that were not in accord with the truth were inserted by these various successive copyists in their work of reproduction. And many of these omitted things and additions were of vital importance to the truth of things spiritual as they had been declared by the disciples as containing the truths that Jesus had taught.

And during the period—and the short period as the lecturer denominated it—between the earliest writings of the fathers of the church, and the times of the actual occurrences of the things to which these writings are supposed to relate and correctly describe, there were many changes made in the writings that I had left, as well as in those left by the other original writers.

Even in epistles of Paul, which these theologians and Bible students claim have more authenticity and greater certainty than the Gospels or other epistles of the Bible, many changes were made between the times of their writings and the times of the execution of the manuscripts or of the sermons of the fathers of the early church.

Within that one hundred and fifty years the truths of the spiritual teachings of the Master, had become to a more or less extent, lost to the consciousness and knowledge of those who attempted to reproduce the original writings, because these men had become less spiritual, and their thoughts and efforts had become more centered in building up the church as a church than in attempting to develop and teach and preserve the great spiritual truths. The moral precepts became the dominating objects of their writings and teachings and were more easily comprehended by them than were precepts that taught the way to the development of their souls and to a knowledge of the will of the Father, and the mission of Jesus to mankind as a way-shower and saviour of souls, rather than as a Messiah to establish his kingdom on earth.

No, I declare with authority that the authenticity of the Bible cannot be established as the word of God, for in very many particulars it is not His word, but on, the contrary, contains many assertions of truth that are not truths and diametrically opposed to His truths, and to Jesus' teachings of the truth.

This Bible has changed and perverted the whole plan of God for the salvation of man, and has substituted a plan that arose from the limited wisdom of those who attempted to convince mankind that they had a knowledge of God and of His designs as to the creation and destiny of man; and they were influenced very largely in this particular by their knowledge of and belief in the teachings of the Jewish church and the history of the Jewish race in its dealings with God, as they supposed, and in the teachings of the Scribes and Pharisees. This fact was conspicuously shown by these writers attempting to substitute Jesus in their plan of salvation in the place of the animals in sacrifice in the Jewish plan of salvation. As the God of the Jews in order to be appeased and satisfactorily worshiped, demanded blood and more blood, so the God, that Jesus declared was the God of all the peoples of the earth, in order to be appeased and satisfactorily worshiped, demand blood and that the blood of His dearly beloved son.

Among these writings of the Bible there are many things declared to be truths, and embodied as the actual words of God, that are contradictory and unexplainable, and which, if they were the words of God, or even the teachings of Jesus, would contain no contradiction, or admit of any constructions that were not consistent one with the other.

As the additions and emasculations and interpretations were made in the original writings of those who declared the truths as they had heard them from the Master, the decreasing want of comprehension of spiritual things and the growing wisdom of their own finite intellects, caused them to conceive a plan on the part of God for man's salvation, and as the recopying continued the thoughts of those who copied, or who dictated the same, became more centered on this plan, and so these copies were gathered together and considered, and efforts to have some agreement in the declaration of this plan; and as the new copies were made they were constructed with the view of showing forth this agreement.

It must not be supposed that the copies from which the manuscripts that are the basis of the Bible were made were executed and preserved in a manner that caused them to be isolated one from the other, and that they were not all known to the persons who copied or caused the copying of the writings from which the manuscripts were made, for that would not be true. These, what may be called the basic copies, were in circulation at the time the Christian fathers wrote, and they had access to them, and quoted from them and helped to give them the interpretations that now prevail in the churches with the additional interpretations since those days.

Men know now that among these Christian fathers were bitter disputes as to what was a part of the word, and as to what should be accepted and what rejected among these writings antedating the manuscripts that form the basis of the Bible and that many manuscripts, purporting to be the word of God were rejected as such, and for the reason that they could not have been the records of God's word, because they did not agree with what the bishops of the church in their human knowledge and reason accepted as God's word should be. Even these bishops disagreed and differed, just as the human minds and reason disagree with one another.

Then I say the lecturer did not prove the authenticity of the Bible as being the word of God. He did not go down the stream of time as he called it, far enough to discover the existence of any authenticity, and that being so, his argument of proof is just as weak as if he had started from the time of the printed Bibles, where their contents are substantially the same, but they not being the originals, the similarity proves nothing.

What I have said with reference to my own writings applies to the writings of all the others. The Bible does not contain their writings as they wrote and left them to humanity.

The Bible contains many truths, and enough to enable man to reach the Kingdom of Heaven, provided they are correctly understood and applied, but there are so many things taught therein as truths, which are just the opposite of truth, that they make it difficult for men to discern and apply the truth, and comprehend the Will of God with respect to men, and the destinies that must be theirs according as they follow and obey that will or do not do so.

John has already written you on this subject with reference to his writings and so has Paul as to his, so that there is no necessity for me to deal with the errors and interpretations contained in their writings.

I will not write more now as you are tired, but will soon come and write a message on another subject that I have been desiring to write for some time.

With my love and blessings, I am,
Your brother in Christ,
Luke.

Celestials must work until the Celestial Kingdom will be closed

March 15th, 1917.

I am here, John.[29]

I was with you tonight at the séance and heard what the medium said, and saw that as she delivered the various messages, she was being dictated to by spirits of a very low order of development, and that they enjoyed very much the deception that they were practicing upon the medium and upon the hearers.

These spirits are not the kind that you should have the association of, and while your band was present and prevented any of these spirits from getting in rapport with you, or from affecting you by their influence, yet it does you no good to mingle with such spirits.

The medium believes that the spirits who came to her are really the relatives of, or spirits interested in the people in the audience, but as a fact, these spirits are mostly impostors who have gotten possession of the medium and use her for their own enjoyment. When she attempted to describe the spirits present, she was not only imposed upon, but the spirits whom she saw, as she said, were not the spirits whom the sitters might suppose them to be.

But there were some of these spirits whom she saw really were the ones that she described them to be, and were interested in the people to whom they came, but they were of the earth plane, having very little development.

When she attempted to tell you of your condition and want of spiritual development in the knowledge of the truth, she was dictated to by some of the fraudulent spirits, who did not know the truth and who were not in condition themselves to read your condition of spiritual development and took you to be one of the usual visitors at their séances, and, hence, caused the medium to commit the error that she did.

The spirits who she says came to you were not your grandparents, for you must know that none of your spirit band manifested themselves, and the ones that she saw and said were interested in you, were some of the spirits who are with her very often, trying to deceive the people.

The medium has the powers of seeing and hearing the things of the spirit world to some extent, and is generally honest in her attempts to convey what she receives, but sometimes she exercises her own thoughts and fabricates the message that she delivers.

It is a pity that such a condition of affairs should exist, but it is a truth and will continue so long as these spirits of deception are given the opportunity to manifest themselves.

---

[29] This message was received by Mr. Padgett after Mr. Padgett and Dr. Stone had attended a séance in Washington. (Dr. S.)

And I will further say that while Dr. Stone had around him a number of his spirit friends, yet they did not manifest themselves, and the Indians that the medium described were not in any way connected with the Doctor. Of course at these séances there are always a number of Indians present who delight in manifesting themselves to the medium, but tonight none of these Indians formed any part of the Doctor's guides or band, and he must not believe that he has around him these howling Indians, for there is nothing in common between him and such spirits, and he is too well protected for these spirits to form any rapport with him.

While at times the Doctor may do some good to some of these wandering spirits who attend these séances yet, as a general thing, they are not helped by him, for the most of the spirits who attend such séances do not come there for assistance, but for enjoyment or, if they are thoughtful and anxious spirits, to communicate with their friends.

His work does not lie in the séance room, when great numbers of spirits of all kinds and conditions congregate, but in the quiet of his own room, or as he walks the streets, or in the church meetings where spiritual truths are taught, and where people of some soul development assemble. He has around him many of these spirits who are earnestly seeking for light and relief from their sufferings, and if he, in these moments of quietness or when he is where the spiritual atmosphere prevails, will let his thoughts go out to these spirits of darkness, and his mind formulate and project the advice and knowledge which he has of spiritual things, he will do much good and help many spirits toward progression.

Of course, the mediums of the kind that you visited tonight, have a work to do, and notwithstanding all the undesirable conditions that surround them, they do some good both to spirits and mortals, and they should be encouraged and helped to understand the possibilities that are theirs; but this does not mean that you and the Doctor, who have often gotten into the association of a very different and higher order of spirits, and having before you a work of a different character from that of these mediums, should not seek such places and encounter the retarding influences that are always present, in order to do the good that you can do.

I realize that this may seem unkind to these mediums, but what I state is a fact, and is not stated for the purpose of decrying the work of these mediums, but only to show you that such places for you to frequent, as your work is not there, but is as I have above stated.

You will comprehend the purport of my message, and it is not necessary to write more upon the subject, but understand this, that in order to do your work most effectively, it is meant that you go not where these low and vicious, or merely dark spirits congregate and seek control of the mediums, and of the sitters as well, but on the contrary, demand that these dark spirits shall come to you where the influences are more helpful and seek your help, and you need not fear that they will not come, for, as a fact, they are with you whenever they get the opportunity, when possible. Every mortal for his own work and in his own place.

Well, I was there, because, as I have told you, I am your especially appointed guardian to direct in your soul development, and it is not a waste of time or a descending to places that you may think I should not attend to do this work of looking after you, and accompanying you in your visitations to séances or churches or wherever .you may happen to be. You are the instrument that we are using to do our great and vital work for the salvation of mankind, and I can do greater work to help and protect that instrument. Because I come to the earth plane and engage in this work, I am no less the John of the Celestial Heavens.

And what I have said in reference to you applies to the Doctor for James was with him, protecting and looking after him, and doing the work that, as the Doctor's special guardian, he takes delight in doing.

We are Celestial Spirits of the highest order, but that fact does not prevent us from realizing the necessity of the salvation of man, and even though we have to come to earth to bring about this salvation in work and association with spirits of the earth plane, yet it is a labor of love, and humility is the touchstone that brings to us happiness in our work.

No, we are with you often and in close association and we would not be fellow workers with the Master, if for one moment we should have the feeling that because of our high estate, we should not come into rapport and helpful association with sinful mortals; and so long as the Father requires His great truths to be taught, and men's souls to be Saved from the effects of the great fall and made angels of Divinity, our work will continue.

But some time our work on earth as well as in the spirit spheres will cease, and then our homes in the Celestial Heavens will be our only places of labor and love. The kingdom will be completed, the doors of the Heavenly Kingdom closed and the angelic hosts be separated from the spiritual and perfect man. Such is the decree.

And as the Father desires all men to become at-one with Him in His Divinity of Love, we must work until the day of the great consummation of the kingdom arrives, and the spirits who have not on the wedding garment shall suffer the doom of the second death.

And when Jesus said *"Work while it is day for the night cometh when no man can work"*, he meant that while the kingdom is open for men to enter we must work, for when its doors shall be closed the work of the angelic laborers must cease, and man and spirits be left to an eternity in the spiritual spheres.

And so we work, and so you must work until the time of the (great) separation, and as the Master said, the wheat and the tares must be permitted to grow together until the great time of the harvest, so must the soul with only the natural love and that with the Divine Love be permitted to mingle together until the reaping of the harvesting shall take place. And until then, we must mingle and work and pray without ceasing.

Well, my brother, I have written enough for tonight and will stop, but do not misunderstand what I have said in reference to the mediums of the séances. They have work to do, and they must do it, and not be discouraged. You have a work to do, and you must do it in the way that we have pointed out, and the work that you can do they cannot, and hence, you must do your assigned work, and that alone.

So with my love, and the Blessings of the Father, I will say good night.

Your brother in Christ,
John.[30]

Describes the difference between the spirits of the Celestial and the spirit spheres and their happiness, etc

September 25th, 1915.

I am here, St. John. (Apostle of Jesus.)

I come tonight to write a short time about the truths of the Celestial Spheres in which I live and enjoy the happiness which my Father gives me.

As you may know these Celestial Spheres are above the spiritual spheres, and are inhabited only by spirits who have received the New Birth and who believe in the Truths as taught by Jesus. No other spirits are permitted to enter these spheres, and no other spirits could possibly find any happiness in them, for in them Divine Love is so developed in the souls of the spirits who live there that any spirit not having that Love would find that he is in an atmosphere that is entirely foreign to his qualifications, and he would be most unhappy. But as I say, no spirit who has not that Divine Love, which we tell you about, can possibly enter into these spheres. The walls of demarcation are just as solid and forbidding as are walls of demarcation in your prisons on earth from the outside world.

I live in a city that is most wonderful in its beauty and

---

[30] This message is a composite of three, being published in Volume I and Volume II and in Volume IV. (G.J.C.)

magnificence, and is filled with structures that surpass anything that you can possibly conceive of. This city is inhabited by spirits who have a wonderful soul development, and are capable of understanding the deep truths of God, which are not given to mortals or spirits in the spiritual spheres.

This may seem a little strange to you, but it is true; for it would be utterly impossible for the spirits of these lower spheres, or for mortals, to understand these higher truths. They cannot be comprehended with what you call the intellectual faculties or the mind, but can be only understood by the soul's perceptions, developed to such a degree that nothing that partakes of the purely material can have an abiding place in that soul.

The mind must stop in its progress at the sixth sphere, and after that only the soul can progress. But this does not mean that the spirit who makes such progress in the Celestial Heavens does not increase in knowledge and understanding, for he does to a greater extent than it could be possible for the mere mind to progress; but this progress of a spirit in knowledge and understanding is a progress of the soul perceptions, of which I speak. The faculties of the soul are as far superior to and above the faculties of what you call the mind as are the heavens above the earth.

So you see the soul does not merely embrace the affections and love of a spirit, but also qualities which enables it to understand and develop the qualities of knowledge at a place where the progress of the mind ceases. It is hard to explain this to you or for you to comprehend its meaning, but this you will understand that as the soul progresses in its development of its perceptions, knowledge and understanding of all things pertaining to the Celestial World increases. When you properly consider this you will find that it is a wonderful provision of the Father's Love and Grace.

What an important thing to both mortal and spirit is the soul. It can be starved on earth and also in the spirit world; and on the other hand, it can be developed on earth as well as in the spirit world. If mortals would only understand that as regards eternity, the soul is the great thing which they possess, and should be given more care and development than any and all other parts of man's being.

I may come again soon and go fuller into a statement concerning the soul and its functions and importance.

Tonight I will not write more.
With my love and blessings, I am
Your brother in Christ,
John.

Condition of spirits and their experiences and beliefs that are below the Celestial Heavens; how they congregate together

September 25th, 1915.

Let me tell you a few things concerning the spirit world that is the world that is below the Celestial Heavens of which John wrote.

In the several spheres, which are seven in numbers, are many planes, inhabited by spirits of many nations and races of mankind, and these various races have to a certain extent the customs and beliefs that they had when on earth. The lines of demarcation are just as strictly drawn as are those of the several nations on earth. The result of this, that many spirits who live in this exclusive manner never learn anything other than what their own leaders tell them and what their various sacred books may teach them.

The Mohammedan is a Mohammedan (Muslim) still, and so likewise the followers of Zoroaster, and also those of Buddha and of Confucius, and all of the various founders of religious sects.

Sometimes these spirits in their wanderings will meet spirits of other races than their own, and interchange thoughts, but very rarely do they discuss matters pertaining to their respective beliefs. There are undoubtedly truths in the sacred writings and beliefs of all these races of spirits, and to the extent that these truths are taught and understood these spirits are benefitted. I am now speaking of spiritual truths, because as to the mere truths pertaining to the natural or material world, they all have the same opportunity to investigate and understand them. There are no race or creed or doctrinal beliefs and teachings as to these truths affecting the material, and by this I mean, material as it exists in both the spiritual and earthly worlds.

But as I say, each of these races or sects has its own ideas and doctrines of the truth, and it can progress no further than the limits of these ideas permit it to progress. No founder of any race or sect has ever taught the New Birth, or the inflowing of the Divine Love in contradistinction to that of the natural love. And the teaching of Jesus are the only ones that reveal to man the existence of this Divine Love, and how to obtain it. So you see the importance of this Truth coming to man. I must say here, that without the possession of this Love no spirit can enter the Celestial Spheres.

The teachings of the other founders will show men the way to a life of happiness, and to what they may suppose, continuous existence. But the teachings of Jesus are the only ones that declare and lead men to a realization of the true Immortality of the soul.

I have written too long already, and must stop.

True Gospel Revealed anew by Jesus

Your brother in Christ, St. James.
Yes, I am that James. No the Saint is only used as a means of identification—it has no significance in our Spirit World.

An ancient spirit, tells of his beliefs when on earth. Sacrifice to the Devil

September 25th, 1915.

I am a spirit who has never written you before, and would not now, except that I have the opportunity to tell you of some things that you may not know.

I am a spirit who lived as a man when the earth was young, and men had not become so filled with sin and error and all those evil things which cause so much unhappiness on earth.

In my time men had not the ambition and greed for accumulating worldly possessions that they have now, and consequently worth—individual interior worth—determined a man's standing in our community and his real character before us.

I don't want to write much at this my first coming, as I desire to come again and write. I am not able to tell you how many thousand of years ago I lived, but it was before the time of the Bible description of creation.

I now live in the Celestial Spheres, for I am a Christian and a follower of Jesus.

I was an Indian and lived in the Himalaya mountain country, far removed from where your large cities now are. We were pastoral people and hunters. We were followers of our own doctrines which were not those of any sect or people that you know of. My race is not now in existence, and the teachings of our seers have never been preserved.

My name was Inaladocie. I was a ruler of my people when I lived on earth. We believed in one God only, and in doing justice to our fellow man. We did not believe in any possible blood atonement or in any Messiah to come who would save us by his death and sufferings.

We had our creeds too, and elaborate ceremonies and even sacrifices, but these were not exercised to avert the wrath of any angry God; but rather to preserve us from the evil influences and harm of a Devil. We loved God, but feared the Devil.

Now, I know how the plan of salvation teaches no such doctrine of sacrifice and vicarious atonement.

I must stop now, so good night.
Inaladocie.

Various experiences of spirits when they arrive in the spirit world

February 25th, 1915.

I am here, Prof. Salyards.

Well I am very happy and desire to write you on some phases of spirit life that I have observed in my experience of progressing.

I have noticed that the spirit when it first comes into this life, is very often in a condition of darkness, not realizing where it is or what its surroundings are, and in many instances, it requires quite a long time for the spirit to realize that it is not still of earth. But in many cases this is not the condition of the spirit, for it seems to have an immediate understanding of its condition and surroundings. I attribute the first mentioned condition to be due to the fact that, when on earth, the mortal had no definite belief as to what the future life might be; and in many instances believed that the soul went into the grave with the body, to await the great resurrection day.

Some of your religious denominations are preaching that doctrine now, and, the consequence will be that all those who believe the doctrine will experience the condition of darkness and the want of knowledge of the continuity of life that I have spoken of.

The second class of spirits, or those who appear to realize immediately that they have passed from earth to spirit life are those, who, while on earth, believed that the spirit when it left the body passed immediately into the Heavenly Spheres, or into the opposite—I mean the place of the wicked. I know that many of this class have hardly realized that they were in heaven or hell, for some little time after their entrance into spirit life.

Well, as soon as the spirits realize fully that they are no longer of earth, they commence to inquire as to where they are, and many of them ask questions that indicate that they are disappointed in not realizing the expectations that they had while on earth. It is very difficult at times to convince them that there are no such places as the heavens and the hells as taught by the churches; for while our spirit world may be a heaven or hell to them, yet the heaven or hell that they expect to find is not here.

Some, on the other hand, do not seem to understand that they have really left the earth, because, they say, if we had left the earth life, we would know nothing—quoting Job and some of the preachers: "the dead know nothing."

I have been very much interested in observing these different phases of the departed spirits' beliefs and thoughts. Now all this shows the absolute necessity of mortals understanding the truths pertaining to life and death.

This affords a very strong argument why Spiritualism should be more extensively and earnestly taught to mortals and why the false doctrines of those who teach either that the dead know nothing, or that the departed spirit goes either to heaven or to hell in the orthodox sense, should be shown to be not only a false belief, but injurious to mankind.

Let the believers and teachers of Spiritualism make greater and stronger efforts to refute these harmful teachings, and they will be doing the cause of truth and of man's happiness a great good.

I am not only interested in these phases but in all others, which show that the spirits, even after they realize that they are still alive, and must live as spirits continue to show the fact that their orthodox teachings are false. Some say that they may yet be able to go back into the body and await the great resurrection day for deliverance, and say that they will soon see God, and that He will take them into His heavens, where they will find that eternal rest and peace that they were taught to expect when on earth; and the wicked, even, look in dread to have some devil come and carry them to the hells where torture of the most terrible kind they think awaits them.

From all this you may understand that we spirits who know the truth have a great work to do, to enable these darkened spirits to understand and believe that their false hopes and dreadful fears have no foundation in truth and will never be realized.

This work many spirits are engaged in doing and these spirits are not necessarily of the higher kind, for many spirits who occupy the earth plane and have no real spiritual enlightenment, are engaged in this work.

I am not now engaged in causing these dark spirits to see the truth, for I have progressed to higher things, and my mission is to teach the truths of the higher life, which I have been taught by spirits who live in higher spheres.

This work to me is one that is not only interesting, but which gives me the great happiness that comes with the realization that I have been the means of leading a spirit to learn to love God, and to receive the happiness which the love of God gives to spirits. I tell you that this teaching is the grandest that I ever engaged in in all my life. When on earth, as I taught and saw the young mind develop, I found much happiness in the knowledge that I was doing some good, but here, in my teachings, when I see a soul develop, I realize that I am doing a spirit that greatest of all good in bringing it at one in love with the Father; and happiness here and that of earth, is as the soul development is so much greater than the development of the mere mind.

My work is not confined entirely to this teaching; I also am engaged in trying to assist mortals to a true conception of the life here—I mean the spiritual part of this life. No man is entirely without spirit influence, whether good or evil. Many are susceptible to the influence of the evil spirits, and for that reason the work of the good spirits is so much more difficult. There is in man's nature that which leads him to evil thoughts so much easier than to good thoughts. This is an old saying, I know, but is a true one, and the fact that it has been said so often and for so long a time, does not decrease the importance of it as a truth. So while men have felt this evil inclination in their nature, the fight between the good and evil influences will be somewhat unequal. The advantage though with the good influences is that what they suggest is truth which will never die, while the suggestions of the evil influences last only for a comparatively short time.

When the material gives up the spirit being which it clothes, that being will then be relieved of many of these natural tendencies to evil thoughts and deeds; and while this mere separation does not make a devil a saint, it makes it so much easier for the spirit to get rid of many of these evil tendencies, and makes him more susceptible to the influence of truth and goodness.

You must not think from this, as soon as they have been in the spirit world for a little time, they become good spirits, for that is not true. Many evil spirits have been in the spirit world for a great many years, and yet have their evil thoughts and desires, and all the evil qualities of hatred, malice, envy, etc., as when they were on earth.

Their giving up the earth life did not deprive them of their will, the greatest force or power that God gave to man, except that of love. And many of these spirits refuse to exercise their will in a way that will enable them to rid themselves of these evil thoughts and desires.

So you see, the mere fact of becoming a spirit does not mean that the mortal has become a good and saintly spirit. No, I am sorry to say that many men who were very evil on earth are still evil as spirits; and their happiness, which they think they have, is only that happiness, which they, as men, thought they realized from the exercise of evil thoughts and acts. Yet there is one great redeeming fact connected with their dark and sad condition, and that is, that in the end, whenever it so pleases God, all evil will be banished from the spirit world, and all spirits will be given that happiness which comes from a nature free from sin and error. Not by the fiat of God, but by men seeking and doing those things that will free the soul from sin and error and again come into harmony with God's laws. Just such I imagine as Adam and Eve enjoyed in the historical Garden of Eden.

But that happiness, while of a character that brings much contentment and peace, yet is not the true happiness which God is waiting to give all His children who ask and seek for the inflowing of the Divine Love in their souls.

I will not discourse on this great happiness tonight, as it would take too long and you are somewhat tired; but will say, that all men should seek for it both on earth and in the spirit world. When on earth I did not have it, but since I came here I found it, and now possess it, thanks be to God and His loving kindness.

You folks all have it, and many others too numerous to mention. Let me stop now as I am tired and you need to rest.

So with all my love and best wishes, I am your old professor, Joseph H. Salyards.

Heaven is a place as well as a condition of the soul

February 27th, 1920.

Let me write a short time tonight as I see that you are anxious to hear from some of your friends in the spirit world.

I have not written for a long time, though I have been desirous to do so, and tonight will say only a few words in reference to my progress and happiness in my condition as a Celestial Spirit, for I am now in the Celestial Heavens, and know the truth of many things that have been written you.

It is a little difficult for me to recite to you the wonders of these heavens and the perfect happiness that is enjoyed by those spirits that have found their home and abiding place in the many mansions that Jesus spoke of while in the flesh. You must know that heaven is a place as well as a condition; notwithstanding the fact that so many of the Spiritualists teach that it is only a condition or state of the soul. No, this is not all of the truth but is a great part of the truth, for the condition of the soul determines just what heaven it shall occupy and find its harmony and happiness in; but the all loving Father has provided that the soul shall have a place, corresponding to its condition, in which it may live and progress. If heaven were only a state of the soul, then it would not be a real, existing thing, with the substance and reality that the soul, even in its state of bliss, must have as a necessary accompaniment to the enjoyment of what the Father has provided for its true condition of living.

Heaven, as a place, is real and independent of the state of the soul, though it is necessary for the soul to be in a corresponding state in order that it may enter into this heaven and fully realize that it is a home suitable for its condition and enjoyment.

If it, I mean heaven, were not a real objective and perceptible place then the soul would be limited by its own condition that would be very narrow, as I may say, and confined to the limits of its own state, and separated from the states of other souls, and without the social intercourse that makes heaven a place of such happiness and contentment. Every soul would then be in the condition of the ascetic in human life, and introspection and contemplation would be the source and only means of possible bliss, and knowledge of those things that are spoken of as beyond the heart of man to conceive of, and which are truly and certainly provided by the Father's Love for the continuous and never ending progress of the soul towards higher and greater enjoyment, would have no real, conscious existence in that soul.

As man in his earth life, in which condition of the soul determines his heaven, is provided with those surroundings and material things that are intended to make him happy or miserable, so in the heavens things material are provided to enable the soul of man to better enjoy its own condition. The things of heaven are not all spiritual, as conceived by so many men, but are partly composed of the material of the universe and are so constituted and formed as to supply the desires and wishes of the soul with that which will satisfy the soul's longings for beauty and harmony and perfect enjoyment. In the several heavens are homes, real and substantial, suited to the states of the souls and differing as those states differ in their requirements.

These material things are not subjective as so many mortals teach, but are objective as are things of earth, and are the objects of sight and touch and of the other spiritual senses.

When I desire to go into a city, and indulge my desires, I find a city with streets and avenues and houses and other things that belong to a city, just as do you mortals of earth when you visit your cities; and so, when I desire to go into the country and enjoy the fields and hills and streams and gardens. They are all here, real and existing, and not the subjects of mere thoughts or state of my soul; and when I am absent from city or country, that city or country continues to exist in all its beauty and magnificence just as truly as when I am present.

Men must know that the soul in its heavenly life requires these material things, and has them, just as a soul when enveloped in a body of flesh, requires the material things of earth. While the condition of the soul determined its place of living, yet that place is also existing and real and awaits the coming of that soul in a condition of harmony. In these heavens there is nothing nebulous or impalpable or only a reflection or image of the soul's condition, but everything is real and substantial and lasting as the eternal hills; and when the soul finds a habitation it is not the effect of its own condition, but a place already prepared for the habitation of that soul and in accord with its true condition. Otherwise heaven would be a place of confusion and of appearances and disappearances, with no stability or abiding qualities, and the many mansions, spoken of by Jesus as existing in his Father's house, would have no real, permanent being, but depending for their creation and existence upon the mere state of the soul. The mansions are there and change not, and whether or not they shall have occupants depends upon the harmony of souls in their correspondence with the harmony of God's laws creating these mansions.

I have written you this short description of the heavens, as based upon my knowledge and experience, devoid of speculation or metaphysical musings.

I am glad that I could write you again. I am very happy and know that the Divine Love of the Father is a thing real and transforming, and the all sufficient thing to create in the souls of men and of spirits that state which will enable them to have and enjoy the mansions of the Father in the Highest Heavens.

I will not write more now. Good night.

Your friend and brother in Christ, A. G. Riddle.

The soul's progression as I have experienced it

January 19th, 1916.

I am here, your old partner, Albert G Riddle.

I desire to write to you tonight upon a subject which I think will be interesting, but it is so late now I hesitate to do so.

Well, as you think it will be all right, I will do so. I want to write on the subject of the soul's progression as I have experienced it.

As you know, when I first came into the spirit world, I was an unbeliever in things pertaining to the soul, except that I thought that the soul, which in my then opinion was the equivalent of that part of man which survived death, would continue to exist, and progress as the mental qualities of the man should be developed. That the mind was the great and only thing in the future existence, and as the mind was developed more and more on earth the condition of the man in his progression would be determined.

I had no conception of the soul as a distinct and independent existence from the mind, and I thought that all the qualities and attributes of the mind were those which belong to the soul, and that I had none others. And so, I say—I entered the spirit world and did not change my beliefs until a long time after I became a spirit.

But, as I continued to live in the spirit world in this belief, I found that the mental faculties and their development did not bring to me the satisfaction which I had anticipated; and also, met some of my friends of earth, who had preceded me by long years, men of great mental acquirements. I found that their condition was not as satisfactory a nature as I had led myself to believe that they should be, for many of these friends were only in the earth plane, and some were in darkness which was wholly contrary to what they should be if my theory of the

True Gospel Revealed anew by Jesus

'allness' of the mind was true. All this caused me to think, and in thinking, I commenced to realize that there might be something wrong in my theory, and that the soul might be a distinct thing from the mind in its nature and functions.

I did not find that these intellectual friends of mine had any very great happiness nor were they satisfied with their condition, and yet they could not by the exercise of any mental progress get out of their condition of darkness. Of course they were engaged in pursuing studies of one kind or another, and such studies gave them considerable happiness and satisfaction, yet, notwithstanding all this, there was some restraining force that prevented them from going to spheres higher than they were then living in.

I found that there were higher spheres where the mind was developed to a much greater degree and where many spirits who believed in the supremacy of the mind, lived and enjoyed the pursuits of their studies. At times, some of these spirits would come to our plane and tell of the wonderful development and happiness in these higher spheres, and urge us to make the effort to progress and become inhabitants of them, and you may be assured we were willing and anxious to make such progress. But try as I would, and as my friends would, the efforts produced no visible effect and we continued in darkness.

Being of an inquisitive nature, I sought for the reason of our inability to get out of the darkness. At last I found that the mind was not everything, but the development of the moral qualities were necessary to enable us to progress as we desired, and that in order to develop these qualities, something more than the mere exercise of the mental faculties were required.

Conscience must be satisfied and our recollection of evil deeds on earth must be gotten rid of, and our qualities of soul which determined our position and condition in the spirit world must be so adjusted to the demands of the laws of harmony, so that we could be able to advance in our progress to that place which such adjustment would entitle us to occupy.

I further found that the darkness in which we lived was not created by any defective condition of the mind, for many spirits whose minds were highly cultivated and possessed of unusual knowledge were in just as much darkness as were many spirits of very meager mentality and information.

All this knowledge came to me and caused me to seek a way to improve my moral nature and to get rid of the recollections of those things which tainted and darkened such nature, and I sought very diligently, but it was slow work and the efforts required were great.

But some progress was made, and if I had continued long enough and used my will powers in urging the cultivation of kind thoughts, and love for the truth and affection, etc., I would undoubtedly have progressed from darkness. This had been the experience of many spirits who believed as I did, that the mind was the thing, and depended upon their own will and exertions to bring the desired results.

But while in this condition of struggle and slow progress, I would occasionally meet spirits who seemed to be of a higher order and more beautiful than was I, and naturally I wondered what the cause was, although, strange as it may seem to you, I never made the inquiry until one day I met some of our folks who had this beautiful appearance, and seemed to be so perfectly happy.

Naturally in our conversation, I asked them the cause of their happiness, and when they told me I was so surprised that I gave very little credence to what they said, because what they told me was so similar to what I had heard on earth in the orthodox churches. I supposed that these friends had brought with them their old orthodox faiths and emotions, and were deceiving themselves as to the cause of their appearances, and that the probable cause was that they were more moral than I, when on earth, and hence, their recollections of earthly sins were less and conscience was not so severe on them, and therefore they had gotten out of their darkness into light with the resultant appearance of beauty and happiness. I would not at first accept their explanations of the cause of their conditions, and continued for sometime longer in the effort to improve my moral condition and advance in my mental acquirements.

But there was one other thing, I noticed, and that is that while these beautiful friends had not the mental development, apparently, that some other spirits who had progressed out of the darkness into the higher spheres of light, yet the beauty, and seeming happiness of these friends were so much greater and of a different nature from the happiness and appearance of those more highly mentally developed spirits.

And again, I thought and concluded that even moral and mental development could not explain the cause of the difference between the appearances and happiness of these friends and those of these more mentally developed spirits; so I again determined to seek the cause and, as a consequence, I sought these friends with the intention and desire to listen more seriously to what they might tell me, and to open my mind to the secret as it was to me.

Well, I listened to them and they told me that their progress and condition was caused by the soul development which they had received in seeking for and obtaining the Divine Love of the Father. That the soul is the great and important part of being spirits. That the condition of the soul development determines the position and appearance and happiness of the spirit,—that the spirit body and mind are both subordinate to the soul, and whenever the mind submits to the control of the soul, and the will of the mind, as you may say, to the will of the soul, that then the progress to the highest sphere will commence, and the spirit who is thus progressing will show the state of his advancement by the appearance of his beauty and happiness.

They further explained to me the nature and power of the Divine Love and its great developing potentialities and the absolute necessity of its entering into and possessing the soul, in order for it to make its greatest progress. That as this Divine Love became more and more a part of the soul's possessions, the soul took on itself the Divine Nature of the Father, and all these things which had a lodgment therein, and which tended to make it dark and sinful disappeared, and as these things disappeared, the soul mounted to higher spheres, and became happier and more beautiful, and the spiritual body correspondingly manifested this happiness and beauty.

All these things and many more these friends told me, and urged me to seek for the Divine Love of the Father and offered in every way to help me. At first I could not understand what seeking this Divine Love meant, but they took great pains to instruct me, and told me that only through prayer and faith would it come to me. That while this Love was waiting to fill the soul of every spirit and anxious to do so, yet only by earnest, sincere, seeking would It enter the soul and fill it with Its Great Essence.

At last they persuaded me to pray to the Father and then prayed with me, but it was hard to have faith in that which my mind did not understand and could not grasp. But they said, the soul has its faculties and is not dependent upon the mind for this faith, and upon my exercising these soul faculties would depend the question of my receiving this love and this faith, for as love came, faith would come also, which faith was not a mere mental belief, but something greater and different.

Well, I continued to pray for this love, and after awhile, I felt a sensation which I had never felt before, within my soul, and as I prayed this feeling increased, and faith in a small degree came to me, and I realized that there was a love possessing me that was never with me before. I continued thus to seek and pray until at last, this Great Love came to me in great abundance, flooding as it were, my whole soul, and happiness unspeakable came to me and, as these friends said, light and beauty also.

Well you can imagine that my longings and desires became insatiable—the darkness disappeared—my recollections of the evils of my life became fainter and fainter and suddenly I found myself in the third sphere, which then appeared to me to be the very heaven of heavens and the very fountainhead of beauty and happiness.

Now during all this time, and it was not accomplished in a day, I gave no attention to the development of my mind, or to the acquiring of knowledge of the material things, as I might say, of the spirit world, but when I found myself in the beautiful sphere that I have mentioned, it seemed to me that my mental faculties had expanded beyond all possibilities of belief and knowledge of things that I had never before heard or conceived of; came to me with wonderful clearness.

But the soul and not the mind was the thing! And Love—this Divine Love of the Father—made happiness mine and everything beautiful and satisfying. He who seeks only the development of the mind, and lets the soul slumber is poor indeed; but he who seeks the development of the soul finds that as his soul develops his mind does also, and rich he is beyond compare.

Well, I continued in this soul development, and in the increased happiness and the attainment of great brightness, and more than all the possessions of this Great Love, until I passed through the fifth sphere, where everything was much more beautiful, and Love so more abundant than in the third sphere, and entered the seventh sphere where I now am. I will not attempt to tell you the glories of this sphere, for I feel that words are inadequate to do so. Then in a faint, unsatisfying way, have I attempted to rehearse to you the soul's development, and the wholly sufficient thing that it is.

And my advice to all mortals, based on my own personal experience, is to seek with all their might and earnest efforts the development of the soul, and that of the mind will follow. This they can commence while yet on earth, and they will find that progress after they have crossed the border line will be much more rapid and easier.

Well, it is late and I have written long enough. But I wanted so much to write to you tonight upon this subject of the soul development as I see its vital importance to the future happiness of man and to his immortality.

So with all my love and blessings, I am
Your brother in Christ,
Albert G Riddle.

Says he never when on earth accepted Christianity. Is now a Celestial Spirit

September 5th, 1916.

I am here, Constantine.

I was the Roman Emperor and died as the head of the Christian Church. I wasn't really a Christian and did not understand the true

True Gospel Revealed anew by Jesus

principles of the Christian teachings, but I adopted Christianity as a State religion because of political purposes added to my desire to destroy the powers of my antagonists who were believers in and worshipers of the gods of paganism. I was a man who cared not in the slightest whether the cross or the symbol of the oracles was the true sign of religion, or whether the followers of religious beliefs belonged to the Christian church or the worship of the gods which our country had for so many years adopted and followed.

My great desire when I made Christianity the State religion was to obtain power and the allegiance of the majority of the people of the empire. The Christians were very numerous and were persons of such intense convictions—so intense, that not even death could remove or change these convictions—I knew that when they once gave me their allegiance, I should have a following that could not be overthrown by those who were worshipers of the old gods. The latter people were not so interested in their religious beliefs, individually, as to cause them to have such convictions as would interfere with any religion that I might establish, when they realized that their material interests would be advanced by at least, formally recognizing that religion as a state establishment. Their beliefs were not the results of conviction but merely those of what had been accepted by their ancestors and transmitted to them as a kind of inheritance. They believed in the gods and the oracles as a matter of course, without ever having made the objects of their beliefs matters of investigation in order to learn if those beliefs were true or not. Truth was not sought for, and hence conviction was a mere shallow acquiescence.

During all the time of my office as Emperor, I never changed my beliefs and never accepted the teachings of the Christians as the revelation of truth, and in fact, I never considered such a matter as religion, worthy of my serious consideration. Many doctrines were proposed and discussed by the ecclesiastical teachers and leaders of this religion, and those doctrines were approved by me which were adopted by a majority of these leaders as true and the correct declarations of what the Scriptures of the Christians contained. I let these leaders fight their own battles as to doctrines and truths, and when they decided what should be accepted and declared by the church to be true doctrines, I approved the same and promulgated them as binding upon all the followers of the Christian faith.

So I, though it has been frequently said, did not establish the canonicity of the Bible, or determine and legalize the doctrines which were declared and made binding by the conventions of the leaders of the church. Of course, I gave them my sanction and official approval, but they were not mine and should not be said to have been established by me, for if the doctrines of the Arians had been accepted and declared by a majority of these ecclesiastics as the true teachings of the Christian scriptures, I should have sanctioned and given them the State's authority. As I said, I was not a Christian when I lived and I did not die a Christian, notwithstanding all the fantastical and miraculous things which have been written about me and my conversion to Christianity.

When I came into the spirit world, I found myself in great darkness and suffering, realizing that I had to pay the penalties for the sins thought and committed by me on earth; and all the masses which were said for the benefit of my soul never helped me one particle to get out of my unhappy condition.

I knew nothing about the Divine Love or the mission of Jesus in coming to earth, and I found that my sins had not been washed away as the teachers had often told me on earth would be done for me. Many long years I remained in this condition of darkness and unhappiness, without finding any relief by reason of the mystical workings of Jesus' atonement of which the priests had told me, and which I did not believe, nor the help of the gods in whom I had been taught to believe by our philosophers and religious teachers. No, I found no relief and my condition seemed to be fixed, and hope of the Christian heaven that was never mine, and of the fields Elysian that would be mine in a hazy way, did not cause me to feel that my sufferings would at sometime come to an end and the glad face of happiness appear.

But after a time the light of the truth in which Jesus came to teach, broke in on my understanding and soul, and the Divine Love of the Father commenced to flow into my soul and continued until I became a possessor of it to that degree that I was carried to the Celestial Spheres, where I now am, a redeemed pure and immortal soul, having undoubting knowledge and conviction that I possess in my soul the Divine Essence of the Father, and the certainty of eternal life in the Celestial Kingdom.

I cannot tonight write you of my experience in either the dark planes or in the successive progressive spheres, but sometime I will come and detail that experience. But before ceasing my writing, I wish to say with all the force that I have, that only the Divine Love of the Father can save a soul from its sins and make it at one with the Father in His Divine Nature.

Let creeds and dogmas and manmade doctrines take care of themselves, and learn the Truth, and in that Truth abide, for Truth is eternal and never changes, and no decrees of man or dogmas of church tradition of the early fathers or writers, or creeds of ecclesiastical conventions, so solemnly adopted, and declared, can make that a truth which is not a truth. Truth existed before all these things and is not subject to them, nor by them can it be added to or taken from.

I must not write more now, and thank you for having permitted me to write.

So with my love, I will say good night.
Your brother in Christ, Constantine.

Affirms Constantine's writing

September 5th, 1916.

I am here, St. Luke.

I am glad to write once more and feel that very soon you will be able to receive our messages. I will not attempt to write at length tonight, and will only say that as you may doubt the identity of the one who has just written you, I desire to confirm the fact that it was Constantine, the Roman Emperor, who wrote you. He was very much pleased that he could write and in a hurried way correct some of the historical errors that have existed concerning his true position as to Christianity.

He is now a very bright spirit and an inhabitant of the Celestial Spheres, and of course, a possessor of the Divine Love. I desire to tell you though, that he was scourged by his conscience as it were, before he got out of his condition of darkness and suffering, superinduced very largely by pride. In his own conceit, he was an emperor for a very long time after he entered the spirit world, and retained all the pride of an emperor. But I will leave all this for him to write about as he promised, and stop writing for the time.

Well, you must not become discouraged for the Divine Love is a reality, and you have some of it and may have more. Only pray the Father for His help and guidance. We all love you and trying to helping you. Only believe.

Your brother in Christ,
Luke

Helen affirms that Constantine and Luke wrote

September 5th, 1916.

I am here, your own true and loving Helen.[31]

Well, my dear, you had an unusual message tonight, or rather, I may say, an unexpected one, and I see that you doubted the identity of the author; but as Luke is acquainted with him you can rest assured that what Luke said is true.

But he is only one of a great number of spirits, who as men were prominent on earth, are here in the spirit world, and if given the opportunity would write to you, but as we have work to do—which will

---

[31] Wife of Mr. James Padgett, who is a Celestial Spirit. (Dr. S.)

take a great deal of your time and energy—these spirits will not be permitted to write at this time, of the truth that we wish to convey. The one who wrote is or was an important personage in the history of Christianity, and hence we thought it advisable to let him write.

Your own true and loving
Helen.

What actually happened at Jesus' crucifixion

March 27th, 1921.

Let me write a few lines tonight, as I have not written you for a long time, and desire to tell you of the scene that was depicted to you tonight by the words and music at the church.[32]

I was present at the time of the crucifixion of Jesus and saw all that took place and the wonderful display of the forces of nature that were presented to you tonight in the drama of the crucifixion.

Well, as you may not know, many of the scenes that were so forcibly presented to your imagination never had any reality in fact and the drama was the production of the oriental mind which was so often used to depict things that had their origin only in such eastern imaginations.

When Jesus was crucified there was no great concourse of people; because he was considered as a common malefactor, paying the penalties that followed the violation of the law that he was charged with violating. Of course there were soldiers and a large number of the members of the Jewish Sanhedrim and a few followers present, but there was no unusual crowd to witness the execution. He was not the only one crucified at the time and the other two were considered just as the Jews considered him—violator of their laws and one to be punished by hanging on the cross. The words that he is supposed to have uttered at the time of his extremis were not uttered by him and no words that he may have spoken could have been heard by any of his followers, for they were kept away from the immediate scene of his execution, and it was only after he had been pronounced dead and found ready to be removed from the cross, that his followers were permitted to approach his body and remove it from the tree. The others, who were engaged in the execution did not hear any words of his, and as I have said, his followers could not hear and thus be able to report any supposed saying of his. So far as known, he died as bravely—that is without fear or doubt as to the future as did any other who has suffered the same fate.

The words that he is supposed to have uttered, were not so

---

[32] Mr. Padgett attended an Easter Service in the Year 1921. (Dr. S.)

uttered, and he did not call upon the Father for His help, or to cause the bitter cup to pass from him, and all reports of what he said or did at that time are not true, but merely the imaginings of those who wrote of him in later times.

There was no sudden breaking up of nature or things material, and the accounts of the graves opening, and the bodies arising there from and being seen and talked with in the city are purely fiction, and have no foundation in fact.

I know that Christians of today will not be ready to receive these statements as true, because of the long years of belief in these things that have obtained during the centuries. Why men should want to believe in these representations of things that never happened it is hard to understand, for in themselves that have no significance except that mere endeavor to make as dramatic and impressive on humanity the wonderful circumstances that they allege surrounded the death of Jesus. If they will only think, they must realize that the death of Jesus, accompanied by all the startling environments described in the Bible did not afford one iota of help in way of saving a human soul or teaching that soul the true way to the Father's Kingdom. His life is what had the effect and not his death; and the sooner men learn that Truth the sooner will they learn the fact that no death of Jesus could save them from themselves, or show them the way to the Celestial Kingdom.

I know that men will not want to believe what I have written, and continue in their belief that all these tragic circumstances surrounded the death of Jesus. And I suppose that this belief will continue with them for a long time to come. But what I have said is true, and no man can by any possible workings of God's laws find any hope or assurance of immortality in these things. You may ask me how I know that Jesus uttered no words at the time of his death, and I can answer by saying that he told me so himself.

He has not been present tonight at any of the churches where his death on the cross is celebrated, and will not be until after the time of the great worship and adoration of him by the churches has gone by. This worship is all very distasteful to him and are such that he does not desire to witness, and hence, he remains in his home in the high Celestial Spheres. He desires men to worship only the One True Father that he worships, and thus receive the true benediction of the Father.

Well, I see that you are tired and I will not write more.
With my love, I will say good night.
Your brother in Christ,
Samuel.

Affirming that Samuel wrote the preceding message

March 27th, 1921.

I am here, your true and loving Helen.

Well dear, I see that you are tired and I will not write much.

The message that you received is from Samuel, who was present at the crucifixion in spirit and heard and saw what took place, and so can be believed. I know also that what the Bible contains as to the crucifixion of Jesus is very erroneous, and written by men to impress their followers of the importance of Jesus' death.

I will not write more now. So believe that I love you with all my heart and want you to be happy.

Good night.

Your own true and loving

Helen.

Minister of the Gospel: His beliefs were merely intellectual. After awhile became skeptical

I am here, a poor, miserable man who is without hope in this dark and dreary world of lost souls, and surrounded by spirits who are like myself—suffering from the effects of an evil life and a lost soul.

I come to you because I have seen others come, and apparently receive some benefits and, as you know, hope is a thing which will come to us at all times, even though for a moment; and when I came to you that moment was mine. But to be frank, I do not expect that you can help me any, for the moment of hope has gone, and only my dark and fixed despair is with me.

But as I have commenced to write, I will be polite enough to continue, and show to you that I am not unmindful of the realization of the benefit of the opportunity which you give us to come to you, and of your kindness in listening to our tales of woe. And so if not too troublesome I should like to tell you a little of my condition and what brought it about. I mean as I now see things in their true nature and relationship to cause and effect, and why I am in the condition of darkness and suffering that now holds out to me no hope of succor.

Well, when on earth, I was at one time a minister of the gospel of Christ, and for a number of years preached, as I thought, his truths of salvation to men; and at the same time actually and truly believed in what I taught. But now I see that my belief was wholly intellectual and not arising from the soul's inspirations; and my teachings were also merely those, or rather my condition as teacher was merely that of the teacher of a school or similar institution.

True Gospel Revealed anew by Jesus

I never enjoyed religion in its true or soul sense, and all my endeavors to teach others were made because I had a kind of realization that I was called upon to pursue that course of life.

But my teachings, while others have been benefitted by them, never benefitted myself. Well, after a while I got tired of this life of the ministry, and in an evil hour, forsook it, and became a lawyer; and then my thoughts were taken entirely away from things religious, and as I progressed in the studies and thoughts of my legal profession, there developed in me the mental condition of mind that required every proposition asserted to be proved by convincing and irrefutable evidence.

And this condition of mind grew in me, and to such an extent, that nothing would I accept as true where faith merely was all that was given upon which to base the truth. And, as a consequence, I became a reader of books that were called scientific, and showed me the absurdity of receiving as an established fact, anything which could not be demonstrated by my five senses in conjunction with my reasoning faculties.

After a while, the question of God's existence and the truth of the genuineness of the Bible, and the reality of religion came before my skeptical mind in a new light, and as I had associates whose minds were in a similar condition to my own, I rejected the truth of all these things, and became an infidel without a God or savior even in a mental sense.

And so I continued to live in this condition of mind, which all the time became as the years went by, more skeptical, and my soul's development, as I now see, what little it then had been, ceased and I became dead, and dead beyond resurrection.

In my ministerial life I taught, and mentally believed in, the ministrations of the Holy Spirit, and its functions in awakening man's soul to a realization of the necessity of seeking the love and favor of God. And I also preached that without the work of the Holy Spirit it was impossible for any man to become the possessor of God's Love, or to be accepted by Him as a child redeemed. And I also preached that to reject the benefit or the work of the Holy Spirit or as the Bible says, to blaspheme against the Holy Spirit, was to become guilty of the unpardonable sin, for which there was no forgiveness. And after I became a skeptic, as I have said, I was guilty of this very sin, for I, while ever respectful in my declarations as to things religious, often vowed and asserted that the Holy Spirit was a myth, and that it did not work to save men's souls, and could not. That all who believe in such silly tales, were of shallow minds, and needed to be educated to the truths which could only be obtained by developing their minds and be made to realize that whatever their senses, together with their reasoning powers did not prove, or rather accept as proved should be rejected.

So you see, I, according to the Bible teachings committed this unpardonable sin, though while on earth I did not believe that I had; and, in fact, did not believe there was any such sin to commit; but, alas! how many of my associates, men of bright minds and loving and kindly souls committed the same great sin.

I died, and when I died and became a spirit my beliefs came with me and remained with me for a long time; and I enjoyed considerable happiness in the exercise of my mental qualities in the pursuit of certain studies in regard to the spirit world. I met many congenial spirits, and in our interchange of thoughts, I found much that was interesting and profitable. But after a while for some unaccountable reason these pleasures of intellectual enjoyment ceased to have the satisfying properties that they had at first, and I felt that there was something wanting though I did not realize what it was, and my companions could not tell me. In my wanderings I met many spirits, and always being eager in the search of truth, I did not hesitate to ask questions of those whom I thought might be able to enlighten me, and at last, in my pursuits, I came across a very beautiful and bright spirit—the most beautiful that I had seen—and being curious in its best sense, I asked what was the cause of his beauty and brightness and apparent happiness, and in a voice that was all love and with a look of great pity and sympathy, he told me that there was only one cause and that was that through the ministry of the Holy Spirit he had received the Love of God in his soul, and that as a result of that Love from an ugly and dark spirit he had come into the condition in which I saw him.

You can imagine my surprise. It was like a thunderbolt out of a clear sky. It was proof, plain, palpable and convincing that the Holy Spirit was a real thing, that it does cause the love of God to flow into the souls of men and spirits and that its work brings such glorious results. Where now was my belief that only five senses and the reasoning powers of my mind were the only things that could show me the truth. Oh, I tell you it was a shock! And then there came back to me the teachings of the Bible and my early life as a minister, and with these recollections came the conviction of the awful mistake that I had made while on earth. And worse than all, and what sounded my everlasting doom, came the memory that I had blasphemed and committed the unpardonable sin against the Holy Ghost, and that for me, never through all eternity was there any possibility of forgiveness.

Why should not all hope die within? It did, and can you be surprised when I tell you there can be no hope, and that I must suffer and remain in this condition of darkness and soul death through all the long years of the future.

So you see that, that one moment of hope when I came to you, or rather which caused me to trouble you with my unhappy story of why

I am beyond all hope of forgiveness or expectation of any happiness or life in the outstretching future.

So my friend, I am in the position of Dives; I cannot myself be benefitted by his knowledge of the truth of the Holy Spirit, and the certain doom which arises from blaspheming its work and mission, yet I can tell you to sound the warning to all mortals that they must not deny the Holy Spirit or speak words of blasphemy against it.

Well I have taken up more of your time than I should have done, and I will stop writing.

My name was S. B. C._____. I lived in Glasgow, Scotland, and I died in 1876, in a fatal and false belief, and a traitor to my young faith. I would say, that if you could show me that what you say is true, I would be the happiest man in all the spirit world, and that I would seek for this love of God with all my heart and soul. But I feel that you are raising in me false hope. Well, if you are speaking what you know, I will try to believe what may be said to me; and I assure you that I will listen most attentively, and respectfully to what may be said, and of course, if there is any hope held out to me I will grasp it and never let it go away from me. But it will be hard for me to believe that there is any forgiveness for me.

Yes, I promise that I will try to listen without having my present beliefs influence me, as far as I can.

Well, I see a great number of spirits—some are very unhappy and some not so unhappy, but dark and forbidding.

Yes, I see some bright ones, just like the one who told me that his beauty and happiness came from the work of the Holy Ghost in his soul. I have told her what you said, and she says to me: "My dear brother you are mistaken in thinking that you are beyond forgiveness, for the Father's mercy is so great and His love so abundant that they are sufficient to redeem the vilest sinner that ever existed or ever will exist in all His great universe. So if you will come with me, I will show you the results of this Mercy and Love of the Father, and you will soon realize that this mercy and love is for you, even though you now believe that you are past redemption." And she looked on me with such love and sympathy, that I already feel that I may be wrong, and I am going with her. So my very dear friend, I will come to you again and tell you my experience with your grandmother.[33]

So believe that I am so thankful to you for your interest, and permit me to subscribe myself.

Your thankful friend, and so good night.

S. B. C.___

---

[33] Ann Rollins, a Celestial Spirit. (Dr. S.)

Affirming that dark spirits were helped

April 5th, 1915.

I am here, Helen.

I am very glad that you helped so many spirits tonight, and some of them were very much in need of help.[34] The poor spirit that you sent to me was truly penitent and cried such bitter tears of grief and sorrow. I know that she will soon be forgiven and receive the light. She is now praying to the Father and her whole soul seems to be in her prayers. Oh, I thank God, that you can help them as you do. It is to me, so surprising that I wonder what you have about you that God should give you such power to help.

Well, sweetheart, you are tired, and I must stop.
So believe that I love you and am with you.
Your own true and loving
Helen.

---

[34] Mr. Padgett gave one evening a week to allow the dark spirits to write and cause them to visualize the bright spirits. These spirits, after receiving instructions, would make their progress to the Celestial Heavens. (Dr. S.)

Hell

Hell and the duration of punishment

November 19th, 1916.

I am here, St. Paul. (Of the New Testament.)

I merely want to say that I was present at the church tonight and listened to the preacher (Dr. Ratcliff) tell his congregation what he didn't know about hell, because what he said, in many particulars was untrue and it was pleasing to hear him tell his people that there was no physical suffering, although he didn't explain to them why there could be no such suffering, and I mean that no spirit, when he goes into hell carries with him his physical body, or any other body, that has such substance as would be affected by fire and brimstone and the other unreasonable things that the churches have for so many years taught and terrified their members with—and as a consequence caused them to believe that the Father is such a cruel and wrathful Father, demanding that His cravings for satisfaction be supplied by the sizzling in fire of the bodies of His children. No, this damnable doctrine is not true and I am glad to see that the churches are ceasing to believe or teach it.

But the doctrine that the preacher taught is quite as bad, and as useless as the former, for the reason, that punishment of sinners and those who are out of harmony with God is a fact which they all will realize when they come to the spirit world, and that being so, to teach that this punishment is everlasting is as harmful as the one that I first mentioned. How strange that preachers and teachers will try to cause their people and listeners to believe that God is such a wrathful and vindictive being, having less love and mercy than the most wicked and earthly father has for his children. It is so very deplorable that such attempts are made by these supposed instructors of what God is, to blaspheme Him in His great qualities of Love and Tenderness, and the desire that all His children become happy.

Oh, I tell you that these preachers will have a woeful sin to answer for when they come to an accounting, and that will not be at the great judgment day, as they teach, but just as soon as they enter spirit life and realize the great harm that they have done to many who have followed them in their teachings—and they will realize that awful result very soon after their entrance into the spirit world, for they will have come to them, as clouds of witnesses, the spirits of those who were under their instructions on earth, bringing with them all the evidence of the results of their erroneous beliefs and the stains of this great sin of blasphemy.

I, Paul, write this for I know I have suffered from this very cause myself, because, when on earth, I taught some doctrine like unto the one that these preachers are now teaching, and even now I realize that to some extent I am responsible for many false beliefs; but I thank God that all that is ascribed to me in the Bible, I am not responsible for, and that if my true teachings were known and taught, the blind and erroneous beliefs that are now so prevalent among Christians would not exist. I tell you that mortals do not conceive the great harmful and deplorable results that flow from their beliefs in the Bible, in many particulars.

This Book is one of falsehoods and forgery and imputations that have no resemblance to what the Master or any of his apostles taught, and you can readily realize how anxious we all are that these errors and untruths be removed from the minds and souls of men. But I must not permit myself to become too enthusiastic in considering these things tonight, or I might not stop as I should under the circumstances.

I will come, though, very soon and write you on the subject, as it is a vital one to mankind, and I will explain the truths connected with it as fully as is possible for men to understand. I should like to write more tonight but I must not. So with my love, I will say, good night.

Your brother in Christ,
Paul.

Hell and the duration of punishment—continued from preceding message

November 20th, 1916.

I am here, St. Paul.

I come to write you on the subject that I commented on last night, namely: Hell and the duration of punishment, and if you feel that you are in condition to receive the message I will begin and finish the same. Well, as I said last night, the hell of the orthodox preachers as formerly taught, that is a hell of brimstone and fires, is not the true hell and has no existence save in the minds of these orthodox believers.

The true hell is a place and a condition and one is not separated from the other; and while the condition of the soul and the beliefs of men create the hells to a very large extent, yet hell is a fixed abiding place, made and established and of such a character as to suit the inhabiting of it by the soul according to the condition of that soul. To illustrate a soul that is less vile and filled with evil thoughts and the recollection of evil deeds and false beliefs, is in a very different place from the soul that has more of this evil in it. The former soul would not find its habitation in the same place as the latter soul would, any more than would the highly developed soul find its home in the same place as would the soul that is less developed. Heaven is a place or many places suited to the development of the soul, so hell is a place suited to the souls of degradation and evil condition. I mean to be understood as saying that place and condition of soul are correlative terms, the home of the soul depending on the condition of the soul. As these different hells vary, so they are suited for the souls of spirits according to the defilement of soul.

I see that you are not just in condition to write or to receive my thoughts, and I will not write more. But I will come soon and write fully on these matters. So with the hope that soon you will be able to take my message. I will say good night.

Paul.

Hell—what it is and what the purpose is. Continued from preceding message

November 21st, 1916.

I am here, St. Paul.

I desire tonight to finish my message on Hell—what it is and what its purpose is. As I said before hell is a place as well as a condition, and, the man who believes that it is nothing more than a condition of his mind or soul will be wonderfully surprised as well as disappointed. I know the condition of mind and soul to a very large extent creates a man's hell and is the chief source of his suffering and the darkness that surrounds and envelops him; yet this condition is not the only source of that suffering or of darkness in which he finds himself.

Hell is a place, and a place that has all the appearances and ingredients that are in exact agreement with his state as produced or caused by the condition of his mind or soul, and is not a place of universal character and fitted for the habitation of souls, irrespective of conditions of degrees of defilement and sin and darkness. It is not a single place forming a common home for all fallen souls, but is composed of many and different places, and as has been said, there are many hells having gradations of appearances and surroundings that are suitable for causing additional sufferings which souls may have to endure.

The expression, "the lowest depths of hell" is not a meaningless one, but portrays a truth, a real existing fact that many spirits are now experiencing the reality of. In its broadest sense, hell is every place outside of heaven, and heaven is that place where everything entering into it—its appearance and qualities and its inhabitants—is in perfect harmony with the respective laws of God and His will concerning the same. And this statement involves the fact that there are several heavens, because the heaven of the redeemed, or those who have received the Divine Essence in their souls and become of the divine nature of the Father, is a distinct heaven from that wherein live those who have been restored in their natural love to the perfect condition that the first parent possessed before the fall—the condition of the restitution to mankind of that perfection which was lost by the disobedience of the first man and woman.

Mortals usually believe that heaven is a condition, and the Bible, in which so many believe, attempts to describe this heaven with its streets of gold, and pearly gates, etc., and as a fact it is a real, substantial place, having all the elements and appearances of a home of bliss, which help to bring to its inhabitants happiness and joy in addition to the happiness which their soul perfection and development cause them to have.

Then, as heaven is a place, having real substance, perceptible to the spirits that inhabit it, why should not hell be a place of real substance also, with those qualities and appearances, exactly suited to add to the unhappiness of those who are fitted for it? The spirit world, both heaven and hell are places of substance, having their planes and divisions and limitations of occupancy, and not mythical, invisible conceptions of mind as you mortals ordinarily conceive ghosts to be. The spirits of mortals are real and more substantial than are the physical bodies of mortals, and these planes and divisions, whether of heaven or hell, have a more real existence, than have the mortals in their places of habitation or confinement in the earth life.

The hells are places of darkness and sufferings but in them are no fires or brimstone, etc., as have been so commonly represented by the preachers and teachers of the orthodox churches, because there is nothing therein that would feed fires or that fires could affect, and there are no devils or Satan, though there are evil spirits of men that are more wicked and vicious and horrifying than have ever been pictured of the devil and his angels. In your communications you have had some very realistic descriptions of hell from those who are actually living therein and are realizing its tortures and realities, and I will not take the time here to attempt to describe it in detail, and will only say that as it has not entered into the minds of men to conceive the wonders and beauties of heaven, neither have they ever conceived of the horrors and sufferings of hell.

But from all this men must not understand that the punishment and darkness which the spirits of evil endure in the hells are specifically inflicted by the Father because of any wrath that He may have towards these spirits, or to gratify any feelings of revenge, or even to satisfy any outraged justice, for it is not true. Man, when he becomes a spirit, is his own judge and executioner, submitting to and receiving the inexorable

True Gospel Revealed anew by Jesus

results of the law, that whatsoever a man sows that shall he also reap. This is a law that is necessary to preserve or bring about the harmony of god's universe, which, of course, is absolutely necessary, and while it may appear to man, at first sight, to be a harsh and cruel law, yet in its workings and results, even to the individual spirit who may suffer in the reaping, it is a most benign and beneficial law, for the darkness and sufferings of a few years, as you mortals say, bring about an eternity of light and happiness.

The law must rule; and in all the apparent harshness and suffering and want of mercy, the Great Divine Love of the Father overshadows the sufferer and finally makes the defiled and wicked soul become one of purity and goodness. Men may never have thought of the fact; that if it were possible for these evil spirits to live in heaven, their sufferings and unhappiness would be greater than what they endure by living in the place that is more in agreement in its surroundings and appearances, with their own distorted conditions of soul. So even in their hells, the Father is Merciful and Good.

And regarding the second proposition of the preacher (Dr. Ratcliff) in his sermon, namely, the duration of suffering or of the life of the spirit in hell. His conclusion was, that this duration of the spirit is eternal, everlasting and without end. How it must have hurt and violated the teachings of his soul and his conception of the loving Father, to come to such a conclusion! But, yet, being bound by his creeds and the domination of his belief that the Bible is the sole authority upon hell, as well as heaven, in the conviction of his mind—and here I want to emphasize mind, for his heart was not in agreement, he declared that the duration of the sufferings and life of the hells is eternal, and the saying of Jesus proved it to be, not only because it was in the Bible, but because the true meaning of the original Greek word, can have no other translation; not knowing, or if knowing, not recalling, that Jesus, even if he used such expression, did not speak in Greek, and that back of the Greek word, in order to obtain the true meaning of the word used by Jesus, he, the preacher, must go to the word as it was uttered by Jesus and its true meaning.

So many preachers and commentators on the Bible attempt to determine a most vital truth by a shade of meaning that they conceive a particular word in its original, may have, when they are not justified in concluding that such word had at the time used, such shade of meaning, or that the original as they conceive it to be, was the original word actually spoken or written. They seem to lose sight of the fact that the writings of the Bible, I mean the manuscripts to which they make reference to prove the correctness of their conclusions, are far removed from the original writings, and that by reason of the copying and recopying of the word upon which they rely, and the shade of meaning that they give it in their interpretations may not have been the word originally used. Of course, they have no way of learning this fact, and, consequently, they have to resort to the best authority that they can have access to. But under such circumstances, it is not a justifiable thing to have a vital question of man's future and destiny determined by the shade of meaning that may be given to one word or more words, without reference to other declarations of the same Book, having relation to the subject matter of the inquiry.

The preacher said that in his conclusion as to the question he must be governed by the Bible alone, and had no right to indulge in speculation of the philosophies of other men, and that in the Bible he could find nothing that would justify him in coming to any other conclusion than that the duration of punishment in hell is eternal. Well, he was not honest with himself, for if he had searched a little more deeply and have given as much credence to other parts of the Bible as to the passage that he quoted, he would have found a strong statement to the effect that the evil spirits in hell have the possibility of leaving it, and not only that but that a part of the great mission of Jesus, upon whose supposed declaration the preacher based his conclusion, was to show the way and induce these spirits of evil to leave their hells. This was the Master's first work after he became a spirit, and he would not have attempted to preach to these wicked spirits in hell,[35] so wicked, according to the Bible, that God because of their great sins when mortals, punished them as He never punished any other of His children, for their disobedience, utterly destroying them as a race and His only living human creatures from the face of the earth, by one great catastrophe, leaving only Noah and his family as a reminder of the great failure of God in His creation—the most perfect and the "very good." So I say, if the preacher had searched the Bible he would have found that the hell that contained the spirits of all the human race that was living at the time of the flood, except Noah and his family was not in its duration eternal.

And again, had the preached searched further he would have found that the Master Himself, declared by necessary implication, that, at least, for some of the wicked who became inhabitants of hell, there was possibility of release, and certainty upon conditions. I refer to the declaration attributed to him where he said, "*He that sinneth against the son of man, it shall be forgiven him, but he that sinneth against the Holy Ghost, it shall not be forgiven him, neither in this world, nor in the world to come.*"[36]

Now, to any reasonable man there is only one interpretation of

---

[35] First Epistle of Peter—Chapter 3—Verse 19-20. (Dr. S.)
[36] Matt. Chapter 12—Verse 32 (Dr. S.)

this declaration and that is, that for any and all sins, except that against the Holy Ghost there is forgiveness in the next world as well as in the mortal world, and that being a fact, it is an irresistible conclusion that the Father would not compel a spirit to remain in hell after He had forgiven that spirit's sins.

No, the preacher had not searched the Scriptures, as he was in duty bound to do, else his conclusion, could he have ridden his mind of the beliefs that the creeds of his church had driven into his intellect, and of the teachings of the ancient fathers, and of the churches that had taught such false and damnable doctrines for so many years, would have been very different. The preacher repudiated the old teachings that there would be physical suffering in hell, or fire or brimstone, etc., and expressed his commiseration for those preachers and others who had taught such doctrine, and for their awful responsibility and accounting, and his commiseration was needed and appropriate. But I want to say here that he needs as much, if not more, commiseration for the preaching of his false doctrines, as did those preachers to whom he refers. He has more light, or may have, and his accounting will be correspondingly greater.

I have written a long letter, and you are tired and I must stop, but before doing so, let me declare the truth to be, that hell is not a place of eternal punishment. That all the hells as well as other parts of the spirit world are places of progression and the privilege of probation is not taken from any spirit no matter how wicked, for all are God's children and in His Plans for the perfecting of the harmony of the universe, and man's salvation, all the hells will be emptied and the hells themselves destroyed. But men must not think from this that the duration of suffering in these hells is necessarily short, for that is not true; some of the evil inhabitants of these places have been in such darkness and suffering for centuries, as mortals count time, and may be for centuries more, but the time will come when they will have the awakening to the fact that they may become children of light, and then when they make the effort to progress, they will succeed. The sooner that mankind learns that hell is not a place of punishment to satisfy the wrath of an angry God, but merely the natural and necessary living place of the spirit, whose condition of soul and mind demands, and that condition changes, and it will change, the hell of its habitation will change until finally for that spirit all the hells will disappear.

You are tired and I must stop. So thanking you, and leaving you my love and blessings, I am your brother in Christ,
Paul.

Experience of an orthodox minister after he passed into the spirit world

July 1st, 1917.

Let me say only a few words as I am anxious to write and tell you that I was with you tonight on your last visit to the home of my son, (Mr. Fontaine), and was hoping that the opportunity would present itself for me to write; but, as you know, I was disappointed, and I know that my daughter was also, for she expected that in the event that you should call at her brother's home, she would be able to get a communication from me.

As I could not write there, I thought I would accompany you home in hope that I might write, as I am now doing, for I heard you say that you had received a letter from your wife every night, and if that should happen tonight that I might have the chance to write.

Well, I want my daughter to know that I approve her searching for the truth which she may find in spiritualism, if properly sought for; and, notwithstanding, that some of my family do not believe in it and treat it with indifference or disbelief, yet, in it many truths may be found. It is a truth itself, and is waiting for mortals to investigate and learn that it is true, and that in it are those truths that will lead them to much greater happiness than they now have on earth, and infinitely more than they can possibly find should they come to the spirit world without a knowledge of these truths.

As they, I mean my family, know that I was a strict orthodox and believed in the teachings of the Bible as the church to which I belonged taught, and which I, myself, taught, and died firmly established in that belief and came into the spirit world wholly impregnated with this belief, expecting to meet Jesus and be admitted to the presence of God; and, according to my beliefs, I was justified in having such expectation. But alas, how different was my experience when I left the mortal world and how my expectations shattered in a moment, as it were!

As my spirit left my body, I was fully conscious of the change that was taking place, and knew that I was dying, but was perfectly calm and without a particle of fear. I suffered no pain, or dread of what I should meet, but rather felt a happy expectation in the thought that my troubles of the earth life were past forever, and that soon I would be at rest and find my home among the chosen children of God, and have Jesus welcome me and take me in his arms of love. All the expectations that I possessed before my passing were with me, and much accentuated, and no doubt of my realizing the same, for a moment, entered my mind to disturb my hopes. I also expected to meet my loved ones who had gone before and enjoy the happiness of their presence and purified condition of soul.

Well, I soon found myself a spirit, dissevered from my body, possessed of joy and, as mortals say, lighter than air. Figuratively speaking, I seemed to be walking on air, with nothing to interfere with my ascension to the bright realm where I expected to find my beloved ones and the Christ of my beliefs and love.

I hardly realized my separation from my body before some of my loved ones met me and welcomed me with love and cheer, and told me that they were so happy that I had come over, and that I must not be afraid or doubt that I was then an inhabitant of the spirit world. I could scarcely tell you how happy I was and how the memories of the cares and burdens of my earth life left me, and how I seemed to be in an atmosphere of love and heavenly joy. The meeting with them was more than I had anticipated, and I thought how it had not entered into my mind when on earth to conceive of the beauty and grandeur of the spirit home[37] which Jesus had said he was in heaven preparing for all those who believed in him, and in the great sacrifice and atonement that he had come to earth to make for men and which he did make.

But soon, I remembered that my great expectation was to see Jesus, and feel the influence of his love, and also, get into the heaven where the Father was and join with the mighty hosts in singing halleluias and songs of thanksgiving. And I then asked my angel loved ones, where Jesus was and when I should enter into the presence of the Father, and receive His benediction of approval as a faithful and obedient child.

And then, in a loving way and in a manner to make my disappointment less intense, they told me that Jesus was in the Celestial Spheres, and the Father, they had never seen—that He was a way up in the Spheres where no spirit had yet entered, nor had any Spirit seen His face or heard His voice—no matter how exalted and developed that spirit might be. That I was mistaken in my beliefs and that it was only by the development of my soul in love, could I possibly ascend to the Celestial Spheres where the Master was. That belief in the blood washing or in the vicarious atonement would not fit my soul for the Celestial Spheres and that only the Divine Love in my soul and the freedom from my erroneous beliefs would enable me to become a possessor of the mansions that Jesus was preparing for those who became in atonement with the Father. That what they told me was the truth, and that sometime Jesus would tell me the same thing; and while I could not go to his home, yet he frequently came to the earth plane and endeavored to help and comfort spirits who had not the soul love that enable them to become children of the higher spheres.

---

[37] This is a temporary place before the spirit goes to the plane that the soul condition determines. (Dr. S.)

Well, you can imagine my astonishment and disappointment, and how the nakedness of my beliefs appeared to me. And as I thought of the long life that I had given to the cultivation and establishment of these beliefs and expectations in my own mind, and that I had no other knowledge or hope of salvation, I become doubtful of everything that was told me; and my God became no God, and Jesus, as my savior, became no longer my savior, but a man who had deceived me during all the long years of my life; and I became resentful and hardened, and refused to believe in anything. For I thought that while on earth I was honest with myself and honest with God, and that when the Bible had been certified to me as God's true revelation, with the certain and only plan of man's salvation, and I had devoutly believed in its plan and endeavored to live the life that entitled me to salvation, thus, as I say, I thought of these things and the realization of my deception made me rebellious, and I almost hated spirits and God.

For a while, I was permitted to indulge in these thoughts without interruption, and then my friends told me that these thoughts were very harmful, and would prevent me from learning the true way to salvation and happiness, and that the longer I indulged in my feelings of resentment and thoughts of having been deceived, the greater would be my stagnation in my progress, and the darker would become my surroundings.

Very soon they told me that all things in the spirit world were controlled by the unchangeable laws of God, and that these laws required that I should go to the place that my soul's condition fitted me for, and that they would have to leave me for the time being. And they said further, that all the beliefs in all the world will not determine the place in which a newly arrived spirit will have to find its home, unless those beliefs be true; and that the beliefs that I had and on which I depended for my salvation were not true.

Well, I found my place, and with it darkness, in which I remained for a long time, refusing to believe what was told me as to the true way to light and happiness, and, just here, I want to say, that it is not an easy thing to lay aside or get rid of the beliefs of a life time on earth, even though the surroundings and disappointment of the spirit show that such beliefs must be false; and that belief—a merely intellectual belief—is a very important factor in determining the temporary destiny of the soul.

I have written a long time and I will not relate in detail how I learned the truth and found the light, and was started on my progress to the higher spheres or how Jesus came to me and showered on me his love, and told me of the things that would be mine, if I would only follow his advice.

He said that the great stumbling block to the progress of a spirit in its search for the truth and the mansions in the higher spheres is this erroneous and damning belief in his vicarious atonement etc., and which so many spirits who come to the spirit world, bring with them.

I am now very happy, and am in the fifth sphere, where there are beauty and happiness beyond all conception; and if the opportunity was mine tonight, I would endeavor to give you some faint idea of my home and its surroundings, and of the beautiful spirits who are my associates.

Some day, I know this home will be hers, for she will not have the burdens of the beliefs that I had to overcome. And just here, I must say, that as she knows how very dear she is to me, and how much I, who have so much of this great love of the Father in my soul, must love her, she must also know that I would not deceive her for all the world; and knowing this must take my advice and seek for this Great Love of God, which made such a happy spirit of her father. Let these old orthodox beliefs as to the plan of salvation leave her, and pray direct to the Father for His Love, and she will receive all that is necessary for a great earthly happiness and for a joy unspeakable in the spirit world.

I am with her very often in her earthly troubles, and try to help and console her, and sometimes I do succeed a little. She must remember that these trials are only for a moment, and then will leave her forever, and that the love and influence which her father is throwing around her will never leave her; and that in that moment which mortals dread the most—I mean of death—her father and other loved ones will be with her and take her in their arms of love, and she will have never a fear or dread as to where she is, for love will be so great that her soul will respond in such a way that all else will be forgotten. So tell my daughter to try to not let her troubles and cares worry her so that she will neglect the presence of the consolation which we try to bring to her.

Well, I have written as much as I feel that I am justified in doing as your time is needed for others as well, but your wife, who is so good, says that I must not fear that I have consumed too much, for she is always interested in the making known to mortals those things that will make them happy on earth and certain of heaven. I should like to say something to my wife, but I see that she is not in condition to receive my message, for she is suffering as I suffered, unconsciously, in the dogmatic beliefs of her church. Oh, if I could only come to her in my appearance of earth and tell her of the errors of her beliefs, and of the truths that have made me free and a true child of the Father, I would do so with the rapidity of light, and with the hope that my love for her would give me. I never loved her on earth as I do now, and when she comes to the spirit world she will not come a stranger, for a greater love than she has ever conceived of will meet her, and she will know the lover.

Tell my daughter to read what I have written to her mother, and even though her mother will not believe, yet some of the things that I have said will find a lodgment in her memory, which will come with her to the spirit world, and help her in her disappointment in not having her expectations realized.

And what I have said to you, my daughter, I say to my sons, and urge them to think of these things that are so vital to them as mortals as well as when they become spirits.

Sometime, with your permission, I will come again and write to my folks. So thanking you and with my love to all my dear ones, I will say good night.

Your brother in Christ,
Rev. Fontaine.

Affirmation that the orthodox minister wrote and gave his experience in the spirit world

July 1st, 1917.

I am here, your own true and loving Helen.

Well dear, you are a little tired and I must not write much. The spirit who wrote you was at the home of his son, as he says, for as you know I was there and I saw him there. He came home with you and I told him to write, for I knew that he was very anxious.

He is a very bright spirit and has much of the love in his soul and is anxious that his wife and children should believe what he wrote. What a privilege they have in having such a father to be with them, and give them the influence of his love. If mortals could only understand the great fortune of having a dear one in the spirit land who has the amount of love in his soul that the spirit who wrote you has.

Your own true and loving
Helen.

Book of Revelations is only a mere allegory of some one or more writers and is not the same as St. John wrote

March 12th, 1916.

I am here, St. John—Apostle of Jesus.

I was with you tonight and heard the sermon of the preacher on heaven and what it is and, as his text was founded on some expressions in a book of the Bible ascribed to me and which I did write, though not just as is contained in the Bible, I thought it appropriate (meet) that I should come and write you as to the truth of the sermon, and as to the value of the book as descriptive or suggestive of what heaven is and what its appearances are, and what the spirits of the redeemed are doing

True Gospel Revealed anew by Jesus

in what the preacher designated as service.

Well, I first want to say that while I did write a book of the nature of the one in the Bible named Revelation, yet this one does not contain my writings to any great extent, nor are my ideas set forth or followed in this book of Revelation. As you may now know, in my time, and for a long time previous, the Jewish writers, because of the great troubles and persecutions their nation was undergoing, were accustomed to write books in the nature of the one contained in the Bible, and called Revelations, for the purpose of encouraging their people to believe that all the wrongs that they were suffering would be avenged by God, and their enemies made to suffer and become destroyed, and that in the end their nation would be rescued from its condition of servitude and sufferings and become the ruling nation of the earth; and these writings were accepted by the Jews as having the authority of divine inspiration and conveying to their nation the truths of God and the same promises of His intervening in their behalf. The writings were always ascribed to some prophet, seer, or man of God who had the special privilege of coming in contact with God or some of His angels through the mysterious and sacred means of visions.

Of course, these writings were merely intended to encourage the Jews to establish their faith in God and in the belief that He would send them a Messiah who would have the power to redeem them from the punishments and thralldom that they were undergoing under the tyranny and strength of their heathen captors and persecutors.

Always were these writings prophetic and held forth the promises for the future, without ever attempting to fix a time for their fulfillment, or the ending of the nation's woes and the coming of its deliverer, so that time went on and the promises were not fulfilled, hope continued to exist and the belief of the Jews was not lessened, and non-fulfillment was explained by the further belief that the time for the consummation of their eagerly wished for expectations had not yet arrived. That God was all knowing as well as all powerful and careful for their race and that He and He alone understood just when the proper and fitting time should arrive.

This hope upon hope was a wonderful force in keeping up the beliefs and expectations of the Jews, and so effective was it that to this day they remain a nation or rather a race in belief and expectation of this coming Messiah. But, alas, as they did not recognize and accept him when he did appear, they will never again see his appearance, for he will never come as their Messiah as expected of old, but only as the great teacher and redeemer, not only of their race, but of all the peoples of the earth. He has already come as such a redeemer, and is working now to lead men to the true and only way to life and happiness and immortality. But never will any Messiah come to the Jews to establish them on earth as a great and chosen nation, as nearly all of them believe and still look for.

Thus, as I say, many books or manuscripts were written by the claimed Jewish prophets holding forth to the Jews the results of visions claimed to have been experienced by these writers. But as the prophecies, in the sense that the Jews understood them, have never been fulfilled, neither will they be fulfilled in the future, and their value has no reality.

This custom as I may call it, continued from these early times down to the time in which I lived and wrote, and my book of prophecy was written by me, not with the purpose of establishing the Jews as a nation on earth, or causing them to believe that their hopes or longings would be fulfilled, but for the purpose of encouraging the Christians to believe that notwithstanding their persecution and sufferings and martyrdom they would in the future life, when they should meet the Master and the saints, find joy and peace and heaven. But in my writings nothing was said about the wrath of God being visited upon the persecutors of the Christians or of their having to go into a hell of fire and brimstone, so that from that fact the happiness of the redeemed would be increased.

My writings have been added to and all kinds of grotesque imagery interpolated so that the whole design and purpose of my writings were changed and destroyed and the present Book of Revelation is only a mere allegory of some one or more writers who were gifted with some knowledge of the Christian teachings and unusually oriented imaginations. This book is of no value, but on the contrary is doing much harm to the cause of the truth as taught by the Master; as we who are in the Celestial Heavens and have knowledge of things heavenly as well as things earthly know to be the fact.

It should not be accepted as a truth of the revelation of truths, and not be believed in for any purpose. It has lead many good men and honest and earnest seekers after the truth astray, and caused them to believe and teach false doctrines that have resulted in much darkness and stagnation in the development of human souls in their longings for the truth. So, I say, let men entirely discard its teachings, and any and all lessons that the preachers or others, who think that they can understand its meaning, attempt to teach.

The writings that I gave to my people, of the kind mentioned, have long ago served their purpose, and the writings called the revelations contain in it no truth that will help mankind to the Heavenly Kingdom or to their eternal happiness and at-onement with the Father. Let it die the death of a falsehood, born out of time.

I also was interested in the struggle of the preacher to explain what heaven is, and what his people who may consider themselves redeemed children of God, will find when they become inhabitants of that heaven.

Well, he spoke truly when he said heaven is a place as well as a condition, for it is inconceivable that any condition of the spirit of a mortal could exist unless there be a place where that spirit could find a habitation. All space in the universe of God is a place, or contains places where things of existence must find localities. There is no such thing as a vacuum in God's economy, and all parts of space are fitted with something having substance, either material or spiritual, and wherever such substance is, there is a place for its abiding.

Yes, heaven is a place, or a number of places, for the preacher is far from having the true conception of heaven when he supposes it is one large place, where all believers go after death, irrespective of their condition of soul and moral perfections. As I say, there are many heavens and many places, all as real and substantial as are the different stories and rooms in your home of earth. And the partitions, if I may so speak, between these different places are just as impassable for spirits that have not the proper qualifications to pass through as are the partition walls between the various rooms in your earth homes for you mortals to pass through. These places are distinctive, and the many mansions that the preacher referred to, are situated in many heavens or more correctly many spheres of the heavens.

Strictly speaking, there are two heavens in God's spirit universe, namely, the heavens of the redeemed and transformed soul by the Divine Love called the Celestial Heavens, and the heavens of the restored perfect man, called the Spiritual Heavens,[38] each and all of them being places of real perfection and substance.

As one star differs from another star in glory, so these several heavens within heavens differ from one another in glory and appearance and in those things which help to make the mansions of their inhabitants beautiful and attractive and glorious.

It would take too long for me to attempt to describe any of these heavens, for they each and all excel any conception that the mortal is capable of having; but I will say this, that there are no streets of gold or pearly gates, or suns or stars in any of them; only the light of God's love and mercy illuminates them.

I will postpone my further writing, but will come very soon and complete what I intended to say about the sermon of the preacher, and attempt to show the real appearance of some of the heavens, and what service the redeemed children of God render when they come to the spirit world.

So my dear brother, I will say good night.

---

[38] The highest plane of the Sixth Sphere. (Dr. S.)

Your brother in Christ,
John.

Description of the Third Sphere. Affirmation Jesus wrote the Prayer

December 8th, 1916.

I am here, St. John, Apostle of Jesus.

I desire to finish my comments on the preacher's (Dr. Ratcliff) sermon on heaven. (Message of November 26th.) As I said, these Apocalyptic (Book of Revelation) writings were made for the purpose of encouraging the people of those days to believe that God would intervene in their behalf, and save them from their sufferings and persecutions, and in the one case establish a Messiah's kingdom on earth that would cause the Jews to become the ruling nation of the universe, and in the other, to establish a kingdom in heaven where the Christians would find rest and happiness in becoming inhabitants of that kingdom, and children of the Father, and participants in the glories of Christ's reign as king and priest. Well, as the subject of the sermon was that Kingdom or Heaven and the preacher endeavored to tell his people what that heaven is, I will consider that subject.

In the first place, as I have said, that heaven is not one universal place where all the Christians, irrespective of their soul development, go, but in that heaven are many heavens or spheres in which the spirit of mortals will find homes and also happiness according to their soul development or their spiritual development. And in order that there may be no misunderstanding, I must say that the soul development comes only through and by the operation of the Holy Spirit. The spiritual development involves only the result of the correct workings of the moral faculties of a man and the purification of his natural love which, of course, comprehends the development of his soul, so far as the same may be developed by this purifying process. The results of each operation is very different, and lead to a perfection and relationship to the Father, which is in harmony with the laws controlling the respective heavens—for the place of final habitation of each may be called heaven.

But my object tonight is to describe to you the appearance and condition of one of these heavens, and as mortals have heard more about the third heaven, which we in our information to you have called the third sphere, than of any of the other heavens, I will confine my description to that place.

Well, it is occupied by the spirits of mortals who have received considerable of the Divine Love, as well as by those who have progressed to a great extent in the purification of their natural love and the expansion of their minds and intellects, though the latter do not remain very long in this heaven, but progress to the fourth where there are more opportunities and more instructions in those things which have to do with the mind's advancement. While those who have made progress in the soul development and those in the intellectual are all in the third heavens, yet they occupy different and distinct planes in that heaven, for those things that attract the one class do not attract the other, and there is very little intermingling of these spirits except that those who know that the Divine Love is real sometimes attempt to show those, who do not, the desirability of obtaining it and the happiness that it brings to spirits.

As we have already told you, the condition of the soul—not of the mind—to a large degree makes the heaven of the spirit, and in the providence of the Father, He has made the surroundings and the appearances of the environment suitable to the condition of the soul and fitted to increase the happiness of those spirits who may, because of their soul progress, be attracted to the particular places in which they find themselves—their homes.

The appearance of this heaven to those who have this Divine Love in their souls is far excelling the capacity of your mortal language to explain, even if I had the ability to describe the same. But in one general statement I may say that for these spirits there is everything to make them happy to the extent of their capacity to receive and enjoy. There are trees and flowers, and hills and dales, and rivers and lakes, and beautiful landscapes, and above all the wonderful atmosphere, as I may express it, that is created by this wonderful Love of the Father, and a glorious light that illuminates and gives life to all who live in it, which comes from this Love of the Father. It is the sun, moon and stars, and sunrise and sunset, and summer clouds, and evening shadows and morning glories. Your material sun and moon and stars do not appear in this heaven, for the effulgence of the light from the Father's love eclipses and eliminates the light of these material creations of the mortal world.

And then there are homes of the grandest splendor and beauty suited to the conditions of the various spirits, which have in them everything that will tend to cause happiness and joy to their occupants and visiting friends. Musical instruments and books, and paintings and furniture of every kind fitted to bring to the spirits contentment and joy, and a realization of peace and rest from the cares that you mortals have with you all through your earth life. And above and more important than all, a wonderful atmosphere of love which makes all these spirits realize that they are the children of the Father and brothers of one another and lovers of all humanity.

And in addition, the social life is beyond all conception. The spirits have their times of visiting as well as those of staying in their homes; and many pleasures as well as of work and helping spirits and mortals; of singing and music and laughter as of prayer and contemplation of deep spiritual truths. Yes, in the lighter social pleasures as well as in the solitary meditations and aspirations of the soul's progress, there is happiness and enjoyment and freedom from those things which defile or make inharmonious the thoughts and heart's desire of these spirits. All is gladness and there are none who have solemn downcast countenances that many of earth imagine portrays the truly righteous and redeemed of mortals. No, love knows no sadness, and as the soul speaks its condition by the appearance of the spirit body's countenance, the soul being so full of gladness and joy, the countenance can express only those emotions of the soul. This is the result of the law which declares nothing can be hidden, and every spirit must show forth the truth of its condition. There are no walled cities or streets of gold or pearly gates or other of the material things which the book ascribes to me sets forth, so that man can get some conception of what heaven is. These things in heaven would not be gold or pearls or diamonds or jasper, for when they are compared to the real beauties of the things which it contains, they are as the faint light of the candle compared to the light of your noon day sun. Truly the mind of man cannot conceive of the glories that await the love lit soul when it comes to its heavenly home.

There is another misconception that the preacher had, following the teachings of Revelation, and that is that the Kingdom of Heaven is a walled city—the New Jerusalem—in which all the spirits of the redeemed live, singing their loud hosannas to God. There are cities of which your earth cities may be called correspondences, but there are also villages and hamlets and homes in the country, as you would say, surrounded by green fields and shady vales through which run rivers and streams of silvery hue and clear as crystal, and also placid lakes which afford the pleasures of boating and sailing and other amusements. For each spirit is provided the place that is most attractive to him and it is optional with him where his home shall be. But all love and worship the Father, and endeavor to make their neighbors happy and help the development of the soul towards a progression to the heavens which are higher yet. All spirits are controlled by law, but that law is the Law of Love, and that love is the Love Divine—the essence of the Father's Divinity.

I have written enough for tonight, and I hope from what I have said that you may catch some faint conception of what the glories of this third heaven is for those who have found, to some extent, this Love and possess it; and then, when as you must know there are many heavens above this, each successively possessing increased glories and happiness, and beauties of place as well as beauty of spirit, you may imagine what the Master meant when he said, "In my Father's house are many mansions—."

I know that my attempted description may be unsatisfactory to some mortals, but it is the best that I can do, because mortal words cannot convey and mortal thoughts cannot conceive the realities; and man in his imaginings may better get a spiritual view of these things. I will not write more tonight.

I am with you quite often, throwing around you the influence of my love, and endeavoring to help and encourage you. Let your faith in us and in our communications increase, and believe above all that the Master wrote you the prayer[39] which you received a few nights ago. Study it deeply and grasp its spiritual meaning, and let your longings and aspirations go out to the Father as suggested by the prayer, and you will find a wonderful and satisfactory response to them. We are praying for you and your friends, and you must believe that the love is coming into your souls. So with my love and blessings, I will say good night.

Your brother in Christ,
John.

Changed his erroneous beliefs that he taught on earth and is now in the Celestial Heavens

August 8th, 1915.

I am here, George Whitefield.

I was a preacher of England and a contemporary of John Wesley. I am in the Celestial Spheres where are only those who have received the New Birth that has been written about by other and more ancient spirits.

I merely want to say that I am still a follower of Jesus, but a little different in my knowledge of what he was and is. I do not now look upon him as God, or a part of God, but as His true son, and the greatest of all the spirits in the spirit world. There are none to be compared to him in beauty or spirituality or in his knowledge of God's truths.

I used to preach to thousands about his vicarious atonement and his blood sacrifice, but now I see his mission in a different light. it is not his death on the cross that saves men from their sins, nor his sacrifice that appeases the wrath of an angry God, but his life and teachings of the Divine Love bestowed on mankind and the way to obtain that Love, that saves men from their sins. There was no need to appease the wrath of an angry God for there was no angry God, only a Loving and Merciful God; and when men think that unless they turn from their sins they will be forever burned in a fiery hell, they are the dupes of preachers such as I was and will never get the Love of the Father by such teachings. God is

---

[39] The Prayer is on page 36. (Dr. S.)

Love, and men must know it—and His Love is for all of every race and clime.

I see now, what a great mistake I made in my conception of God and of Christ's mission on earth, and how much harm I did to mortals in my preaching and how I slandered the Father of love. But I was honest in my beliefs and taught as I thought the truth to be, yet that does not alter the fact that many a mortal after he became a spirit, was retarded for a long time in his spiritual progress, because of these false beliefs, which in order to progress he had to give up and start anew in his efforts to find the truths of God.

And as I worked hard and preached eloquently to make mortals believe these injurious doctrines while on earth, so now I am working hard and preaching eloquently to make spirits who come over with these beliefs, unlearn them and see the truth as it is.

I am in sympathy with the movement which the Master is now making to spread the truth of these spiritual things on earth and am ready to follow him in all his efforts to bring about the salvation of men not only from sin but from erroneous beliefs.

So I come to you tonight to express my sympathy and interest in the cause.

Let your work proceed, and do your best to make known to men the great truths which the Master shall teach. We will all join in the work and do everything in our power to speed the great cause of men's redemption from sin and ignorance.

The man must have the soul development by obtaining the Divine Love, because you cannot inspire a man to preach grand and sublime spiritual truths unless he has the capacity in his own soul to feel and understand the truths.

I will not write longer tonight.
I am your true friend,
George Whitefield.

How all mankind can become Divine Angels and how erroneous beliefs prevent this consummation

May 28th, 1916.

I am here, your grandmother.

I will tell you tonight of a truth that may be of interest to you, and I know that it is of importance to all who may long for happiness in the future life.

As you know, I am now in the Celestial Spheres, in a place higher than the third Celestial Sphere, and where are no special lines of demarcation separating it from what you may call the higher planes.

In my plane, the inhabitants are those who have received the Divine Love in their souls to an extent that makes them know that they are of a nature that is Divine and in at-onement with that of the Father. Of course, those who have entered the first Celestial Sphere[40] have the knowledge of having partaken of the divine nature, but they are not so filled with this love as we are who live in the sphere that I am in.

It is not possible for me to tell you of the extent of our happiness, because you have no words in your language that can possibly convey a faint conception of this happiness, and I will not attempt to describe it; but if you will combine all the emotions of joy and happiness which you have received or experienced in all the years of your life, you would not be able to realize the meaning of our happiness in the faintest degree.

I merely recite this truth to show to you and all mankind what is possible for you and them to obtain, if you will only pursue the course that the Father has provided, and the Master has pointed out in his messages to you.

The great instrument that causes this great happiness is love, and by this I mean the Divine Love of which we have so often written, and without which it is impossible for a soul to obtain this condition or to become a dweller in the Celestial Heavens.

Man, as you have been instructed, was not created with this Love, and could only obtain it by his own longings and aspirations being exercised in the way that the Father had provided—in no other way could these desires for this love be realized. But the great pity is that the first of the human race declined or rather refused to pursue this way, and thought that they were wise enough to know a better way; and in attempting to pursue this way brought about their own fall and the loss of the privilege of obtaining this Love; and in all the long years until the coming of Jesus, no man, after the first created, had the privilege, and hence, it was not possible for them to find any greater happiness than that which might come from their natural love.

At the coming of Jesus, men again had bestowed upon them this great privilege, and a possibility of the knowledge of the way in which the privilege could be exercised. This was not declared to all men, for the territory in which Jesus taught and proclaimed this important truth was very limited, and the great majority of men died without knowing that this gift had been re-bestowed. But God in His goodness and love did not restrict the bestowal of this love to those who might be fortunate enough to learn of it from Jesus and his apostles, but sent His Holy Spirit to implant it in the souls of all men who might be in such condition of soul aspiration and longing as to permit this Love to enter their souls.

---

[40] First Celestial Sphere is immediately above the Seventh Sphere. (Dr. S.)

When spirits became possessed of this knowledge they commenced the work of trying to influence men in such a way that there arose in them a longing for a closer unity with God, and an opening up of the soul perceptions, and as a result many men, in various parts of the world, received this Love in their souls without knowing that it was this Divine Love; but it was, and when these men in their spirit forms entered the spirit world, they soon found that, to some extent, they were possessed of this Love, and it was not difficult for them to listen to the explanations and teachings of those spirits who had received it, as to the truth of its existence.

Now all this may not appear to be of much importance to present man, and hardly worth attention, but my great object in writing in this manner is to show that God had no special or peculiar people, and that it was not even necessary that all peoples should learn from Jesus the fact of this gift, for in such a case, the great majority of mankind could not possibly have heard of this Love while they were yet mortals. No, this was not a necessity, but the knowledge which came to mortals through Jesus enabled them, who possessed it and believed, to the more readily pursue the way to obtaining this Love.

Many spirits had received the benefit of the rebestowal of this Love, or rather the privilege of seeking for and obtaining it, before Jesus came to the spirit world, yet they understood that the greater extent of the possession of this Love was in Jesus; and no spirit now possesses it to the degree that he does.

But whether the souls of mortals or spirits received the knowledge of this truth from Jesus or from the workings of the Holy Spirit in its ministrations, they all know that the seeking for and getting this Divine Love are the only means by which the soul may become an inhabitant of the Celestial Heavens.

I realize that what I have written conflicts with the orthodox belief that it is only through the death and blood of Jesus that men can be saved from their sins and become children of God and at one with Him.

If this belief were true, then by Jesus' sacrifice all men would he saved, irrespective of their obtaining this Divine Love, or only those would be saved who had heard of Jesus and accepted him as their savior. Neither of these propositions is true, for without this Divine Love entering into the soul of a man, it would be impossible for him to partake of the divine nature of the Father, and become fitted to occupy a home in the Celestial Spheres. This love in the soul, whether it is a result of the workings of God's ministering spirits, causing a real soul longing, in conjunction with the Holy Spirit, makes the man of a nature divine, and a redeemed child of God.

Now from what I have said it must not be inferred that the

mission of Jesus, and his work on earth and in the spirit world are not the great things connected with man's redemption, for they are. It was not until Jesus' coming that this Great Gift was rebestowed, and it was not until his declaring this fact and teaching the Great Truth of the New Birth could either mortals or spirits receive this privilege. The ministering spirits could not influence the souls of men to seek for the inflowing of this Divine Love until they had first received it themselves, and understood its existence; and here let me declare a fact, that when Jesus preached to mortals on earth the necessity for the Second Birth, myriads of spirit beings heard these teachings and became possessed of this knowledge.

And to-day, men are attended by hosts of spirits of all kinds, and the sayings and teachings of men are heard by more spirits than men, and the influence of such teachings has its effect upon spirits as upon men, for the spirits of men which are existing in the earth planes are the same spirits substantially, that they were when on earth, and an earthly friend frequently has more influence upon them than do other spirits no matter how high their condition may be.

I am so happy to be able to write you again, and let you know that I have not forsaken you.

I am with you quite often and am trying to help you. Pray more to the Father, and exercise more faith and you will grow in soul development and happiness.

I will not write more now.

So with all my love and blessings, I am your grandmother
Ann Rollins.

What Jesus meant when he said: He that liveth and believeth on me shall never die

August 15th, 1915.

I am here, Jesus.

I was with you tonight at the meeting of the Christians and I saw that you were thinking of several things that I had written and wanted to tell the preacher of my truths. But of course you could not. He took a bit from the Bible which I am credited with having uttered and I did, but I did not mean exactly what he explained it to mean when I said *"he that liveth and believeth on me shall never die"* I meant that the man whose soul was not dead in sin and believed in the truths that I had disclosed, that is that God's Divine Love was waiting to enter into and fill his soul with its essence and substance and that man by prayer and faith received that Divine Love, he should never die. That is he would become immortal as God is immortal.

No mere belief in me as Jesus the man or as the son of God is sufficient to give a man eternal life for while he must believe that I was sent by the Father to proclaim the great truth that He had again bestowed on man, the possibility of obtaining this Divine Love by his prayers and faith, yet unless he believed this and became the possessor of this Divine Love, he could never claim eternal life.

I wish that the preacher would pay more attention to the truths which I taught, that is, those truths which showed men the Fathers Love waiting to be bestowed and the way to obtain it, than to my personality.

I, Jesus as the son of man or of God, do not save any man from his sins and make him at-one with the Father, but the truths which I taught and which were taught me by the Father are the things that save.

I know that the preachers attempt to explain these things by the light of the Bible as they understand that light, but so often it is so obscured that instead of preaching from light they preach from darkness.

For these reasons among others, I am so anxious to declare to you my teachings of these truths that the world may know what truth is, and what the individual must do in order to attain eternal life or immortality.

I know that you are anxious to do this work, and that your soul is trying for the inflowing of this Great Love and the enjoyment of a close communion with the Father. So keep up your courage and trust in the Father, and the end of your worries will soon cease. I will try with all my power to bring about this opportunity for your receiving my messages and believe that very soon I will succeed.

So believe in my love and my desire for your success.
Your brother in Christ,
Jesus.[41]

Jesus: Faith and how it can be obtained

October 10th, 1915.

I am here, Jesus.

I came tonight to tell you that you are nearer the Kingdom than you have been for a long time, and that if you pray to the Father in more earnestness you will soon realize the inflowing of the Divine Love, that will make you free indeed and fit you to enjoy that close communion with the Father that will enable you to forget all your worries and disappointments, and see with your soul perceptions the great truths which I and my followers may endeavor to teach you.

I know, that at times, it seems difficult to grasp the full meaning

---

[41] This message is a composite of two, being published in Vol I and Vol III. (G.J.C.)

True Gospel Revealed anew by Jesus

of faith in the Father and His Love, but if you will earnestly seek for His Love, you will find that there will come to you such a belief in His Wonderful Love and in the nearness of His presence, that you will be free from all doubt.

You have asked me "what is faith" and I will answer: Faith is that which when possessed in its real and true meaning makes the aspirations and longings of the soul a real, living existence; and one so certain and palpable that no doubt will arise as to its reality.

This faith is not the belief that arises from the mere operation of the mind, but that which comes from the opening of the perceptions of the soul, and which enables its possessor to see God in all His Beauty and Love. I do not mean that the possessor of this faith will actually see God in form or feature, for he has none such, but his soul perceptions will be in such condition that all the Attributes of the Father will appear so plainly to him, that they will be as real as anything that he can see with the eyes of the spirit form. Such faith comes only with constant earnest prayer and the reception into the soul of the Divine Love.

No man can be said to have faith who has not this Divine Love. Of course, faith is a progressive quality or essence of the soul, and increases as possession of this Divine Love increases, and is not dependent on anything else. Your prayers call from the Father a response that brings with it faith, and with this faith comes a knowledge of the existence of this Love in your own soul.

Many persons, I know, understand this faith to be a mere belief, but it is greater than belief, and is existing in its true sense only in the soul. Belief may arise from a conviction of the mind, but faith never can. Its place of being is in the soul, and no one can possess it unless his soul is awakened by the inflowing of this Love.

So that, when we pray to the Father to increase our faith it is a prayer for the increase of Love. Faith is based on the possession of this Love, and without it there can be no faith, because it is impossible for the soul to exercise its function when Love is absent from it.

Sometime, as you progress in these writings, you will be in soul condition to understand just what faith is, but until that time your faith will be limited by your possession of this Love.

Well, in my healing of the sick, and the blind and the others of earth, who needed a cure, when I said: "as your faith so be it unto you," I meant that they must believe that the Father had power to bring about the cure; but I did not mean that if their minds merely had the belief that I might cure them, that then they would be cured. Belief was not sufficient of itself, but faith was required.

Faith is not a thing that can be obtained by a mere exercise of the mind, but has to be sought for with the soul perceptions, and when obtained will be enjoyed only by the soul perceptions.

I am with you in all my love and power, for I love you as I told you and desire that you shall become free and happy, so that you can do my work.

With all my love and blessings I will say good night.
Your brother and friend,
Jesus.

Jesus is not God, but an elder brother. Sin has no existence except as it is created by mankind and man must pay the penalties

December 25th, 1915.

I am here, Jesus.

I come tonight, because I see that you are lonesome and feel the need of companionship, and I come to you as a brother and friend to cheer you and make you feel that though you have no mortal friend with you, yet you have a friend in the spirit who is closer than a mortal brother and who loves you with a deep and abiding love.

Today has been one in which the people of your land have celebrated what they suppose is my birthday, and have also worshiped me as one of the triune Godhead, as they believe. But as I have told you before, such worship is all wrong and is very distasteful to me, and only makes me the more anxious and determined that this great falsehood shall be exposed and not believed in any longer.

There is only one God and that is the Father, and He alone, must be worshiped, for He alone can save mortals from the result of their sins and from the consequences of the great fall of the first parents. I do not want men to look upon me as anything more than an elder brother who is filled with the Divine Love of the Father, and very close to Him in the Qualities of Love and Faith.

I am a spirit who is possessed of a knowledge of the Attributes of the Father, that no other spirit is, and yet am only one of his children as you and the rest of mankind are, and for my own brothers to worship me as god makes me very unhappy, seeing that they can have such a little knowledge of the Truths of the Father.

Tomorrow this worship and praise will be continued and I must look upon it with all the distaste that I have, and realize that I am not able to set men aright in their beliefs and worship. Oh, I tell you the harvest is ripe and the laborers are few, but very soon, I hope this truth of the oneness of God, and the brotherhood of myself with all humanity may be revealed to mankind through the messages that you may receive and transmit to men.

The one Great Truth that is the foundation of men's salvation is the New Birth, and the fact that the Divine Love of the Father is waiting for every man to let it enter his soul and make him at one with the Father.

I am with you very often and am trying to impress you with the great necessity of having these truths revealed, as men's souls are longing for the truth, and their intellects are dissatisfied with the present teachings of theology, and the sayings of the Bible in many places. While this is to be deplored, yet the time will come when the light that I came into the world to disclose, will shine for every man who may come within the reach of my teachings.

Last night, I was reading, as you read an article, which advocated the eliminating from the Christian teachings of a large part of the New and nearly the whole of the Old Testament, and the formulating of a faith based entirely on my sayings and the writings of some of the Bible writers. Such a plan is one that should be investigated by the thinking Christians of the present day, and in a modified way adopted.

The only difficulty in carrying out this plan effectively and having it produce the results desired, is that the Bible does not contain many sayings of mine disclosing the truths, and does contain many sayings attributed to me which I never said.

Take that saying over which a controversy is now being had, and which is referred to in another article contained in the book mentioned, that is, that I said, I came not to bring peace to the world, but rather a sword.

Now, while it appears in Matthews' Gospel as coming from me, I never said, it nor used any expression that would convey the meaning that some of the commentators are endeavoring to place upon the words. I never taught war upon a man's neighbors and never at any time was such a thought a part of my teachings to the disciples or to any others.

No, militarism is all wrong, and against all the precepts of truth, and it should not, for a moment, be believed by any Christian or by anyone else that such action was ever advocated by me.

While the truth will cause a division, as I know, among men as to what the truth is, and may even separate and cause bitter thoughts and even hatred to arise in the souls of men towards their fellow men, and even brother may come to dislike brother, yet the accomplishing of such results was not the object of my coming to earth and teaching the truths, but rather are the results of the unavoidable conflict between truth and error. Truth cannot compromise even for the sake of peace, and error will not submit or acknowledge its untruth so long as it can get any mortal to believe in and advocate it.

And because of the great gift of free will to man, truth itself, with all the power and knowledge of the Father back of it, will not compel a man to accept it against his will, and hence, as man is very fallible and thinks and believes according as his finite, mental faculties convince him that a certain thing is or is not true, he will not be willing to surrender his convictions until the truth shall come to him in such a way as to persuade him of its reality; and as men differ so much in the operations of their minds and reasoning faculties there will necessarily be a great division among them as to what is and what is not true. And hence there will arise disputes and hatred and even wars among them in maintaining their respective beliefs and opinions as to what is truth.

While these feelings of discord must necessarily follow the advent of Truth, yet I did not come for the purpose of bringing a sword, but for the purpose of showing men what the Truths are and of causing harmony and belief in these Truths. Never is hatred, nor discord nor war among men justified—no matter what the cause—and if men will only learn the Truth there will never exist such feelings or acts.

Truth is of itself, a thing apart, and admits of no variations or modifications, and, hence, the minds of men must submit to and embrace Truth; it will never accommodate itself to the beliefs of men. One is fixed and unchangeable, and the other is always changeable, and until founded on a knowledge of the Truth, will at sometime or other have to change, because in the end Truth will be established in the hearts and minds of men, so that harmony and peace shall reign in all God's universe.

Error does not exist in the world because God created it or permits it to exist, but solely because there belongs to man an unrestricted will, which controls and influences his thoughts and acts, and which in turn is influenced by the desires and appetites of the mortal.

I know it is said that if God did not permit evil and carnal thoughts and desires to exist in the world, there would be no reason or possibility for man to exercise his will in a way that would bring him to all these feelings of hatred, etc., that I speak of. But this is merely saying that if a man had not the power of free will he would commit no sin and indulge in no error, for you must know that in his creation he was given not only the privilege and the power, under certain conditions, to become a being entirely free from sin—which is merely the violation of God's established laws—but also the privilege and power to violate these laws. As he wills so shall he be.

Everything in nature may be turned into an instrument of harm if the laws which establish the functionings and workings of these things are violated. Sin as an abstract thing, does not exist, but is the result of disobedience to some law whose operations in conformity to its creation must be pursued, and should always be pursued; and men who violate it must suffer the consequences of such violation.

Mortals may not fully realize that every law carries with it a penalty for its violation and this applies to the smallest law in the material universe as well as to the greatest law in the Spiritual Kingdom, and this penalty is just as sure in its operation as is the law itself.

A man may be created, physically, almost perfect and so long as he lives in that way which does not violate some physical law which is operating to keep him in that physical perfection he will suffer no pain or in-harmony in his being; but just as soon as he does violate this law, the penalty therefore asserts itself, and he suffers. Now this arises not because there was existing in the abstract any pain or suffering and had not man violated this law he would never have known that there was such a thing as pain or suffering; but when he did violate the law, there came into operation the penalty which, as I said is always the result of violating the laws of harmony.

And the same principle applies to the moral and spiritual universe. As I said, there is no such thing as sin or error in the abstract, for so long as a mortal may know and follow the truth he will never realize the existence of any such thing as sin or error, but the moment that law of truth is violated, the penalty asserts itself, and man realizes that sin and error do exist; not as an abstract entity, but as a concrete sensitive thing, which will continue to exist, until the violation of that law ceases, and harmony in its operation is again restored, or rather until man in his thoughts and acts is brought into harmony with the operations of the law.

So you see, God did not create or permit sin or error to exist in the sense that it is an independent entity, waiting to influence men to do wrong and violate His laws of perfect harmony, but rather that when men in the exercise of their will, which He will not compel, violates one of His laws, and thereby, as to themselves, interferes with that harmony, they cause the in-harmony to arise, which brings with it the pains and sufferings and sins and errors which are prevalent in the world.

Let men think, if they can, of sin or error in the abstract, and then try to describe it. What is the result? Only vacuity.

So I say, God did not create sin or error, but gave to man that great gift of will, free and not subject to His control, and then man became the responsible being that he is. But in giving man this great gift, He did not relinquish or subordinate His will to that of man nor did He confer upon man the power to change or modify His immutable laws, which He, Himself, will not do. And within the limitations that man can exercise his will, that is when such exercise does not interfere with the will of God or His laws, man may exercise that will with impunity, and without responsibility, as it were, but when in the exercise of that will he infringes upon the will of God or violates one of His laws, then, while man is not controlled in the exercise of his will, yet for such violation he must pay the penalty which such violation calls into operation.

God has decreed that His universe shall be one of harmony in its workings, and that no man shall destroy or interfere with that harmony, and no man can; but as man is a part of that harmony, his every act which tends to interfere therewith—and it does not, except as to himself—brings upon himself the penalty of that interference.

Let a man who has violated this harmony, and thereby as to himself, becomes inharmonious, again get into that harmony, and as to him there would be no sin or error; and let every man do this and there would be no sin or error in all God's universe.

So, I repeat, there is no sin or error, in the abstract, in all the universe, and they appear only when man in the exercise of his will, interferes, as to himself, in the harmony of God's laws. It makes no difference what the cause of this interference may be, or in what way the will of man may have been exercised, or for what reason, to bring about this in-harmony, the effect is the same. Because harmony and in-harmony cannot exist together no matter what the cause may be. No matter that in one case the cause may appear excusable or even, apparently forced on the individual. The excuse for, or apparent justification of the cause will not make what is inharmonious unite and work in unison with God's laws of harmony.

And hence the man whose will may be excused in the way mentioned by reason of heredity, or environments, or want of proper mental or moral instruction is just as much out of harmony with the violated law, as is the man who willfully violates the law. The penalty must be enforced just the same in each case, as the only remedy is the restoration of the harmony.

But there is this difference between the individuals of what may be called the involuntary class and the individuals of the voluntary class, the former will find it easier, and with more rapidity, to get into this condition of harmony than will the latter.

So men must not accuse God in permitting sin and error to exist in the world, as they do not exist, except as man brings them into existence by the wrongful exercise of his will. All sin and error bring their sufferings, and if there were no sufferings, and men were permitted to exercise their wills irrespective of the laws which govern the universe, without incurring the penalties then the only result would be that anarchy would prevail in all God's universe where men live, and in the spirit universe as well, for the will and its great franchise of unrestricted exercise pass with the mortal when he leaves his material body.

So with all my love I will say, good night.
Your brother and friend,
Jesus.

Worship of Jesus as part of the Godhead is wrong and sinful—how much Jesus deplores this erroneous belief of mankind

April 23rd, 1916.

I am here, Jesus.

I come tonight to tell you that you are in a much better condition of soul than you have been for several days, and the inflowing of the Divine Love has been working to-day in greater abundance in your soul.

I do not intend to finish my message tonight as it is rather late and you are not exactly in the condition to receive it. But turn your thoughts more to God and pray in more earnestness and very soon will come to you the power and soul perception which will enable you to receive my message as I desire to deliver it to you.

Today has been one when mortals—and I mean those who profess to be followers of me—have offered their worship and songs of praise to me and to God, but I am sorry to say, that He has been worshiped in a secondary sense, and I brought into prominence as the Savior of mankind, and as the important one of the three that constitutes the Godhead. How wrong and sinful this all is; and how I deplore these erroneous beliefs and understandings of men. If they would only know that I am not God, and no part of the Godhead, but only a son and spirit filled with His Divine Love, and one having knowledge of Him, and His plans for the salvation of mankind, they would get nearer to God in their worship, and receive more of His Divine Love in their souls and partake more of His Divine nature.

But I realize that this belief in me as God, and that my death and sacrifice on the cross were necessary to their salvation, will be hard to eradicate, and that many who now live will pass into the spirit world before the truths which I come to teach and declare will be published to the world.

We must make more speed in our work of writing and receiving these messages, for the importance of the world knowing the truths as regards me, and the true and only plan of salvation is now pressing and must be shown to man in order for him to turn to the Father's love and gain an entrance into the Kingdom. I want you to give more time to our writings, and instead of reading those books of philosophy and the speculations of, what are supposed to be, wise theologians and philosophers and scientists, let your hours from your business cares be devoted to my communications and those of the other writers of the Celestial Spheres.

Of course, I do not intend that you shall not permit the dark spirits to write on the nights that you have set apart for them, because such prohibition would prevent much good from being accomplished. These spirits are greatly benefitted by having the opportunity to write, and many of them have been greatly helped thereby, and have been turned to the light and instructed to seek for the Divine Love of the Father. The spirits here, who are engaged in the work of instructing and helping these spirits have rescued many from their condition of darkness and sufferings, and have shown them the way to light and to their salvation. The work is a great and important one and must not stop; and here let me say that this work will be a part of your duty and also your pleasure, as long as you may live a mortal life. You will, undoubtedly be the means of helping mortals to see the truth, but your work among these dark spirits will be even greater, and the harvest more abundant, and when you come to the spirit world you will be surprised and gratified at the great host that will meet you, giving you thanks for the great help and assistance that you rendered them. Yours is a wonderful work and is now spoken of and wondered at in the spirit world. Well, I will not write more tonight, but must come soon and finish my message, as I have many yet to write.

In my Father's house are many mansions, as I said, when on earth, and for your consolation and that of your two friends, I am preparing for each of you such a mansion; not as you may suppose by erecting in the Celestial Heavens actual houses for your reception, but by helping to build in your souls that development of the Divine Love and the nature of the Father that will, when you came over, make your souls in that condition that will necessarily and absolutely cause the formation of these mansions to receive you. No one else can build these mansions for you, only your own soul development. But while this is true, yet these Celestial Heavens have a locality and surroundings and atmosphere that will contain all those things that will give your mansions the proper settings. The fields, and trees and waters and sky, and all these things that you in your earth life find necessary to your happiness and peace are in the Celestial Heavens, only quite different from those that you are acquainted with.

So, believe what I say, and believing trust me and my love, and you will never be forsaken. A man's life on earth is but a span; but in our homes eternity means immortality, with always progress and increasing happiness.

So with my love and blessings, I will say good night.
Your friend and brother,
Jesus.

The Vicarious Atonement

The belief in the efficacy of the vicarious atonement of Jesus by his death and crucifixion by the churches has caused much harm to mankind and the loss of the True Way to the Celestial Kingdom

March 18th, 1916.

I am here, St. John, Apostle of Jesus.

I wish to write tonight on a subject that is of importance to the members of the orthodox churches as to the belief in the efficacy of the atonement of Jesus by his death and crucifixion.

All the orthodox believe and their preachers and evangelists teach in their sermons and addresses, and the teachers of Bible classes instruct their students, that the blood of Jesus and his death on the cross were the two factors in his career on earth that save men from their sins and satisfy the great penalty of death which overhangs them, because of man's first disobedience and the sins that followed there from.

Well, this doctrine has prevailed in the beliefs and teachings of the church ever since the church became established by the convention that met in pursuance of the orders of Constantine, when the books that now constitute the Bible were given the sanction of the church as canonical. Before this time some of the early fathers believed in the doctrine of the atonement as above stated, and the controversies between them and others who did not subscribe to this doctrine were very bitter, and at times, very unchristian according to the Christianity that prevailed among the early followers of the Master, or according to his teachings.

From that time until the present, although the great Roman church has been seceded from and reforms have been made by churches founded on such reforms, this doctrine has been incorporated in and believed by most of the churches, no matter what name they may have adopted and what form of government they may have prescribed.

This doctrine constitutes the foundation principles of these various bodies of church entity, and to-day, these principles are as much a part of faith and teachings of the churches as they ever were in all the centuries that have passed.

Of course, with this cardinal doctrine there have also become incorporated in these faiths and teachings certain other principles, which apply more to the individual members of the church than to the church itself as a body. I mean belief in the truth that there is a close relationship between God and the individual which may be established by prayer and the longings of the soul for the inflowing of God's love, and the regeneration of the nature of man by the influence of this love by the Father.

But in these latter days, this truth has been known to and its workings experienced by a comparatively few of those who call themselves orthodox Christians. The large majority has depended upon the belief in the doctrine that Jesus, by his sacrifice and death, paid the debt which man owed to God; and when the members of the church in an intellectual belief assert that they believe in and accept Jesus as their Savior because he paid the debt, and by the shedding of his blood washed away their sins and made them at one with the Father, and thereby became saved from the wrath of the Father, and in a moment become the truly redeemed and accepted children of God, and that as long as they maintain that belief and attend to their duties as such members and observe the regulations of the church, they are safe and fitted for the enjoyment of heaven and the presence of the Father.

They also believe that unless a man accepts Jesus as his Savior, in the way I have mentioned, that man will be eternally lost, and in the beliefs and teachings of some of these members, will be sent to hell to be eternally damned and punished.

Well one view of this doctrine is just as true as the other, or rather just as untrue because both of these phases of belief have no foundation in fact, and are not in accord with the teachings of the Master, or with the fact as I know it to be, not from any mere belief but from personal experience and observation.

Oh, how the pure teachings of the Master have been distorted and made the means of preventing so many human souls from reaching the heaven of happiness that they wished for, and that they thought would be theirs when they should give up their mortal lives.

This doctrine, so long believed, has worked the damnation of many a man, as regards his soul development and his becoming at one with the Father and reaching the heavens that are prepared for those who obtain that soul union with the Father.

I know it may seem surprising to some, who are really, true, believers in this doctrine and, as they think, in the truths of God and the teachings of Jesus, which are believed to be infallibly contained in the Bible, that I announce the falsity of these beliefs and their utter ineffectiveness in enabling these sincere people to obtain that which they so earnestly desire.

But such is truth, and truth never changes, never compromises with untruth, and never permits the erroneous beliefs of a really sincere mortal to swerve in one iota from the results and consequences of that false belief. And the great injury that this false doctrine has done to humanity, and is now doing, will continue in the world to come, until the belief in truth shall supersede the belief in that which is false. And thus not everyone who shall say "Lord, Lord," will enter into the Kingdom of Heaven.

These false beliefs have operated in two ways to injure man and render him unfit for an entrance into the Kingdom. First, by the belief that brings about the injury that results from the positive operation of error, which is great; and next by the want of belief in the truth, which prevents progress in the acquirement of those qualities which belong to and are necessary parts of that truth.

When men believe in the doctrine that I have stated they become satisfied, and, knowingly or not, remain in a state of false security, not attempting to develop the soul qualities, which are the only ones that are in relationship with God. Their mental beliefs are strong and may increase in strength, but their soul communions with the Father and their growth and expansion in the soul development, becomes stagnant and, as it were, dead.

This is the great injury that these false beliefs do to the man and to the spirit. I mean in his individual capacity, for it must be known as a truth, that the salvation of man or his soul progress towards an at-onement with the Father is an individual matter solely, and men as aggregations or in church communities are not redeemed from sin, nor as such, can they have any relationship with the Father or receive His Divine Love, which is the only salvation.

There is only one possible way in which man can come in unison and at-onement with the Father, and thereby fitted to enjoy or inhabit the mansions in His Kingdom, which Jesus spoke of when on earth, and that is the way that will make the soul of man like the soul of the Father, and a partaker of his Divine Qualities of Love and Life. No belief that will not bring about this uniting and commingling, as it were can possibly make the soul of man a partaker of these qualities that are a part of the soul of God.

Then let man consider for a moment what possible connection there can be between these Soul Qualities of God and the death and blood of Jesus. God is the creator of life and death, and also of blood and flesh, and He can destroy as well as create. Had the sins of man called for the sacrifice of that which was mere flesh and blood, or the extinguishment of a life that God had created in order to pay the penalty of that sin, then a God who demanded such a payment—and this implies of course, that such a God was wrathful and could only be appeased by something that He could not of and by Himself obtain—would not possibly be satisfied with that which He had created and over which He still had absolute control, and which He could destroy and make non-existent at any time He pleased. Jesus' life was already a possession of God, and when he surrendered that life he did not give to God anything that he did not already own and could not have taken. And when his blood flowed on the cross, it was not that which God could not have made flow at any time and in any manner.

So the absurdity of such a doctrine is too apparent for serious consideration. For its logical meaning is that God was demanding a debt that had long been unpaid, all wrathful and insatiable, and would be satisfied only with the death of a living being and the flowing of his blood; and that death and that flow of blood in one way or manner only, namely, on the cross. And yet with all this demand that has been sounding down the ages for centuries, relentlessly and unpityingly, He became satisfied and His wrath assuaged by seeing His own creature die—and that creature His best beloved son—and by hearing the trickling of the blood of that creature from a wooden cross; by all which, the life and the blood being already His to let live or destroy as He might see fit, man became at one with Him.

The simple reduction of such a proposition is that God, in order to pay a debt that was owing to Him, accepted in payment thereof that which was already His, and which no power or being in all His universe could have taken from Him.

Now, I say all this reverently as your preachers say, but the fact is, that the mere assertion of such a doctrine, as I have been dealing with, is so blasphemous that no treatment of it, showing its falsity, could be irreverent.

And again, the absurdity of believing that God demanded that Jesus should die on the cross as one of the necessary accompaniments of his death, in order to carry out God's plan for this death and make the payment satisfactory, is so apparent and absurd, that I and all of us spirits in the Kingdom of the Father wonder that mortals can believe such an unreasonable dogma.

To follow this absurd proposition to its logical conclusion, it was necessary not only, in order that the debt might be paid, that Jesus should die on the cross, but that Judas should become the traitor, that the Jews should clamor for his death and that Pilate should pronounce the sentence. These were all necessary means to the satisfaction of the debt, and being so, why is it then that Judas and Pilate and the Jews are not saviors of mankind also, even if you say in a secondary sense. Jesus could not have clamored for his own death, or erected his own cross or nailed himself thereto, or pierced his side with a spear in order that the blood might flow, for if he had done this he would have been a suicide; but it may be, there would have been more of the elements of the payment of a debt in that method of dying than in the way in which his death was brought about.

True Gospel Revealed anew by Jesus

No, I tell you, I, John, who loved the Master more than all the others and who was closer to him, who was with him when he was nailed to the cruel cross, which I think of with horror, and who was among the first to take his body from the tree and first felt his blood upon my hands—tell you that the death of Jesus on the cross did not pay any debt that man owed to God, nor did his blood wash away the sins of any man. And oh, the pity of it all is that mortals for all these long years have believed that they were saved by his sacrifice and blood, and by such belief have never come any nearer to the Master or in at-onement with the Father.

As I and others have written you, the only way in which man can be saved from his sins and become in at-onement with the Father, is by the New Birth which the Master has described to you as being the result of the flowing into the soul of a man of the Divine Love of the Father, and the disappearing of everything that tends to sin and error. As this Love flows into a man's soul it permeates that soul as does leaven the batch of dough, and that soul partakes of this Divine Love and thereby becomes like the Father in His Divine Nature, and fitted to inhabit His Kingdom.

Now, you can readily see that there can be no possible relationship existing between the death of Jesus on the cross and his blood, and the giving to the soul of a man those Divine Qualities that belong to the Father's Nature. These Qualities are not imparted to man by death and blood, but by life and love and faith which comes with that Love—and here when I say faith, I do not mean the mere intellectual belief of which I have spoken.

As we have before written, when the first parents were created they were not given this Divine Love, but the mere possibility of obtaining it upon their seeking for it in the Way that God had provided. It was not forced upon them, but it was optional with them whether they would receive it and become fitted to inhabit the Kingdom of Heaven. When they committed their act of disobedience they forfeited this privilege, and, as to it, died, and were left without a mediator between themselves and God. And here I don't mean any mediator in the way of paying a debt, for they owed no debt to God—they were merely, as you mortals might say, disinherited children; and the only mediator that man needed after that time was one through whom might come the Glorious Tidings that the Father had changed His Will, or forgiven the disobedience to the extent of restoring his original state, which is the re-bestowal of the privilege of obtaining into their souls His Divine Love.

And, in this sense, never was there any mediator between God and man until the coming of Jesus and his announcing to man that the Father had changed His Will and had restored to mankind the great privilege of partaking of His Divine Nature and Immortality. And thus, as in the first man, Adam, all men died, so in the man Jesus, were all men made alive. And Jesus was the mediator not only in declaring to man the re-bestowal of this Great Gift of the Divine Love and Immortality, but, also, in showing the Way by which men could and must seek for that Gift in order to possess It.

The Great Gift of God to man was not Jesus, but the potentiality of obtaining the Divine Love of the Father and thus becoming Divine and fitted to reside in the mansions of the Kingdom of Heaven.

And thus Jesus became the Resurrection and the Life and brought Immortality to light. How much greater a savior than by paying a supposed debt by his death and blood.

No, he is the savior of man by his living and his teachings, for he was the first to receive this Divine Love and to become Divine himself, and the first fruits of the resurrection. We have explained to you before in detail, some of the truths that I have declared in this message, and it is not necessary to further explain them here.

In closing, I wish to declare with all the emphasis that I possess, arising from a knowledge based upon the teachings of the Master and my personal experience as a possessor of this Divine Love and a partaker of the Father's Divine Nature, that no vicarious atonement of Jesus, nor the shedding of his blood, saves any man from sin or makes him a redeemed child of the Father, or fits him for a home in the mansions of the Celestial Spheres.

With a love that can come only from a redeemed and Divine nature I love all mankind, and am working to help them find the way to life and immortality and happiness beyond the conception of mortals or spirits who have not received this New Birth of the Divine Love of the Father.

I have written enough for tonight and you are tired.

So my dear brother, with all my love and the blessings of a heart filled with the Love of the Father, I am

Your brother in Christ,
John.

What is the use in believing in the sacrifice of Jesus on the cross as salvation from sin

June 4th, 1916.

I am here, St. Luke, writer of the third Gospel that was.

I desire tonight to write a short message on the question:—"What is the use in believing in the sacrifice of Jesus on the cross as a salvation from sin?" I know that this belief is at the foundation of the so-called Christian religion and is the cornerstone of most of the churches as they now exist, but as such a belief is false and does not effectuate the object claimed for it, I must declare the utter uselessness of such a belief and the great harm it is doing to mankind.

A thing is just what its internal qualities make it. I mean by this, what the ingredients of its composition causes it to really be, and these ingredients cannot be supplied unless they have in themselves, an existence of those qualities which are sufficient to make that composition just what is necessary and required to produce the thing in its genuine substance.

This applies to things of the soul, and unless the qualities of the soul are such as to eliminate the elements of sin and everything that prevents that soul from coming into harmony with the laws of God, that soul will continue in sin and separation from the Divine nature of the Father.

The soul is in each individual an entity, which is distinct and separate from the soul of every other man, and is dependent for its qualities, not in what that other man may do or not do, but upon that which will make those qualities like, or in substance the same as the qualities of that thing which is desired or sought for, as a necessary acquirement in making the substance of that possessed and that desired, similar.

According to the belief of which I speak, the sacrifice mentioned causes the salvation of man by appeasing the wrath of God and lifting from man the condemnation under which he was suffering, and by accomplishing such an object man became a new creature in his soul qualities, and was given the qualities that are required to make him like unto the Father, and, therefore, he (man), has nothing further to be done for him in order to relieve him entirely from the possession of this sin, and from the demands of God—the sacrifice is sufficient to bring about these results.

But as we have told you, and as even the followers or possessors of these beliefs assert, Love is the great necessity to effectuate the union between God and man, and this Love must dwell in the soul of man as well as in the bosom of the Father, waiting its bestowal on man.

It can be obtained only by sincere seeking on the part of man, and no other way is provided by which it can be obtained. The sacrifice or the shedding of blood does not cause the inflowing of this Love into the souls of men, and the mere fact, even if it were true, that an angry God had been appeased, or debt paid, or a mortal is redeemed would not cause this Love to become a part of the souls of men.

I know that it is asserted that these things, in some mysterious way, reconciles God to man, and thereby causes the acceptance of man by God, and when that is done, all the sins and depravity of a man's soul immediately become no longer a part of his soul's qualities, and the soul is perfected and its condition is that which enables it to become of a nature like that of the Father.

But a difficulty with this conclusion is that only Jesus and God are the one that are participating in this great work of redemption, and man is eliminated from the necessity of doing anything, except to believe that the sacrifice is sufficient to cause his full salvation, and all that it means.

How this belief that the sacrifice or the flowing of the blood can make a sinful soul pure, or become a partaker of the Divine nature of the Father, has never been explained by the teachers of the Christian doctrines in any way that is consonant with reason, and cannot be so explained, for the one reason that is of itself sufficient, and that is, that the sacrifice does not work such a consummation. No one man, not even Jesus, can do the work of another or for another that will produce the results necessary to insure the reconciliation mentioned.

It is claimed that Jesus died to save all men from their sins, or that he that believeth on the name of Jesus shall be saved from their sins. But the question again arises, how—in what way? Can it be argued that his death made the impure man clean, even though he believed it did? Can his blood shed on Calvary cleanse the soul of any man? I know that it is claimed that in some mysterious way it does, but no one explains the how. Can anyone of the great theological teachers tell you by what mysterious or other process this blood operates on the Mercy or Love of God, so that the sinner is saved from his sins or from the penalties which the violation of God's laws entail? I know that they cannot, and for the same reason as before stated, that the blood does not accomplish these results. Then what is the use in accepting such belief when it cannot be understood or explained, and is the blindest of blind beliefs of mortals?

No, no sacrifice of Jesus, no shedding of his blood and no vicarious atonement as it is called, can save a human soul from sin, or bring it into the Love of the Father, or cause it to become a partaker of the Divine Nature. We have already in previous messages declared and explained to you what and what only brings to men salvation, and I will not here repeat, but will say this, that "except a man be born again, he cannot enter into the Kingdom of Heaven." nothing less is sufficient and nothing added to can in any way bring about man's salvation.

I will not write more tonight, as what I have said should cause men to think and understand upon what false and baseless foundation they stand when they rely upon the belief in Jesus sacrifice to save them from their sin.

With all my love and blessings I will say, good night.
Your brother in Christ.
Luke.

Denies the vicarious atonement—this belief doing much harm—Bible contains many false statements

October 26th, 1915.

I am here, St. Paul.

Yes I am and I want to say just a few words. The book on the "vicarious atonement" (by Pastor Russell) that you have been reading—about the ransom price and the blood of Jesus and the sacrifice on the cross—as to these things is all wrong, and you must not believe what it says.

Well, I know the Bible ascribes to me the teaching of these things, but I never did; and I tell you now, as I have before told you, that the Bible cannot be depended on as containing things that I wrote, for there are many additions to what I wrote, and many omissions of what I wrote; and so with the others whose names are stated as the writers of the New Testament. Many things contained in that book were never written by any of the alleged authors of the book. The writings of any of us are not in existence, and have not been for many centuries; and when they were copied and recopied, great additions and omissions were made, and, at last, doctrines and dogmas were interpolated that we never at anytime believed or wrote.

I have to say this, and I wish to emphasize my statement with all the conviction and knowledge of the truth that I possess: Jesus never paid any debt of man by his death or his blood or vicarious atonement. When Jesus came to earth his mission was given him as he progressed in his soul development, and not until his anointing was he wholly qualified to enter upon his mission or the work thereof.

The mission was twofold, namely:—to declare to mankind that the Father had rebestowed the Divine Love which Adam or the first parents had forfeited; and secondly, to show man the way by which that love could be obtained, so that the possessor of it would become a partaker of the Divine Nature, and Immortal.

Jesus had no other mission than this, and any statement by the preacher or teacher or church doctrines or dogmas or by the Bible, that his mission was other than I have stated, is untrue. He emphatically never claimed that he came to earth to pay any ransom for mankind, or to save them by his death on the cross, or to save them in any other way than by teaching them that the great gift or privilege of obtaining immortality had been bestowed upon them, and that by prayer and faith they could obtain it.

The author of the book is all wrong in his theories, but if you accept the statement of the Bible as true, he makes a very forcible presentation of the Scriptures. But the Scriptures do not contain the truth on this subject, except by the New Birth that Jesus taught, and that being so, his explanations and theories must fall to the ground. Some day and that very soon, he will come to the spirit world and have an awakening, which will cause him much suffering and remorse, because of his teachings of the false doctrines that his book contains.

I did not intend to write so long a letter when I commenced, but your questions required answers, and I could not give you answers in less space. But nevertheless if you shall obtain any benefit from what I have written, the time consumed will be compensated for.

I must stop now, but will come again sometime.
Your brother in Christ,
St. Paul.

Affirms what Paul wrote about the vicarious atonement

October 26th, 1915.

I write to corroborate what Paul said, both as to the errors of the author of the book (Pastor Russell) that you have been reading, and also of the Bible, upon which he bases his arguments and conclusions.

There are some of the epistles credited to me, and I did write some to the members of the church, over which I had supervision, but the epistles as contained in the Bible are in many particulars untrue and conflicting with my beliefs, then and now, and I never wrote such conflicting statements. I never wrote that Jesus paid a ransom for mankind, or that his death on the cross saved men from the death which they inherited from Adam, or anything of the kind that insinuated that men were saved by any act of Jesus which satisfied the wrath of God, or, as the author said, satisfied Divine justice.

Justice was not an element in the Plan of man's salvation, only Love and Mercy, and the desire of the Father that man become reconciled to Him—that is, come to Him and receive the Great Gift of His Divine Nature. No blood shedding or death of Jesus or vicarious atonement could have accomplished this, for none of these things would affect the soul development of a man. The matter of soul development is an individual matter, and can only be accomplished when man seeks for the Great Gift of Divine Love, and receives it in his soul and develops it. Then he becomes a partaker of the Divine Nature and one with the Father.

How deplorable that man will teach this erroneous doctrine of blood atonement. How very much harm it is doing to mankind and to spirits as well, for many spirits come into the spirit world with their beliefs so firmly established in this doctrine that they frequently remain for years in that condition of belief, and consequent stagnation of their soul's progress, and of their obtaining a knowledge of the truth.

This author, when he comes to the spirit world, will undoubtedly have to pay the penalty of his erroneous teachings, and very probably that penalty will be that he will have to unteach them, if I may use the word, to all the spirits who when on earth believed in and followed his teachings of these false doctrines.

But some day men will know the truth, and the truth will make them free. You must try your best to get in condition to take the messages which the Master desires to write so they can be published to the world.

I am, your brother in Christ,
St. Peter.

Various Subjects

What men can do to eradicate war and evil from men's souls. Jesus never came to bring a sword but to bring peace through his teachings

December 24th, 1916.

I am here, Jesus.

I desire to say that I was with you tonight at the church, and listened to the preacher's sermon,[42] and was somewhat surprised that he should have declared that all the wars and persecutions and outrages that, in the manner described, have been perpetrated on mankind since my coming, can be ascribed to my coming and my teachings. I, of course, can only resent the imputation and declare that the preacher has misconceived the cause of these wars and persecutions, and to charge that they are due to my truths or the truths that I taught, is not only an injustice to me, but a great injury to the truths and objects of my mission to mankind. Never did I attempt by force or constraint to compel a human soul to believe in my truths, or to became a follower of me, in or out of the church.

My mission on earth was to show men the Way to the Father's Love, and to declare to them the Great Gift of this Love, and also to break down and destroy the erroneous beliefs and ignorance that then existed among men as what was necessary, in order to seek for and obtain this Love of the Father and their own salvation. And so far as the truths, moral or spiritual, which I taught, antagonized the false beliefs and practices of men, there was and necessarily would be a conflict in the thoughts and lives of those who followed me and those who persisted in their existing beliefs. To this extent I brought a sword into the world, but it was not the sword that called for bloodshed and murder and persecutions. It was the sword that pierced men's souls, where this great conflict should and must be fought to the end.

No nation can be more spiritual in its government or in its treatment of other nations, than are the individuals composing it, spiritual. The nation cannot be greater than or different from the individuals who control it, be such control centered in one or more individuals, or in a secular or religious head. The ruler, if he be not a real follower of me, although he may claim to be, cannot in his acts or deeds,

---

[42] This sermon by Dr. Mitchell was entitled: "The Great Paradox—Jesus the Prince of Peace and the Troubler" (G.J.C.)

attribute to me the results of the carrying into action his thoughts and desires and ambition.

The present war,[43] of which the preacher spoke with such horror and lamentation, is not due to my coming into the world as an iconoclast or destroyer of sin and error, but to the fact that men refused to be controlled or persuaded by my doctrines of peace, and acted because of the sin and evil desires and immoral ambition that they possessed and permitted to control them. The sword which he claims I brought into the world did not cause these sinful and inhuman desires and ambitions to manifest themselves in the form of war and all the evils that follow it. No, this war is not a part of my warfare or the plan of the Father to bring salvation to mankind.

The cause is this and only this: The exercise by men in control of the nations of their desires for increased power and territory and subjugation of nations, together with their sinful cravings for what they call glory and unsatisfied ambition. Had they understood my warfare, each of these men would have found his enemy in himself and nowhere else, and the Great War would be a war of the soul and not the war of nations.

Each nation claims that its war is right and that God is on its side, and prays to that God to assist it in overcoming its enemies. But I want to say here, and it may astonish those who believe that if they conceive that they are in the right and pray to God for success that their prayers will be answered, that God hears only the prayers of the righteous, or of the sinner who prays for mercy and salvation. Never in all the history of mankind has God responded to the prayers of men or nations to assist in the destruction of other men or nations, and this, notwithstanding the accounts in the Old Testament of the many times that he was supposed to have helped the Jews to destroy their enemies.

If men, for a moment, will think that God is a God of Love and that all people are His children, the equal recipients of His Love and Care, they will realize that His Love would not permit Him to sacrifice the happiness or well being of one class of His children to satisfy the desires of revenge or hatred or outraged justice as they conceive it, of another class of His children. In all the beliefs of this kind, men have misconceived God and His Nature—with men like other creatures His powers are governed by God's immutable Laws, and those laws are no respecters of persons. Man was given a free will which he could exercise righteously or sinfully and God does not forcibly control such exercise, but the same exercised rightly or wrongly is subject to law, which imposes penalties or rewards according as the law is violated or obeyed.

This war, which so many mortals believe and declare is a

---

[43] World War—1914—1918. (Dr. S.)

punishment inflicted on men because of their sins and disobedience—that is, that it was specially caused by God because of such condition of men—and some expounders of the Bible teach that it was prophesied centuries ago—this war, I say, is solely the result of the sinful conditions and workings of men's souls and thoughts, and the natural effect of the causes that men themselves created, and the exact workings of the laws that such causes brought into operation. And in a similar condition, where the same causes exist, laws will invariably operate, wars will occur and recur until the possibility of the causes cease to exist.

God never ceases to love and care for mankind and always He desires that men shall be happy and at one with Himself, and that they shall exercise their wills in accordance with His Will and His Laws; but just as certainly does He never by compulsion or force endeavor to compel men to exercise their wills in a manner that is not voluntary with them. Should He do this, men would cease to be the greatest of His Creation and incapable of giving Him that voluntary love and obedience which only is acceptable to Him.

But from what I have said, it must not be inferred that the Father is indifferent to men's sufferings and the calamities that wars bring upon mankind, for He is not; and, if, in His Wisdom, He saw that it would be for the lasting good of the men who are engaged in the present war,[44] that He should intervene by the mere force of His Powers and end the war, He would do so. But in that Wisdom He sees, that there is a good which men should have, greater and more eternal than their mere physical and material good, and that greater good cannot be obtained by them through His suddenly bringing this war to an end without regard to their souls, and thoughts and desires. The law of compensation must work, as well for nations as for individuals, even though apparently the innocent suffer as well as the guilty.

On earth, as men are now constituted—that is in their condition of sin and disobedience to the laws of their being—exact justice cannot be expected and is not received, because this justice is the subject of men's dispensation and not that of God. A man is influenced by his desires, which in turn, control his will and results in his acts and deeds, which must of necessity, bring their results. These results can be avoided only by absence of deeds, and these by a different exercise of the will, and this, by the change of desire. So when a man so desires and wills, God will not set aside the law of compensation, and cause results to follow that are not the consequences of such desire and will.

But God is always willing that these evil results shall have no existence, and through the influence of His Love and Holy Spirit is calling

---

[44] World War—1914—1918. (Dr. S.)

men to learn the way to wholly prevent the possibility of these results coming to them, either as individuals or as nations. He has provided the Way and is teaching men the knowledge thereof, through and by which the causes that produce these harmful results may be utterly destroyed and prevented from ever arising to bring to them, the deplorable results such as are manifested in the present war.

God will not interfere by His mere fiat to cause the one side or the other of those who are engaged in this war of bloodshed and carnage to become victorious. The law of compensation must work and as the leaders of the respective nations have sown so must the nations reap, and in this the innocent must suffer in this reaping, because as conditions are, the law could not work its fulfillment unless all within the scope of its workings should feel its operation. But the Father and the hosts of His angels and the spirits of men are working to bring this terrible catastrophe to an end. You have written long, and it is late, so I will postpone the further consideration of the subject to another time. Believe that I am with you and love you and will sustain you in your desires to do my work.

Your brother and friend,
Jesus.

Comments on Jesus' message on the cause of war

December 24th, 1916.

I am here, your own true and loving Helen.

You have received quite a wonderful message from the Master tonight and it will cause some surprise, no doubt, to many who believe that God confers a special dispensation for every prayer, irrespective of the workings of His laws.

But the Master has clearly shown that this belief is erroneous, and that man, himself, can prevent God from answering prayer. I do not mean that it will not be possible for Him to do so, if He should choose to exercise His power, but that man by his own will and deeds places himself in such a condition that God would have to violate His own laws to make a response in accordance with the prayers of men, which He will not do.

I know that you will find the message very interesting, but not so much so as what will follow, for the one places man in the condition of having to depend on himself without expectation of the Father's help, and the other will show that the Father is not only willing and ready to help men in their distress, but also the way in which He will help, and the absolute certainty of that help being given.

Your own true and loving

Helen.

Comments on Jesus' message on the cause of war

December 25th, 1916.

I am here, Elias, Prophet of Old, (Elijah). I will write a short message tonight, as it is late and you are tired. Well, I desire to say that the message you received from the Master contains some of the most important truths affecting the relationship of God to man in his worldly or material living.

Every Truth that was uttered has in it an element which shows that man to a certain extent must expect and know that God will not interfere with the Law of Compensation as to its effects and results. Only will He help man to remove the causes that so certainly entail the results, [45] and the sooner men know this and more thoroughly understand it, will they become able to avoid the consequences of sin and the violation of law, and also understand that no prayer will cause God to respond, where a suspension or setting aside of his Laws or their workings are necessary. He will respond to prayer, where that prayer asks the removal of causes, but never when it applies only to effects.

This Truth men should learn and in their prayers ask that those things or causes which in compliance with the Law of Compensation bring about results that are harmful to them be removed, or eliminated from their acts and deeds as well as from their desires. I could write a long message on this subject but will not do so now, as you are not just in condition to receive it. I will come soon and write at length. So with my love I will say, good night.

Your brother in Christ,
Elias.[46]

There are no devils and no Satan considered as real persons and fallen angels

January 3rd, 1916.

I am here, Jesus.

---

[45] Causes are for example the causes of sin. As an example, if someone is an alcoholic, God will assist to remove or lessen the desire for drink, if the mortal truly wishes and prays for this assistance. However the results of alcoholism are not likely to be removed, as this is part of the Law of Compensation. So praying for relationships to be healed, which were damaged as a result of alcoholism or healing a damaged liver may not be effective, unless and until the primary cause is totally resolved. And even then, it is possible it may not be resolved if it is part of the compensation due. (G.J.C.)

[46] This message is a composite of two, being published in Volume I and Volume III. (G.J.C.)

I am with you tonight to warn you against letting any doubt enter your mind or heart, as to our actually writing to you, for we and none other are actually in communication with you.

The book that you read (Pastor Russell—On Spiritualism) is a snare and a lie, for there are no angels who have become devils as the author of that book declares. Never were there any angels who through ambition or any other reason revolted against the power of government of God, and thereby lost their estate as angels. Never was there any Lucifer, and never were there any angels who were thrown from the battlements of heaven into hell, as it has been written and as I told you before, there are no devils and no Satan, considered as real persons and fallen angels.

The only spirits in the spirit world are those who at one time were mortals and who lived lives on earth, shorter or longer, and whenever angels are mentioned in the Bible, or rather in the New Testament in places which contain my sayings or those of the apostles, and I mean those sayings which were actually said, the word angel always refers to the spirit of some mortal who had passed the line between life and death as commonly understood.

I desire to tell you of these things at large very soon and to instruct you as to who were the angels of God that are supposed to have had an existence prior to the creation of man and of the world; and who the inhabitants of heaven were before the Spirit of God entered into man and caused him to become a living soul as the Bible says. But the time is not yet ripe for me to instruct you in these matters, because there are so many more important truths to be first taught you, truths which are vital to man's salvation and happiness to those on earth and in the spirit world.

But this you must believe, that no devils ever write you or in any manner manifest to or through any of the numerous mediums who are used to show the existence of spirits of men in the spirit world, no matter whether these mediums be good or evil. There are spirits of all kinds just as there are mortals of all kinds, having all the traits and characteristics of mortals, and some of these spirits may be justly called wicked or evil spirits, and even devils. But they are nothing more or less than spirits such as I describe.

I know that the belief of the majority of mankind is that there are such things as devils and that they are independent creations of God, made by Him to tempt and inflict all kind of trouble and unhappiness on mortals, and because of the great number of years that these beliefs have existed, and the fact that many of the churches still teach that such devils do exist, and are at all times trying to tempt and injure men, it is hard and will be difficult to induce men to believe that there are no such things as devils, which is the truth.

I know that the Bible in many places speaks of my casting devils out of men, and of men being possessed of devils, and of the apostles casting out devils, and of their not being able to cast out some of these devils, but I tell you now that the Bible is all wrong in this regard, and the writers and translators of the Bible never understood what the word devil, as used in these various instances, meant or was intended to mean. As I have told you, there was never any devil or devils in the sense mentioned and taught by the churches, and consequently, they never could have possessed mortals nor have been cast out of them. It is true, that by the workings of the law of attraction, and the susceptibility of mortals to the influence of spirit powers, mortals may become obsessed by the spirits of evil—that is evil spirits of men who once lived on earth—and this obsession may become so complete and powerful that the living mortal may lose all power to resist this influence of the evil spirits, and may be compelled to do things that the mortal will not desire to do, and to show all the evidence of a distorted mind, and present appearances of a lost will power, as well as of the ability to exercise the ordinary powers given him by his natural creation. And in these instances referred to of casting out devils, wherever they occurred, and they did occur in some of the instances mentioned, the only devils that existed were the evil spirits who had possessed these mortals.

And this obsession obtains today just as it did then, for the same laws are in operation now as were in existence then, and many a man is in a condition of evil life and disturbed mind from the obsession of these evil spirits; and if there were any men of today in that condition of soul development and belief that my disciples were in, they could cast out these so called devils just as the disciples cast them out in the Bible days.

But men have not this faith, though there are many who have been blessed with the inflowing of the Holy Spirit; but they have not the belief that such work as the disciples performed can be performed by them now, and, in fact, the most of them believe that it would be contrary to God's will to attempt to exercise such powers, and hence, they never attempt to do such work.

But when men learn that in all ages God is the same, that His laws work the same way, that mankind is the same so far as the soul's possibilities are concerned, and that the faith which God made possible for man to attain to, may be possessed by him now just as it was possessed by my disciples, then they will attempt this work of beneficence and will succeed, and the sick will be healed and the devils cast out, the blind made to see, and the deaf to hear, and the so-called miracles will be performed as they were in my days on earth.

There is not and never was such a thing as a miracle in the sense of having an effect produced by a cause which was not the result of the ordinary workings of God's laws, for these laws in their workings never vary, and when the same law is called into operation upon the same condition of facts the same results will always be produced.

So, let a mortal have in his soul the same amount of God's Divine Love which the Bible writers meant or should have meant, when they spoke of being endowed by the Holy Ghost, and let him have the necessary faith, that when he prays to God, he will give him the power to exercise this Love in a sufficient degree to produce the desired results, and then try to exercise the power of casting out devils or healing, etc., and he will find that success will attend his efforts. God is the same at all times and under all circumstances, and only mortals vary in their conceptions and conditions.

So I say, there are no devils as independent creatures of God, in contradistinction to the spirits of men who once lived on earth, and you must believe that there are not.

I tell you now, that the teachers of such false doctrines will have to pay the penalties for their false teachings when they come to the spirit world, and see the result of these false teachings, and no relief will be granted until they have paid the last farthing. To believe such doctrines entails results that are bad enough for any spirit to endure, but to teach others these beliefs and convince them of their truth, entails upon the teacher, whether he actually believes them or not, sufferings and duration of sufferings of which men have no conception.

I will not write more tonight, but will, in closing, say that you have my love and blessings, and my promises I will fulfill, so that you will realize your expectations and be in condition to perform the work that you have been selected to do.

Well, you let doubt come into your mind, and as a consequence, your soul does not respond, although, strange as it may seem, the Divine Love is there, but when this mental doubt exists, it is as if it were a covering which prevents the existence of the Love in the soul to shine forth and produce the great feeling of happiness and joy which otherwise you might experience. The mental condition of the mortal, undoubtedly has a great influence on the consciousness of the man as to his possession of this soul development and the Divine Love, and consequently, there will have to be this continuous fight as long as life lasts on earth, between the mental conditions and the soul's consciousness. But as the mental beliefs are brought into harmony with the soul's condition, more and more the fight will grow weaker and less frequent, and it is possible that they will cease altogether, and the mental beliefs become entirely and absolutely subordinated or rather absorbed in the soul's consciousness of its being possessed of this Divine Love of the Father.

So my dear brother, I will say good night.
Your brother and friend,

Jesus.

Happiness and peace that passeth all understanding comes to the possessor of the Divine Love

September 10th, 1916.

I am here, Samuel.

I come to write you that I am with you in love and hope for your present blessing and happiness. I know that the worries of life prevent you from realizing the influence of this Great Love which is surrounding you and which is ready and waiting to fill your soul to its fullness. But if you will pray more to the Father and exercise your faith, you will find that your worries will lessen, and peace will come to you in such abundance and beauty that you will feel like a new man.

As John said, with this faith, Love will flow into your soul, and you will realize to some extent the joys of our celestial conditions; for the Love that may be yours is the same Love, in its nature, that we possess, and that has made angels of us all, and inhabitants of the Father's Kingdom. Only believe, and you will realize how willing this Love is to take possession of your soul, and make you so happy that even the troubles that you have will not be sufficient to take from you the great peace that surpasseth all understanding.

I have been in the spirit for many years and have possessed this Love for a long time, and know by actual experience what it is, and what great joy it brings to its possessor, so that you can rely on what I promise you, and feel the certainty that actual knowledge gives. I am now, a wholly redeemed child of the Father, and one who knows that His Divine Love in the soul makes the man or spirit of the Essence of the Father. When this Love enters the soul of man it increases like the leaven in the dough, and continues in its work until the whole soul is impregnated with it, and everything of sin or error is wholly eradicated.

Love worketh all things that man can wish for or conceive of, and more besides. Paul's description of Love and the wonderful qualities and conditions that emanate from it, does not contain all its emanations and resultant happiness.

But I must not write more tonight for it is late and you are tiring. So believe what I have said, and try to follow my advice, and you will soon experience that peace and happiness which only this Love can bring to the souls of men. So with my love and blessings I will say good night.

Your brother in Christ,
Samuel.[47]

---

[47] This message is a composite of two, being published in Volume I and Volume II. (G.J.C.)

Jesus did not perform all the miracles claimed in the Bible

May 30th, 1917.

I am here, St. Peter, Apostle of Jesus.

I have seen what you were reading (Luke's Gospel) and must inform you that many of the supposed miracles of healing and raising of the dead and the controlling of the laws or expressions of nature never occurred.

No, these accounts are not true and are the results of the imaginings of men who attempted to add to the book that Luke wrote. Of course there is a true foundation for some of these alleged miracles, but as to others, there is no foundation in fact.

Jesus did heal the sick and cure the blind and the deaf and the withered hand and the palsied man and resurrected the supposed dead, but not in the way described in the New Testament; and it is not good for men to believe in the truth of all these miracles.

Well, that incident never occurred, for Jesus in casting out evil spirits would have had no authority or power to permit them to enter into the swine, and it would not have been in consonance with his love and ideas of what was just, to have allowed the swine to receive these spirits and thereby perish as the account says. And besides, the result of such an happening would have been, that the property of the innocent owners was taken from them and lost.

In all Jesus' performance of miracles or in any of his teachings did he ever do or say that which worked wrong to a human being. All men were to him the objects of his love and the salvation which he came to earth to show men the way to.

Sometime, I will consider these miracles in a message, and inform you of those that he actually performed and those that are the mere fancies of some of those eastern teachers who had a very wonderful imagination and used them in adding to the truths of Luke's original writings.

Well, there is some little truth in that for we were in a storm and were afraid and he slept, and we awakened him, but he did not rebuke the storm and the waves and cause them to subside, but rather he allayed our fears by his talk and example and to us it became as if there were no storm, for when fear left us it was as if we were not sensible of the storm so far as the dread of drowning or perishing was concerned.

No, this is another interpolation and should not be believed. Many wonders ascribed to Jesus were never performed, although it appeared to us as if there was no limit to the powers of Jesus. But sometime I will come and write fully on this matter. I must stop now.

Your brother in Christ,

Peter.

The wandering Jew

June 21st, 1917.

I am the man who said to Jesus as he bore his cross to Calvary, "Pass on," and to whom he said, "Tarry thou till I come;" and for years and years I waited, until at last he came to me, not as the reincarnated Jesus, but as my brother and friend in the possession of the Divine Love, which I received in my soul after the long years of waiting and suffering on earth.

I know that this is considered a legend by mortals, but to me it was a vital and painful fact. I was truly the wandering Jew and found rest nowhere, and even death would not come to me to release me of a life that was a torture, and a cause of recollection of my inhumanity to the truly Jesus.

I have now been in spirit life for many centuries and am in the Celestial Heavens, for the Divine Love of the Father is sufficient to redeem the vilest of mortals and the perpetrators of the greatest sins from their conditions of darkness and sufferings.

If I had only known what a beloved son of God the Master was when I uttered my vile words and cruel curses, I would never have opened my mouth, except to bless him and comfort him as he walked his weary way to the cross; but, I did not know, and thought that I was serving my God, when I reviled him, who, as I thought, was a blasphemer and destroyer of our religion.

But, I paid the penalty even while on earth, and suffered the tortures that no man can understand, for as I continued to live, and death was always fleeing from me, I commenced to and did realize that I had committed a sin against the chosen of the Father, and his, I mean Jesus' sentence upon me became a thing of wonderful and ever present reality.

But now, I know that he loved even me, and that while I was wandering and suffering he was with me trying to help me open up my soul to the Divine Love, which was my only liberator from my doom.

I know that this may seem strange and unbelievable to you, and not possible in the workings of God's economy in dealing with His creatures, but it was true, and I know. But the Wonderful Love! Oh, how can I ever express my feelings of gratitude to the Father and to Jesus! While I remained in my ignorant and disheartened state, that very Jesus was with me many times in his love, trying to help me. Many spirits have told me this, and it is true.

I write this because I want you and the world to know that this

Love is waiting for all mankind, and that there is no sinner so vile that it cannot turn him into the Divine Angel of God's Celestial Heavens.

I will not write more now, except to say that whenever you read of me, remember that I am no longer the wandering Jew but a redeemed child from sin and error, and much beloved by that very Jesus whom I treated so cruelly.

With my love I will say, good night.

I will sign myself as I am best known,

The Wandering Jew.

Confirming the experience that came to the "Wandering Jew"

June 21st, 1917.

I am here, St. John, Apostle of Jesus.

Well, you were surprised at the last message and it is not to be wondered that you were, for I know that to you this story was a mere legend, as it is to most others of the mortal life, who have thought on the subject.

And again, the wandering Jew was not in your mind as I know, for I was present before you commenced to write and know just what the contents of your mind were, and what expectations you had.

I recite these facts to impress you that this message is not the result of any subconscious mind that the philosophers speak of, but the message came solely because the spirit who wrote came to you and took control of your brain and hands and actually wrote the message.

He is truly the man known as the Wandering Jew, and the legend is true so far as his having treated the Master as he said and the Master's sentence upon him to "tarry until he should come."

Naturally the question arises, how could the Master have imposed such a sentence, or what power had the Master to do that which is so contrary to all the ordinary known laws of God?

Well, the question is a pertinent and proper one and is entitled to an answer. At the time of the Master's crucifixion he was surrounded by a great host of spirits, in whom was vested the most wonderful powers of the spirit world, and they accompanied him in his weary march to the cursed cross, all trying to sustain him, and listening to his words, and many of them knowing his thoughts and the travail of his soul; and when he rested because of the burden of carrying the cross, they were with him and heard the inhuman command of the Jew and the Master's reply, and then they determined that the sentence should be carried out and never end until the Jew had traveled the weary road of suffering that he saw Jesus was travelling, and until he should seek relief in that way

True Gospel Revealed anew by Jesus

that the very Master came to earth to make known to mortals, and this Jew was among them.

The spirits were with the Jew continually sustaining him in his physical life so that the friend that he hoped and prayed for—I mean death—should not come to him, until first should come the Great Love of the Father to redeem him from the results of the sentence. And strange as it may seem to you, at the very time that these spirits were exercising their powers to prolong the physical life of the man, they were also trying to influence him so that he would open up his soul to the inflowing of the Love; and among those who thus worked was the Master himself.

But the old beliefs of this Jew in the teachings of the laws of Moses, and in Abraham as his father and the great medium of his salvation, and that great power which he possessed—the human will—prevented the opening up of his soul for many long years, and not until he was convinced that the sentence of the Master was being carried out, did he commence to realize that the teachings of his church and father Abraham were not sufficient for his salvation from the awful doom pronounced upon him; and there came to him the thought that the man whom he had cursed might be the truly son of God, and that his teachings of the only way to the Father and happiness was through this Love; for in the meantime he had lived among the Christians and had learned what the teachings of this love were, and that it was waiting for all, and could be obtained by all through prayer and the submission of the human will.

Well, he suffered and sought in every way to obtain this death, but it always evaded him, until at last his will broke and the truth came to him and with it prayer, and then came freedom; for I must tell you that when the soul of a mortal prays in earnestness and with true longings, all the powers of all the spirits in the spiritual or Celestial Heavens cannot prevent that Love from responding to the prayers, and from making the longing soul free and at one, to a degree, with the Father.

The sentences of spirits and angels cannot exist contrary to that Love's demands. And this being so, mortals can readily understand that all the powers of the hells and the evil ones cannot prevail against that Love. And thus further will you understand that the true prayers of a longing soul are more powerful and will bring the response from the Father, than all the powers of angels, and spirits and devils combined. Thus you may comprehend what an important creature is one poor mite of a mortal when in truth and earnestness he comes to the Father, seeking His Love.

Well, when I came tonight, I had no thought of writing such a message as I have written, but as I realized that you may in thinking about the message of the Wandering Jew, and doubt that the laws of nature may be set aside even at the command of the Master, I thought it best to write you as I have. No laws of nature were, in fact, set aside, but the powers of the spirits were exercised upon preserving the physical organs and functions of this Jew, so that life would remain, and the vitalizing principle perform its work in preserving the Jew as a living mortal.

Do not wonder at this, for I must tell you that before these messages shall be completed you will be told of many truths that will be more astonishing and contrary to what men call the laws of nature, than is the case of the Wandering Jew.

I will not write more now, and with my love to you and your friend, I will say good night.

Your brother in Christ, John.

Comments on the message of the Wandering Jew.

June 21st, 1917.

I am here, your own true and loving Helen.

Well, dear, you have had some very surprising messages tonight and I don't wonder that you think they may not be just from whom they represent themselves to be, but the fact is that the persons professing to write actually did so.

The Jew is a very bright spirit of the Celestial Spheres, but one who is very humble, and the effect of his great suffering an earth is plainly shown in his great humility. What a wonderful thing such an experience is! And when he told you of his long weary years on earth, he seemed for the moment, to be going over the experience again; but of course, he was not, for the love that is in him prevented the grief of those years from finding more than a temporary lodgment in his recollections. Well the truth of what he wrote you can be believed in, not only because John corroborated him, but because many other spirits who were present at the time, say that it is true.

Your own true and loving,
Helen.

Why the churches refuse to investigate that spirits can and do communicate with mortals

April 23rd, 1916.

I am here, St. John, Apostle of Jesus.

Yes I come to tell you that I have been with you to-day in your attendance on the church services, and as the preachers declared their

True Gospel Revealed anew by Jesus

ideas of what immortality means, I suggested to you thoughts showing how unsatisfactory their reasonings and conclusions were. Of course, what the morning preachers said about the reasons for inferring that immortality must be the lot of man had in it a considerable force and also consolation, and I am glad that he dealt with the question as he did, but when all is said, it was merely hope and belief, knowledge was absent, and men so often realize that their hopes are not fulfilled.

How regrettable it is, that while men may know—and I emphasize know—the truth of immortality if they will only seek for it, yet they will not seek, although it is open to search even without the information that our messages give you. And in speaking of immortality in this writing, I mean continuous life upon the death of the physical body.

Of course immortality, as it has been explained to you, can only be learned from the teachings of our communications. But immortality in the former sense, continuity of life, can become established as a matter of knowledge, and to the satisfaction of these orthodox preachers, if they will only seek with open minds, divorced from the beliefs that keep them from accepting, as true, any and everything not contained in the Bible.

It has been established as a fact, for a long time that in its beginning antedating even the Bible that spirits or angels communicated to men; and the Bible has many instances where such occurrences were declared. But while these orthodox teachers accept all these instances as true, yet they say that the occurrences were caused by some special interposition of God, and to a certain extent this is true. But this cause applies to all instances of spirit communication that have taken place since these Bible manifestations.

As we have told you many times, law—unchangeable law—governs all God's universe, and nothing happens by chance; and so every instance of spirit communion is the result of the operation of some law working in an orderly manner. No spirit could communicate and no mortal could receive the messages, unless the law worked in such a manner as to permit or cause the same. And here I must say, that the same principle of law that enables the evil spirit to communicate or manifest enables the higher spirit to do the same. There is no special law for one and not for another.

Your land is filled with mortals who have developed in them such powers as enable the spirits to become in rapport with them, and thereby make known the fact that the supposed dead are alive and able to declare the fact to mortals. These facts have been established to the satisfaction of men of all kinds and characters. To the scientist as well as to the man of ordinary intelligence, and even less; and to the open-minded orthodox preacher as well as to the infidel.

And all these things are not merely matters of chance but are designed to show him that he is a living, never dying being, as far as known, whether in the flesh or out of it, and what is thus designed and provided for man's consolation should not be looked upon with suspicion or fear of being against God's will. No, this great privilege is a part of God's goodness to man, and he must so understand it, and to his hope and desire for continuous life, add knowledge.

So I say these leaders of the worshipers at the orthodox shrines may, if they will learn the truth of this immortality or continuity of life after the death of the body, make certain that for which they have only a hope, backed by their faith in what their Bible tells them is the truth. Of course this hope and faith may become so strong as to satisfy their doubts on the question, but even then it is not knowledge. This faith and hope will pale into insignifance, when the mother, mourning for her recently departed loved one, hears his voice declaring to her that he is still alive, and has all his love, and longings for her, and that he is with her feeling her love for him.

But these teachers will not seek, or if they do, and feel their hope and faith turn to knowledge, they will not declare the truth to their flock; and why not declare the truth to their flock; and why not? Because the creeds and dogmas and iron bands of erroneous beliefs forbid them doing so. They will preach of the press, and, if necessary, will lay down their lives for such a cause, but yet, when they come to deal with this question of supreme and vital fact, they are afraid to seek the truth, or, in seeking, to find and declare the freedom of their beliefs from the bondage of their creeds.

What a responsibility they have, and what an answer they will have to make! They bury the talent which is given them, and the accounting will be grievous.

But some day and soon, this truth will seek them with such overwhelming force, that their creeds will crumble, and in addition to hope and faith there will come to them knowledge, and with knowledge freedom, and with freedom, the pearl of great price which to them has so long been hidden in the shell of fear and bigotry. I must not write more tonight.

I felt that I must say these few things to you to encourage you in your work of bringing truth to light. So with all my love and blessings, I am

Your brother in Christ,
John.

Discourse on the devolution and evolution of man—scientists only know of evolution after man reached the bottom of his degeneracy or devolution

July 22nd, 1917.

I am here, St. Luke, writer of the Third Gospel that was.

Well, I desire to write a few lines on the subject contained in the book which you were reading tonight. I mean the book dealing with the "Creation and fall of man."

Well, the man who wrote the book is endeavoring to reconcile the Bible doctrine of the creation and fall of man with the scientists' doctrine of evolution, and to show that these two views of the subject are not antagonistic, and if properly understood, may be used, one to support the other. But in this he has not succeeded, nor can he, for this reason, if there were no others, that man did not evolve from the beast or lower animal, but was always man, the creature of God, perfect in his creation and wholly natural.

There was nothing of the supernatural about him and he never possessed any nature of the superman from which he fell at the time of his disobedience. He has never been anything more or less than the perfect creation of his Maker, although he has degenerated in his qualities and in the exercise of his will.

Evolution or the doctrine of evolution has its limitations, and its founder, or those who follow him either wholly or in a modified way, are not able to retrace this doctrine to the fall of man, and hence, when they attempt to pass beyond that stage when man seemed to have been very degenerate and a product of the animal progenitors, they get into the field of speculation, and knowledge ceases to exist.

Man was not created with any of the Divine qualities, as the writer seems to think but was made the merely natural man that you see now, without the defilement of his soul qualities which involves only the elimination of those things from his soul that cause the departure from the condition of his creation. That is, when he was created he was in perfect harmony with the will of God and His laws and when he shall be restored to that harmony of unity with these laws, he will then be in what was his before the fall.

So the idea put forward by the author that man was created with something of the divine in him, which took him out from a kind of physical condition of imperfection, and that when he lost these Divine qualities he fell into that imperfect condition, is all wrong. The great truth connected with man's creation, is that man was created perfect, that as regards his order of creation or the qualities of his moral and physical nature there could be no progress, for the next step in progression would be the divine.

Thus you will see that he was so wonderfully and perfectly made, that he was only a little lower than the angels, and by angels I mean the souls of men which have ceased to be incarnate and have partaken of the Divine Love and become a part of the Father in His Divinity of Love—not the mere souls in the spirit world which have only the development of their moral qualities, because these, whenever they have become purified and in harmony with the laws and will of God, are only men perfected in their natures and organisms as they were at the time of man's creation.

I say, the perfect man possesses those qualities and attributes that were his at the time of his creation, and he cannot progress or become greater or other than he was at the time of such creation. He was made perfect as a creation, and beyond the perfect there can be nothing greater evolved from the qualities and faculties, one and all, that made him perfect.

And to progress, there must come into his nature, from without, the Divine Love, that which will add to these qualities and faculties, which you may understand is no part or method of evolution.

When the first parents fell, they lost that which destroyed the harmony of their existence with the laws of God, and also were deprived of the great potentiality of becoming Divine in their natures of Love and Immortality, like unto the Father—but as mere created men they fell from perfection and not from divinity. Nor were they by that fall deprived of the possibility of living forever in the physical bodies, because those bodies were made only for the purpose of enabling the souls to individualize themselves, and thereafter die and become dissolved into their derivative elements.

The physical body was never created to live forever, and men were never created to live on earth forever, for a greater and larger world was provided for their eternal habitation, where things are real and only the spiritual exist. The earth is a mere image of the realities of the spirit world, and exists only as the nursery for the individualizing of the soul. That you may not misconceive my meaning, remember the soul is the man—the ego—and that when man fell, it was not the physical part of man that fell, except as it was influenced by the soul, but, it was the soul that fell; and the sentence of death was not pronounced upon the physical, but upon the soul potentialities, and, hence, you may see, that when man shall again become the perfect man, it will not be necessary that the physical body be restored.

Even if it were not contrary to the physical laws of the universe, or, to speak more correctly, to the laws controlling the material part of the universe, that the material body of man be resurrected and again be housed, the soul, it would not be necessary, for the soul has its spirit body which manifests its individuality. There is no necessity for the resurrection of the physical body, and there will be no such resurrection, for God never does a useless thing.

As I say, man has never ceased to be the man of God's creation, although he has become degenerate and defiled, and at one time in the history of his existence devoluted to that degree, where, save for the essential qualities of his creation, he appeared to be lower than the brutes; but he was always the man of God's creation, and never an animal of the lower order. The scientists in their geological search and research and in their finds of fossils and traces of ancient man, and in their biological theories, conclude that man was of a lower degree of intelligence and manner of living, and they may be justified in so concluding, and also that he has gradually evolved from that condition and state, and draw apparent correct theories there from, yet when they attempt to go further, they enter only into the realm of speculation and become lost in the darkness of mystery. They can rightly acclaim the evolution of man from where they lose him in their retracing of that evolution, but can know nothing of his devolution anterior to that time; and, hence their speculations are without foundation of substance.

No, man has not evolved from the lower animal, but only from himself when he reached the bottom of his fall. In this particular, the history and experience of man is this—he was created perfect,—he sinned, he fell from the condition of his created state—his condition at the bottom of his fall was inferior in some phases to the brute animal—after long centuries he commenced to rise from his base condition, and had made progress when the scientists by their discoveries found evidence of his then condition,—and since then he has been the subject of their "evolution." But the scientists and all mankind must know that all during these centuries of descent and ascent, man was always man, the greatest creation of God, and the most fallen.

Well, I have written enough for tonight but as I was with you to-day as you were reading and saw the misconceptions of the writer of the book, as well as those of the scientists to whom he referred, I thought it advisable to write the few incomplete truths about the subject.

I will soon come and write.
So with my love and blessings, I will say good night.
Your brother in Christ,
Luke.

The relationship of man to the creation of the world, and the origin of life

January 15th, 1916.

I am here, Jesus.

I come tonight to tell you that you are in a very much better condition than you have been for some time, and your rapport with us is so very much greater, that I feel that I should write you a message upon an important subject which is vital to the salvation of man from the sins and errors of his life on earth, and I will write a portion of what I desire to write.

Well, I will first say that there are so many men and women on the earth, who believe, or assert that they believe, that through their own efforts they can develop those soul qualities which are necessary to bring them in accord with the Soul of the Father, that I find that the task of convincing these persons of the errors of their beliefs, or assumption of beliefs, will be a very great one. This task will not be confined to those who have given real and deep study to the mysteries of life, both on earth and thereafter, but also to a much greater number who have a kind of smattering of this supposed knowledge, which the wiser or more learned publish to the world as a result of their investigations.

It is more difficult to convince the ignorant, who think that they know the laws of being and the plan of the workings of God's universe, than to convince those who have given sincere thoughtful study to the same, because the latter, generally, as they progress in their investigations become convinced that the more they should know as a result of their investigations, the less they really know.

I do not know just what is the most important subject for comment tonight relating to these matters, for there are so many, all of which I must at same time instruct you about; but I will write tonight about "The relationship of man to the creation of the world, and the origin of life."

Your Bible says: in the beginning God created the heavens and the earth, etc., out of a void, and continued that creation until there was a perfect heaven with all its glories, and a perfect earth with inhabitants of every kind—all perfect and made just as an all wise and all powerful God would create; and as a climax to all, man, who was so perfect that he was made in the image of his Creator.

Well, this story is just as good and satisfactory as any that has been conceived and written by man, and is just as worthy of belief, but as a fact it is not true, for there never was a time or period when there was a void in the universe or when there was chaos.

God never created anything out of nothing, but His creations, such as are perceived by and known to men, were merely the change in form or composition of what had already existed, and always will exist as elements, though there will undoubtedly be changes in form and appearance and in constituent elements in their relation to one another.

God was always existent—a Being without beginning, which idea the finite mind, I know cannot grasp, but it is true; and so also everything which is in the universe to-day always existed, though not in form and composition as they now are; and as they are they will not continue to be, for change eternal is the law of his universe. I mean as to all things which may be spoken of as having a substance whether they be material or ethereal.

Of course, His Truths never change, and neither do the laws by which the harmony of the universe is preserved and continued perfect. Now, the earth on which you live did not always have an existence, as an earth, and neither did the firmament and the great galaxy of planets and stars, but they were not created out of nothing, and neither was there chaos, for in God's economy of being there is never any chaos, which if it should be, would mean the absence of the workings of His laws and harmony.

But the earth and the firmament were created—at one time they had no existence as such, and at a coming time they may cease to have such existence, and this creation was in an orderly way, according to design, with no element of chance entering into it; and such creation was not through what your wise men may call accretion or evolution—that is self evolution—for every new or additional exponent of growth or manifestations of increase was the result of God's Laws, which he operated in the creation of the creature.

There is no such thing as self evolution, or that development which arises from the unassisted growth of the thing developed, and this applies to all nature as well as to man. To grow, to become nearer perfection, implies the decay and disappearance of some elements which have performed their missions and work in the growth of the thing created, and never do the same elements continue in the development of that which the laws in their operations, bring to greater and greater perfection.

But in all this work of creation there are laws of disintegration and apparent retrogression operating, as well as laws of positive construction and advancement; and again these former laws do not operate by chance, but by design just as do the latter class of laws. The All Creator knows, when for the purpose of bringing forth the perfect creature—be it man or animal or vegetable or mineral—the laws of decay and retrogression as well as the laws of advancement and increased effectiveness shall operate, and He never makes a mistake in setting into operation these laws, and never pronounces the result of His work, "Not good."

As has been said, a thousand years are as a day with God, and while for many long years it may appear to man, there are retrogression and delay in bringing to perfection a creature of the Creator's works, yet that apparent retrogression is not such a fact, but only a course or method adopted for bringing forth the higher or greater perfection. I know it is difficult to explain these workings of creation to the finite, earthy mind but you may grasp some conception of what I desire to make known.

Man, in his creation, was not the slow growth as were some of the other creations of God, but was from and at the beginning made perfect, with the exception of the qualities of Divinity and Immortality. He did not grow from a lower creature, as some of your scientists have proclaimed, by the slow process of evolution, and this a self evolution, resulting from inherent qualities which were developed by experience, but he was created the perfect man.

I will stop for the present.
Your brother and friend,
Jesus.

Previous message continued

February 6th, 1916.

I am here, Jesus.

I come tonight to resume my discourse of several nights ago. As I was saying man is the creature of God, made in perfection and instantaneously, as it were, not having a slow growth as other creations, and when he was created he needed no evolution or additional attributes to make him the perfect man. His physical body was perfect, and also his spiritual body and his soul.

He had, in addition to these three constituents, a gift which, by his disobedience, he forfeited, and which was never restored to him until my coming, and which when possessed by him made him more than mere man. As to those things which were made constituent and absolute parts of him, they were perfect, and no evolution was necessary to give them any increased perfection. Man then was a more perfect being than he is now, or ever has been since his fall from his condition of perfection.

After his disobedience and the consequent death of the potentiality of partaking of the Divine nature of the Father, which is the gift above mentioned, man was left in a state where he depended exclusively upon the qualities which he then possessed for his future happiness, and freedom from those things which would cause him to lose the harmony that then existed between him and the laws governing his being.

The greatest of all the qualities bestowed upon him was that of the will power which was wholly unrestricted in its operations. Although, when exercised in a manner which brought this will in conflict with the laws controlling this harmony, man had to suffer and pay the penalties of such violations. But notwithstanding that these perversions of the exercise of the will brought the sins and errors which now exist on earth, God did not place any limitations on this exercise.

Man, in his creation, had bestowed upon him appetites and desire pertaining to his physical nature, as well as desires of his higher or spiritual nature, and they were all intended to work in harmony and not in antagonism; and in such workings, man was kept pure and free from sin—which is merely the violation of God's laws of harmony. But after the first disobedience, which is the greatest demonstration of the power of man to exercise that will, even when God had forbade him to do so, and after man lost this great potentiality that I speak of, succeeding disobediences became easier; and as these disobediences occurred man lost to a great extent the desires for the spiritual things, and the animal or physical part of his nature asserted itself, and then, instead of exercising these appetites which belonged to the physical nature in such a wise way that no in-harmony would ensue—and here let me say that even after the fall it was possible and even expected that man would exercise these appetites in the way mentioned, he indulged them beyond their proper functions, and increased such indulgence, until he commenced to find, as he thought, more pleasure, in such indulgence, than in the thoughts and exercise of his higher nature, and the aspirations which belonged to it.

This deterioration of man was not sudden, but gradual, until, at one time, he became in a state or condition of being bordering on that of the lower animals, and in fact because of this increased indulgence of these appetites he seemed to be transformed into the lower animal; but yet he remained man, a being created in the image of his Maker.

And from this position of low degradation or degeneracy man slowly commenced to progress towards the attainment of his original condition before the fall. Never in all this time, was his freedom of will taken from him, nor attempted to be controlled by God—but always the laws of compensation worked, and man suffered as he continued to create sin and evil.

But as man on earth continued to degenerate and to permit, what is sometimes called his animal nature to dominate his spiritual nature, many men died, and continued to die, and their physical bodies went back to the dust of which they were created, and their spiritual selves became inhabitants of the spirit world, where they were freed, in a longer or shorter time, from the desire to exercise these animal appetites and the spiritual part of man again asserted itself, until many of these spirits became free from sin and evil and in harmony with the laws of God, controlling their natures and conditions as they existed before their degeneracy and before the disobedience commenced.

And these spirits thus made free and in their spiritual dominance commenced to try to assist men while living on earth to direct his will in such ways as to rid himself of submission to these appetites, and to become again a true man as in his creation state, minus the potentiality that I have mentioned. But these efforts on the part of spirits have been slow in their effects, and while men in individual cases, have been almost regenerated, yet as whole the progress has not been as rapid as is desirable—sin and evil still exist in the world, and men's perverted appetites and desires still control then to a large extent.

Of course, this progress from the bottom of degeneracy has taken place in some parts of the earth, faster than in others, and, hence, you have your distinction between the civilized and the uncivilized races or nations; but this does not necessarily mean that the civilized people, as individuals, have made greater progress in the manner indicated, than have the individuals of some of the so called uncivilized nations, for it is a fact, that among some men of the former nations are perversions and manifestations of perversions of these appetites that do not exist in the latter nations.

Advancement in the intellectual qualities do not necessarily mean progress in the spiritual asserting itself over the perversions of these appetites, for will is not a thing entirely of the mind, and neither are these appetites and desires, because back of the mind are the affections usually called the heart's desires, which is the seat of these appetites, and from which these desires arise; and as they arise the will is influenced by them and as the will is influenced come positive thoughts and deeds.

It is not surprising that your scientists believe and preach the doctrine of the evolution of man from a lower species of animal, or from an atom or from something that they cannot just understand or give a name to, because in their studies of the history of mankind, and of the created world, they find that man has developed and progressed amazingly from what appeared to have been his condition in some ages past.

But history does not extend to the time when man was in this lowest condition of degeneracy, and hence all the conclusions that these scientists reach are based upon facts, sufficient unto themselves, which show the progress of man only after the turning point of his degeneracy. They have no fact, and, of course, when the word "facts" is here used, it refers exclusively to the material things of nature—showing them the gradual decline of man from his state of being a perfect man to that when his retrogression or degeneracy ceased, and his progress of return to his former estate commenced.

So, if the scientists will believe and teach that man, instead of evolving from an atom or some other infinitesimal something, or from a lower species of animal than man, evolved from his state or condition when he was at the bottom of his degeneracy, to which he had descended from the perfect man, then they will believe and teach the truth, and their theory of evolution will then have as its foundation or basis, a fact, which now it has not—only a speculation.

This in short, is the history and truth of the creation of the universe of man—of man's fall and degeneracy, and evolution and progress. And through all this creation and subsequent existence, runs life, permeating it and always with it, and the origin of Life is God.

I have finished and I hope that you will find some instruction as well as entertainment in what I have written. I will come again soon and write you another truth. The fact that you waited for sentences to be formulated to express my thoughts, merely means that I was manipulating your brain so that the proper expression or idea could be conveyed to your hand as I wrote it.

You have my love and blessings, and I am more interested as time passes in you and your work. Keep up your courage and your desires will be fulfilled.

Your friend and brother
Jesus.

Ancient Spirits give their Testimony

The importance of the Jews learning the truths of God proclaimed by Jesus

November 9th, 1915.

Moses, the Prophet of God of Ancient Days.

I have been with you on several occasions when some of the ancient spirits wrote you, and I was much interested. I am still the faithful servant of God, but in addition, a believer in Jesus, who is the greatest of all the sons of the Father, and the only one of all God's messengers who brought to light, life and immortality.

I could not have said this before his coming. I mean that I could not have said that other great reformers and teachers of the truths of God had not done this, because I did not know before the coming of Jesus what life and immortality meant—and no man or spirit before that time knew this great truth.

I am now in the Celestial Heavens with many of the old prophets and seers who have received this great gift of the Divine Love, and many who lived and died since Jesus' time are also Celestial spirits—partaking of immortality. I now see that many of my teachings were not true—that love did not enter into them, but rather the spirit of retaliation which is absolutely no part of the truths of the Father. The Jews still look upon me as their great teacher and law-giver, and many of them observe literally my laws.

And I want to tell you this fact, because I believe that when you publish the messages of the Master, should you publish also what I may write, many Jews will believe me, and that I and many of those who taught my teachings, are now engaged in showing the spirits of Jews who come into the spirit world the truths as taught by the Master.

The Jewish nation is the most strict of all people in their beliefs in and observations of their religious doctrines as set forth in the Old Testament; and, hence, will be among the last of all men to accept the truths which I now understand and teach. But I hope that something which I may communicate to you will cause them to think and become believers and observers of this New Revelation of the Truth.

They have fought and suffered for their religion in all these centuries and are still doing so, and the one great thing that more than any other, has prevented them from accepting the teachings of Jesus and believing in his mission to mankind, is that his followers, or those who attempted to write his teachings, and those who interpreted the same, declare and maintain that Jesus is God—that the true God was three instead of one, as I in the Decalogue declared. this has been the great stumbling block to the Jews, and when they read, as they may, that Jesus himself declares and proclaims that he is not God but only his son, and that they are also his sons, they will look upon his teachings with more tolerance, and many of them will be inclined to accept his Truths and the Truths of the Father; and Judaism in its religious aspect will gradually disappear, and the Jews will become a part of the one great religious brotherhood of men, and as in our Celestial Heavens, there will be on earth no more Jew and no more Gentile, but all will become one in their belief in the Father and the mission of Jesus. He will be accepted as the Messiah not only of the Jew but of the whole world, and then God's Chosen People will not be a very small minority of God's children, but the whole world will be his Chosen People.

I am so interested in this phase of the Great Truths that shall be given to and accepted by men, because I was more than any other man responsible for the present beliefs of the Jews, which causes them to hold themselves separate and apart from all the rest of mankind as the chosen and specially selected of God's people.

I will not write more tonight, but I feel that I must ask you to permit me to write again, as I have a mission to perform on earth to undo a work which I so effectively performed when I was the leader of my people.

As Jesus is teaching and will teach all mankind the way to the Father and immortality, I must teach my people the way to get rid of these erroneous and false beliefs which are contained in the Old Testament.

So thanking you, I will say, good night.

Moses—the law-giver of the Jews.

Writes of his experience in the spirit world, and his life on earth

July 21st, 1915.

Daniel, the prophet of God of the Old Testament.

I am with you tonight because you have reason to believe that you have been selected to do the work of Jesus in transmitting his messages to mankind; and I want to add my testimony to that of the others who have preceded me.

I am a follower of the Master, although I lived on earth many years before he came to announce the rebestowal of the great Divine

Love of the Father, and show the way by which every man who so desires may obtain it.

I never knew what this Love was until Jesus came and declared it to man and to spirits, as he did; and when he came to the spirit world, after his crucifixion, he preached to us who were in the spiritual spheres the great doctrine of God's plan of salvation.

Men must not think that mortals are the only recipients of this Love, or that they are the only ones that had the privilege of learning the way to this Love, for, as I tell you, Jesus came to the spirits who lived in the spiritual heavens, and made known this great plan and taught the way to Immortality.

I was, before his coming, a spirit who enjoyed the favor of the Father to the extent that my natural love was developed to the highest degree, and in that love I was comparatively happy. I also possessed great intellectual development but as to the Divine Love, which I now possess, I knew nothing of, nor did any spirit then living.

This may seem strange to you, because from my history as contained in the Old Testament, you would naturally suppose that I was in high favor with God, and so I was; but that favor extended no further than in receiving from Him a very great amount of the natural love which He had bestowed on all mankind, and in knowing by my spiritual perceptions and the power of a psychic nature, which I possessed, that God was caring for me and using me to convince the heathen nations, that there was only one God, and that He alone should be worshiped.

Never did I know the reality of what the Divine Love was, or that I was not in position other than I might have been, had not that Love been taken from mankind when our great earthly father committed his fatal act of disobedience. No spirit in those times before the coming of Jesus, could possibly progress higher than the sphere where this natural love and intellectual development existed in their greatest degree of perfection.

So you see, I was never a spirit possessed of this Divine nature, until after the coming of the Master; and you will find nowhere in the Old Testament, any declaration or promise the man should possess this Divine nature, and we who lived in the days of my earthly life, were satisfied with and expected only the favors and gifts of God as they might affect our earthly prosperity and happiness.

I was a prophet, as it is written, and God spoke to me through His spirits the things which I declared to the people, and also enabled me to foretell many things which would and did happen. But this great favor and gift did not bring to me the possession of the Divine Love or nature of the Father; and when I came to die, I passed to the spirit world a spirit possessed only of the natural love and the great moral development which my communications from my associations with the spirits of the

Father had given me.

So man must not think that we of the Old Testament, no matter whether prophet or seer or the specially favored by God, ever had this Divine Essence of His, while we lived on earth or while we existed as spirits, before the coming of Jesus.

Abraham, Moses or Elias never possessed this Divine nature, although they were the specially chosen of God to do His work in the particulars in which they were chosen; and they never understood that their lives after death were to be anything more than a mere existence in the spirit world as spirits, or, as it was expressed, they were gathered to the home of their fathers. Rest was then understood as the great condition of the good men of God, and this rest meant to them a relief from all earthly troubles and a happiness that would result from such freedom.

So that, when the Master came into the spirit world and preached the great truth of the re-bestowal of the Divine Love, the spirits were as much surprised as were mortals; and there was just as much unbelief among them as among mortals.

The Jews still believe in their doctrines which had been their rule of faith when in the flesh; and the laws of Moses and the declarations of the prophets control them as spirits just as they had controlled them on earth.

Of course, after they became spirits, they learned many things which pertain to the spirit world of which they had no knowledge as mortals; and among the laws which they learned as spirits was the great law of recompense. Of course, Moses had in a way taught the principles of this law as instanced in his decree of "an eye for and eye, and a tooth for a tooth" but this was merely a shadow of what the law of recompense means in the spirit world.

This law was then in existence just as much as it is now, but then spirits had only the natural love to help them get out of their condition of suffering and darkness, and, in many cases, it required centuries and centuries for this love to work out their salvation.

And I must tell you also, that when this natural love had done its work, the spirit came into a condition of happiness and satisfaction. So much so, that many of them remain contented; and some who lived on earth when I lived and became spirits when I became a spirit, are still in that condition of happiness which this natural love in a pure state gives them. They did not awaken to the great truth that the Divine Love had been offered them at the time of Jesus' coming to earth, just as many, yes, as the large majority of men, have never awakened to this fact.

So you see, while God in His goodness and mercy has provided a way by which all may become partakers of His Divine nature and of the corresponding great and never dying happiness, yet, He has also provided a natural love which may become free from all sin and earthly grossness, and when so purified enables the spirit to enjoy a happiness far beyond what mortals may conceive of.

But this latter condition does not bring immortality, and no spirit with only this natural love has any assurance that it is immortal. Well, I have written very much and must stop for this time.

Well, at the time Moses and Elias met Jesus in the Mount of Transfiguration, they had received a portion of this Divine Love, because they had learned previous to that date of its re-bestowal on mankind. And as they were very spiritual beings, in the sense, that they had developed their natural love to its supreme excellence and were very near the Father in their soul development, so they were ready recipients of this Divine Love when it came again to man and spirits. But they were not so filled with it then as many spirits who were mortals in your time, are now.

As I understand the meaning of the Transfiguration, it was to show to the disciples of the Master, that while Jesus was the possessor and embodiment of this Divine Love in the mortal world, so Moses and Elias were the possessors of it in the spirit world. In other words, Jesus' appearance showed that it had been bestowed on mortal man, and the appearance of Moses and Elias showed that it had also been bestowed on the spirits.

Sometime I will come and relate to you my experience in finding this Love and in becoming convinced of the real mission and truth of Jesus' teaching—and how this Love came into my soul and resulted in my becoming a Christian. The sphere in which I live has no number,[48] but it is high in the Celestial Heavens, but not as high as that in which the apostles live. They have wonderful soul development, which means the possession of this Love to a great degree, which determines their place of living.

Well, I am grateful that I could write to you tonight, and I feel that by having done so, I am opening the way to my being able to do good to mortals, for we are now forming an army, as you would say, to make a great and successful onslaught on the powers of evil and darkness as they now exist in the mortal world. Jesus will be the leader of this army. He is the greatest spirit in all God's universe, and we, who are his followers, realize that fact and follow him without question. So, my friend, I must stop.

With the love of a brother, who to you may seem ancient, but is very young, I will say, good night.

Daniel.

---

[48] All spheres above the third Celestial sphere are so graduated that no number is used. (Dr. S.)

His teaching and experience when on earth. Did not get the Divine Love until Jesus came to earth

July 21st, 1915.

Samuel, the Prophet of God of the Old Testament.

I am the same Samuel whom the woman of Endor called from the spirit world to show Saul his doom; and as I come to you tonight, I came to her at that time, only my purpose is not the same, and I am not the same spirit in my qualifications.

I am now a Christian and know what the Divine Love of the Father means, while then, I did not, and was a spirit living in comparative happiness and existing in the consciousness that I had done my work on earth, and was then enjoying the repose of the righteous; for as we understood that word then in both the mortal and spirit worlds, I was a righteous man.

I come to you tonight, because I see that you have been chosen to do the great work of the Master in His efforts to redeem mankind from their lives of sin and error, and to show them the way by which they may partake of the Divine nature of the Father and obtain immortality.

How much more mankind, and spirits too, are blessed now than they were when I was a mortal, and for a long time after I became a spirit. My God then and your God now, are the same, but His Great Gift of Divine Love was not in existence then as It is now. And so you and all other mortals should realize the great privilege you have because of this Gift and the gift of Jesus to explain, and show the Way by which that Love may be obtained, and that freely without mental exercise of a high order, but merely by the longings and aspirations of the soul in its desires to become a part of the Father's Divinity.

I tell you that the ways of God are wonderful and mysterious, and His Plans, while to us may seem to be working slowly, yet they are working surely, and will be accomplished in His Own fullness of time.

I never knew when on earth, that God was such a God of Love and Mercy. He was our Jehovah and ruler. He was a God of anger and wrath and a jealous God, as I thought, ever ready to punish those whom He thought to be His enemies with massacre and death. I obeyed Him and performed His work as I understood I should, more through fear than love. In fact love was never with me a weapon or instrument to be used in bringing the disobedient Jew to a compliance with what we thought was the will of God.

In such a method of procuring obedience the soul was never developed, and love was a minor factor in making the Jews obedient to the Father's requirements.

Our principal desires were for the success of our earthly

undertakings, and when these were accomplished, we had no further use for our God, except to keep Him in reserve for occasions that might arise when, as we thought, we might need His assistance.

I know that Moses commanded the Jews to love God with all their souls and mind and strength, and many of them thought that they were doing so, but in reality their love was limited by the extent of their desires for worldly gain. And this I know, for when they had succeeded in obtaining what they wanted, they forgot to love God; and, hence we prophets were so often required to instruct them, and so frequently did call them to a recollection of God, and the danger they ran in forgetting Him and His laws. But we seldom attempted to have them call back in their recollections of Him through love, but nearly always through threatenings and the portrayal of dire punishments that would be inflicted upon them should they continue to forget Him.

And thus it was that Saul sought my help and advice. He thought that not only had God forsaken him, but that he had forsaken God, and he expected the punishment that he thought would result from such neglect to serve and obey God. And he thought, that as I was in the spirit world and probably very close to God, I would exercise some influence and have the great threatened calamity arrested. But he did not seek me through love of God, but through fear of his enemies and dread that God would direct His wrath upon him.

So you see, fear was the ruling sentiment that actuated the Jews in my time in their dealings with God, and when that fear was allayed or forgotten God was forgotten, and only again remembered when danger appeared. Of course, there were many exceptions to this class of Jews, for there were some who really loved God and that in a way that no fear of wrath or anger on His part formed a part of their love.

So, you will see that the laws of Moses were not so much intended to regulate the spiritual or soul part of the Jews, but to control them in their dealings with one another in the practical affairs of life and in their dealings with the heathens and strangers.

The moral laws thus taught were taught for the purpose of making them righteous as between themselves, and then, as a consequence, so they thought, they would be righteous towards God. But the great essential to make them one with God by obtaining the Divine Love was missing, and never sought for, and could not then be found, for it did not then exist for mankind. I am now a Christian and know that the Divine Love is a reality and that all men may have it if they will only seek for it.

Well, the woman of Endor was not a witch and did not practice the black art. She was a good woman possessed of powers to call up the dead, as they were called. She did not engage in practices of doing harm to mortals, such as putting spells upon them or using charms, but she was a true medium and, while not possessed of much spirituality, yet she was a woman of good morals, and had around her many spirits of the higher order whose only desires were to do good to mortals. She was the one who was careful to have no evil spirits come and communicate, and her powers with the higher ones were very great. Had she been of what you call the lower class of mediums, I would never have responded to her call; she was in rapport with men and other spirits whose thoughts were turned to the higher things of the spirit world, and, hence, she had no difficulty in having us appear when she desired it for the consolation of help to mortals.

Saul, I had instructed and advised when alive, and naturally after I became a spirit and he needed help, he would seek my advice.

In those days mediums were more numerous than most people suppose, and because of their being so common and of such different kinds, and the most of them engaged in necromancy and evil arts, there were passed strict laws against them pursuing their calling or engaging in the practice of consulting spirits.

But not all were bad, and many of them did good in the world, and among these was the woman of Endor, notwithstanding that she has been so vilified and abused by the churches and preachers. You may be surprised when I tell you that she is now living high up in the Celestial Heavens and a redeemed spirit enjoying the Divine Love of God.

Well, I must stop, but I will come again sometime and tell you of the things that I know in reference to these higher spheres.

I will say good night.
Your friend and brother,
Samuel.

Affirming that Daniel and Samuel wrote

July 21st, 1915.

I am here, Helen.

Well, sweetheart you must stop for tonight. You are tired and it will do you harm to write more.

They are powerful spirits and look as young as do the spirits of those who died recently, and were very young. I mean they looked like young men—and really are; and they are very highly developed in their souls and intellects. Daniel is especially beautiful and also very powerful.

With all my love, I am
Your own true and loving
Helen.

Elias on the history of the times when he lived on earth. He never knew of the Divine Love until Jesus came to earth and made known its rebestowal

October 1st, 1916.

I am here, Elias. (Elijah of the Old Testament.)

I was the prophet of old and now I am an inhabitant of the Celestial Heaven and an immortal child of the Father. I have been present on several occasions when the high spirits were writing to you, and have been much interested in the work which they are doing and in the work which you are doing, for you are doing a wonderful work in helping the dark spirits of suffering,[49] and in bringing these spirits in close communion with the higher spirits who can show them the way to the Father's Love.

I would like to write you a long message tonight upon the history of the times in which I lived, and the knowledge that we, who were looked upon and written about as prophets, had as to the relationship between God and man; and what some of our experiences were with the spirits of the heavens who came to us and communicated some of the truths of the Father. And I will say, in all our knowledge of truth, we never understood what the Divine Love of the Father was as distinguished from the love that He bestowed on all men irrespective of their seeking for His Love, and irrespective of the fact that they were sinful and disobedient to His commands. As I now know we could not have understood what this Divine Love meant, or ever have possessed it, for in my time and until the coming of Jesus, the privilege of men receiving it did not exist. The Father had withdrawn this privilege from humanity.

But we did receive spiritual knowledge of those things that would make man better in his moral nature, and bring him closer to the Father in his natural love; and our efforts were directed towards making the people understand these things and the necessity of complying with the moral laws.

As I said, I should like to write you a long message, but there is another present who desires to write and I will stop. But I will come soon and deliver my message, and in the meantime I will pray for you and try to help you in your soul development and in your work. With all my love and blessings I will say good night.

Your brother in Christ,

---

[49] Mr. Padgett gave one evening a week for the dark spirits to write. He would then cause these spirits to visualize the bright spirits who would help and instruct them so they could progress. (Dr. S.)

Elias.

His experience while on earth and the spirit world. Transfiguration on the Mount a reality

October 11th, 1916.

I am here, Elias. (Elijah, Prophet to the Hebrews.)
I will write a short message tonight as I promised. While on earth I was a prophet to the Hebrews and tried to warn them that God was not pleased with the manner in which they were living, especially in not obeying the commandments as to their worship and the individual lives they were leading. I was not a man who knew the attributes of God as I now know them, for then, to me, He was more a God of wrath and jealousy than of love and mercy, and the most of my teachings were to warn the Hebrews of the wrath that would certainly fall upon them unless they were more obedient and followed the laws of Moses.

I now know that the wrath of God is not a thing to be feared, and that His wrath is not a thing of reality. That when men disobey His laws and neglect to worship Him in truth and in spirit, His feeling towards them is one more of pity and sorrow than of wrath, and that instead of punishment He extends to them His Mercy and Love.

In my time the God of Love was not known to the people in any practical way although He was written of as a God of Love, and the people were not looking so much for love as the fearing His wrath; and it was only by threatening them with His wrath could they be made to realize that they were disobedient and aliens from Him.

They had not that soul development that comes with love, and their aspirations were almost wholly for the possession of the things of life and for a happiness that such possession could give to them, as they thought. They expected a Kingdom of God on earth and such Kingdom was to be one that should rule and govern the earthly affairs of men. Of course they believed that when such Kingdom should be established, sin and the troubles of life would be eradicated, and all the world would be subject to the dominion of such Kingdom.

Their hopes and aspirations were in the nature of national hopes and aspirations and not in those of the individual. The individual was swallowed up in the nation and happiness was to be a national one instead of an individual one, except so far as the national happiness might be reflected upon and partaken of by the individuals. I, myself, knew nothing of the Divine Love, and could not possibly have known, for then it was not open to man's seeking, as it had not been restored by the Father. But I knew of a higher development of the natural love than did most of the people, and realized what increased happiness such development would give to the individual who might possess it. I also knew that prosperity and power of the nation, as such, would not bring the happiness of love, but only the pleasures and satisfaction which increased possessions would naturally create.

The Jews were a carnally minded race and the development of the spiritual side of their natures was very slight. Their acquisitiveness was large both as individuals and as a nation, and when they were prosperous they lost their sense of dependence on God, and resorted to those practices and that manner of living that would enable them, as they thought, to get the most enjoyment out of their possessions. The future, that is the future after death, did not enter very much into their consideration of existence, and they lived emphatically for the present. If you will read the Biblical history of those times you will find that most of the warnings of the prophets came to them when they as a nation were most prosperous, and, as they thought, independent of God, or at least, of not being compelled to call upon Him for help and succor.

What I have said showed the characteristics of the Jews, and they still have these characteristics although since the coming of Christ and the teachings of his doctrines that have become so widely known, the spirituality of the Jews have been increased and broadened. At times they would heed my warnings and at other times they would not. Sometimes they considered me as a friend, and sometimes as an enemy.

Well, I was psychic and frequently heard voices of instruction and admonition from the unseen world, and, as was our knowledge in those days, supposed that such voices was the voice of God, and so proclaimed to the people. But now I know that such voices were those of spirits that were trying to help the people, and bring them to a realization of the moral truths which Moses had taught.

When Jesus was born into the flesh, there came with him a rebestowal of the Divine Love, and through his teachings that fact became known to men. We who were in the higher spirit spheres also came to know of that gift, and while none of us received it to the degree that Jesus did, yet we received it and became pure and holy spirits, free from sin and error, and partakers of the Divine Essence of the Father and possessors of immortality.

And so, at the time of the transfiguration on the mount, some of us possessed that Love to such a degree that our appearances were shining and bright, as described in the Bible. But Jesus was brighter than Moses or myself, for he had more of this Divine Love in his soul and could manifest it to the wonderful degree that he did, notwithstanding his physical body.

Our appearance and his appearance on the mount were to show to the mortals and spirits that the Divine Love had been rebestowed and received by both mortals and spirits, and this was the cause of our meeting. And while accounts of that event have been disseminated in the mortal world ever since its occurrence, so also, had that fact became known in portions of the spirit world, and many spirits as well as mortals, have sought for and found that love to their eternal happiness.

Its existence was a fact then and it is a fact now, and the Love is open to all mankind as well as spirits. The voice that the apostles heard proclaiming that Jesus was the well beloved son was not the voice of God, but that of one of the Divine spirits whose mission it was to make the proclamation. This incident was not a myth but an actual fact that formed a part of the Plan of the Father to assure man of his salvation.

I will not write more now, but will come later and write you further on this subject of the rebestowal of the love and of my experience in receiving it. So with my love and blessings, I will say good night.

Your brother in Christ,
Elias.

Elias was not John the Baptist, neither was John a reincarnation of Elias

February 7th, 1917.

I am here, Elias.

I want also to encourage you in the belief that you have the great work to do, and that you must not falter or delay the coming of the messages, for if you will only think for a moment, you will realize that there is no other way in which these truths can at this time be conveyed to mankind.

You must not doubt, or cause yourself to hesitate for a moment to believe that the work has been imposed upon you as one not fitted to receive these truths. I know that sometime it is hard for you to believe that you have been selected to do this great work or that you are fitted to receive these great spiritual truths that are to be given to the world, but you must not let such thoughts linger in your mind, for it is a fact that you have been selected to do the work, and you must not shirk it, for if you do, mankind may remain a long time in ignorance of what the truth is, and the way in which it can take on the Essence of the Father, and become His true children, and partakers of His nature, so that the very Essence and Divinity of the Father may become a part of the people.

The work must be done by you and you must not doubt, but have a firm conviction of its truth and try your best to receive the messages. I merely wanted to say this much, as I am much interested in the work. Yes, there are a great number present, and you have around you a wonderful spiritual influence which should cause you to believe that these spirits are present trying to help you.

I was Elijah of the Old Testament, and I actually lived and was a prophet among the Jews, and was not John the Baptist, nor was he a reincarnation of me as some of earth teachers claim. John was himself alone. He was in the flesh only once and was not a reincarnation of me or anyone else. I will not write more now, so good night.

Your brother in Christ
Elias.

Much interested in the work and the importance of mankind knowing the Truth

February 7th, 1917.

I am here, Cornelius. (The Centurion)

I want to write merely a few lines tonight. I am so very much interested in you and your work, that I feel that I should give you some encouragement in the way of letting you know that there are many spirits present here tonight who love you very much and desire that you should receive their messages of love and truth.

As I have told you, I am in the Celestial Spheres and know what the Love of the Father is and what immortality means, as I am the possessor of the Love, and the conscious owner of that immortality. The world is now so anxious to know the truths that pertain to God and to man's relationship to Him, and the messages that you are receiving will give to the world what it so much longs for.

I know that the Christian doctrines as contained in the Bible and taught by many preachers and priests, are the only doctrines that the Christians have any knowledge of, and, consequently, are accepted by them as being the inspired revelations of God, and the truth of what He is, and what man must do in order to obtain salvation. And these people rest securely in these beliefs, and in the assurance that the Bible way is the only way to salvation; and resting in these beliefs the world does not see the necessity for obtaining the only thing that will make them in at-onement with God, and make them inhabitants of His heavens.

I merely write this to show you that it is of the greatest importance that the truths of the way to salvation be revealed to all mankind. I do not think that I have anything more to say tonight, and so will leave you. With all my love, I am

Your brother in Christ
Cornelius.[50]

---

[50] This message is a composite of two, being published in Volume I and Volume II. (G.J.C.)

The truth of the Bible as to the things that are contained in the Old Testament

March 18th, 1917.

I am here, Elias.

I come tonight to write a short message on the subject of "The truth of the Bible as to the things that are contained in the Old Testament." And by this I do not mean that I will discuss this portion of the Bible in all the views and declarations that are contained therein, but only as to that portion which has to do with the times in which I was supposed to live.

In the first place my entrance on the scene of Jewish life and history was very abrupt, and little was written about my antecedent life, and in fact, nothing except that I was a Tishbite who lived in that portion of Palestine where the acts and doings of the prophets and men of the Hebrew race are very seldom referred to, and little is known of these people.

When I came into notice, as portrayed, I was not very widely known, and to the writers of the Scriptures it appeared as if I had come out of the unknown, where God had taken special pains to instruct and communicate to me the truths of His laws, and also the acts of disobedience of those Jews among whom I appeared. But a very great deal of the accounts of my appearing and things that I declared and did are imaginary and the result of the workings of the minds of those who produced the stories of the lives of the Jews at those times, and in the way told in the Bible.

I was a real existing person and of the prophet class and warned the kings and rulers of the wrath of God that was impending upon them, and of the evils of their manner of living, and was listened to by these kings, who sometimes heeded my warnings and sometimes did not; and some of the consequences were suffered by them in a way similar to that described in the Bible.

But I never claimed to have direct communication with God, or to deliver any messages that He had directed me to deliver by His own word of mouth, or that I had ever seen God, or knew who or what He was.

I was a man who lived a rather secluded life, and was versed in the teachings and beliefs of the Israelites, as they were known at the time, and was also given to much meditation and prayer and possessed much of the religious instinct, and, in fact, to such a degree, that I really believed that the thoughts and perceptions of truth that came to me, were actually the messages from the unseen world; and possessing the knowledge of the moral truths, as declared in the Decalogue and as taught by the priests of the temple, I could readily discern and understand the acts and doings of the kings and of the people, as well, to be a violation of these moral truths. And so when I learned of these violations, I appeared to these rulers and people and denounced their acts and doings and threatened them with the wrath of God, unless they ceased their acts of disobedience and returned to the worship of the one true God that the Hebrew race distinctly declared and worshiped. Sometimes I was received as the true prophet of God and sometimes I was not and, as a consequence, my messages, at times, were received and believed in, and at other times they were not.

The foundation stone of my belief and office was that there was only one God, and He was the God of the Hebrews, and all other Gods that were believed in, and worshiped by a part of the Jews and by the Gentiles, were false gods, and should not have obeisance made to them or worshiped. And, hence, when I appeared to Ahab and denounced the gods of Belial, I was performing, as I believed, the duties that my God had imposed upon me, and which were so necessary to cause the turning away of the people from their false beliefs and worship to an acknowledgment of the one true God.

Well, there are many things related in these writings that never occurred and the one that is often referred to and accepted as proof of the superior power of my God over the god, Ba-al, that is the consuming by fire of the offerings at the altar by the power of God, after the priests had called upon their false god to answer their prayers and he neglected to respond, never occurred, but it is the result of the endeavor of some Jewish writer to demonstrate to his people, the wonderful power and activity and closeness of that God to His prophets. Such an incident never took place, and there are many other occurrences related to the powers that I possessed as the prophet of God, that never had any existence.

While I considered and believed myself to be a prophet of God, yet I never had any of the supernatural powers, nor were any such ever displayed by me, as recorded in the supposed history of my life as a mortal.

There is one other instance to which I desire to refer and that is my supposed ascension into heaven in a chariot of fire in the presence of Elisha. This is merely a tale, as I may say, well told, but it never had any existence in fact; and I did not ascend in my physical body, or did any other mortal that I have heard of, not even the Master, for it would be against the laws of God that such a thing should take place, and He never violates His laws for the purpose of demonstrating to mortals His power, or the greatness of any of His followers or for any other purpose.

No, I died as other mortals died, and was buried as was necessary for me to be buried, having with one at the time of my death, friends and relatives; and since that time my physical body has never been resurrected and never will be.

I ascended into the spirit world in my spirit body, as has every other mortal at the time of the death of his physical body since the world of human existence began, and in the future, the spirits of men will so continue to ascend and their physical bodies go to the elements out of which they were composed.

It may be supposed, that because I was versed in the teachings of the religious laws of the Hebrews and the precepts of the decalogue and believed myself to be a prophet and especially delegated by God to denounce the sins and evils of the kings and people that had forsaken the beliefs and practices of their fathers, that I went into the heaven of perfection and into the supreme happiness that the obedient child when in perfect harmony with the laws of God, would enter. Well, if I had been such child, I might have done so, but not being such, I went merely into the spirit world and found my place just where the condition of my soul in its harmony with God's laws and His truths, fitted me for and determined that I should be placed.

The condition of soul determines the destiny of the spirit. No mere belief in self-righteousness, or the conviction that I—the individual—have been specially favored by God to do His work, or that I am closer to God and deserving of His special mercy and favor, or that a special dispensation is exercised in my behalf, can ever place me in different surroundings or conditions or degrees of happiness, from what the actual harmony of the qualities of my soul with the laws of God and the workings thereof, entitle me.

The law of fitness works invariably and under all circumstances, and the conditions and qualities of the soul in the spirit world can never be hidden nor counterfeited. Then is seen face to face, and the law in its application and effect never makes a mistake so that the soul not having the fitness cannot enter into the Kingdom of Heaven by crying, Lord, Lord, did I not prophecy in Thy name, etc.

Many of these stories of the Old Testament may be profitably used to draw a moral or adorn a tale, but when the question arises, as what shall determine the destiny of the human soul, then the truth never changes, and only the truth will decide the question. Only a pure, perfect soul can find its home in a pure perfect heaven, and only a Divine soul can find its home in a Divine Heaven; which latter, is the home of the soul that possesses the Divine Essence of the Father to that fullness that the created qualities of the soul have disappeared and been replaced by the Divine Substance.

So that, we may be prophets and preachers, wise in the intellectual knowledge of religious truths, and saints on earth, and apostles and disciples, and yet, not having the purification of the soul or the Divine Essence, we cannot enter the home which the one or the other of these possessions will fit us for.

Let the prophets of Old, and the sacrifices and the blood and the vicarious atonement rest in the memory of forgetfulness, and seek and obtain the inflowing of the Divine Love of the Father, and then the home of the soul will truly and certainly be the Heavens Celestial where only things Divine can exist.

Well, I have written enough for tonight, and hope that you will find my message both interesting and helpful. It is true, and you can believe that it is and in its truth rests the certainty of what the destiny of your own soul may be.

I will come again very soon. So good night.

Your brother in Christ, Elias (Elijah).

He now knows the difference between the spirit who has in his soul the Divine Love and one who has not

December 4th, 1916.

I am here, Esau, son of Isaac.

I was the son of Isaac and the brother of Jacob, and the one whom the Jews regarded as having sold his birthright for a mess of pottage, but I was misrepresented in this regard, as I did only that which necessity compelled me to do. But all that is long past, and now I am an inhabitant of the Celestial Heavens, for in the world of spirits all things are made right, and I became a possessor of the Divine Love after I had received knowledge of its rebestowal at the coming of Jesus.

Many of the characters of the Old Testament have never yet realized this great transformation, because in their conception, of self righteousness, are contented in that conception, and worship God as they did on earth, although they have ceased to offer sacrifices of animals, because they have none in spirit life to offer, yet they still have the belief that sacrifice is necessary, and in their imaginations, they offer what to them is symbolical of the offerings that they made in the earth life.

Yes, that is quite a natural supposition, but you must know that mind and the beliefs of mortals continue with them when they become spirits and who will not permit themselves to be convinced of the errors of their conceptions of Deity, and many of these spirits of old, are in that condition now. They refuse to believe or even listen to the truths of existence and their relationship to God, as they did when on earth. They have eyes, but they see not, and ears but they hear not, and enveloped in the darkness of their beliefs, they decline to let in the light, or to permit the truths[51] that are so apparent to others to illuminate their souls. A mind that is shut in by bigotry and intolerance is just as persistent after the mortal becomes a spirit even though a change in its surroundings in what you might call its physical existence and in its possibilities for learning the truth, yet many of these spirits, absolutely refuse to recognize any change or possibility of change in their spiritual condition.

It is not surprising that you may not understand how it is possible that these spirits of the kind mentioned could live all this great period of years, as you estimate time, in this condition, surrounded by spirits[52] who have found the truth, and display that possession in their appearances and happiness, and especially by some of their old associates who have entered into the light, and not be influenced by these appearances and the experiences of these associates, but, nevertheless, it is true, and the difficulty of converting these bigoted spirits seems to grow the greater as they advance in their progression of mind and natural love. They are happy in a relative sense and in their beliefs they can conceive of no other belief or cause of progress that could bring to them greater happiness; and besides they are firmly convinced that they are doing the will of God in their manner of worship and in their symbolical sacrifices.

These ancient spirits, as you call them, but who are young as compared to many in the spirit spheres; have their synagogues and temples of worship, and their priests and servants and worshipers according to their old beliefs. And the ceremonies attending their gatherings for worship are very little different from what they were on earth. They have all their vestments and attire and other accompaniments that on earth distinguished them from the common people, and they say their prayers in public and delight in appearing as holy spirits, the specially chosen of God, just as they did on earth, and as they are developing more and more in their natural love, and taking on the condition of perfection, so far as the perfection of the first parents as they existed before the fall, they may remain in this condition of belief as to their relationship to God, and as to their proper and only way to worship Him throughout all eternity.

They decline to receive the knowledge of the truth of the New Birth, and as that is a thing that is optional with them and its rejection does not prevent them from becoming the "perfect man," as you have had explained to you, there is no absolute necessity as they think they

---

[51] This refers to the spirits who have obtained the New Birth. (Dr. S. in the errata published with the First Edition)
[52] Those who have partaken of the Divine Love in their souls. (Dr. S. in the errata published with the First Edition)

should be born again in order to enable a restoration of the harmony of that condition and relationship that they may have to the Father. Of course, until the day of the consummation of the Kingdom of the Celestial Spheres they will have the opportunity to become recipients of the Divine Love and the transformation into angels redeemed, but it is doubtful if very many of them will ever elect to accept this great privilege.

I am glad that I could write to you tonight, as it is a new experience with me, but one that gives me great satisfaction, and I will come again, if agreeable to you, and write further. I wish to say in closing that I know the difference between the spirit who has in his soul the Divine Love, and one who has not, and that the mere time of a spirit's existence in the spirit world, does not necessarily indicate that the spirit possesses the Divine Love. As Jesus said when on earth, "the first shall be last, and the last shall be first," and I may add, that some will never be first or last, but only the reminders of what might have been. I will not write more.

Your brother in Christ
Esau.

What is the greatest thing in all the world?

April 20th, 1916.

Solomon, of the Old Testament.
I come only to say, that very soon I desire to write you another message, conveying to you some great truth of the Father. I will not write more now, but will soon come.

(What is the greatest thing in all the world?)

Prayer and faith on the part of mortals; and Love—the Divine Love—on the part of God. The latter is waiting, and the former causes it to enter into the souls of men. No other truths are so great and momentous to men. Let what I say sink deep into your memory, and try the experiment. I know you do try, but try and then try and never cease trying. Love will come to you and with It faith, and then knowledge and then ownership.

I could write for a long time, yet, but I must not as you are tired. So with my love and blessings, I will say good night, and may the Father's Love take possession of you.

Your brother in Christ,
Solomon.

Adds his testimony and experience in the spirit world.—Jesus is the ruler of the Celestial Heavens

August 10th, 1915.

Lot, of the Old Testament.

I come because I now am a follower of the Master, and want to add my testimony to that of others of olden times who have written you that Jesus is alive and the ruler in the Celestial Heavens, and is now working among men and spirits to show them the way to eternal life, and the Divine Love of the Father.

I am not a Hebrew who would have denied him had I lived when he came to the earth for in my thoughts and belief, I expected the coming of the Messiah and to me Jesus was that Messiah in all the qualities and spiritual possessions that I expected him to have.

Of course, when I lived we had not the privilege of knowing what the Divine Love of the Father means,—we only knew that there was a God and that God loved us as we thought, as His chosen people and wanted us to live correct lives on earth, and thereby receive His blessings as mortals, and all the rewards that an obedient life might bring to us. But as to this Greater Love which makes angels of us all who possesses it, we had no knowledge, nor had we ever been taught by our seers or prophets that such a Love existed and as I now know the privilege of obtaining it did not then exist. Only with the coming of Jesus came that Love again to man and spirits.

But God had for us a natural love in contradistinction to the Divine Love and we had for Him a love which when fully purified makes us spirits with a happiness that is beyond all conception of human happiness. But even of that happiness we were not taught, and only did we have glimpses in the teachings of our prophets that such happiness might exist in the future life.

I was a lover of God as I then understood what God was; but such love was not that which arose from my conception of Him as a tender loving Father, but more as a stern wrathful God—one of jealousy and always watchful and ready to punish for disobedience to His commands. And yet we also learned that when we obeyed Him and did His will He would reward us.

So you see the God of my days and the God of the present, as we now conceive Him to be, are not similar. And all men should now understand and believe that Jesus Christ brought to light, and by that I mean to the knowledge of men, the possibility of their knowing the True God of Love and Mercy; and also, that because of that Love and His Great Mercy in the re-bestowal upon mankind of the possibility of men becoming possessed of the Divine Love of the Father which would make them one with Him and with certainty of Immortality.

It was long years after Jesus came before I received this Divine Love or believed the great truths which Jesus taught. I was so satisfied in my happiness as a spirit possessing merely this natural love which had been purified and freed from sin and error, that I thought there could be no greater love or no greater happiness. But in the course of time I had reasons to think that there might be another if not greater love in operation in the spirit world, because of the wonderful beauty and brightness of some of the spirits that I at times met. And I started to make investigation of the matter, and as a result, I learned of this Divine Love, and at last sought for and found it. And what a treasure I found!

I am now so filled with it that my happiness is beyond all conception of not only man, but of spirits who live in lower spheres than I do. I must not write more tonight, but I will tell you that I am one of the many Celestial Spirits who are interested in and now are engaged in doing the great work for the redemption of mankind.

Jesus is our leader and we are all following him in the effort to redeem the world, and by that I mean the individuals who comprise the world. For you must know that redemption is an individual matter and not one that can be accomplished in the way of redeeming a nation or a race as a whole. So you see back of this work is the great power of the Celestial as well as of the spiritual heavens. I have written enough for tonight.

Well, the incident of my wife turning into a pillar of salt is like a great many others related in the Old Testament—these incidents are mere figures of speech used to illustrate some moral or spiritual truth. My wife was never turned into salt, but died a natural death and her remains were buried where mine were buried. She is now in the Celestial Heavens also.

So my dear brother, I must say good night.

Lot.

An ancient spirit, wrote a book—description of creation and of the fall of man—Genesis was copied after his writings

August 10th, 1915.

I was a native of Arabia and lived before the time of Abraham, the Jewish patriarch. I come to you tonight to tell you that before the Jewish Testament was written, I had written a book containing a description of creation and of the fall of man, and that the book of Genesis was copied after my writings, which were founded on traditions older than were the description of Genesis.

These descriptions of the creation of the world were not the works of men inspired by the angels or by any other instrumentalities of God, but were the results of the imaginations of the minds of men who lived long before I lived, and who left only tradition of their writings or teachings. I say all this to show you that the world has existed for many thousands of years longer than the account of its creation in the Jewish Scriptures would lead you to think.

I don't know when it was created and I have not found any spirit in the spiritual world who does know. Of course no spirit would know of his own knowledge because in the natural order of things, man must have been created subsequent to the creation of those things which were necessary for his sustenance and comfort. I have never seen any angels who were not at one time mortals, and hence I could not learn from them when the world was created and I have never seen any angels or spirits to whom God has made this revelation. So I say the creation of the world or rather any account if it is all a matter of speculation and tradition.

Yes, I have been informed as to the fall of man. My information is as follows:—when man was created he was made two-fold,—that is there were male and female beings—which was intended to make a perfect one without losing any individuality on the part of either. Their names were not Adam and Eve, but Aman and Amon, which meant the male Am and the female Am. Am meaning the exalted creation of God.

These beings were made perfect physically and spiritually. But these souls were not possessed of all the qualities of the Great Creator Soul, and in that particular were inferior to the Great Creator. But as regards this soul part of their creation, they were made in the image of their Creator. The physical or spiritual part of their creation was not in the image of their Creator, for He had no physical or spiritual body. But their soul part was only made in the image of their Creator—and not of the Substance—but this image was given a potentiality of obtaining or receiving the Substance of the soul qualities of their Creator and provided, if they pursued that course in their existence or living which would cause their souls to receive in accordance with certain operations of the laws which their Creator had prescribed, this soul Substance. And only in obedience to these laws or their operations could this Substance of the Creator Soul, be obtained.

Well, these creatures were not equal to the test, or rather requirements, and after living awhile they became possessed of the idea that they needed not to comply with these prescribed laws, but could of their own will and power obtain this Substance by doing that which they had been forbidden by these laws to do, and so in their efforts to obtain this Substance or Divine Love they disobeyed these laws, and, as a consequence, these potentialities of obtaining the Substance of the Creator Soul were taken from them, and then they became beings still possessed of the spiritual and physical forms and continued souls, but not of these great potentialities—and this was the fall of man. The story of the apple is a myth.

No apple or anything else that was intended to be eaten formed any part of the fall. It was wholly the fall of the soul's potentialities. The disobedience was the great unlawful desire on the part of these two, to obtain this soul substance before, in accordance with the operations of the laws prescribed, they were fitted or in condition to receive it; and as a consequence, they became disobedient, and being possessed of wills which were not in any way bound or limited by their creator, they exercised these wills in accordance with their desires, and from this disobedience the wills of men and women have continued to act in accordance with their desires and in violation of the great laws of truth, which were made for the two creatures at the time of their creation and are the same unchangeable laws of this time.

The soul substance that these two forfeited was the Divine Love of their Creator, which, had they by their obedience became possessed of, would have made them a part of His Divinity, and thence like Him not only in image but in Substance and reality. The potentiality that was taken from them was the privilege which they had to obtain this soul Substance or Divine Love by complying with obedience which these laws prescribed. So you see the story of genesis is merely symbolical. I have nothing further to say tonight.

I live in a sphere which is part of the Celestial Heavens. I have, through the mercy of God and His gift, declared by Jesus, received this potentiality and through it the Soul Substance which our first parents forfeited. The name which I have given you was mine when on earth. It is Arabic and nothing else. You must know that many of the names of my time were in after centuries incorporated in the nomenclature of other nations and races.

So I will say good night.
Your brother in Christ,
Leytergus.

Woman of Endor was not a wicked woman as many believe

August 7th, 1915.

Saul of the Old Testament.

I am the same Saul that called up Samuel, or rather who caused the woman of Endor to do so. I was a wicked man in those days, and knew not the love of God, and very little of my fellow mortals. I was a cruel man and a worker of iniquity, and violated God's laws in many ways. As you have read, I came to the end of my resources and went to consult Samuel as the last resort. I did not know that God had abandoned me until Samuel had told me.

Yes, He did and was my protector as long as I obeyed Him and did what was right in His sight. I know that He did, because when I obeyed Him, I was successful and happy. I only knew from what the prophets told me, and they claimed to have communications with God in some way. I believed this, and hence thought that God was protecting me.

I am a redeemed spirit now and am happy in the Love of the Father. I became a lover of the Father and an inhabitant of His Kingdom long after Jesus proclaimed the Great Truth of Divine Love restored. Before that I was a spirit who lived in the happiness which I experienced in developing my soul and becoming a good spirit, free from sin and error. But this happiness is not that which I now enjoy.

I want to confirm what Samuel said as to the woman of Endor. She was not a witch or evil woman, but was a medium and received communications from the higher spirits of the spirit world. She had been abused for centuries, and should not be further thought of as a wicked woman. I will not write more tonight.

Well, do you suppose that we of the spirit world stand still in our mental advancement? I know all the important languages of the earth and can write them and understand them. Do not think that spirits do not learn here just as they learned as mortals. The only difference is that they can learn so much more rapidly and can retain their knowledge more easily than mortals can.

So I will say good night.

Your brother in Christ, Saul.

Writes his experience in his progress

July 8th, 1915.

I am here, Socrates, the Greek.

I knew that you thought of me and I was attracted by your thought. If such spirit is in rapport with you or has a similar soul quality; the soul condition is the great medium of attraction. I have been with you before, and there is a rapport growing out of your soul qualities. I am now a believer in the Christian doctrine of the soul's immortality, and in the teachings of Jesus as to the way to obtain the Divine Love of the Father, as you are, and, hence, our qualities of soul are similar.

I am now a follower of the Master and believe in his Divine mission on earth, although he had not come to earth when I lived. After I became a spirit I realized my belief in the continuity of life after death, and lived in the spirit world a great many years after Jesus came before I learned and believed his larger truth of immortality.

Of course, when I taught I had only a hope which was almost a certainty that I should continue to live through all eternity, but I had no other foundation for that belief than the deductions from my reasoning powers and the observations of the workings of nature. I had heard of the visitations of the spirits of the departed, but had never had any personal experiences in that direction, but I readily believed it to be true.

My conviction of the truth of a future continuance was so strong that it amounted to a certainty, and hence when I died, I comforted Plato and my other friends and disciples, by telling them that they must not say that Socrates will die but rather that his body will die; his soul will live forever in fields Elysian. They believed me, and Plato afterwards enlarged on my belief.

And Socrates did not die, but as soon as his breath left the body, which was not very painful even though the fatal hemlock did its work sure and quickly, he went into the spirit world a living entity, full of the happiness that the realizations of his beliefs gave him.

My entrance into the spirit world was not a dark one, but full of light and happiness, for I was met by some of my disciples who had passed over before me and who had progressed very much in the intellectual development. I then thought that my place of reception was the heaven of good spirits, for there were good spirits to meet me and carry me to my home. I was then possessed of what I thought that I was in the home of the blessed; and I continued there for many years and enjoyed the exchange of minds and the feasts of reason.

And as I continued to live, I progressed, until at last, I entered the highest intellectual sphere and became a beautiful and bright spirit, so they told me, and taught the things of a mind developed. I met many minds of great power of thought and beauty; and my happiness was beyond my conception when on earth. Many of my old friends and disciples came over and our reunions were always joyous. Plato came and Cato and others.

And the ages went by, and I continued in my life of intellectual enjoyment and profit, with many spirits developed in their minds and powers of thought, until our existence was a continuous feast of bright and momentous thoughts interchanged. I traversed the spheres in search of knowledge and information without limitation, and found the principles of many laws of the spirit world.

I found in many spheres spirits, who said they were the old Hebrew prophets and teachers; and they were still teaching of their Hebrew God, who they claimed was the only God of the universe and who had made of their nation his favorite people; but I did not find that they were much different from the rest of us—I mean what they called the spirits of the pagan nations. They were not superior to us in intellect, and they lived in no higher spheres than we lived in, and I could not learn that their morality was any more exalted than was ours.

But they insisted that they were God's favorite people, and were in their own estimation, superior to the rest of us and lived in a community all to themselves. I did not know just what the conditions of their souls were, but, as I observed the condition of the soul determines the appearances of the spirit, I did not perceive that their appearances were any more beautiful or godlike than were ours, and I concluded that their God was no better or greater than was ours.

No one, that I could find, had seen any God and I had not; so who or what God was became merely a matter of speculation, and I preferred to have the God of my own conception to the one that they claimed to have.

For long years my life went on in this way, until in my wanderings I found that there was a sphere I could not enter, and I commenced to make inquiries and was told that it was one of the Soul Spheres in which the great ruler or Master was a spirit called Jesus, who had, since my coming to the spirit world, established a New Kingdom, and was the chosen son of God in whom he lived and had his being; and that only those who had received the Divine Love of this God could enter this sphere or become inhabitants thereof. I then sought for more information and, continuing my search, I learned that this Love had been given to men and spirits at the time of the birth of Jesus on earth, and that it was free for all who might seek it in the way taught by him. That he was the greatest true son of this God, and that in no other way than the one shown by this son could this Love be obtained or the Soul Spheres entered.

I thereafter thought of this new revelation, and let many years go by before I became convinced that I might learn something, and become benefitted by seeking this way and this Love; and after awhile I began to seek; but you must know that I and spirits like me, who lived in the spheres where the mind furnished our pursuits and enjoyments, could not enter what was called this Soul Sphere, yet the inhabitants of that Soul Sphere could come into our sphere[53] without let or hindrance.

And I sometimes met and conversed with some of these inhabitants; and on one occasion I met one called John,[54] who was a most beautiful and luminous spirit, and in our conversation he told me of this Divine Love of his God, and of the Great Love and mission of Jesus, and showed me some of the truths taught by Jesus, and the way to

---

[53] Spirits in this sphere have developed their natural love to a pure state but do not possess the Divine Love which is necessary to obtain in order to enter the soul spheres and the Celestial Heavens. (Dr. S.)

[54] St. John, Apostle of Jesus. (Dr. S.)

obtain this Divine Love, and urged me to seek for it.

Strange to me, there were not any of the intellectual qualities required to be exercised in seeking for this Love—only the longings and aspirations of my soul and the exercise of my will. It seemed so simple—so easy—that I commenced to doubt whether there was any reality in what I was told, and I hesitated to follow the advice of this spirit, John. But he was so loving and his countenance was so wonderful, that I concluded to try, and I commenced to pray to this God and tried to exercise faith as I was told. After a while, most surprising of all things, to me, I commenced to have new and unaccountable sensations, and with them a feeling of happiness that I had never experienced before, which made me think that there must be some truth in what I was told. And I continued to pray the harder and believe with more surety. I continued to make these efforts, until, at last, the great awakening came that I had in me a Love that never before was in my soul, and a happiness that all my intellectual pursuits had never been able to supply.

Well, it is not necessary to tell you further in detail my experience in getting and developing this Love. But I became filled with it, and at last entered the Soul Sphere, and what I saw is beyond description.

I met Jesus, and had no conception that there could be such a glorious, magnificent and loving spirit. He was so gracious and seemed to be so much interested in my welfare and progress in the truths that he taught.

Can you wonder that I am a Christian and follower of him? Thereafter, I learned what True Immortality is, and that I am a part of that Immortality. I see how far short my conception and teaching of immortality were. Only this Divine Love can give to spirits Immortality, and anything less is but the shadow of a hope, such as I had.

I am now in a Sphere that is not numbered; but it is high in the Celestial Heavens and not far from some of the Spheres where the disciples of the Master live. I am still progressing, and that is the beauty and glory of the soul development—where there is no limit—while my intellectual development was limited.

I must stop now as I have written more than I should have done. But I will come to you sometime in the not distant future and tell you of some of the truths which I have learned.

Your friend and brother,
Socrates—the one time Greek philosopher but now a Christian.

Confirmation that Socrates wrote through Mr. Padgett

July 8th, 1915.

I am here, your own true and loving Helen.

Well, sweetheart, you have had some wonderful messages tonight, and should feel that you are highly favored in having received such wonderful writings. The message from Socrates may have been a surprise to you and caused you to wonder at the truths and description that he gave of his conversion.

You are certainly a wonderful medium, and you must consider yourself blessed in having such high spirits write to you.

Have faith in the Master and his promises and that is sufficient.

Your own true and loving

Helen.

Plato, disciple of Socrates, is now a Christian

November 11th, 1915.

Let me be the one to tell you of the truth of what you want to know. I am one of the first of the great philosophers of ancient Greece, and was known as Plato. I was a disciple of Socrates and a teacher of his philosophy, with additions.

He was not only a great philosopher but the nicest and best man of his time. His teachings of immortality were then far in advance of those of any teacher, and no man has since surpassed him in his conception of the soul's destiny or its qualities, except the great Master, who knew and brought to light the great truth of immortality.

Socrates and I are both followers of the Master and inhabitants of his Heavenly Spheres where only those who have received the Divine Love of the Father can live. As I followed Socrates on earth, so I followed him in the knowledge of the New Birth, and in the possession of the Great Love which brought to us Immortality.

I cannot say much more tonight as you are too tired to receive any thoughts, but sometime I will come and write you of this great truth, and how far short my philosophy was in its attempts to teach immortality.

I see that you have received many messages from the spirits who are higher than I, and who know more about these Divine Truths but, yet, I think that my experiences in regard to the teachings of this great subject may do some good.

I will not write more, but will say good night.

Your brother in Christ,

Plato.

Various subjects continued.

What does the spirit of man do when it leaves the physical body for eternity?

May 29th, 1916.

I am here, St. John, Apostle of Jesus.

I come tonight to tell you a vital truth, which I know you will be interested in. The question has often been asked: "What does the spirit of man do when it leaves the physical body for eternity?"

Many spirits, I know, have written you about this matter and some of them have described their personal experiences, yet in all the information that you have received there are some facts that have not been referred to, and I will in a brief way describe them.

When the spirit leaves the body, there is a breaking of the silver cord, as it is called, and thereby all connection between the spirit and the body is severed for all eternity—never again can that spirit enter that body, and neither can any other spirit, although, I know, it is claimed by some spiritualists that another spirit may inhabit the cast-off body. But this is all wrong, for no spirit ever enters the body which has once been the home of another spirit, and, hence, claims made by some of the wise men of the East that such a thing can be, have no foundation in fact.

When the silver cord is once severed, no power that is known to the spirit world, or among spirits of the highest sphere, can again resuscitate that body and cause the manifestation of life, and, hence, in the miracles mentioned in the Bible, where it is said that the dead were brought to life, it must be understood that this tie between the spirit and the body was never broken.

In those ancient days, as now, there were persons who had the appearance of being dead, and so far as human knowledge was concerned were dead, but who were really in a state of what may be called suspended animation. With no signs of life appearing, to the consciousness of men, death was thought to have taken place. Yet in no case where the supposed dead were raised to life, had the mortal really died.

As Lazarus has already told you, when Jesus commanded him to come forth, he had not died, and so of all the other supposed dead who were called to life. When this tie has been once severed, there are certain chemical laws affecting the physical body, and certain spiritual laws affecting the spirit, which absolutely render it impossible for the spirit to again enter the body; and as you have been informed, we all, mortals and spirits and angels as well, are governed by laws which have no exceptions, and never vary in their workings. So I say, when once the spirit and body separate, it is for all eternity, and the spirit then becomes of itself, a thing apart, controlled entirely and exclusively by laws governing the spirit body.

With the spirit's entry into the spirit world, comes the soul, still enclosed in that spirit body, and to an extent controlled by that body, which latter is also, in certain particulars controlled by the soul. The spirit body has not, of itself, the power to determine its own location or destiny, as regards place, for the law of attraction which operates in this particular, operates upon the soul, and the condition of the soul determines the location of itself, and as the spirit body is the covering of the soul, it must go where this law of attraction decrees the soul shall abide.

While the mind and the mental faculties and the senses have their seat in the spirit body, yet the law that I speak of does not operate upon these faculties, as is apparent to every spirit which he knows from observation, as well as from experience, that the combined power of all these faculties cannot move a spirit body one step in the way of progress, unless such faculties have, in their influence upon the soul, caused its condition to change; and in the matter of mere mental or moral advancement this can be done.

So, I repeat, the condition of the soul determines the locality as well as the appearance of the spirit body, and this law of attraction is so exact, that in its operations, there is no opportunity for chance to interpose, and place the spirit body in a location which is not its, by reason of the operation of this law. So that when the spirit body enters the spirit world it must go to and occupy the place which its enclosed soul determines that it shall occupy. No interposition of spirit friends or love of parent or husband or child can prevent this destiny, although for a time, until the soul has really has an awakening as to its condition of severance from the mortal life, these relations or friends may retain the spirit body near the place of its entrance into the spirit life, even though that place be one of more beautiful surroundings and happiness than the one to which it is destined. But this situation does not last long, for the law works, and as the soul comes into full consciousness, it hears the call and must obey.

And thus you see, friends and loved ones in spirit life meet with love and kindness and consolation, the newly arrived spirit, but the parting must come, and every soul must find its home according as its own qualities have determined. And yet the consolation mentioned is a real one, for in many instances, if it were not so, the lonely spirit would experience fear and bewilderment and all the unspeakable sensations of being deserted.

Then there comes a time, when every soul must stand alone, and in its weakness or strength realize that no other soul can bear its sorrow or take from its burdens or enter into its sufferings, And thus is realized the saying that each soul is its own keeper and alone responsible for its own condition.

Of course in many cases the loving friends may visit that soul in its place of existence and offer consolation and help and encouragement and instruction, but in some cases this cannot be, for as this soul is then laid bare to itself, all its deformities, and sins and evil qualities come before it, and thus throws around it a wall, as it were, that prevents the good friends and loving ones from appearing to it.

And thus again comes into operation the great Law of Attraction for while these more elevated friends, cannot come to that soul, yet other spirits of like souls and qualities may become its associates, and render such assistance as the blind can lead the blind in their movings about. And I wish here to say, notwithstanding what some of your spiritualistic teachers have said that the soul has its location as well as its condition.

The above condition that I have described is the destiny of some souls shortly after becoming spirits, and it is a deplorable one, and you may think that such souls are deserted by the loving influences of God's ministering spirits, and left all alone in the dreary places of their habitations. But such is not the case, for while they are deprived of the presence, to them, of the higher spirits, yet the influences of love and compassion are flowing from these spirits, and at sometime will be felt by the lonely ones, and as these influences are felt the poor souls commence to have an awakening which gradually causes the wall of their seclusion to disappear until at some time, the higher spirits find that they can manifest their presence to these unfortunate ones.

And, besides, this, every spirit, no matter how fallen, has a work to do, even though it may appear insignificant, and among these spirits of similar conditions some are a little more progressed than others, and by reason of a law which causes the more progressed to help the lesser, the latter are frequently helped from their low estate.

Now what I have last written applies of course to the spirits who are wicked and vile and without any soul development in the way of goodness, but a similar principle enters into the conditions of all the spirits in the earth plane, although the higher they are in that plane the greater opportunities they have for receiving help and progressing. Of these latter, and the operation of the mental thoughts and moral qualities upon the condition and progress of the soul, I will write you later.

I have written enough for tonight, and leaving you my love and blessings, I will say good night.

Your brother in Christ,
John.[55]

The condition of the world when Jesus came to teach

May 24th, 1915.

I am here, Jesus.

You are feeling better tonight, and I will try to write a little. I do not know that you are in condition to take a formal message, but I will tell you some things that will be of interest to you and mankind.

When I came to the world to teach the truths of my Father, the world was almost devoid of spiritual conception of the true relationship of God to man, and God was a being of power and wrath only. It was because of this conception of Him that the Jews were so devoid of the true knowledge of His nature and attributes. They only knew Him as a God who was interested in their material welfare, and did not realize that He was a God who wanted them to know Him as their Spiritual Father and Savior from the sins and evil natures that they possessed. And consequently when I came they looked upon me—I mean those who accepted me as their Messiah—as one who would redeem them from the slavery which their Roman conquerors had placed them in and make them a great and independent nation; more powerful than all the nations of the earth, and fitted to rule the whole world.

They had no conception of my true mission on earth, and even my disciples, until shortly before my death, looked upon me merely as a savior of them from the burdens which the Roman yoke had placed upon them. The only one of my disciples who had any approximate realization of what my coming to earth meant, was John, and that was because of the great amount of love that seemed to be a part of his nature and being. To him I explained my real mission and taught him the spiritual truths which I came to teach, and the only way in which mortals could receive that Love of the Father, which was necessary to make them one with the Father and enable them to partake of the Divinity of the Father. Hence, only in John's Gospel is written the one necessary requirement to a full salvation and redemption of mankind. I mean the declaration that men must be born again in order to enter into the Kingdom of Heaven. This is the only true way by which a man can become a true child of the Father, and fitted to live in and enjoy the Father's Kingdom to the fullest.

The other disciples had more or less conception of this necessary truth, but not the full comprehension of what it involved. Peter was more possessed of this Love than were the other disciples, except John,

---

[55] This message is a composite of two, being published in Volume I and Volume III. (G.J.C.)

and with it he also understood that I was the true son of my Father; but he never understood nor declared that I was God. He was a man filled with zeal and ambition, but his development of love was not sufficient to enable him to fully realize that my Kingdom was not to be an earthly one, until after my death, and then the conviction came to him in all its truth and fullness, and he became the most powerful and influential of all my disciples.

After the Pentecost, all of my disciples understood what my real mission was, and they went into the world and preached the true doctrines of my mission on earth, and the Love of the Father for His children, and the fact that that Love was waiting for all who should seek for it.

So you see that many of my disciples when on earth were not possessed of the true conception of my mission, and were not true followers of me in that inner meaning of what the Love of the Father meant, and what I tried to preach to them.

I have on earth now many mortals who understand my teachings better, and with a greater extent of soul knowledge, than did my disciples when journeying with me through Palestine.

But there are a great many men and women now living who do not understand my teachings, even though they think they understand the Bible and the interpretations of its discourses in accordance with the accepted doctrines of the learned and so-called teachers of its truths.

I don't feel that you can write more tonight and so will stop, and say that you must continue to get stronger, spiritually and physically, so that we can continue our writings more rapidly and with greater satisfaction. So believe that I am Jesus and your true friend and brother who is with you very much trying to help you and make you happy and contented.

With my love and prayers, I am
Jesus.

Affirmation that Jesus wrote

May 24th, 1915.

I am here, Prof. Salyards.

I would like to give you another installment of my discourse, if you feel inclined to take it at this time.

It was the Master, you must not doubt.

Well there is another law of the spirit world which provides that no spirit can ever progress to the higher sphere until he realizes that he must seek the Love and help of the Father.

You may say that there are many spirits in the higher spheres who have never received this Love, and who, notwithstanding, have progressed and are now comparatively happy spirits. This is true, but their progress is merely intellectual and moral. They can progress to a limited degree only and then must stop in their progress, as the progress of the mind and the natural love has its limitations. But such progress is not the progress that I speak of—this is without limitations and leads to spheres without end, progressing nearer and near to the very Fountainhead of the Father, as the Divine Love increases in greater abundance in the soul to progress higher. This I am told by spirits from these Celestial Spheres.

Well, I am sorry that you became sleepy, for it broke the thread of my discourse so that I cannot resume.

Yes, I understand and do not blame you, but the effect is just the same.

As your wife wants to write I will stop.

Your old friend and teacher,

J. Salyards.

Corroborates Jesus wrote

May 24th, 1915.

I am here, Helen.

Well, you had a message from Jesus and I am glad that you could write for him, though it was not one of his formal ones as he said, but it was full of truth and interesting. So you must think of it and you will get benefit from it. Professor was disappointed that he could not finish his message, but he was not at all offended that you went to sleep—he understood that you could not keep awake, and so he will try again.

I am very happy and am almost with your mother in her new home, and feel that I will soon be with her. So you must rejoice with me in my progression.

I see that you are not in a very good condition to write tonight, and I will not write more now.

With all my love, I am,

Your own true and loving,

Helen.

The religion of the future and a comprehensive and final one, founded on the truths that Mr. J. E. Padgett is receiving

November 6th, 1917.

I am here, Jesus.

True Gospel Revealed anew by Jesus

I have been with you part of the time as you were reading the different explanations of the various religions,[56] and tried to direct your mind so that you might conceive the difference between the things taught in those teachings and what we are revealing to you. Many things that are set forth in those teachings that are mysteries and the results of speculation will be revealed to you in their true existence and meaning, so that all defects or desiderata that arise because of the insufficiency of these teachings will be corrected and supplied. I am glad that you read these sermons, for they demonstrate to you a number of truths that were known to the ancients but which fall far short of the truth. At those times there was no source from which our truths could come, either in the spirit world or in the mortal world, and hence humans could not become inspired as to the vital truths that we are revealing.

The men who appeared as reformers and gave forth the truths that were unknown to their fellowmen were inspired by the intelligences of the spirit world, but that inspiration could not be greater or higher than the knowledge of the spirits by whom these men were inspired. And what I here say applies not only to the prophets and teachers of the Old Testament times, but to those of all the times and among all races preceding my coming to earth and making known the great truths which were revealed to me by the Father.

I noticed that some of these teachers and writers of essays at the great religious gathering attempted to speak of a future or world religion, and their claims were divergent but were based mostly on those foundations that will never support such a religion. They almost entirely based their concepts on principles of morality as understood by them, and the churches based their beliefs on the teachings of the New Testament, which in many and vital particulars are erroneous, especially, the basic one that I am God the Son and that my vicarious atonement and sacrifice must be the touchstone of the future great and ultimate religion. Well, as their claims are not true it is certain that any religion based upon them cannot be true or lasting.

There will be a religion of the future and a comprehensive and final one, and it will be founded upon the Truths which you are now receiving, for it will be inclusive of all the other religions, so far as the truths that they contain are concerned, with the addition of the greatest of all truths affecting mortals—the New Birth and transformation of the human soul into the Divine. When men shall come to make a comparative analysis of these existing religions and the one that I shall make known, there will be very little conflict in the vital principles, and my teachings will only add to the old teachings that which all men can

---

[56] Mr. P. had been reading—The World's Parliament of Religions at Columbian Exposition of 1893 (Dr. S.)

accept.

Hence, you see the importance of our working more rapidly in our efforts to disclose and disseminate the truth. I will come in a few nights and deliver another formal message, and others also will come and write you. Many of the Celestial Spirits are qualified to teach the truths of the Father, and they are ready and anxious to do so.

I will not write more now, but with my love and blessings will say, good night.

Yes, I am with you as I promised and will continue to be.

Your brother and friend,
Jesus.

Difference in his beliefs now and what his beliefs were when on earth

January 5th, 1916.

I am your friend in Christ and desire to write a few lines, but it will not be about religious matters, for I heard what the Master said, and he knows what is best.

Well, I am in the seventh sphere[57] and am very happy and enjoy all the delights of a soul redeemed, and am in the way of progress to the higher spheres where some of your band live. How beautiful must be their homes, because, when they come to the lower spheres, they have such beauty and are so filled with the Father's Love that I know they must live in homes of transcendent beauty where happiness is supreme.

I am not one who knows all that there is in the heavens provided by the Father, but I know enough to say, "that no eye of man has seen and neither has his heart conceived of the wonderful things that the Father has prepared for those who love Him and do His will." In our sphere the glory of our habitations and surroundings that we have are beyond all conceptions of mortals, and beyond all the powers which we have to describe. Your language is poor indeed when we attempt to use it, to describe our homes and our happiness.

Never a sigh, nor a thought tainted with the slightest flavor of unhappiness or discontent. All our wishes are gratified, and love reigns eternally and without stint. Never, when on earth, did I conceive that one man could love another as one spirit here loves his brother spirit. The mine and thine are truly the ours, and no spirit is so happy as when he is doing something to make another spirit happier; and then, love between the opposite sexes is so pure and glorified.

My home is not in any of the cities, but is in the country, among

---

[57] Seventh Sphere is the highest before entering the Celestial Spheres. (Dr. S.)

beautiful fields and woods where the purest waters flow in silver streams of living light, and the birds of paradise in all their glorious plumage sing and make merry the echoes of the hills and rocks, for we have hills and rocks as well as plains and beautiful meadows and placid lakes and shining waterfalls, all praising God for His goodness.

So why will not every mortal try to attain to this heavenly condition of love and happiness, when it is so easy for him to do so? The Divine Love is waiting for all, and needs only the seeking and the believing in order to make the mortal an heir to all the glories of this heavenly place.

But the mind of man, in its superimposed importance and in the conceit of the wonderful powers of his reasoning faculties, keeps the simple childlike faith from making him a child of the Kingdom.

Oh, I tell you, if mortals only knew what is here ready for them to obtain and make their own, they would not let the supposed greatness of their minds, or the cares and ambitions and desires for earthly possessions keep them from seeking this great and glorious inheritance, which is theirs by merely claiming it in the way made known by the Master.

And he—what can I say of him—the most glorious and beautiful and loving of all the spirits in God's universe. When on earth I looked upon him and worshiped him as God, sitting on the right hand of the Father—way up in the high heavens, a way off waiting for the coming of the great judgment day; when he would separate the sheep from the goats and send each to his eternal place of habitation—whether to hell or heaven only he knew, and I did not and could not until the great judgment should be pronounced. But now, when I see him as he is, and know that he is my friend and elder brother, a spirit such as I am, with only love for his younger brethren, be they saints or sinners, and a great longing that all may come and partake of the feast which the Father has prepared, I feel that the loving brother and friend is more to me and my happiness is greater than when I looked upon him as the God of judgment, having his habitation away off beyond my vision or reach.

He is so loving and so pure and so humble. Why his very humility makes us all love him almost to adoration, and if you could only see him, you would not be surprised that we love him so much.

Well, my friend, I have written a little more than I intended, but I am so filled with love and so happy in having such a friend as the Master, that I can hardly restrain myself. I will come again sometime and write you upon some spiritual truth, which I so much want you to know.

When on earth I was not an orthodox to the full extent, but my early belief that Jesus was a part of the Godhead I did not succeed in getting rid of, although my mind often rebelled at the thought; but the early teachings of my mother lingered with me, and maturer thoughts and development of mind could never entirely eradicate this belief in Jesus as being part of God. Some have said and thought that I was almost an infidel, but this is untrue, for I always believed firmly in the Father and, as I have told you, in Jesus.

I was also to some extent a spiritualist[58]—that is I believed in the communications of spirits with mortals, as on numerous occasions I have had such communications, and have acted on advice that I received through them. But I never learned from any of these communications any of the higher truths which I now know, and which are so important for mortals to know, and which, if men only knew and taught, would make their religion a live, virile, all pervading and satisfying religion. We are all interested in your work, and are co-workers with you in revealing these great truths.

May God bless and prosper you and cause you to see the realities of the great Divine Love, is the prayer of your brother in Christ,
A. Lincoln.

The great world teacher will be the Master again come to earth in the form of his Divine Revelations

October 11th, 1917.

Let me write a line or two. I have been present with you since you returned from the church, and have listened to your conversation.

I was with you tonight at the prayer meeting and heard what the preacher said, and was particularly interested in his ideas about the coming of the great world teacher, and saw that his idea of what constituted greatness in this particular, arose from his estimate of human greatness.

The teacher will not be a great preacher or a magnificent specimen of physical development or a man with a wonderful voice, but a man who can reveal to the world the Truths of the Father, regarding the relationship of man to the Father and the plan provided for the redemption and reconciliation of man to the Father. It is a fact, and I know whereof I write, that the regeneration of the human soul is caused more by the quiet meditations of mortals of the truths of the Father and by the silent longings of the soul than by the emotions that arise from the fervid and persuasive sermons of the preachers and evangelists. These latter may arouse the dead souls to a realization of their need of a reconciliation to God, but not so often do these emotions bring the soul into rapport or unison with the Father, as do the silent meditations of

---

[58] See a book by Mrs. Nettie Maynard Colburn—"Was Abraham Lincoln a Spiritualist?" (G.J.C.)

True Gospel Revealed anew by Jesus

which I speak. There must be the true soul longings and aspirations for this love of the Father, and in such cases these longings do not arise from the emotions produced as I have mentioned, and especially where such emotions are the results of fear created by the picturing of an angry and revengeful God. No, in the silence of the home chamber, where the mortal is, as it were, alone with God, and lets his longings go to the Father for the bestowal of His Love, because of the love that the mortal may have for the Father, does this Divine Love come in response and regenerating power. Only the mortal and God need be alone. Excitement or the magnetism which the preacher may give to the mortal does not create the true longings or aspirations, and for the preacher to suppose that the great world teacher must be a man with this great personal magnetism or with a voice that can cause the feelings of the mortal to vibrate with emotion or excitement, is a mistake. Jesus when on earth, I am told, never tried to create emotion or excitement in this manner, but his teachings were as the still small voice that enters the soul and draws it to a contemplation of the Father's Love in all the power of a soul's longings—hungry and craving.

So I say, the preacher's conception of this teacher was not a true one, and besides, while there will be a revelation of the truth, there will be no world teacher, but only a revealer of truths that will be disclosed. The Master, himself, will be the great teacher come again to earth in the form of his revelations.

I wish that I could come and proclaim these truths, but I cannot, and only through the instrumentality of a human can my thoughts be made known, and they will not be my thoughts either, any more than will they be the thought of the mortal, because what I may attempt to impress upon the minds and consciousness of men will be only those truths that I have learned from the same source as will come the Revelations.

Of course these truths will have to be preached and taught to men, but this will not be done by any great teacher, but by many preachers who shall learn the truth from what the Master shall disclose; and no man of himself, will be able to claim to be the great teacher. The greatest will be those who shall have the most of the Divine Love in their souls, and the greatest knowledge of the truths.

I also heard the preacher say that he would believe in any truths that might be confirmed by miracles, such as were performed in the time of Jesus—the instantaneous healing, etc. Well, you need not be surprised of such a demonstration, for it will surely take place. When a man shall receive in his soul sufficient amount of the Divine Love, there will come with it to that man a power and knowledge of the laws governing the relation of spirit to material organism that will enable that man to perform these same acts that are called miracles; and further, there will be some who will have that power and will demonstrate the same in confirmation of the truths that you are receiving.

The spirits who are now working to make known to man and convince them of these truths, have determined that such so-called miracles shall take place in confirmation of the New Revealment. The Master is the leader in the movement and he will not cease to bring about this great demonstration or rather not cease to work to this end, and he will not fail, if the human agents will follow his leading.

Well, I must not write more tonight, but as I am interested in this great work, and saw that the preacher's conception of this great world teacher is incorrect, I deemed it wise to write you as I have; and what I have written is not the result of my individual belief or opinion, but the result of what these high spirits have determined shall come to pass; and back of it all is the will and help of the Father, for in His Love and Mercy He desires to see all men become His true children and redeemed from the sins and evils of their present human condition.

So with my love and as a co-worker I will say good night and subscribe myself,
Your brother in Christ,
George Whitefield.[59]

Comments on message from Whitefield

October 11th, 1917.

I am here, your own true and loving Helen.

Well, dear, I see that have had a very happy evening and it is not to be wondered at, for there were many spirits present filled with the Love of the Father and throwing around you their influence.

Whitefield also wrote you and he was very much in earnest in what he wrote, and what he said is true and you can place the utmost confidence in the truth of what he wrote you.

As he said, we all say, the only great world teacher will be the Master, and his teachings will be through the messages that you receive. There will be a great responsibility in disseminating these truths, and thus making known to the world not only the truth but the identity of the Great Teacher. It is not reasonable for men to believe that any mere man can possibly be such a teacher as the preacher referred to, for only he who has the truth can teach the same, and no man in all the world has this truth, and will not have it, except as he may learn the same from the Revelations of the Master.

I know that it is difficult for you to believe that this can possibly

---

[59] Preacher of England at the time that John Wesley lived. (Dr. S.)

be, but it is not the miracle, as you call it, for that is the transformation of the human soul into the Divine Soul, which is the result of the Power of the Holy Spirit in its operations. No, the miracle, the great miracle is the changing of the human into the Divine.

Good night my dear husband.
Your own true and loving,
Helen.

Refers to the nominal Christian and the need of the Divine Love in the soul, so as to become a true Christian

February 11th, 1917.

I am here, John.

I come tonight to tell you that your condition of soul is very much better than it has been for some time, and you are more in unison with the Father's Love than you have been for some time and you realize that this Love is working in your soul and making you happy.

I have been with you a great deal today as you copied the messages and saw that you enjoyed the truths that they contained. The message describing "the progress of the soul"[60] is one that contains the truth of how the soul finds the true way to the Love of the Father and to progress to the Celestial Spheres. It is a very clear and convincing portrayal of the necessary course that every soul must pursue, which comes into the spirit world devoid of the Divine Love. There is no other way in which that soul can find its true development, and the message is one that will appeal to the honest seeker after salvation and the happiness which only a perfect atonement with the Father can give. (Mr. Riddle on the Progress of the Soul.)

I also see that you have been thinking a great deal about your future on earth in carrying forward the work that you have been selected to do, and I am glad that the great work is becoming to you a matter of such importance and seriousness; for important it is, not only to the world but to you; and this you will realize when you consider what was told you a few nights ago—that there is no one else in all the world at this time who is fitted to do the work which you are now doing and which you must continue to do during the whole time of your stay on earth.

As you progress in this work and as these truths come to you and your soul becomes more filled with this Love, you will to a greater and greater degree realize and understand the wonderful importance of the work; and you should now bend all your energies to developing your

---

[60] The souls progress as I have experienced it. Page 154 in this volume. (Dr. S.)

soul, and its perceptions and to carrying forward the work.

We understand as well as you the disadvantages under which you are now laboring and the necessity for getting into that position with the harmonious surroundings that will enable you to give your whole time to the work, and we are endeavoring to bring about these necessary conditions and will succeed in our efforts, and you must have faith; for faith will help you very much to work in conjunction with us and so cause the consummation of our desires and plans much more rapidly.

To us the accomplishing of this work is infinitely of more importance than to you, because we realize as you cannot, what a failure to have these truths made known to men would mean to them in the way of depriving them of opportunities that are so requisite to their future salvation, both on earth and in the spirit world.

So I say, let not yourself become discouraged, but believe, and you will find that our promises will be fulfilled, and the work will go on, and the truths be made known to humanity.

I am with you a great deal, trying to develop your spiritual nature, and by this I mean your soul, for as this develops the better able you will be to receive our truths and properly transmit them to the waiting world, so that men may readily see and understand the truths of God and the only way to His kingdom of Love and immortality. Doubts as to the teachings of the churches are now penetrating and permeating the minds of many, very many of those who are nominally Christians, and the perception of God is almost blunted, and they attend worship only because of a kind of feeling of duty and impression that it is right for them to do so. They know nothing of the Divine Love of the Father's nature and of the plan for their salvation.

Their prayers and worship are only those which come from the lips or a kind of blind intellectual belief. Their soul longings do not enter into their prayers and as a consequence, their petitions for God's Love and mercy go no higher than their heads, as has been said. This condition of men is very injurious to their future welfare and cannot possibly lead them to the Father, and so long as it exists men can never become in an at-onement with Him. Only the inflowing of this Love can reconcile men with God in the higher and desirable sense. Of course they may become in harmony with Him by a purification of their natural love, but that is the harmony only that existed between Him and the first parents before their fall, and is not the harmony which Jesus taught and which was the object of his mission to teach. When he said "I and my Father are one", he did not refer to the atonement between the mere image and the substance, but to the at-onement which gives to the souls of men the very substance of Father.

I should like to write more tonight, but you are tired and should not further be drawn on as it will make you feel bad physically.

So I will say good night and stop.
Your brother in Christ,
John.[61]

"Verily, verily, I say unto you, he that believeth on me, the works that I do, shall he do also; and greater works than these shall he do; because I go unto the Father. If ye ask anything in my name I will do It."

September 24th, 1916.

I am here, Jesus.

I have been with you a great deal to-day, and know just what have been the workings of your mind, and tried to influence you as to some of your thoughts. I was with you at church in the morning and heard the minister's sermon and saw that he did not rightly comprehend the meaning of the words of the text. "Verily, verily, I say unto you. He that believeth on me, the works that I do shall he do also: and greater works than these shall he do; because I go unto my Father." "If ye shall ask anything in my name I will do it."

His explanation of what was meant by "greater works than I do," was not in accord with what I meant, or with the meaning that I intended to convey; for when I referred to works I meant those works which the world considered as miracles. I intended to assure my disciples that they would have power to do similar works or perform similar miracles to a greater extent than I had performed them. "Greater" referred to quantity and not to quality.

But this power or the successful exercise of it was not dependent upon belief in my name, but upon their faith in the Power of the Father and in the fact that He would confer upon them that Power. There was no virtue in my name or in me, as the individual, Jesus, but all virtue rested in the faith that they might have in the Father. I never performed any of the so-called miracles of my own self, but they were all performed by the Father, working through me; and just as He worked through me He would work through my disciples who should acquire the necessary faith.

As I have told you before, all acts that are apparently miracles are controlled by law just as are those things which you call the workings of nature, controlled by law, and when sufficient faith is acquired there comes to its possessor a knowledge of these laws; it may not be, as you would say, a knowledge, or consciousness that is perceptible to the ordinary senses of man, but perceptible to that inner sense, which is the

---

[61] This message is a composite of two, being published in Volume I and Volume III. (G.J.C.)

one that enables men to comprehend the things of the spirit. And having this knowledge of the inner sense men may so control these laws that they will work those effects which seem to be contrary to the accustomed workings of the laws of nature. Until my disciples had acquired this faith that brought to their inner sense this knowledge, they could perform no miracle and do no work of phenomenon that other men could not do.

The Bible expression, that belief in my name is sufficient to cause the workings of miracles is all wrong, and I never said that such belief was what was required, neither did I say, "that whatsoever should be asked of the Father in my name would be given to men."

I was not a part of the Godhead and I had not of myself any power, and neither did my name have any miraculous influence with the Father. I was a man as other men are men, only I had become filled with the Divine Love of the Father, which made me at one with Him, and, consequently, had that knowledge of His Love and laws that enabled me to bring into operation those laws that would cause the desired effects to appear as realities.

But belief in my name caused no working of these laws, or the response of the Father to any supplications. Prayer must be made to the Father in the name of Truth, and to His Love and Mercy. Every individual is dear to Him, and He is ready to bestow this Love upon every one who asks in faith and pure desire. And in response to the earnest prayer will come Love, and with it knowledge of things spiritual, and with this, power that may be used for the good of mankind.

My name is not a mediator between God and man, and neither is belief in one, the Jesus, a means to reach the responsive Soul of the Father. If men will understand my teachings of truth, and when they ask in my name mean that they ask in the name of these truths, then such askings will have its results—but so few men, when they pray to the Father in my name, have such intention or understanding.

Only a knowledge of the Truth of the Plan for men's salvation will enable them to seek in the right way to obtain the Gift of the Father—and when I say knowledge of the Truth of the Plan, I do not mean that men shall understand all the minutiae of this Plan, and how one element or part of it may operate upon another, and what results may flow there from. But that knowledge must be sufficient in the beginning which shows to man that the Father is a God of Love, and that this Love may be obtained by man through earnest prayer for Its bestowal. This is all that is necessary, for the response that will follow will cause the New Birth, which when experienced by a man will place him in that unison with the Father, that will lead to a knowledge of the other Truths that form a part of the Plan of Salvation.

There is nothing else that will bring about this knowledge of that inner sense of which I write. A knowledge of the mind, except in conjunction with this inner knowledge can never bring about this necessary at-onement with the Father. It often exists that a man will have this inner knowledge and at the same time have a knowledge of the mind which is wholly at variance with the truths of the plan for his salvation. And the mind of man, being a thing of wonderful power, can for a time retard the growth of the knowledge of the inner sense, or, as I will say, the soul sense. But only for a time, for at some time the soul sense will progress to that knowledge of the truth, so that the erroneous mind knowledge, will entirely disappear, and man will possess only the truth.

Of this erroneous mind knowledge, or, perhaps rather, conviction, is the belief that in my name, that is supplications made in my name, will bring about the realization of the desires of the supplicant. Also that in my blood or in the power of the cross, or in my alleged vicarious atonement, the salvation of men can be obtained. If any name must be used in man's supplication then use only the name of the Father, for His is a name high over all, and the only name in heaven or earth that can bring to man salvation and at-onement with His being.

And what I have said applies to many other declarations contained in the Bible, such as *"he that believeth on the Lord Jesus Christ shall be saved." "There is no other name under heaven whereby men can be saved"* etc. This is the enunciation of a false doctrine and misleading to the great majority of mankind for they accept the declarations as literally true. Of course if it be interpreted as meaning that he that believeth on the truths that I teach, then the objection is not so great, but even then the declarations do not go far enough, for men may believe in these truths, and that belief may be a mere mental one, acquiesced in merely by the mind's faculties, without any exercise at all of the soul sense. If to all these declarations shall be added the vital Truth, that *"except a man be born again, he cannot enter into the Kingdom of Heaven,"* and to this mental belief be added the soul's faith, then the doctrines will be truly stated and men will understand what is necessary to salvation.

Belief and faith are not the same; one is of the mind, the other of the soul—one can and does change as phenomena and apparent facts change, the other when truly possessed, never changes, for faith possessed by a soul causes all the longings and aspirations of that soul to become things of real existence—which like the house that is built upon the solid rock can never be shaken or destroyed.

I write thus tonight to show that the preacher in his sermon did not explain the true meaning of the text, and did not comprehend the truths that were intended to be conveyed of which the text was susceptible, though it did not set forth my expressions or in its literal interpretation declare the truth. I will not write more now except to say, that I love you with a great love, and pray to the Father to bless you. Believe in the Father and trust me for you will not be disappointed, and pray that this Divine Love of the Father shall come into your soul so that you shall know that you are an accepted son of the Father. Keep up your courage and have faith that whatsoever things you shall ask the Father in the name of His Love and Truth shall be given to you. I am with you in all my love and care and you will not be forsaken.

So my dear brother, rest assured that I am
Your brother and friend,
Jesus.

Affirming that Jesus wrote

September 24th, 1916.

I am here, your own true and loving Helen.

Well, my dear, you have had a wonderful message from the Master tonight, and you may study and understand it thoroughly, for it contains in it more truth than you may see on a cursory reading. It is so contradictory to the beliefs of Christians and therefore so important, that knowledge of its meaning to the fullest is desirable. So good night.

Your own true and loving
Helen.

God is a God of Love, and no man can come to Him, unless he receives the Love of the Father in his soul. The time will come when the privilege of obtaining the Divine Love will be withdrawn from mankind

March 3rd, 1915.

I am here, Jesus.

You are in a better condition tonight and I will continue my messages.

"God is a God of love, and no man can come to Him, unless he receives the Love of the Father in his soul." As men are by nature sinful and inclined to error and the violation of God's laws, they can be redeemed from that sin only by obtaining this Love; and that can be obtained only through prayer and faith in the willingness of God to bestow this Love upon whomsoever may ask for it. I do not mean that there must be formal prayers or compliance with any church creeds or dogmas; but the prayer that is efficacious is that which emanates from the soul and earnest aspirations of a man. So let men know, that unless

they have the real soul longings for this Love, it will not be given to them—no mere intellectual desires will suffice. The intellect is not that faculty in man that unites him to God. Only the soul is made in the likeness of the Father, and unless this likeness is perfected by a filling of the soul with the Divine Love of the Father, the likeness is never complete.

Love is the one great thing in God's economy of real existence. Without it, all would be chaos and unhappiness; but where It exists, harmony and happiness also exists. This I say, because I know from personal experience that it is true. Let not men think that God is a God who wants the worship of men with the mere intellectual faculties; that is not true. His Love is the one thing that can possibly unite Him and them. This Love is not the Love that is a part of man's natural existence; the love that men have who have not received a part of the Divine Love is not sufficient to make them one with the Father; nor is that love the kind that will enable them to enter the Celestial Spheres and become as the Angels who are filled with this Divine Love, and who do always the Will of the Father. This Love is found only in the souls of those who have received it through the ministrations of the Holy Spirit—the only instrument of God's workings, that is used in bringing about the salvation of men.

I have seen the operations of the Spirit upon the souls of men, and know what I tell you to be true. No man must rest in the assurance that any other instrumentality or medium than the Holy Spirit will enable him to obtain this Love. He must not rest in the thought that without this he can become a part of God's Kingdom, for no love but this Divine Love can entitle and qualify him to enter that Kingdom.

When on earth I taught the doctrine of salvation only through the workings of the Holy Spirit in fulfilling the commandments of the Father. Mere belief in me or in my name without this Love will never enable any man to become the possessor of this Love. Hence the saying; "that all sins against me or even against God's commandments may be forgiven men, but the sin against the Holy Spirit will not be forgiven them, neither while on earth nor when in the spirit world." This means that so long as a man rejects the influences of the Spirit he sins against it, and such sin prevents him from receiving this Divine Love; and hence, in that state he cannot possibly be forgiven, and be permitted to enter into the Celestial Kingdom of the Father.

God's Love is not that which needs the love of man to give it a Divine Essence, but on the contrary, the love of man in order to become Divine in its nature, must be completely enveloped in or absorbed by the Divine Love of the Father. So, let man know that his love is but the mere shadow of what the Father's Love is, and that so long as he refuses to receive this Love of the Father, he will be compelled to remain apart from the Father, and enjoy only the happiness which his natural love affords him.

I am so certain that all men may receive this Love, if they will only seek for it in the true way and with earnest desire and faith, that I know it is possible for all men to be saved. But men have the great gift of free will, and the exercise of that gift towards the seeking and finding of this Love seems to be a difficulty that will prevent a large majority of the human race from receiving this great redemptive boon.

My Father is not desirous that any man should live through all eternity without this Love; but the time will come, and very soon, when the privilege of obtaining this Love will be withdrawn from mankind; and when that great event takes place, never afterwards will the privilege be restored; and men who are then without It will be compelled to live through all eternity with only their natural love to comfort them and get whatever happiness they may be able to obtain from such love. Men may think that this time of separation will never come, but in that they are mistaken, and when too late, they will realize it.

The harmony of my Father's universe is not depending on all men receiving this Divine Love because in the workings of God's laws of harmony on men's souls all sin and error will be eradicated, and only truth will remain; but the mere absence of sin does not mean that all parts of God's creation will be peopled by spirits and men who are equally happy, or who are filled with the same kind of love. The man, who is free from sin and has only his natural love, will be in perfect harmony with other men possessing the same kind of love; but he will not be in harmony with those spirits who have this Divine Love and the supreme happiness which It gives. And yet, such differences in love and happiness will not create discord or want of harmony in the universe.

Adam and Eve, or whom they personify, had not this Celestial Love—only the natural love that belonged to their creation as human beings, and yet, they were comparatively happy; but their happiness was not like that of the angels who live in the Celestial Heavens where only this Divine Love of God exists. They were mortals, and when temptation came to them, the love that they possessed was not able to resist it, and they succumbed. So, even though man may hereafter live forever and be free from sin and error, yet, he will always be subject to temptations which this natural love may not be able to resist. I mean that his nature will be merely the nature that Adam and Eve had—nothing greater or less.

Even in that condition he may be able to resist all temptations that may assail him, yet, he will always be subject to fall from his state of happiness, and so become more or less unhappy. This is the future of men who have not received the Divine Love.

But the spirit who has this Divine Love becomes, as it were, a part of Divinity Itself, and will never be subject to temptation or unhappiness. He will be free from all powers that may possibly exist for leading him to unhappiness—as if he were a very God. I mean that His Divinity cannot possibly be taken from him by any power or influence or instrumentality in all the universe of God.

This love makes a mortal and sinful man an Immortal and sinless spirit, destined to live through all eternity in the presence of and at one with the Father.

So, if men would only think and realize the importance of obtaining this Divine Love, they would not be so careless in their thoughts and aspirations concerning those things which will determine their future state through all eternity.

The importance of these truths cannot be too forcibly placed before men for their consideration; and, when the time comes for them to pass over, the more they have pondered on and obtained a knowledge of these truths, the better will be their condition in the spirit world. The spirit world will not help them so very much to obtain a more enlightened insight into these spiritual matters, because in this world men differ and have their opinions just as on earth.

Of course, they have not all the temptations to indulge their passions and appetites, which they had when in the flesh; but as regards their opinion of spiritual things, the opportunities are not very much greater, except in this, that because of the freedom from the passions and influences of the flesh, they may sooner turn their thoughts to higher things, and in this way sooner realize that only this New Birth in Love of the Divine can save them entirely from the natural results that follow the possession of only the natural love.

A spirit is only a man without an earthly body, and the cares that necessarily belong to the obligations of earth ties. Even as a spirit, some retain these cares for a long time after coming over, and then are relieved of them by paying the penalties of a violated law.

Well, I have written long and must stop. So I say with my blessings and love, good night.

Your fellow spirit,
Jesus.

Tells of her great happiness in her progress

March 3rd, 1915.

I am here, Helen.

Well, was not that a wonderful message of the Master? It was so full of things that should make men think and work to get this Divine Love that he spoke of.

I am happy to say that I have it now to a considerable degree, and the more I get of it the happier I am. I thought that I was happy when I entered the third sphere, and more so in the fifth, and then supremely so in the seventh,[62] but, really, I did not know what happiness was, until I got into my present home in the Celestial Heavens; and I suppose as I go higher, the happiness of each succeeding progressive sphere will be so much greater than that from which I progressed.

But, of course, the Master has been the Great Teacher, whose love and power have helped me more than all the others. He is so wonderful in love and wisdom that I almost adore him, although, he says that I must worship only God, and I follow his directions.

My experiences here are so wonderful that I hardly realize what it all means. My time in the spirit world has been so short, and yet, the wonderful knowledge of spiritual truths and the great happiness that I have received, cause me to wonder in amazement that such things could be.

You have had a long writing tonight, and I think I had better stop.

So good night.
Your loving wife,
Helen.

Jesus is not God or to be worshiped as God. Explains his mission. These messages that Mr. Padgett is receiving is his "New Gospel to all men, to both mortals and spirits."

January 24th, 1915.

I am here, Jesus.

You are now in condition, and I will give you a short message. When I was on earth I was not worshiped as God, but was considered merely as the son of God in the sense that in me were imposed the Truths of my Father and many of His wonderful and mysterious powers. I did not proclaim myself to be God, neither did I permit any of my disciples to believe that I was God, but only that I was His beloved son sent to proclaim to mankind His truths, and show them the way to the

---

[62] In the second, fourth and sixth spheres are found those spirits who are developing their natural loves to a pure state but do not possess the Divine Love. The spirits who are developing their souls by obtaining the possession of the Divine Love do not stay long in the second, fourth and sixth spheres but make their progress to and through the third, fifth and seventh spheres and into the Celestial. When they progress above the Third Celestial the spheres higher are so graduated that no number is used. This information is given in a message from Mr. Padgett's grandmother, (Celestial Spirit, Ann Rollins) and published in Volume II (4th Ed.) page 86. (Dr. S.)

Love of the Father. I was not different from other men, except that I possessed to a degree this Love of God, which made me free from sin, and prevented the evils that formed a part of the nature of men from becoming a part of my nature. No man who believes that I am God has knowledge of the truth, or is obeying the commandments of God by worshiping me. Such worshipers are blaspheming and are doing the cause of God and my teachings great injury. Many a man would have become a true believer in and worshiper of the Father and follower of my teachings, had not this blasphemous dogma been interpolated into the Bible. It was not with my authority, or in consequence of my teachings that such a very injurious doctrine was promulgated or believed in.

I am only a son of my Father as you are, and while I was always free from sin and error, as regards the true conception of my Father's true relationship to mankind, yet you are His son also; and if you will seek earnestly and pray to the Father with faith, you may become as free from sin and error as I was then, and am now.

The Father is Himself, alone. There is no other God besides Him, and no other God to be worshiped. I am His teacher of truth, and am the Way, the Truth and the Life, because in me are those attributes of goodness and knowledge which fit me to show the way and lead men to eternal life in the Father, and to teach them that God has prepared a Kingdom in which they may live forever, if they so desire. But not withstanding my teachings, men and those who have assumed high places in what is called the Christian Church, impose doctrines so at variance with the truth, that, in these latter days, many men in the exercise of an enlightened freedom and of reason, have become infidels and turned away from God and His Love, and have thought and taught that man, himself, is sufficient for his own salvation.

The time has come when these men must be taught to know that while the teachings of these professed authorities on the truths of God are all wrong, they, these same men, are in error when they refuse to believe in God and my teachings. What my teachings are, I know it is difficult to understand from the writings of the New Testament, for many things therein contained I never said, and many things that I did say are not written therein. I am now going to give to the world the truths as I taught them when on earth and many that I never disclosed to my disciples or inspired others to write.

No man can come to the Father's Love, except he be born again. This is the great and fundamental Truth which men must learn and believe, for without this New Birth men cannot partake of the Divine Essence of God's Love, which, when possessed by a man, makes him at one with the Father. This Love comes to man by the workings of the Holy Ghost, causing this love to flow into the heart and soul, and filling it, so that all sin and error must be eradicated.

I am not going to tell tonight just how this working of the spirit operates, but, I say, if a man will pray to the Father and believe, and earnestly ask that this Love be given him, he will receive it; and when it comes into his soul he will realize it.

Let not men think that by any effort of their own they can come into this union with the Father, because they cannot. No river can rise higher than its source; and no man who has only the natural love and filled with error can of his own powers cause that natural love to partake of the Divine, or his nature to be relieved of such sin and error.

Man is a mere creature and cannot create anything higher than himself; so man cannot rise to the nature of the Divine, unless the Divine first comes into that man and makes him a part of Its Own Divinity.

All men who do not get a part of this Divine Essence will be left in their natural state, and while they may progress to higher degrees of goodness and freedom from sin and from everything that tends to make them unhappy, yet, they will be only natural men, still.

I came into the world to show men the way to this Divine Love of the Father and teach them his spiritual truths, and my mission was that in all its perfection, and incidentally, to teach them the way to greater happiness on earth as well as in the spirit world by teaching them the way to the purification of the natural love; even though they neglected to seek for and obtain this Divine Love and become one with the Father.

Let men ponder this momentous question, and they will learn that the happiness of the natural man, and the happiness of the man who has obtained the attributes of Divinity, are very different, and in all eternity must be separate and distinct. My teachings are not very hard to understand and follow, and if men will only listen to them and believe them and follow them, they will learn the way and obtain the one perfect state of happiness which the father has prepared for his children. No man can obtain this state of Celestial bliss, unless he first gets this Divine Love of the Father, and so becomes at one with the Father.

I know it is thought and taught that morality and correct living and great natural love will assure a man's future happiness, and to a degree this is true, but this happiness is not that greater happiness which God desires His children to have; and to show the way to which I came to earth to teach. But in some hearts and minds my truths found a lodgment, and were preserved to save mankind from total spiritual darkness and a relapse to worship of form and ceremony only.

I have written you this to show that you must not let the teachings of the Bible, and what men wrote or professed to have written therein, keep you from receiving and understanding what I write.

I shall write no more tonight, but I will continue to tell you the Truths which will be "my New Gospel to all men," and when they have heard my messages they will believe that there is only one God, and only one to be worshiped.

With my love and blessings I close for this time.

Jesus.[63]

The spirits who have little development of soul can help those who have less development than themselves

November 23rd, 1915.

I am here, St. John, Apostle of Jesus.

I want to tell you tonight about the things that spirits who have not received the Divine Love of the Father do, or have done to them, as you may say, in order to get out of their darkness and suffering and progress to a happier condition.

Well, when these spirits of evil or sinful life first come into the spirit world, they enter what is called the earth plane; and when I say the earth plane I mean those spheres which are nearest the earth and partake very largely of the material. They are received by their friends who may have been with them at the time of their passing, and are, to a certain extent, comforted and made familiar with their surroundings. This may last for a shorter or longer time according as the spirit is capable of understanding his changed condition from mortal to spirit. After this condition of consciousness is assumed by the spirit, these friends leave him, and some guiding spirit, whose duty it is to perform the task, shows or conducts him to the place or plane which he is fitted to occupy, and which by the workings of the law of equalization, he must occupy. In this place he is surrounded by and must associate with spirits of a similar condition of development as his own, until some change comes to him which fits him for a higher place.

Of course, this change may come in a short time, or it may require a longer time to bring it about—all this depending upon the realization by the spirit as to what his condition is, and the fact that there is a possibility of progressing. Of himself he cannot bring about this change, for the law which fixes his place or condition does not cease to operate until there is called into operation another law which permits and helps the change.

The only way in which this changed condition can be brought about is by the influences of other spirits of a more enlightened and higher position than that of the spirit whose position I have spoken of. These influences do not necessarily come from spirits who have received

---

[63] This message is a composite of two, being published in Volume I and Volume III. The correction suggested by Judas has been applied. The original text of "so that all sin tends to make them unhappy." is now "so that all sin and error which tends to make them unhappy, must be eradicated." (G.J.C.)

the New Birth, but may come from spirits who know nothing about it, and who have only the natural love, and even they may not necessarily be of a high order of development of either intellect or soul. But they must be in such condition that they know and are able to tell the lower spirit of the possibility of progress and the way in which it can be made.

Many spirits, who are themselves in a dark position or condition can help others who are in a darker condition, just as on earth a student of a lower class in school may not be able to teach all that is taught or may be learned in that school, yet he can teach those in a lower class than his own, things that he has learned in progressing to his own class.

All spirits have a work to do, and these spirits of little development are engaged in teaching those of lesser development the way to get in the same condition as those who teach are in. But of course these latter cannot teach anything that belongs to a higher condition than the one in which they are. In such cases the progress is very slow for many reasons, and it sometimes takes centuries for a spirit to progress from this very low plane to a higher one where only the lowest grade of happiness exists.

So you see that in order to help these dark spirits, it is not necessary for the helping spirit to be one who has in his soul the Divine Love. But all this means that the spirit who is helped in this way cannot possibly progress higher than its natural love and moral conscience and intellectual endowments will permit—no progression of the soul to a realization of the Divine Love of the Father, or to the Celestial Spheres.

This is important for you and all mankind to know, for the reason that you and others may learn what the true soul development means, and how effectively spirits possessing this soul development may help all other spirits, good or bad. Aside from this you may suppose that the spirits who hear you talk at the séances, where all kinds and conditions of spirits congregate, and promise to help both mortals and spirits, may not be able to do so because some are in a dark and low condition themselves. Yet all spirits may help other spirits, to some extent, who are in a lower condition, and sometimes in the beginning of the progression, more satisfactorily, than can the higher spirits, because these dark spirits who try to help the darker spirits, are more in harmony with them, and the darker spirits will listen to them with more interest and belief that they can help them.

But this is a help that does not work in such a way as to cause the spirits who are so helped to lose their desires and recollections very rapidly and to progress into the higher planes, without the great suffering that you have been told of.

I thought I would write this to you, for the reason that you might not in your investigations and teachings of the spirit life, give due importance to the possibility of one dark spirit helping another. All the phases of mediumship, when honestly conducted, have their proper places and work in God's plan of redemption, and none of them must be considered as useless or without special design.

Of course, the above mentioned phase of assistance to spirits is of the lowest form and is merely preliminary to the great work which the higher spirits do in carrying out the great plan of redemption, which has been explained to you. The important work is that of the spirits who know what the Divine Love of the Father is, and what fits spirits and mortals for the enjoyment of the great happiness which obtains only in the Celestial Spheres, and also in the soul spheres, to a lesser extent.

When a spirit who is dark learns of this Great Love and strives to obtain It, and earnestly prays for the help of the Holy Spirit, which is God's messenger of Love, it will progress much more rapidly, and its sufferings and darkness will leave it sooner and greater happiness will come to it.

But still I say, the work of these lower spirits, that I have spoken of, is a great work and must not be underestimated. So remember what I have written and give due credit to this work.

I will not write more, but will with all my love and blessings say good night.

Your brother in Christ,
St. John.

The necessity for men turning their thoughts to things spiritual

October 16th, 1916.

I am here, St. Luke, of the New Testament. I desire to write my promised message, and if you feel that you can receive it, I will try to write. Well, I desire to declare certain truths with reference to the necessity for men turning their thoughts to things spiritual, and letting the material things of life consume less of their time and thoughts.

In the first place, that which is eternal is of more importance than that which is temporal and has an existence for a short time only, even though these things of time are necessary to sustain and preserve man while living his life on earth.

I would not be understood as implying that these material things are not necessary and important for man to acquire and use to the best possible advantage, for they are a necessity to his earth existence, and it is not only a privilege but a duty for man to make the best use of these material gifts that is possible, and to place himself in that condition which will enable him to enjoy to the utmost these things that have been provided for his material comfort and happiness. And further, it is his duty to bend his efforts to develop the use and application of these things, so that the greatest possible benefit and utility may be derived from the proper use of them. And to do this, I understand that man has to give a portion of his thoughts, and devote a part of his time to their consideration, and to the means and methods by which the best results may be brought about, and in doing this man is not disobedient to the Father's laws, or to the requirements which the laws of his own being calls for.

The discoveries of the inventors are desirable and men's work in making these discoveries is commendable, and so are efforts of the merchant and mechanic and financiers to succeed in their different undertakings and as a result accumulate money and use it for their comfort and sustenance. But these things, or the thoughts and efforts used to accomplish these results, do not help the soul development, or even the development of the spiritual side of man's nature, and if man devotes himself for the greater number of his hours of living to these pursuits, when he comes to lay these burdens down and pass into the land of spirits, he will find that he is very poor indeed, and that the eternal part of his being has little developed, and his soul fitted for a place where those who have laid up their riches on earth must necessarily go.

So attractive is this accumulation of money, and the gaining of fame or position to man, that when once engaged in, and especially when accompanied with what he calls success, he naturally devotes his whole waking time and thoughts to these efforts, and as a consequence, very little of this short time on earth is given to thoughts of and striving for things of the higher kind.

If mortals, and especially those who are so arduously and constantly engaged in the effort to win the success that I have just mentioned, could only see and know the condition of those who when on earth were engaged in similar pursuits with like aspirations, and who are now in the spirit world, they would realize the utter futility of such efforts, and the great soul-killing harm that the so-called success on earth, has brought to these spirits.

And while we may assume that many of these spirits did not do affirmative wrong or injury in their work, and did not enter into the condition to which I refer because of any such among or injury, yet they are in a stagnated and shriveled condition of soul and spiritual qualities, and all because when in their earnest pursuits of these material things they neglected the development of their souls or the cultivation of their spiritual qualities. Their sin was that of omission and it is a sure one in its results, and the more common one among men who think too much of material things, or think not at all or are indifferent to everything, and are satisfied to live in an atmosphere or state of vegetating contentment.

The law operates the same upon the man who neglects his spiritual nature because of his absorption in the things material as upon the man who is guilty of such neglect because of indifference, or contentment with the pleasures that these material things give him. In both cases the results are the same—the soul remains stagnant and the spiritual qualities lie dormant; and the man of such neglect will find his place in the spirit world to be one of darkness and suffering.

Life is short and time is fleeting, even though a man may live his allotted time of three score and ten years, and there is no place in all God's universe where it is so important that man should start on his way to eternal progress as in the earth life. There the soul should have its awakening and be fed with thoughts and strivings for the things spiritual. When the start is thus made on earth, it is so much easier for the continuous progress of the soul in the spirit world, if not the awakening may be delayed for years, and the progress which follows it may be and generally is very slow.

So I say, let men not devote so much of their time to those things which are of time only, and while they remain in the world of time until the mortal becomes a spirit. Thoughts are things and when applied to man's spiritual development they are things of the most vital importance. A little thought may start a soul to a dormant, hardly living state, or cause it to grow and increase into a thing of beauty and harmony with the spiritual possibilities of its possessor. And as it has been said, where your treasures are, there will your heart be also, so also will your thoughts that turn man's soul into darkness or light.

So with all my love, I will say, good night.
Your brother in Christ,
Luke.

Explains dematerialization of Jesus' earthly body

October 24th, 1915.

I am here, St. Luke, (Writer of the Third Gospel That Was.)

I was with you tonight at the meeting of the Spiritualists, and heard the statement of the speaker as to the probabilities of what became of the body of Jesus after the crucifixion.

I was not present at the crucifixion, and, of course, do not personally know what became of the body of Jesus, but I have been told by those who were present that the Bible description of his burial in the tomb of Joseph was true. The body was buried in the tomb of Joseph and was left there by those who placed it in the tomb, which was sealed and a guard set over it to prevent anyone from approaching and interfering with the body, because Jesus had predicted that in three days he would rise again.

After the tomb was sealed Jesus arose, and without his body of flesh passed from the tomb and descended into the lower spheres where the dark spirits lived in their ignorance and sufferings, and preached to them the rebestowal of the gift of immortality.

The body of flesh by the power which Jesus possessed became so spiritualized or etherealized that its component parts became disseminated by Jesus in the surrounding atmosphere and he retained only the spiritual body in which he afterwards appeared to the disciples and others.

When he appeared at the meeting of the apostles, where Thomas, the doubter, was present, he recalled to his form, as you will better understand by my using such expression, elements of the material, so that in appearance the body was as much like flesh and blood as when it was placed in the tomb, and before he disseminated these elements, as I have said.

The flesh and blood which encloses the spirit form of man, as you may have heard, is continually changing in obedience to the ordinary laws of nature as understood by man. And when Jesus who understood and had power to call into operation other laws of nature, caused such other laws to operate, that the dissemination of the elements of flesh and blood took place, and he was left only with the spirit form.

This, I know, has been a great mystery to mankind since the time of the discovery of its absence by the watchmen at his tomb, and because of being such mystery, and as an only explanation of such disappearance, men have believed and taught that his body of flesh and blood actually arose from the dead, and, therefore, the real body of flesh and blood of mortals will also arise in what they call the great resurrection day.

But no body of flesh and blood arose, and the spirit form of Jesus did not remain in the tomb after the dissemination of the material body, for no tomb or other place could confine the spirit. You will remember that on the third day Jesus appeared to Mary, who was most intimate and familiar with the appearance of Jesus, and yet she did not recognize him, but thought he was the gardener; and so with the disciples who were travelling with him to Emmaus. Now, if he had retained his body of flesh and blood, do you not suppose that they would have recognized him?

If he had the power to resume that material body into which Thomas thrust his hand and found it to be a body in appearance of flesh and blood, do you think it strange or wonderful that he would have had the power to cast off his earthly body while in the tomb and cause it to disappear into thin air?

This I am informed is the true explanation of the disappearance of the material body of Jesus; and to me and to others who understand the laws of nature—I mean that nature that is beyond the ken of men—it is not surprising or worthy to be deemed a mystery.

I am glad that I went with you to the meeting tonight, as I became impressed with the desirability of making this great mystery a mystery no longer.

With all my love, I am,
Your brother in Christ,
St. Luke.

Comments on what Luke wrote about Jesus dematerializing his body after crucifixion

October 24th, 1915.

I am here, Thomas Carlyle.

I merely want to say that I was present when Luke wrote and heard what he said and was much interested. This very question used to be a great stumbling block to my belief in the resurrection of Jesus, because it seemed to me that the resurrection of the material body was so improbable under the circumstances as narrated in the Bible, that it was difficult for me to believe the story. But now I can understand very readily, because I am acquainted with the laws governing the formation and disintegration of the material things of earth, and I know that there is a law which would enable a person with the knowledge and power that Jesus had at the time of his death, to cause the disintegration of the material, as the scientists say, so that they would disappear into the surrounding atmosphere.

I wish that I had understood this fact when a mortal, for then many other things would have appeared to me as probably true, and I would have been in a different state of belief as to spiritual things, and my progress here towards higher spheres would not have been delayed.

It is to be deplored that this so called mystery was not explained in the Bible, for had it been men would not now be in darkness as to the meaning of the resurrection, and the many thousands who believe that the soul and spirit go into the grave to await the great Judgment Day, would not be in such condition of delusion and have to suffer the consequences of such false belief in the stagnation of their soul progression, which will surely come to them.

I hope you will give this explanation to the world and let men know the truth, that there will be no resurrection of the body of flesh containing the soul or spirit as taught by the churches.

I will not write more tonight, but will come again.
Your brother in Christ,

True Gospel Revealed anew by Jesus

Thomas Carlyle.

Describes what happened after the remains of Jesus were put in the tomb

March 16th, 1916.

I am here, Joseph of Arimathea.

I desire merely to write a few lines to let you know that I really did exist as a mortal, and that I am the same man who laid the body of Jesus in the tomb where never before had anybody been laid.

I was with him at his death, and I was with his body when it was laid in the tomb and sealed, and I know and testify that no man or men or society of men, as it has been said, stole his body from the tomb. His body was entombed as was the custom of my time, and he was wrapped in cerements and fitted for the long sleep in the tomb, as we supposed.

While I was not a full Christian, yet his doctrines appealed to me as containing the truth, having about them a living inspiration, which I did not find in the teachings of the Jewish theology, for I was a Pharisee. I never thought that his death was justifiable or approved it, but I was not able to prevent it; and feeling that a great crime had been committed by the people of whom I was one, I tried to make a small atonement for the great crime by giving him burial in my new tomb.

Of course, I did not believe that he would rise again in the way that he had made known to some of his disciples, and when we buried him, I only thought that that tomb would be his sepulcher until nature had destroyed the body as it had done in the cases of all others who had been entombed.

As you may realize, I was interested in the proceedings taken by the Jewish leaders in their efforts to prove that he, Jesus, would not arise from the tomb on the third day, and I kept watch as well as did the soldiers, and I can testify that no mortal ever removed the stones from the mouth of the tomb.

I was there when the angel came and the soldiers were put in the sleep that the Bible speaks of, and I Joseph say this, knowing that it may not be believed and the Bible makes no mention of it, that I saw the stones rolled away and the shining one standing guard at the entrance of the tomb. I was frightened and I left the place, and was so overcome that I did not return there until the early morning, and then I saw Mary and heard her inquiring for the whereabouts of her beloved Master, and more wonderful, I saw the man of whom she inquired suddenly reveal himself to her, and I can testify also, that it was the same Jesus whom I had helped lay his body in my tomb.

He was not of flesh and blood, as they say, for he suddenly

appeared, and his appearance was not the same as that of the Jesus whose body had been entombed; but when he revealed himself to Mary, there was the same countenance and the same wonderful eyes of love that I was familiar with, and the same voice of love and affection. I know this and I want to tell the world that it is true.

Before Peter came, I went into the tomb, and it was empty and when Peter came I was with him in the tomb and saw his astonishment, and heard his words of wonder and amazement, for notwithstanding what the Master had told him prior to the crucifixion, he did not believe or comprehend, and he was astonished and bewildered as were all of us.

Jesus of Nazareth arose from that tomb, and his fleshly body was de-materialized. As to his disappearance, I could not then explain, as could none who saw him after he had arisen, but now I know that because of his great psychic powers, as you would call them, he caused the disintegration of that body into its elements, as can be done now by many spirits who have that power. Yes, Jesus arose from the tomb, but not from the dead, for he never died, as you will never die, only the physical vestment that enveloped his soul.

I am now in the Celestial Heaven and am with him a great deal, and know that he is the greatest and most wonderful of all the spirits in the Celestial Spheres, and the nearest to the fountainhead of God's Love. He is truly His best beloved Son.

I also want to say that he writes to you his messages of truth, and was with you tonight for a short time. Listen to him and know that you have in him a friend who is closer than a brother, or father or mother.

My brother, I will stop now, and in leaving, say, that you have my love and blessings.

Your brother in Christ,
Joseph.

Faith and works—the Vicarious Atonement—the importance of obtaining the New Birth—his beliefs have changed after he became a spirit

July 6th, 1915.

I am here, a stranger, but a spirit interested in the work that you are doing for the Master, and also for many spirits, good and bad.[64]

---

[64] Mr. Padgett gave one day a week for spirits who desired to receive help and instruction. After these spirits asked for help, he would enable them to visualize bright spirits belonging to his band, who would instruct the spirits what to do to make progress. (Dr. S.)

I am writing by permission of your band, and hence, do not feel that I am intruding. So if you will kindly bear with me, I will say a few words.

I am a spirit in love with the efforts that you and your band are making to help the unfortunates who come to you with such pitying tales of suffering and darkness, and ask for help. I was once, when on earth, a man who suffered much because of my spiritual darkness, and not until late in life did I find the way to my Father's Love through prayer and faith—and even then I had many erroneous beliefs caused by the interpretations of the Bible then obtaining in the church of which I was a member—but since coming to the spirit land I have learned the truth, and have gotten rid of any old erroneous beliefs; and thank God, I am in the way that leads to life everlasting. I was a teacher when on earth of what I thought were Bible truths, and I know that some good resulted from my teachings, although they were mixed with errors—but I have met many spirits of men who listened to my teachings, and believed many things that I taught. So you see, that even if the churches do teach many false doctrines in their creeds, yet mixed with these false doctrines are many truths, and these truths often find lodgment in the hearts of the hearers, and result in their finding the Light and Love of the Father.

I am still teaching mortals whenever it is possible to do. But I find that my task is a difficult one, because there are so few mediums who are capable of receiving the truths of the higher things of life, and the impressions that I make on mortals by the exercise of suggestions are not very encouraging to them or to me. Sometimes the impressions are received and understood but very often they have no effect.

If we could have more writing mediums, such as yourself, who are interested in these higher truths, and would believe that we could communicate such truths to them, the salvation of mankind kind would become much more rapid. But as Jesus said, the harvest is ripe and the laborers are few.

You have a mission, which is greatly to be envied, I mean in the best sense, because you by the exercise of your duties become the medium between the Master and man. And I want to tell you that such a mission is a glorious one, and will bring to you untold blessings because you have now, and will have with increasing power the influences of the higher world of spirits and angels.

The one Great Spirit, I mean the Master, is with you very often, and seems to love you so much, and his love and power are beyond comprehension. He is your friend and brother and the association with such a one will give you much spiritual excellence and power, which men have not often possessed.

At the same time that this mission holds forth so much glory and power, it also brings with it a great responsibility, and one which will demand of you the exercise of all your love and faith and energy. So you see with the great favor comes responsibility.

I have written rather longer than I intended to when I commenced, and I will now stop.

I live in the second Celestial Sphere where live your grandmother and mother and wife.

Well, I did not have the love and faith that they had, and my progress was very slow, and hence, they have overtaken me in my spiritual progress. They are wonderful spirits and have so much of the Father's Love in their souls.

I was a preacher, and lived the life of one after I separated from the church in which I had been taught the doctrines. My name was Martin Luther. Yes, Martin Luther the Monk.

I now see that my teaching of justification by faith, is not of itself, sufficient for man's salvation. The true doctrine is that of the New Birth. I mean that with faith must come the inflowing of the Divine Love of the Father into the souls of men. Merely having faith will not suffice. Without this Love faith is futile, except as it may help to bring the Love.

So you see that while I was in my teachings an improvement on what I had been taught, yet I did not preach the great essential of the New Birth in the sense in which Jesus taught it and which should be understood by mankind.

Faith without works is not sufficient. Works without faith will not bring about the great results desired; and both faith and works without the New Birth or the acquiring of the Divine Love of the Father, are not sufficient to bring salvation to mankind.

Love is the fulfilling of the Law and Divine Love is the Essence of the Father, which, when possessed by men makes them one with Him. Let all men know that of all Divine Things, Divine Love is the divinest and makes man part of Divinity Itself.

Well, I have regretted so very much that my followers, believing in my teachings, worship Jesus as God. Oh, the great error of this belief and how much injury it has done and is now doing to men and spirits!

But, thank God I see the truth breaking into the consciences and minds of many of my followers, and I hope the time is not far distant when this great heresy will no longer be believed.

And the other false doctrine which is common to all the orthodox churches has caused much unhappiness and infidelity and disappointment both in the mortal world and in the spirit world. That is that Jesus' blood saves from sin or that he made a vicarious sacrifice to appease the wrath of an angry God, and thereby removed from men the penalties and burdens of their sins. This false doctrine has caused more men to lose their soul development, and rest secure in a false belief that they were saved from sin and immune from punishment, than has any dogma taught by the churches.

No blood, no death on the cross and no vicarious atonement saves a man from his sins and the resultant expiations, but Love, the Divine Love of the Father, which Jesus brought to the world and declared the way in which it might be obtained, and that it is free for all the Father's children, saves from sin both on earth and the spirit world.

I must stop now and will come to you again if agreeable.

No I am not. To me all men are the children of God, and I have long since forgotten any distinction between the Germans and the other races of mankind.

But war is cruel and unholy and without valid excuse, and should never arise. With the love of a brother who wants all men to seek the light. I am the former monk and reformer.

Martin Luther.

Martin Luther, reformer, is very anxious that the Truths that he now knows be made known to his followers

May 29th, 1916.

I am here, Martin Luther, One Time Monk and Reformer. I desire to continue my message, if it is agreeable to you. Well, we will try.

When on earth I firmly believed what was contained in our doctrines and teachings, and was sincere in trying to induce others to believe as I believed and taught, but after my long experience in the spirit world and my communications with Jesus and his apostles and others to whom the truths of the Father have come, I realize and know that many of my teachings were erroneous and should not longer be believed by those who worship in the churches that bear my name. My doctrine of faith—that is justification by faith—is all wrong when its foundation is considered, and the impossibility of understanding from my teachings and the church's tenets, just what can be intended by faith. Our faith was founded on the assumption that Jesus was a part of the Godhead and the only begotten son of the Father, who so loved sinful man that He caused His sinless and beloved son to die on the cross that divine justice might be appeased, and the burden of men's sins taken from them and placed on Jesus. Oh, the terrible error of it all, and how it has mislead so many of the believers to a condition of darkness and deprivation of the Divine Love of the Father. No, such objects of faith have no foundation in fact, and such a faith does not justify sinful man or bring him in atonement with the Father, so that he becomes a redeemed child of God.

Jesus was not a part of the Godhead, and neither was he begotten in the way that I taught and my followers believe. He was the son of man, and only the son of God by reason of the fact that he had received in his soul the Divine Love of the Father, which made him like the Father in many of His attributes of Divinity.

God did not send Jesus to earth for the purpose of dying on the cross or for the purpose of paying any debt or appeasing the wrath of his angry and jealous Father, for these qualities are not attributes of the Father—only love and sympathy and the desire that men turn from their sins and become reconciled to Him, are His attributes as affects the salvation of men. No death of Jesus could make any man the less a sinner or draw him any nearer to the Father, and faith in this erroneous proposition, is faith in an error and never has man been justified by it.

Jesus came to earth with a mission to save mankind from their sins and that mission was to be performed in two ways only: the one by declaring to man that the Father had rebestowed upon him the privilege of receiving the Divine Love, and the other by showing man the way in which the privilege might be exercised, so that this Divine Love would become his, and thereby make him a part of the Father's Divinity and ensure him Immortality. In no other way could or can men be saved, and made at one with the Father; and faith in these Truths, which makes them things of possession and ownership by men, is the only faith which justifies.

I write this for the benefit, more particularly, of my followers so that they may learn the vital truths of their salvation and change their faith in the death and blood sacrifice of Jesus, to faith in the rebestowal of the Divine Love, and in the further truth that Jesus was sent to show the way to that Love, and that he thereby and in no other manner, became the Way, the Truth and the Life.

I know that the acceptance of these truths will take from them the very foundation of their beliefs, and many will refuse to accept my new declarations of truth, but nevertheless, they must accept, for truth is truth and never changes, and those who refuse to accept it on earth will, when they come to the spirit world, have to accept it, or exist in a condition where they will see and knew that their old beliefs were false and rested on no solid foundation; and the danger to many will be that when they realize the utter falsity and non existence of what they believed to be true, they will become infidels, or wanderers in spirit life without the hope of salvation or of becoming redeemed children of God.

I fully realize the errors of my teachings on earth, and the responsibility that rests upon me for these teachings which are still spreading, and I am almost helpless to remedy them. And so, I write this message, hoping that it may be published in your book of truths.

I, Luther, the onetime monk and reformer, declare these truths with all the emphasis of my soul, based on knowledge in which there is no shadow of error, and which I have acquired from experience not founded on the claimed revelations to man by the voice of God. My knowledge is true, and nothing in opposition can be true, and the beliefs and faith of a man, or of all the inhabitants of earth, cannot change the truth in one iota.

The Roman church taught the communion of saints, and I declare the communion of spirits and mortals, be they saints or sinners. That church taught the doctrine of purgatory and hell, and I declare that there is a hell and a purgatory and that probation exists in both places, and that some time in the long ages to come, both places will be emptied of their inhabitants, some of whom will become redeemed children of God and dwellers in the Celestial Heavens, and others will become purified in their natural loves and inhabitants of the merely spiritual spheres.

I pray and desire that my followers may become inhabitants of the Celestial Heavens and partake of the Divine Nature of the Father and Immortality. To them I say, hearken to the Truths as Jesus has and will reveal them in his messages to you, for in the Truths which he shall thus declare, they will find Life Eternal and the at-onement with God, for which they have for so many years been seeking in darkness and disappointment.

I will not write more tonight, but will come again soon, and reveal other vital truths, if you will find for me the opportunity.

So with my love and blessings, I am
Your brother in Christ,
Martin Luther.

Jesus will never come as Prince Michael to establish his Kingdom

August 13th, 1916.

I am here, Jesus.

I was with you tonight and heard the address of the preacher (Elder Daniels) and the explanation of the cause of the Great War[65] that is now raging in Europe and it was a very intelligent and truthful one and the real foundation of the war.

I will not came as the Prince Michael, as the preacher said, to establish my Kingdom on earth and take into me those whose names are written in the book and destroy those whose names are not therein written, for I have already come and am now in the world working to turn men's hearts to God and to teach them the way by which they may become at one with the Father and receive into their souls the Divine Love.

---

[65] World War, 1914-1918 (Dr. S.)

True Gospel Revealed anew by Jesus

In no other way will I ever come to men on earth for they will not need me as a visible king with the powers and armies of the spirit world in visible form to subdue the evil that exists. There will arise no Satan to fight against me or my followers in the sense that the preacher teaches, for besides, the fact that I am already in the world fighting for the salvation of men, there is no Satan. The only devils or evil spirits who are trying to influence men to evil thoughts and actions are the spirits of men which still retain all their sins and wickedness, and the evil that exists in the hearts of men themselves.

How pitiable it is that the preacher and his followers believe that the spirits of men who have died the natural death are also dead and resting in the grave or in oblivion, waiting for the great day of my appearance on earth, as they say, in order to come again into life and be called by me into my Kingdom. How much they lose by such beliefs, and how great and surprising will be their awakening when they pass through the change called death.

There will be no Battle of Armageddon, only as each man or the soul of each man, is now fighting the battle between sin and righteousness. This is the only battle that will ever be fought between the Prince of Peace and Satan. Each soul must fight its own battle, and in that fight the Powers of God, by His instruments, which never cease to work, will be used to help that soul overcome the great enemy, sin, which is of man's creation. These teachings of the preacher do great harm to mankind in that they cause the individual man to believe, that I, as the Prince of Peace, will come in mighty power, and in one fell swoop will destroy evil and all who personify it, and thereby do the work which each individual man must do.

I know that it will be very difficult to persuade the people of this sect that what they teach and what they conclude the Bible teaches is not true, but I hope that when my truths are brought to light and men have the opportunity to learn the truth, that many of them will halt in the security of their beliefs and attempt to understand these truths, as they must understand them, either in the mortal life or in the spirit world in order to enter the Kingdom of God.

As to these prophecies of Daniel, they have no application to the present condition of the world, and so far as they were written by him or by any other prophet they related only to the times in which they were written. No man, inspired or not, and no spirit, had the omniscience to foretell these wonderful things that are now taking place in the world, and any attempts to apply these supposed prophecies to the happenings of the present day are without justification and the results of the imaginations of men that the occurrences fit the prophecies.

Peace will come, but not as the result of any Battle of Armageddon, or any other battle based upon the principles which the preacher applies to these prophecies. As I have said, this battle is going on all the time, and it is an individual fight between the sinful soul and the creatures of man's disobedience. So do not waste your time in reading or listening to these unreal and foundationless teachings of men who think that they have discovered the intentions of God with reference to the destiny of nations.

I will not write more tonight, but at some time I may say more on this subject, though its only importance is that it attracts men's attention away from the truth and creates beliefs which do harm. I will soon come and write another message of truth.

I am with you, as I told you, trying to help you and to show you the way to that New Birth which is yours and all others who will follow my instructions. I love you as a younger brother and will continue to bless you with my influence and prayers. So doubt not and pray to the Father and you will find the truth in greater fullness and receive corresponding happiness. I will now stop.

Your brother and friend,
Jesus.

Jesus will never come in all his glory and power and take men into his Heaven, just as they are in body, soul and spirit

October 11th, 1916.

I am here, St. John.

I merely want to say that I have been listening to your reading of my message and heard your comments on the same, and you are correct in what you and your friend said.

There is scarcely a greater error in the beliefs of men that retard the development of their souls than the belief that at some time Jesus will come in all his glory and power, and take men into his heaven, just as they are, in body, soul and spirit. This belief has for a long time prevented many men from seeking to develop their soul qualities, either as to the natural love or as to the Divine Love, for as a basis of their faith is that saying in the Bible that "whosoever believes in the Lord Jesus Christ shall be saved;" and many thinking that they have this belief, are contented therein, and further believe that because of that belief, they will be carried into the heavens of Jesus, when he comes, even though in the meantime they may have given up the earth life.

It is deplorable that men should believe these things and live and die in this belief—which, of course, is wholly intellectual. But such is the fact, and we spirits who know the truth, have for all the long centuries been so anxious that men should know the truth, and have been working among men by means of spirit impression, and sometimes by revelation to help them learn not only the truth, but the errors of their beliefs. And as our efforts have not been very successful, we concluded to use the means that we are now using, and to reveal to mankind in our own words and thoughts the truths of God as regards man and all things connected with him.

And here I want to say with all the emphasis that I can, that you and your friends must believe that the communications that you receive as to these Truths are written by us and in our own words, and that your mind does not supply a thought or suggestion, and that you are used only, as a medium to convey our thoughts, and lend your physical organs to facilitate our expressing in our own language the Truths that we desire to convey.

So, no matter how improbable some things may seem to you, you must accept them as true, for nothing but the Truth will be written. And further we will not allow any spirit who is not in our band, or who has not this Divine Love, to write on any of the Truths that are necessary to be revealed to the world. I thought this the proper place to say this, as I desire to assure your friend of the reality of the messages and the source from which they come. I will not write more now, and will say good night.

With my love to you both, I am
Your brother in Christ,
John.

What is the most important thing in all the world for men to do to bring about the Great Millennium, etc

November 30th, 1916.

I am here, Luke of the New Testament.

Yes, I desire to write tonight a few lines upon a subject that has never yet been written on, and I know it will interest you. My subject is:—"What is the most important thing in all the world for men to do in order to bring about the great millennium that the preachers proclaim will come before or after the coming of Jesus?"

Of course, in stating the question thus I do not intend to be understood as consenting to the doctrine that Jesus will come to earth in physical form, on the clouds with a great shout, etc., as many of the preachers teach, for that event will never happen, because, as we have written you before, he has already come to earth or rather to men in the spiritual way that we have explained. Neither do I intend to embrace in the phrase, "the greatest thing," the Divine Love, for that, of course, is the greatest thing in all the earth and in the heavens, as well; but by this expression I mean the greatest thing that men can do, independently of the assistance of the Divine Love.

Well, as commonly understood, the millennium is a time or period of a thousand years when peace will reign on the earth, and the devil, as is said, will be bound and not permitted to roam over the earth, causing sin and destruction of souls, and sickness and the other sins that now so generally beset mortals. Of course there is no personal devil in the sense of a Satanic majesty, but there are spirits of evil which abound in the unseen world and are constantly with mortals, exercising upon them their influence of evil, and suggesting to them thoughts and desires that eventuate in sinful and wrong deeds. But these evil ones are merely the spirits of departed mortals and are not beings of a superior kind in power and qualities.

Sin, as we have told you, was never created by God, nor is it the product or emanations of any of God's perfect creations but is wholly the result of the wrongful exercise of man's appetites and will, when the desires of the flesh are permitted to overcome the desires of his spiritual nature. With sin comes all the evils and discords and inharmonies that constitute man's manner of living his earth life, and until these things, which are not a part of his original nature, but which are the creation of the inversion of that nature, be eliminated from his thoughts and desires and appetites, the millennium will never be established on earth, and neither will Satan be bound in chains and prevented from doing his work of soul destruction.

Now, the converse of this proposition is true, and the possibility of its occurring, is also true, and the question is how can this be brought about, for to bring this about is "the most important thing for men to do. When the cause of the present condition of mankind in sin and sorrow and unhappiness is definitely determined, then will readily appear what is necessary to remedy the condition and remove the cause; and, hence, when the remedy is applied and removal made, the millennium will surely come, for this glorious time of man's desired and looked for happiness is merely one in which peace rules and discord does not exist, and every man is his own brother's keeper in love.

Then what are the causes of the present condition of existence on earth, marred and tainted and controlled by sin and error and disease? These causes are two-fold—the one arising from man's fall from his created perfection of body, mind and soul, in permitting and encouraging the animal nature to subordinate the spiritual and thereby, by the over-indulgence of the former, causing the carnal appetites to grow and transform the man into a lover of sin and things evil; and the other arising from the influences which the spirits of evil, who are always endeavoring to make close rapport with men, and exercise their evil influence over him.

While the personal Satan does not exist, yet the idea conveyed by the necessity of binding him in order to bring about this millennium is a true one, and applies to the actual relationship of men to these evil spirits, except this, that in the case of the latter it is not necessary or even possible to bind them, but to loosen them—that is to loosen their rapport with or influence over men, for when that is done, men become, as it were, free, and these evil spirits are as if they were not.

So you see, as a preliminary to the ushering in of this greatly desired time of peace and purity, men must cease to believe that it will come with the coming of Jesus in a manifested physical way, as a mortal conqueror might come with legions of followers and noises of drums and by force of arms or greatness of power subdue his enemies. This will never be, for no man is an enemy of Jesus, but all are his brothers, and he is not now making and never will make war on any human being, only on the sin and defilement that is within his soul; and this war can never be waged by power or force of legions of angels, for so great is the power of man's will and so respected is its freedom of action by the Father, that there is no power in heaven or earth that can or will change a sinful soul into a pure one by force and threats and conquering legions of angels, even though they might be led by Jesus, which will not happen. No, the soul is the man, and that soul can be made pure and sinless only when that soul desires and consents that such a condition may become its own.

So, it should not be difficult for men to understand that this erroneous belief, that Jesus will come in this semblance of a human conqueror and establish this great time of peace, is doing them much harm and delaying the actual time of the coming of this event. The effect of this belief upon the soul is that everything is to be accomplished by the work of Jesus, and nothing by themselves, except to believe in his coming and wait, and be ready to be snatched up in the clouds, and then help the hosts of heaven to destroy all of their late fellow mortals who had not believed with them, and put on the robes of ascension as they literally or figuratively designate such robes.

They thus believe, and in their minds they may be honest, yet their souls may be disfigured and tainted with sin and the life's accumulation of sin, so that they could not possibly be in condition to enjoy a place of purity and freedom from sin. And some of them expect and claim that they will be the judges of others of their fellow mortals, because of the deeds done in the body, and yet in how many cases would it prove to be the blind and sinful judging the blind and sinful.

But they further claim that Jesus, by his great power, and the fact that they believed that he would come again to earth and establish his kingdom, will in the twinkling of an eye make them fit subjects for his kingdom, and qualified to judge the unrighteous and help cast them out of his kingdom. No, this can never be the way in which the millennium will be established, and the sooner men discard this belief and seek the truth and the true way to purity and perfection, the sooner the hope and expectation of mankind will be realized.

Your brother in Christ,
Luke.

Jesus recognizes Mr. Padgett's grandmother's capability in writing the Truths of the Father

June 5th, 1915.

I am here, Jesus.

I merely want to tell you tonight that you are so much better in your condition for writing my messages and for receiving the Love of the Father in your soul.

You took my message last night in a very satisfactory way, and I am pleased with the manner in which you caught my meaning. So very soon we will have another message and a very important one.

I am with you in your hours of lonesomeness, trying to help and comfort and lead you to the Love of the Father.

Tonight I will not write more, as I desire that another shall write, who will give you a message that will interest you very much. I mean your grandmother. She is a very capable spirit in discussing the things pertaining to the spirit. I mean those things which reveal to men the truths of the Father, as she has learned them and understands them. Not merely in a mental sense but in the way of her soul perceptions.

So you will receive much benefit from what she may write, and you will realize that she is a wonderful spirit in the knowledge of all these things that tell of God's Love, and of His care and mercy towards mankind.

I will now, with my love and blessings and those of the Father, say good night.

Your brother and friend,
Jesus.[66]

Writes on the importance of knowing the Way to the Celestial Heavens

March 12th, 1919.

Let me write a line. I am not going to write a long message but one that is very short.

---

[66] This message is a composite of two, being published in Volume I and Volume II. (G.J.C.)

You are now in condition to receive our messages, and I wish to write for a while on the importance of knowing the way to the Celestial Kingdom which has been written you before, but I wish to add to what you have received. You have been told that the only way to obtain that Kingdom is by the Divine Love coming into your soul and changing it into a thing Divine, which partakes of the very Essence of the Father Himself. Well, this is a correct explanation of the operation of this Love on the soul, but in order to get this Love there must be earnest supplication on the part of the seeker, and a mere mental desire for the inflowing of the Love will not suffice.

This is a matter that pertains to the soul alone and the mind is not involved except, as you might say, to start the soul's longings and prayer. When you think that you are longing for this Love and have a mere mental desire for its inflowing, the Love will not come, because it never responds to the mere mind and must always be sought for by the soul's longings. Many men have the intellectual desire for the Love of God, and upon that desire rest, and believe that they have the Love and that there is nothing further for them to do; but they will find themselves mistaken, and that instead of possessing this Love they have awakened only the natural love, and in a way, started it towards its goal of the purified soul, like the first parents before the fall, and will not experience the transformation that comes with the possession of the Divine Love. It is no easy matter to have these longings possess the soul, and men should not remain satisfied with these mere mental desires for they will not be benefitted by such desires, except as I may say, in the way of having their natural love purified. The longings of the soul comes only from a realization that this Love is waiting to be bestowed, and that the soul must become active and earnest in its endeavor to have this Love come into it, and then the transformation takes place.

From this you will see how utterly impossible it is for the devotee of the church to experience this Love or to have the longings of the soul which are not aroused by the observance of the church's sacraments, and the duties which it imposes upon them. They may be ever so zealous in their attendance upon the church services and in complying strictly with its requirements as to doing those things which it prescribes. It is with them all a mental process but the soul is not affected. They may think that their desires are from the soul, and that a response will come, but in this they are mistaken and the soul lies dead. Only when the soul's longings are started into activity are prayers of the worshiper answered.

So you will see that a man may be apparently devout and full of zeal for his church and the teachings of his creed, and yet will not be benefitted so far as the progress of the soul is concerned.

Let not your desires be only of the intellect, but try to bring into activity the longings of the soul, and do not rest satisfied until a response shall come, and it will certainly come, and you will know that the Love is present working Its transforming power upon the soul. This is all I desire to say tonight.

I am pleased that you are now in condition to receive our messages and hope that your excellent condition will continue.

With my love, I will say, good night.
Your own loving grandmother
Ann Rollins.[67]

The Law of Compensation.

January 9th, 1917.

Let me write a few lines. I am much interested in you and your work, and want to do all that I can to help. I have heard your grandmother's message and it is a beautifully encouraging one, and filled with deep truths, which, if you will grasp and apply, will benefit you very much.

I had my troubles when I lived on earth, but never had the sustaining power of the Divine Love that she speaks of, and, hence, lived my life as best I could with only the help of natural powers and a rather cheerful disposition. Had I possessed this Love, I now know that I should have been saved many hours of worriment, and enjoyed many hours of happiness that were not mine. It seems to be the fate or destiny of mortals to experience trouble; as someone has said, man was born for trouble, but this is not just true, for man to a large extent makes his own troubles, and as men come into a knowledge of the great law of compensation they will realize the truth of what I say. But thank God, even though man makes his own troubles and the law of compensation works impartially, yet the loving Father can relieve him from his troubles and make him happy. And in doing so, I want to say, the demands of this law are not unsatisfied. This law, itself, is subject to another law, and that is, that unless causes exist it cannot demand anything from the mortal; and the Father in helping His children does not say to the law, you shall not demand a penalty from this child whom I desire to help, but says to the child, receive my Love and help, and the causes for the demand of this law will cease to exist.

If mortals would only understand this truth they would not continue to believe that the Father cannot help His children, and they would also see that in order to confer such help, it is not necessary to set aside or suspend this great law in its operations. The Father never grants

---

[67] This message is a composite of two, being published in Volume I and Volume III. (G.J.C.)

a special dispensation to relieve mortals from paying the penalties of this law, but He does give to them His Great Love, and when they possess that the causes that entail the penalties cease to have an existence.

The law of the Divine Love is the greatest law and supplants every other law in the workings upon the souls and minds of mortals. Well, my friend, I must not write more, and so with my love, will say good night.

Your brother in Christ,
John Bunyan.[68]

The true meaning of—"In the beginning was the Word and the Word was with God, etc."

September 17th, 1916.

I am here, St. John, Apostle of Jesus.

I want to say only a few words in reference to what the man said to you about my gospel or rather the gospel attributed to me. His reference to the opening words of the Gospel that "In the beginning was the Word and the Word was with God, etc.," is without any force, to prove that Jesus is God, or one of the Godhead, for it was never written by me or at my dictation, and does not state a truth.

The Word in the sense referred to in that Gospel can mean only God, for He and He alone, was in the beginning and made everything that was made. As we have often told you, Jesus was the son of a father and mother the same as you are son of your father and mother, and was not begotten by the Holy Ghost in the sense ascribed to his birth in the account thereof.

He was born of the Holy Spirit as his soul opened up to the inflowing of the Divine Love and was the first of mankind to receive this Divine Love and the Father's Essence of Divinity and hence was the first fruits of the rebestowal of this Love, and, as a consequence, was the first fitted to declare the truths of the Father and show the way. As his soul became filled with this Love and he grew in wisdom and knowledge of the truths of the Father, it may be said that he was sent by the Father to declare the truths and explain the way to the Celestial Heavens and the at-onement with the Father.

Undoubtedly this Love commenced to flow into his soul soon after his birth, because he was selected to declare the truths of the rebestowal of the Divine Love, and the knowledge of that mission came to him as he grew in love and wisdom—hence, he was without sin, though apparently only a boy—natural as other boys—in his human

---

[68] This message is a composite of two, being published in Volume I and Volume III. (G.J.C.)

instincts and feelings. But he was the son of man—Joseph and Mary—and also a son of God, as all men are, with the addition that he was an heir to the Celestial Kingdom.

He was not God, and even up to this time has never seen God, as the orthodox believe, and as Moses and some of the Old Bible characters are said to have seen God. But with his soul perceptions he has seen God, and so have many others of us who are inhabitants of the Celestial Heavens, and that sight is just as real to us as is the sight to you of any of your fellow mortals. It is impossible to explain this to you so that you may fully comprehend its meaning, but this seeing God by our soul perceptions is a thing of reality, and brings with it increased happiness and knowledge of immortality. Jesus is not God, but he is the most highly developed spirit in all the heavens and is nearest to God in love and knowledge of truth.

So, I say, the Word is God and Jesus is His son, and you may become His son in the same sense, as an heir to the Divine Essence of the Father, and an angel of His Kingdom. As Jesus has written you, all men are His sons, but with a different inheritance, yet one that is provided by the Father.

Let not these doctrines of the teachers of what are called Bible truths trouble you, and listen and believe only what may be written you by us. I will not write more tonight as it is late, and in closing will say that you have our love and prayers. I am

Your brother in Christ,
John.

How the soul of a mortal receives the Divine Love, and what its effect is, even though subsequently his mind may indulge in those beliefs that may tend to prevent the growth of the soul—what is a lost soul?

November 10th, 1916.

I am here, Jesus.

I come tonight to tell you that you are in a better condition than you were last night, and in fact, have been for some nights past. I desire to write you a message on the question of "How the soul of a mortal receives the Divine Love, and what its effect is, even though subsequently his mind may indulge in those beliefs that may tend to prevent the growth of the soul—what is a lost soul?"

As you know, the inflowing of this Love is caused by its bestowal by the Holy Spirit in response to sincere prayer and longings. I mean prayer and longings for the Love Itself, and not prayers in general, for the material benefits that men more often and more naturally, as they believe, ask for and desire. The prayers of mortals for these things that may tend to make them successful and happy in their natural love, are answered also, if it be best that they should be, but these are not the prayers that bring the Divine Love or cause the Holy Spirit to work with men.

As the prayers of the sincere, earnest soul ascend to the Father that soul becomes opened up to the inflowing of this Love, and the soul's perceptions enlarge and come more in rapport with the conditions or influence that always accompanies the presence of this Love, and, consequently, its entrance into the soul becomes easier and its reception more perceptible to the soul sense. The more earnest the prayer and sincere the longings, the sooner faith comes and with this faith, the realization that the Divine Love is permeating the soul.

When once the Divine Love finds a lodgment in the soul, it, to the extent that it receives the Love, becomes as it were a changed substance, partaking, of the Essence of the Love; and as water may become colored by an ingredient foreign to itself, and which changes not only its appearance but its qualities, so this Divine Love changes the appearance and qualities of the soul, and this change of qualities continues ever thereafter. The natural qualities of the soul and the Essence of the Love become one and united and the soul is made altogether different in its constituency from what it was before the inflowing of the Love, but this only to the extent of the Love received. As this Love increases in quantity, the change and transformation becomes correspondingly greater, until at last the transformation may and will become so great, that the whole soul becomes a thing of this Divine Essence, and partakes of its very Nature and Substance, a being of Divinity.

When once this Love enters and truly possesses the soul and works the change mentioned, It, the Love, never leaves nor disassociates Itself from the soul—its character of Divine Essence never changes to that of the mere natural love, and so far as It is present, sin and error have no existence, because it is just as impossible for this Essence and sin and error to occupy the same parts of the soul at the same time as it is for two material objects to occupy the same space at the same time, as your philosophers say. Divinity never gives place to that which is not of the Divine. Man is working towards the attainment of the Divine, when he pursues the way provided for obtaining the Divine Nature, and as he advances, and obtains a portion of this Divine, no matter how small, he can never retrace his steps to the extent of ridding himself of this transforming Essence, and again become without its presence.

But this does not mean that a man may not lose the consciousness of the existence of this Essence within his soul, for he frequently does. The indulgence of his carnal appetites and evil desires will place him in the condition that he may cease to have a consciousness of the existence of the Divine Love in his soul, and to himself, he will be as if he had never had any experience of the change that I speak of.

And while this Love can never be eradicated by the evils that man may indulge in or by the mental beliefs that he may acquire, yet the progress of this Love in his soul may be checked and become stagnant, as if the Love were not, and sin and error may appear to be the only dominant elements of his life and being. But yet, when once possessed, the Love cannot be crowded out of his soul by sin and error, no matter, how deep and intense they may be. I know that this may seem strange and impossible to man's intellectual thinking, and that it is not in accordance with what has been attributed to me as teaching that a soul may be lost, nevertheless, a soul that has once received this Divine Essence cannot be lost, though its want of realization of the presence of this Love and its awakening from its dormant condition, caused by sin and error and its misdirected beliefs, may delay its manifestation of life and existence, for a long time, and much suffering and darkness may have to be endured by the soul that is in such condition. And I must not be understood by this, as meaning that a soul cannot be lost, for it can, and many have been and will be, and many will realize the fact when too late.

Now, what is a lost soul? Not one that a man may actually lose in the sense of being deprived of it,—separated from it actually, or even as regards his consciousness of not having a soul, for while, at times, he may believe that he has lost his soul, in the sense of not having any, yet he is mistaken, for the soul, which is the man, can never be separated from himself, and as long as he lives in the physical body or in the spiritual body his soul will be with him. And yet he may have a soul, consciously or not, and at the same time have lost it. This may seem a paradox to the mortal intellect or to the intellect of spirit, but it is true.

Then what is a lost soul? When God gave to man a soul that soul was made in the image but not in the Substance of its Maker, and at the same time there was bestowed on him the privilege of having that soul become of the Substance of the Father, and to an extent, Divine, and entitled to and capable of living in the Celestial Kingdom of the Father, where everything is of the Divine Essence and Nature. When the first parents by their act of disobedience forfeited that privilege their souls lost the possibility of becoming of the Divine Nature and at one with the Father in His Kingdom, and they thereby lost not the natural soul, which was a part of their creation, but the soul having the possibility of obtaining the Essence of Divinity and Immortality as the Father has

Immortality.[69]

As I have said, heretofore, with my coming this great privilege was restored to mankind, and the lost soul became again the object of man's recovery, and now he has that privilege as did the first parents before the fall; but also men may lose it as did they. As with them their souls were lost until they received into it the Divine Essence of the Father, so with men now, their souls are lost until and unless they receive this Divine Essence therein. As the first parents by their disobedience and refusal, forfeited their privilege of having their souls become a living, Divine Substance, so now, men by their disobedience and refusal will forfeit their privilege to save their souls from separation from the Divine Unity with the Father. The lost soul is as real as the verities of the Father's immutable laws, and only by the operation of the Divine Love can the soul lost, become the soul found.

Men may believe and teach that within them is a part of the Divine that will cause their souls to progress and develop until it reaches the condition of Divinity that will make it a part of the Divinity of the Father. But in this they are all wrong, for, while man was the highest creation of God, and the most perfect, and made in his image, yet in man is no part of the Divine, and having no part of the Divine, it is wholly impossible for him to progress to the possession of the Divine. He, of himself, no matter what his development may be, can never become greater or more perfect or of a higher nature, than he was at his creation.

The Divine comes from above and when once planted in a man's soul, there can be no limit to its expansion and development, even in the Celestial Heavens. Let all men seek this Love and there will be no lost souls; but, alas, many will not do so, and the spiritual heavens will be filled with lost souls,[70] not having the Divine Essence of the Father.

I have written enough for tonight, and I am pleased at the way in which you received my message. Continue to pray to the Father for more and more of His Divine Love, and your prayers will be answered, and you will realize with the certainty of conscious possession of the Divine Essence, that your soul is not lost and never will be. So with my love and blessings, I will say good night and God bless you.

Your brother and friend,
Jesus.

---

[69] First parents have made their progress high up in the Celestial Heavens after the privilege of obtaining the Divine Love was rebestowed at the time of the coming of Jesus on earth. This has been affirmed by the messages from Celestial Spirits. (Dr. S.)

[70] This is the Spiritual Heavens of the perfect man who has only the natural love in a pure state, but does not possess the Divine Love which is necessary to enter the Celestial Heavens. (Dr. S. in the errata published with the First Edition)

Mr. Padgett doing a stupendous work and one which is of the greatest vital importance to mankind and to the destiny of mortals

December 9th, 1915.

I am a stranger but I want to say just a word as I am so interested in the work that you have before you to do. You certainly are a favored man by having been selected to do this work. It is a stupendous work and one which is of the greatest vital importance to mankind and to the destiny of mortals.

I will not write longer at this time, but would like to come again, if agreeable, and write.

Yes, I am a lover of God, and I live in the first Celestial Sphere, and, as you know, am a redeemed child of God and immortal.

I will now say with all love—good night.

Thomas Jefferson. (One time president of the United States.)

Affirming that the ancient spirits wrote, and many came from the Celestial Heavens and the lower spirit heavens

August 12th, 1915.

I am here—George Washington. The same who wrote to you a few nights ago.

Well you are my brother and I am pleased that you call me your brother, for in this world of spirits we have no titles or distinctions because of any fame or position we may have had on earth.

I came to tell you that I have watched with interest the many communications that you have received from the various kinds and orders of spirits, and am somewhat surprised that you could receive with such accuracy these several messages. I never in earth life supposed that such a thing could be, and since I became a spirit, I have never seen such demonstrations of the powers that exist on the part of spirits to communicate and mortals to receive the messages that come to you. I know that very many times such communications have been made by spirits to mortals, but what I mean as surprising is the great variety of spirits who come to you. They come from the highest Celestial Spheres as well as from the earth planes and what they write are not only new to mankind but many of their declarations of truth are new to many of us spirits.

Very seldom do we who are in the Celestial Spheres have the opportunity to communicate with any of these ancient spirits who live high up in the Celestial Heavens and when I see them come and communicate to you so frequently, I wonder at it all.

I know, of course, that such spirits do occasionally come into the earth plane; and try to influence both mortals and spirits to do good, but I want to tell you that usually their influence is exerted through intermediary spirits, and not directly by these higher spirits in person as they do through you.

The messages that you have received from these spirits who lived on earth thousands of years ago were really written by them as they controlled your brain and hand.

I am trying my best to help you in your work and will continue to do so, for the work that you have been selected to do is the most important one that the spirit world is now engaged in—I mean the world that recognizes Jesus as its Prince and Master.

Some spirits [71] come, because they see the way open to communicate to mortals, and they naturally desire to make known the fact that they live and are happy in their spheres. But their happiness is not the real happiness which the true believers and followers of the Master enjoy. So you in your work, when they come to you may have the opportunity to tell them of this higher experience which the redeemed of the Father enjoy. Many spirits are in these lower spheres who would be in the Celestial Heavens if they only knew the way.

We frequently try to show them the way to truth and the higher life, but we find it a difficult task. They think that we are merely spirits like themselves—have our opinions just as they have theirs, and that we are mistaken in ours, and hence we can tell them nothing which will show them truths that they do not know, or will give them greater happiness than they have.

When they notice the contrast in our appearance—that is that we are so much more beautiful and bright than are they—they simply think that such beauty and brightness is a result of some natural cause and that we merely differ from them as do one race of men differ from another. They do not seem to think that there is anything in the contrast in our appearance that is caused by any higher spiritual condition than what they have. And this is the great stumbling block in the way of their becoming interested in the conditions which we have, and which should urge them to investigate and learn the true cause for the same. And hence, I say, that you may do them some good in this regard, for you are a third person and should call their attention to the great contrast and tell them the cause as you understand it. What you say would probably

---

[71] These spirits have only the natural love developed to a pure state but do not have the Divine Love. This natural love in a pure state gives to these spirits a wonderful glory and beauty, but compared to those spirits who possess the Divine Love they are like a dim candle in comparison to the brightness and glory of the mid-day sun. (Dr. S.)

make some impression on them, and cause them to make inquiry, and once they commenced this then would come our opportunity to lead them into the light of the great truth of the Divine Love of the Father.

Well, I have digressed from what I intended to write but it is just as well, for all the truths of God are important to both mortals and spirits. I am very happy in my home in the Celestial Spheres of the Father, and I am trying to progress to those higher. So let me assure you of the truths of what you have had written to you by your band and others of God's redeemed spirits.

I thank you for this opportunity and will come again sometime.
Your own true brother in Christ,
George Washington. (First President.)

Jesus was never in India and Greece studying their philosophies as some claim

June 29th, 1915.

I am here, Jesus.

Well, you must have more faith, and pray more. These are the important things, and the next is, that you must call on me when you get despondent and need consolation, for I will respond and help you. And then you must let that dear wife of yours come to you with her love and cheer. She is a beautiful spirit and loves you beyond any conception that you may have and you must love her.

Yes, I do love you more than you can comprehend and you must return my love and be at one with me.

I pray with you every night when you ask me to, as you do, and I know that the Father will answer my prayers as well as yours. I know what I say and you must believe me.

So let me have your questions no matter what they will be and I will answer before you ask them.

I was never in India and Greece and those other places studying the philosophies of the Greek and Indian philosophers. I never received my knowledge from any other than my Father in my communications with Him and from the teachings of the Jewish Scriptures. I lived at home in Nazareth with my parents all the years of my life after my return from Egypt until I started on my public ministry. Neither John nor Paul ever communicated that I was in these foreign countries studying the philosophies of the teachers they name. John never traveled with me outside of Palestine, and Paul, I never saw while on earth.

John was a man of very affectionate nature and was with me a great deal during my ministry, but he was not what was called a learned man nor was he acquainted with the philosophies of the men mentioned.

He was merely the son of a lowly fisherman, and was selected by me for one of my disciples because of his susceptibility to my teachings and the great possibility for developing the love principle. So you must not believe the statements contained in that book on this subject.

Well you must stop, but remember that I am with you and love you.

Your friend and brother,
Jesus.

Writes of his experience in the hells — "It is hard to learn of heavenly things in hell"

January 8th, 1917.

I am here, Nathan Plummer, and I want to say a word. The Indian tried to stop me, but your wife said let him write, and I am doing so.

Well, I am still in hell, and suffering, and I wish that I could die again, but I cannot and will have to stand it. I can't even be deaf (was very deaf when he lived in the flesh) so that I might escape some of my torments, for I am surrounded by the most hellish beings you can imagine, and I have to listen to them. It is no use trying to fight, for I can't hurt anybody, and they became more annoying when I did try to punch one of them.

It is awful, and so I regret that I did not listen and try to understand what the Doctor so often told me when on earth, but now it is too late. I often hear what he says to you now in your conversations, but for some reason I can't quite understand, and besides, if I did, these damned ugly spirits would knock all the understanding out of me. It is hard to learn what you call Heavenly Things in hell, and I am so unhappy and see no way to relief.

The Doctor's father talked to me and told me some things that were like what the Doctor told me, and I felt better when he was telling me, and some hope came to me, but when I got back into my hell and saw all the horrors and the shrieking, ugly spirits, I forgot, and the hell feelings came to me again, and I suffered. Oh, if I could only find some relief from these torments!

Well, I will try again, for I know that Mr. Stone is kind and wants to help me, but my trouble is, that I doubt if he can, but I will go as you advise and try to believe that he can. I am very thankful to you and the Doctor and will try to hope. Anything to get out of this place and away from these devils. Your wife says I must stop. So good night.

Nathan Plummer.[72]

---

[72] I, L. R. Stone was present when the above spirit wrote. I was well acquainted with him

True Gospel Revealed anew by Jesus

Comments on the spirit writing—"It is hard to learn of heavenly things in hell"

January 8th, 1917.

I am here St. Luke.

I want to write a few lines upon a subject that may be of interest to you both. You have remarked upon the expression obtained in the letter that you have just received, "that it is hard to learn of heavenly things in hell." It is a statement in a succinct way of a great truth, and one, if it were known and fully appreciated by mortals, it would cause them to realize the necessity of thinking and learning of these heavenly things while on earth.

I know that many say, they will not believe in the orthodox hell, or in the necessity of troubling themselves about the future, or that they will take their chance in the hereafter, if there be one. If these persons could realize the meaning of such a course of life, they would not leave their future to chance, but would, while on earth, seek for these heavenly things, and make a start for the realization of these things now, and not wait until they had left the form of flesh.

They say that a just God will not punish them by condemning them to eternal torment, and they are correct; and while this just God does not condemn them at all, yet they are condemned by a law that is just as invariable as is the Love of that God, and that law brings its certain punishment, even though it may not be eternal. But it is certain, and upon the spirit itself depends very largely its duration. If the spirit finds itself in that condition that it cannot make a start towards its redemption, until a long time after its coming into the spirit world, then that punishment will longer continue; and, if the start depends, as it does very frequently, upon the ability and capacity of the spirit to receive and understand those things that will start it upon its progress, then many spirits will remain for years and years in the condition in which they find themselves when they first come to their homes in the hells. There is nothing in these places to induce or help the understanding of these heavenly things, but, on the contrary, everything to prevent and obstruct such understanding; even hopelessness and beliefs in an eternity of punishment, and, frequently, want of knowledge that there is any other or better place than where they find themselves.

And I want to say here, that within the spirit there is nothing

---

for several years before he died and often talked to him on the importance of getting the Divine Love in his soul. He was very deaf before entering the spirit world. After he wrote through Mr. Padgett, I told him to look around for my father who is a bright spirit of the Celestial Heavens. The spirit went with my father to receive help and instruction, and has now made his progress to the Celestial Heavens. (Dr. S.)

that has the qualities or powers to start it on a progression, and in this sense, the old Bible expression, "that as a tree falleth so shall it lie," is true. Even as to the natural love these spirits in the hells, cannot initiate a start towards high thoughts and beliefs, and only when some influence from without comes to them, can they have an awakening of their dormant better and true natures, so that their progress may commence. I don't mean by this that it is necessary that some high and spiritual helper shall come to them, but only that some influence from outside of themselves must come in order for them to have an awakening. This influence may be from a spirit[73] in an apparently similar condition to their own, but which has received some glimpse of uplifting truth that it may convey to the dark brother spirit.

All spirits can help others who are in a lower or more stagnant condition than themselves, and sometimes they do; but the great trouble here is, that unless the possibly helping spirits have some desire to benefit their fellow spirits of darkness, they do not try to help. and so as your friend says, "it is hard to learn of heavenly things in hell." He realizes that fact fully, and even with the help that has been offered and will be given him, he will find it difficult to make a start. The mortal life is not the only place of probation, but it is the most important place, and the easiest for man to make his start in, and understand the beginning of these heavenly things.

I will not write more now, but will soon come and write a formal message. So with my love to you and friend, I will say to you both, have faith and let not doubt come to you as to the heavenly things that we have written you about. Good night.

Your brother in Christ,
Luke.

All sin and error will eventually be eradicated from men's souls

August 8th, 1915.

I am here to tell you that God is love and that all mankind are His children and the object of His bounty and care. Not even the vilest sinner is beyond the boundaries of His care and love.

He is not a God who needs propitiation or sacrifice, but calls to all His children to come unto Him and partake freely of the great feast of Love which he has prepared for them and enjoy the happiness which His presence gives.

---

[73] Luke: And when I used the term spirit, I mean the soul clothed in a spiritual body. (Dr. S.)

So my friend, do not for a moment think that the doors of mercy or the entrance into the delights of His heavenly home is closed by the death of the body, for I tell you that the death of the body is a mere entrance into a higher life with increased opportunities. But notwithstanding what I say, the soul that seeks to obtain this Love while on earth has a great advantage in time over the one that waits until his spirit leaves the body before seeking for the Father's love. The best time for mortals to aspire to attaining this Great Gift is the now, and no time is so propitious. God's love is for the mortal even if he has the passions and appetites which the flesh encumbers him with, and when a mortal fights against the temptations which these burdens impose, and overcomes, he, when he enters the spirit world, is stronger and more able to progress, than when he puts off the great attempt until he becomes purely spirit.

So, while there is no such condition as probation terminated when the mortal enters the spirit world, yet the probation on earth is the accepted time to seek the Great Prize.

I know I am writing like some of your camp meeting preachers, but what I say is a truth nevertheless, and happy is the mortal who realizes this fact and acts in accordance.

Jesus is working among mortals now as He did when on earth, and although they cannot see His physical form or hear His voice of love in tones of benediction and pleading, yet the influence of His love is felt and the persuasion of His spirit voice is heard in the hearts of men.

He is still the Savior of men as He was on earth, and His mission will not cease until the closing of the Celestial Kingdom, and sin and error shall be eradicated from earth and from the spirit world. He will be the Triumphor and Conqueror over sin and everything that tends to pervert man from that which is good and righteous.

Man, having only his natural love, will be freed from all in-harmony and live as brothers and friends in peace and happiness. And spirits having the Divine Love, become as angels of God, and live forever in the bliss of the Celestial Heavens.

So I urge upon all men to seek the Divine Love of the Father and live in His presence forever.

I must stop now, but before I go let me say, that I am working with the Master in the great cause that will make men who seek this Love, one with the Father.

So I will say as your brother in Christ, good night.

John Garner.

I was a Christian preacher of England in the time of the Reformation.

Additional Messages added to the Third Edition

A member of the Sanhedrin and judge at the trial of Jesus states the reasons for condemning the Master at the time

January 22nd, 1917

I am here, Elohiam (Euliam).

I am the spirit of a Jew who lived in the time of Jesus and was a member of the Sanhedrin and sat as one of his judges at the time of his condemnation for blasphemy and iconoclastic teachings against the beliefs and doctrines of the Hebrew faith, and was one of those who voted for the sentence of death upon him, and in doing so was as honest in my conviction and action as it was possible for an earnest believer in his faith to be.

Consequently, I was without prejudice against Jesus as a man and, as I believed, a fanatic; and it was only because I was convinced that he was an assailer of, and dangerous to, our religion and the welfare of my race that I consented to his death. Mortals of these days cannot fully understand the exact relationship of Jesus and his teachings to the security of our religion and the preservation of the faith which we believed had been handed down to us by God direct through our prophets and teachers, and when we were confronted with what we believed to be the destructive and irreligious teachings of Jesus and after making the numerous efforts to suppress him by threats and persuasion without effect, we concluded that our absolute and indisputable duty to God demanded that he be removed from the sphere of his activity even though such result could only be accomplished by his death.

And if mortals of the present day could understand our deep religious convictions and the sense of obligation that rested upon us to protect and keep whole the divine doctrines and teachings of our faith and especially that one which declared the oneness of God,[74] they would not judge the action of the Jews in condemning Jesus to death to be a thing unusual or unexpected. He stood in the position to us and to our religion of a breeder of sedition just as in modern times men have occupied the position towards the civil governments of breeders of

---

[74] Jesus, of course, never brought into question the oneness of God. The spirit's concern here evidently stems from the current misinterpretation of Jesus' teachings, which was found even in his disciples before his death. (Dr. S.)

treason and have suffered the punishments which have been with approval inflicted upon them by such governments.

But to us he appeared not only guilty of treason to our national life, but of treason to the higher and God-given life of the religious government of our race, the chosen one of God, as we sincerely and zealously believed. Even in latter days men have appeared and claimed to be the especially anointed of God with missions to perform and have gathered around them a following of people whom they have impressed with the truth of their character and mission and of their teachings, and for a short time were permitted to declare their claims and doctrines and then suddenly brought to death by the decree of those who were in authority, as trouble-makers and enemies of the church or state, and have been forgotten and their doctrines disappeared from memory. And only in the instance of Jesus has his death been remembered through all the ages, and those who were the cause and responsible for his death have been desecrated and cursed and charged with the murder of God.

Well, I write this to show you that the Jews who took the life and demanded the crucifixion of that just man were actuated by motives other or different from those that have many times since caused the very followers and worshippers of that Jesus to murder and crucify other men who have claimed to be the sons of God endowed with special missions for the salvation of mankind.

The sincerity of the Jews who took part in this great tragedy cannot be assailed, and even their Roman masters at the time understood that the demands for the death of Jesus did not arise from personal spite, or the satisfaction of any revenge against the individual, but solely because they believed and so declared that Jesus was an enemy and would-be destroyer of the divine faith and teachings of the Israelite nation, and a seducer of the people, and it is only because of the subsequent rise and spread of his teachings and the truths that he declared—which have made so large a portion of the inhabitants of the earth followers of him—that the act of the Jews in causing his death has been called the great crime of the world and the people themselves to be hated and persecuted and destroyed as a nation and scattered to all points of the earth.

I do not write this to excuse or palliate the great error which we committed in causing the crucifixion and death of the true son of God, but only to show that they, though as I now know, mistakenly, did that which other men with the same faith and convictions and zealous for the religious preservation of the nation, be these men Jews or Gentiles or pagans, would have done in similar circumstances. But the great element of tragedy in all this is not that Jesus was crucified, but that the Jews were so mistaken and failed to recognize and accept Jesus as their long looked for Messiah and Deliverer, not from their material conditions of bondage, but from the bondage of sin and error in which they have lived for so many centuries. This, I say, was their tragedy, and it has been their lasting and deadly tragedy from that time until the present day, and the prospects are that it will continue theirs for many years to come, and that generations of them will pass from the earth life to the spirit world under the shadow of that great tragedy.

They still believe—and that belief is a part of their existence and as firmly fixed as in the days of the great mistake—that they have Abraham for their father and that his faith and example are sufficient to show them the true way to God and salvation and that they are the chosen people of God, and by worshipping the one and only God and observing the sacraments and feasts and commands of God that were given to them by and through Moses and the prophets and as are contained in the Old Testament, they will find the heaven of God here on earth and after death rest in the bosom of Abraham. That the observance of the moral and ethical precepts of their Bible is all that is necessary to develop their spiritual natures, and that beyond such development there is nothing to be desired or to be sought for. That some time they will attain the Adamic condition of reward and happiness, which is the ultimate of man's future existence.

Some are still looking for the coming of the Messiah who will restore to them their former glory and rule on earth as the king and governor of all the nations and that they will be his chosen subjects and selected to assist in the administration of that Messiah's kingdom. How certain it is that their dreams will never be realized and that unless they have an awakening to the true nature of their God they will never become inhabitants of the Father's kingdom!

And I want to say to my people with the certainty of knowledge arising from experience and actual observation, that Jesus of Nazareth was the true Messiah who brought to the world, and first to the Jews, the truths of God and His plans for the salvation of mankind and their restoration to all that they had lost by the fall of their first parents because of their disobedience, and that if the people of my nation had received him and accepted and followed his teachings, they would not now on earth be the scattered, homeless and persecuted race that they are, and in the spirit world would not now be satisfied with their homes and happiness in the spiritual heavens, but would be, many of them, inhabitants of the Celestial Heavens and the possessors of immortality and God's Divine Love.

You have received many messages describing the plan of the Father for the salvation of men and what the Divine Love is and how it may be obtained and its effect on the soul of man and spirit when once possessed, and I will not attempt here to enter into an explanation of these things, but with all the love that I have for my race, superadded to a knowledge of the great error and insufficiency of their faith to bring them into at-onement with God, I advise and urge them to seek the truth and apply it to their individual souls, and affirm that the truth is contained and the way be found in the messages that you have received from Jesus and the other high spirits.

I am a believer in these truths, a follower of the Master and an inhabitant of the Celestial Heavens; but I want to say that these truths did not come to me as a part of my faith until many long years of life in the spirit world, and that some of these years I lived in darkness and suffering. So I will say good night and subscribe myself your brother in Christ,

Elohiam[75]

Why spiritualism as now taught does not satisfy the soul in its longings for happiness, peace and contentment

December 5th, 1915

I am here, Luke.

I want to write a few lines on the subject about which you and your friend Dr. Stone were talking, and that is as to whether Spiritualism, as now understood and taught, supplies that which satisfies the souls of men in their longings for happiness and peace and contentment.

I have heard in the course of my spirit life a great many preachers and teachers of Spiritualism, both in recent years and all along the ages, from the time of my first entrance into spirit life; for you must know that Spiritualism is not a new thing having its origin or belief in the recent years that followed the manifestations in America. All along the ages spirits have manifested to mankind in one phase or another, and men have believed in Spiritualism and discussed it.

Of course, in former times when the churches had the great power which enabled them to dictate the beliefs of men, Spiritualism was not so openly taught or discussed as in these latter years; nevertheless it has always, during the time that I have named, been known to mankind. Never have its teachings gone beyond the mere phenomena which demonstrated to its believers the continuity of life and the communication of spirits. The higher things of the soul's development and the Kingdom of God, as you have been instructed, were never thought of, or, at least, never taught or believed in. Only the two facts that I have spoken of were discussed and accepted; and even today, the scientific men who are investigating it deal only with the phenomena

---

[75] This message is a composite of two, being published in Volume I and Volume III. This may also have been more correctly "Euliam." (G.J.C.)

and are satisfied with proof that man never dies.

At no time has the existence of the Divine Love or the Kingdom of God been sought for or taught by the teachers of Spiritualism, and in fact such things could not have been taught, for they never have been known. God has never been anything more to the Spiritualist than some indefinable abstract force, whose existence is not of sufficient certainty to make Him anything more than a mere principle, as some call Him; and the laws governing all nature are the only things that men must look to for their ideas of right and wrong and the government of their conduct in life.

The Spiritualists speak of the love of man for one another and the brotherhood of man and the cultivation of the mind, and the moral qualities, but admit of no outside help, or if so, of the help of some departed friend who may not be at all competent to help; or if so, such help is only that which one can give to another; and even when the help of what is called the higher spirits is spoken of, it involves no different quality of help.

I know that spirits do help mortals, and also harm them, but all such help according to the ideas of the Spiritualists is based upon what they suppose these spirits possess in the way of superior intellectual acquirements or moral qualities.

The soul of man, which is that part of him that is made in the image of God, although it may be unconsciously, is longing for that which will make such image become Substance, with its resultant happiness and joy. Yet you will not find that any Spiritualist teaches or attempts to teach how or in what way such Substance may be acquired, or the fact that there is such a Substance. They do not know that the Divine Love, coming through the working of the Holy Spirit, is the only thing that can enable the image to be transformed into the Substance, and hence they cannot teach the truths, and as a consequence, the longings of a man's soul are never satisfied by the teachings of Spiritualism.

Do you suppose that if the great truth of Spiritualism had embraced the greater truth of the soul development, that it, Spiritualism, would now be the weak, unattractive thing that it is, and that men would not have sought and embraced it in vast numbers?

Spiritualism, with all the truths that belong to it, is the true religion of the universe and one which would prove more effective in bringing men into a state of reconciliation with the Father than all other religions combined. But it is powerless and without drawing power as a religion because it has not the teachings which show men the way to God's Love and to the satisfying of the soul's longings.

But some day, and in the near future, this defect will be remedied and then you will see men and women flock to its bosom, so that they can enjoy not only the happiness which communication with their departed friends give them, but also, the happiness which the development of the soul by the Divine Love gives them.

Why the great revelation of this truth has been delayed to Spiritualists so long, I do not know, except it may be that mankind was not ready to receive it before; but now the time has come, and false beliefs of the orthodox churches, and the want of belief of the Spiritualists, will both disappear and men be made free and the possessors of the combined truths of Spiritualism and the existence of the Divine Love, which brings to them not only happiness and peace, but immortality.

I must not write more tonight as you are tired; so I will say good night,

Your brother in Christ,
Luke

This is the first formal message received by James E. Padgett

September 28th, 1914

I am here, Jesus.

You are my true brother and will soon have the Love of our Father in your heart. Do not be discouraged or cast down for the Holy Spirit will soon fill your heart with the Love of the Father, and then you will be most happy and full of light and power to help yourself and fellowmen.

Go to your Father for His help. Go in prayer, firmly believing and you soon will feel His Love in your heart. My teachings, I know, you will receive in the course of time, and you will then see that your understanding will be greatly enlarged so that you will know that I am the Father's son as I explained it to you a few nights ago. You can and will receive the Father's Love so that you will not need to go through the expiation in the spirit world.

I was not conceived by the Holy Spirit, as it is taught by the preachers and teachers who are now leading mankind in the doctrines of the churches. I was born as you were born, and my earthly father was Joseph. I was conceived by God's Spirit in the sense that I was born free from sin and error, while all other human beings were born in sin and error. I never was a human being so far as my spiritual existence is concerned, as I was always free from sin and error, but I had all the feelings and longings of a human being which were not of sin. My love was human as well as spiritual, and I was subject to all the feelings of sympathy and love that any other human being was. Do not understand that I was with desires and longings for the pleasures of the world which the human passions created. I was not, only I was capable of deep feeling, and could feel and know the suffering and distress of humanity.

Yes, I will, and you will learn that many errors were written by the writers of the Bible. I will show you that the many alleged sayings of mine were not said by me or did not express my teachings of the truth. Her teachings of Christian Science do not express the true meaning of truth and love as I taught them. She is in error as to the ideas that God is spirit only, a spirit of mind. He is a spirit of everything that belongs to His Being. He is not only Mind, but Heart, Soul and Love.

You are too weak to write more. You have my blessing and also that of the Holy Spirit.

Jesus the Christ[76]

The Master is anxious that mankind should stop worshipping him as God

December 25th, 1914

I am here, Jesus.

You are my dear brother, and I will tell you what I desire you to do at this time. You must not let the little worries of your business life keep you from giving your thoughts to God in worship and in prayer, and from believing in me and loving me as your friend and teacher, for I am; and wish only to have you do those things which will make you more at-one with the Father and love me more. You must try to let all your thoughts turn to the mission which I have selected you to do, for I have chosen you and you must do my work. As I am the one that God selected to do His work when I was on earth, so you are the one that I now select to do my work by giving to the world my messages of truth and love. I will soon commence to write them and you must preserve them until such time as you shall be in condition to publish the same, which will not be very long, for I have already told you, the means that will enable you to give your whole time to me will soon be at your command.

I do not want you to think that you are not worthy to do this great work, for if you were otherwise, I would not have selected you, and this fact alone should be sufficient to make you not doubt that you are a suitable person for the work.

Let me tell you now that no matter what you may think will happen to your business affairs and work, I will look after you and remove all obstructions so that, as I say, you will soon be able to commence your duties.

In my teachings I want to show that I am only my Father's son as

---

[76] This message is a composite of two, being published in Volume I and Volume III. This is the third message from Jesus received by James E. Padgett. (G.J.C.)

you are His son, and not to be worshipped as God. He is the only God and the people who today are worshipping me in all parts of the world are not doing what I desire, for they are putting God in the background and making me their object of worship, which is all wrong and which I am so anxious to have ceased.

They must look upon me only as a son of God and their elder brother who has received from the Father His full Love and confidence, and which I am bidden to teach to them. You are not to let anyone tempt you to let your love of God be displaced by any love that you may have for me, for your love for me must not be of the kind that you have for Him. He is the only God and you must worship Him alone. So be careful and make the distinction, or you will make a most egregious (flagrant) mistake.

I am your own dear brother and teacher and love you with a love that I have for very few of the mortals. Why? Because I see that you will become a true follower of me and will love God as I love Him. Only, I do not want you to think that you are now in a condition that leaves you free from sin or the necessity of progressing to the Father with all your heart for an inflowing of His Love. You must get all this Love that is possible and that can be gotten only by prayer and faith. So in your prayers, have faith and the time will come when you will become very close to the Father and enjoy His Love to a degree that few have so far obtained.

Yes, it is possible and, as I say, it will take place, only do as I have told you. Yes, I will help you with all my power and love, and you will succeed. Only try to believe and you will realize before you come to the spirit world that God is your Father to a degree that will enable you to live very near Him as I am living. Your faith is now very great as I know, and notwithstanding the fact that at times you have doubts and get despondent, yet your faith is there and it will grow in intensity and become so strong that it will never again be shaken. You must now let me stop as you are tired and need rest.

Yes, there are many things in my life as written in the Bible which are true and many that are not true. These I will tell you when I come to write my formal messages and you must wait until then. Yes, I did, but not in the sense that it is taught. To forgive sin is only to let the true penitent feel that just as soon as he prays God to blot out his past offenses and truly believes that He will do so, the sins are no longer held against him for which he will have to account. I could not myself forgive sin, for I was not God, but I could tell them truly that if they repented, God would forgive their sins. Later I will tell you in detail what real forgiveness is and what it consists of.

As for the healing act which I performed at the pool of

Bethesda[77], I am reported to have said, "Is it easier to say, 'take up thy bed and walk,' than for God to forgive your sin?" Well, that is the way it is recorded, but that is not what I said. Actually I said, "That thou may know that the son of man through the power of God can forgive sin, I say unto you, 'take up thy bed and walk'." It was only as God's instrument in showing man the way to His Divine Love that I could bring about forgiveness of sin, and not by any power of my own. If God did not forgive, I could not and neither can any man.

I know that a church claims that authority, but it is not correct. It has no power to forgive sin or to grant any favor or indulgence to mankind, and its assertions of that power is a mere usurpation of what God alone has the power to give.

So let us stop now—
Your own true friend and teacher.
May God's blessing and mine rest upon you tonight.
Jesus[78]

States that the publisher's soulmate is anxious for him to obtain the Divine Love in increased abundance so that he can make closer contact with her

March 29th, 1917

I am here, Mary Kennedy:

I am here, and I will not keep my own dear soulmate waiting any longer, for he is just ready to explode from the anxiety that he has to hear from me. He may not acknowledge this to you, but it is true, for I can read his soul and do not flatter myself when I tell you this.

Well, it has been some time since I wrote him even if you do not think so, but it has been to me, for if you could only realize the happiness that I experience in writing to him, you would understand that sometimes we spirits know what time means in the spirit world, though many of them tell you that they do not know what time means. Well, it may be so, but I doubt that they who say this have ever had the experience of waiting for the opportunity of writing to their soulmates on earth.

I have been with him a great deal, as he knows, and have become a part of his thoughts, and tried to respond in a sensitive way to his thoughts of love that he has sent to me, and sometimes I realized that I succeeded. Well, tonight I desire to tell him that I am more

---

[77] It would appear, based on a recent message from Judas that the reference to Bethesda above is in error, either a later editing error, or an error of transmission. (G.J.C.)

[78] This message is a composite of two, being published in Volume I and Volume II. (G.J.C.)

interested in his happiness which comes to him from the inflowing of the Father's Love than from any that may come from the inflowing of my love, and while I do love him with all my soulmate love, and want him to realize it in all its fullness, yet I am more anxious that his soul shall be opened up to this greater love that is so necessary to his eternal salvation and a home in the celestial spheres. And besides, I must tell him this—that the souls that have this Divine Love developed within them have a more wonderful capacity for this lesser love than those who have only the development of the natural love. To the former there is no end of happiness and to the possibilities of progress.

From my writings, and especially from those in which I attempt a little pleasantry, Leslie may sometimes think I may be a little frivolous or not so serious as a spirit of my development and possession should be, but of this I want to disabuse his mind, for he must know that when there is great joy and happiness growing out of love, even the Divine Love, there will be gladness and pleasantry, and sadness or continued seriousness will have no part in that happiness. I am very serious at times, and meditate with great earnestness and soul longings on the truths of the Father and the meaning of His great Love, and my soul goes out to Him with all the reverence and adoration that He would ask of me, and when I pray for my soulmate and for his progress in this love, then am I most serious and let the longings of my soul go to the Father with all the earnestness that I possess.

No, he must not think that I am a frivolous soulmate flitting from sphere to sphere as one of the spirits wrote you in reference to us who have the Love of the Father in our souls, and seem to he so bright and airy. Only those who are in darkness or who are bereft of this great Love are habitually serious looking with never a laugh or a song to make glad the heart of some other spirit or perchance mortal. Why, if I had to always be serious or apparently an angel of deep thought trying to solve the problems of the universe, I would not be the possessor of the Love that I have, and my face would not shine as the sun, which is the appearance of those spirits who have this Love of the Father in their souls as I have it. I am not flattering myself, as you mortals say, but am stating to you a truth that cannot be gainsaid by any in our spirit planes where we of the redeemed souls live and love and pray.

Of course, when I come to your room or into the earth plane, I do not bring with me my real appearance which my soul produces, for I would not be what the spirits who live on this plane could endure and, then, I am only a beautiful spirit as we are sometimes described by those who write, but, as I am, only those who are like me or higher than I can see or understand. And so I am trying to help my dear one to get so much of this Love in his soul that, when he comes to our spirit world, it may not be long until he can be in condition to see his Mary as she really is. Well, I am thankful that I could write this tonight for I so much desired that he should have some conception of me as I really am.

Tell him that my love is with him all the time, whether I am his Mary in the lower plane or his Mary in the higher heavens, where she appears to her spirit associates in all the beauty of her glory, a glory that can come only with and from the possession of the greatest of all loves.

I thank you and will not write more. So, my dear friend, with my sister's love to you and my soulmate's eternal love to him, I will say good night.

Your sister in Christ,
Mary

How small is the human mind, even of the most learned, as compared to that of the spirit who possesses in its soul the great Love of the Father

January 29th, 1918

I am here, Mary Kennedy:

Well, my dear, I mean Leslie.

You may think that I am a simple little English girl without having any knowledge of what the wise men of earth call psychology. Yet I know more about the soul than the scientist as he is known on earth, for I know that my soul is immortal, and not only that, but the reason why it is so. How small a thing is the human mind, even of the most learned, as compared to the mind of a spirit who has received the great Love of the Father in his soul, and realizes that it is a part of the very essence of the Father's Being.

I know that you would rather have your Mary be an angel of the Celestial Heavens than to be one of the wisest of the wise in the spiritual planes.

Well dear, this is all interesting to us from a certain viewpoint, but really not so interesting as the great love that binds us so closely together. A knowledge of the soul, as I know it, is very vital, but a knowledge of what makes the soul at one in perfection with its true soulmate is equally, if not more, important.

How poor are those spirits who are investigating the subject of the soul in a mere intellectual way as compared with those who know what the soul is, without having to investigate with the mind. And when Love is known and realized how rich is the spirit who possesses and realizes the truth of the reality of that Love, proof comes without seeking proof, and speculation is a thing unnecessary and unknown.

Tonight I am very happy that I can write to you, and tell you what you already know; but to tell you is a joy, for when I do so, you must say, "sweetheart I love you in return," and then you see I am happy in giving and receiving. If it were not so late I would write you a long letter, but the writer tells me that he must not write more tonight.

So believe that I love you with all my heart, and trust in my efforts to help and comfort you, and above all pray more to the Father for His Love, and have faith that it will be bestowed upon you.

Good night, dear heart,
Your own loving
Mary

This message informs the publisher through Mr. Padgett that she is now in a higher plane of the Celestial Heavens, with increased soul understanding of what the Father's Love means

February 16th, 1920.

I am here, your own true and loving Helen.

Well, dear, the Master will not continue his messages tonight as you are not so well and he does not feel it best to draw upon you as he would be compelled to do if he were to continue, or attempt to continue, the message of last night, and so I will write you for a short time and tell you of someone here and very anxious to communicate with her soulmate.

Of course I mean Mary, and she is all aquiver with excitement, as you mortals might say, at the prospect of writing to the Doctor; and so I will let her come and write, but you must be careful and not let her write too long, for what she has to say would require you, in order to receive it, to write for the balance of the evening.

Mary now writes.

I am here, Mary. Well, I am here and want to say a great deal, but as Helen has warned you, I will not trespass very long, and Helen did me an injustice when she said I would want to write all the evening. I am as considerate of you as is possible and notwithstanding my opportunity, I realize your capacity.

Tell my dear one that I have waited a long, long time to communicate with him, and that although I have the advantage of him in that I can see what his thoughts are and know just how much he loves me, yet I also desire to tell him of my love for him, and how much i am interested in him and want him to know it. He is my own true lover, and I realize that no other woman can come between him and me, even as to any earthly love that he may have. And just here let me say that I am not reflecting on you, (James Padgett) for I know the circumstances in your case, and how it is best that you should have someone to comfort your last years on earth.[79] But Leslie does not need such a one, and I shall always be sufficient for him, as he is for me. Tell him that I am very happy in the knowledge that he is all mine, and that my love for him is always increasing, and that my efforts to make him happy never cease.

I am now in a higher sphere than when I last wrote him, and realize what the wonderful Love of the Father means more than ever. Also with this increased Love in my soul, I have greater love for him. I am with him more often than he is aware of, and am pleased that the thinks so much of me and loves me as he does. His life will at the longest be very short,[80] and then I shall have him with the full consciousness that no earthly pleasure or condition can ever for a moment separate us, and that the bliss which I have will be nearer his than he can imagine. I really believe that when he comes over it will not be very long until he will find his home with me, and enjoy the happiness of my home—a wonderful home, not like anything on earth, or that has been conceived of by man.

No, it is beyond description and the nearest approach to a description that he can understand is that the Father's love is in and about it to a degree that renders everything beautiful and grand. He must not despair of coming to me, for he will come as surely as your sun will rise; and then he will know what happiness means in the experience of actual enjoyment.

I am so very happy that I can write to him tonight and encourage him with the knowledge that all these things will be his and forever. He, I know, is not surrounded by those things which ordinarily make men happy, but he has greater wealth than these things can possibly give him, for he has much of not only the Father's Love, but the love of a soulmate who is all his and ready to give him the real true happiness that only a union with a soulmate in the Celestial Heavens can give. He must continue to pray for an increased inflowing of the Father's Love, and as that shall come to him, I shall be able to see that the soulmate love for his Mary will increase also.

I would like to write of many things that are here in such reality and grandeur, but as you must not write much more, I must forego the pleasure. But this he must know, that my love is all his and the many mansions spoken of by the Master will prove to him to be a reality, and not the mere hope that so many mortals rely on. I send him a kiss, yes,

---

[79] It is apparent from the daily dairy that James Padgett had another woman in his life, Ella, and that Helen was quite happy about this. See the entries for Oct. 16th, 1919. That particular message from Helen has not been published. (G.J.C.)

[80] Mary Kennedy got that very wrong, unless it is simply a convoluted turn of phrase. Dr. Stone passed at age 90, on the 15th January 1967. (G.J.C.)

many kisses, such as only angels can send, and if his soul be opened up to their coming, he will realize what it means.

Good night, I thank you, and with my love to him and the assurance that I am watching over him, and sympathize with him in all his earthly worries, will sign myself his loving Mary.

Helen now writes.

Well dear, she has written and says she feels much better, and I know she does, for she looks very happy and grateful for the privilege. I am with Mary in her expressions of love and hope and certainty, and you must believe that these things that she has spoken of will be yours when you come to join us. Why dear, you cannot appreciate what all this means to you and to us! We are truly thankful to the Father for the privilege of knowing that we have on earth a soulmate—the very necessary part of ourselves with whom we can talk and communicate the innermost feelings of our souls.

It is a privilege that not many mortals enjoy, and it is no wonder that men and women are earnestly seeking a way by which they can come into communication with their loved ones, even if these are only their loved ones for a short time.

If they only knew what it means to be able to talk to a soulmate, and have that soulmate tell him of her love and the wonders of it all, they would become more anxious than ever, and the faith that they now have would cease to satisfy. But this cannot be so at this time, and it may be well that men and women generally are not fitted for such an experience.

You know how much I love you and what this love means, and that there is no other love in all the spirit world, except the Father's love, that can so satisfy and make happy.

I must stop now, for you have written enough. But do not forget that Baby is anxious to write, and you must give her the opportunity to do so before long. You will soon feel well again and be in condition to perform your work, which to you just now is the important thing. So I will say good night.

Your own true and loving, Helen[81]

A New Year's Eve message from Helen. A time of thankfulness to the Father for His great Love and Mercy

December 31st, 1917

---

[81] This message is a composite of two, being published in Volume I and Volume IV. (G.J.C.)

I am here, your own true and loving Helen.

Well, dear, I see you are not feeling so well tonight and I will write only a short letter.

As Dr. Stone said, the year has nearly gone never to be recalled and the thoughts of the year have found their places in the great eternity, some to have gone forever never to be remembered, and others to live to face you when you come to the spirit world. I am glad to be able to state that the large majority of these thoughts are such that you need not dread to face, for they have been of things that will help you in your progress in the spheres of love, and what I say of you I say of the Dr., for we have been very close to him during the year that is passed. While your account books have something that do not savor of the spiritual and true, and are to be forgotten as soon as possible, yet many of them are those which only the possession of the Father's Love could have engendered and which will meet you with influences of encouragement and give you great satisfaction, and cause you to thank the Father that you were so susceptible to the influence of that Love and to the impressions of the high spirits who have been with you both so much during the year. You have much to congratulate yourselves, for your souls will not show the condition of underdevelopment that they should even a year ago. You may not be able to appreciate the extent of your development or what your real condition of soul is, and I who can see and now desire to tell you that I rejoice with you and am so thankful to the Father for His mercy and Love which have been so bountifully bestowed upon you.

Not only do I myself rejoice in this fact, but many bright spirits who love you both so much are praising God for His great goodness to you. And tonight many are present, but none happier than your soulmates who, of course, have a love for you that the others cannot have. So notwithstanding the material troubles and worries that you may have had during the year, you have so much to be thankful for, yes, so much more than you realize.

And when you consider from a moment the great number of Celestial Spirits and with them the Master who have been such constant companions all through the year, loving you and trying to help and comfort you, you must see that you have been wonderfully blessed. Scarcely any human being has had such companionship as have you two, and none consciously, for to no man or woman on earth have these messages of love and truth been conveyed as they have to you.

I know that while these high spirits have been in close companionship with other mortals whose souls have received the Father's Love and trying to help them with their presence, yet not one has received to his sensory consciousness the realization of the presence of such spirits, and no word of their great love and solicitude have come to any mortals other than to you, Dr. Stone and Eugene.[82]

When you come to think of this, you must see how great has been the privilege and how with that privilege has come a responsibility that calls for your greatest concern and desire to do the work. Let me advise you three to think of this great fact.

Well, I must not write more, but Mary Kennedy says to tell Dr. Stone that she loves him more than ever before and that her love and happiness in knowing that he is her true soulmate is greater as the year goes out. She wishes him a Happy New Year and knows that it will bring to both of them a closer companionship and a greater happiness than ever, and also a greater and more wonderful development of his soul in love and a consequent greater nearness of the soulmate love.

All your friends send their love and wishes for a Happy New Year, one that shall be filled with an increased possession of the Father's Love and a clearer understanding of His truths and the work that is before you.

May the Father Bless you both is the prayer of
Your own true loving
Helen

Relates how Washington helped him to a knowledge of the Father's Love and his resultant changed attitude towards the Germans

April 23rd, 1916

I am here, Lafayette—I have been anxious for some time to write you again and let you know the results of your advice to me when last I wrote. After our last communication, I sought General Washington and told him of my conversation with you and asked him to explain what this Divine Love meant and how it could be obtained.

He was so pleased at my inquiry that he actually took me in his arms and called me his boy as he had on earth and with his face beaming with love and happiness he told me what this Love meant and what it had done for him, and what happiness it had brought him and how he was now progressing towards the Celestial Heavens of light and truth.

Well, I commenced to consider what he had told me and to have a longing in my soul for that Love and the happiness which he said it would bring me, and I commenced to pray for the Love and tried to have faith. Well, without taking up your time by rehearsing the steps of my progress, I am glad to tell you that I have this Love to some extent and that I am now an inhabitant of the third sphere and enjoying the

---

[82] Eugene Morgan, associate of Dr. Stone and Mr. Padgett. (Dr. S.)

associations of spirits who also have this Love and are striving to progress.

My happiness is very different from what it was before this Love came to me and I realize that the soul and not the mind is the man, especially of God's redeemed children. I never thought that the soul was capable of such Love and happiness and of the knowledge that the Divine Love is the one absolutely necessary thing to bring spirits into unison with the Father.

I want to express my gratitude to you and to say that I will never forget your kindness and love in turning my thoughts to this great truth.

Yes, I am still interested in the war, but now I do not have any hatred for the Germans that I had before. I see that they are all brothers, and children of the Father, and that only the ambitions of some and the passions and hatred of others are prolonging the war. But it will soon close for I see before me the collapse of the German campaign against Verdun and then the end will come rapidly.

I wish it were tomorrow, for then the slaughter and death and added misery would cease. There are so many spirits coming from these battlefields who are all unfit for the spirit life and appear in great confusion, and when they realize they are no longer mortals they become bewildered and miserable. But we are trying to help them. We know no enemies and all are helped alike. I will not write more tonight and in closing give you my love and sign myself with a new name, which is,

Your brother in Christ,
Lafayette

The publisher's father states he is making earnest efforts to reach his wife's home and be with her through prayer to the Father for His Love

November 23rd, 1915.

I am here, your loving father.

I am the father of that boy, and I want to say to him that I am happy too, as well as his mother but not as happy as she is. I am not in her high sphere, but I am striving to get there and enjoy her home. Leslie, my son, I am also happy that you are trying to follow the steps of the Master and in your love for the Father, and in your soul aspirations.

Believe in this truth, and you will not be disappointed, and when the great day of reunion comes you will find more love waiting for you than you ever thought possible for a spirit to receive. So trust in God and follow the teachings of the Master, I know the importance of this, as one who was ignorant when on earth and now have learned only since coming into the spirit world.

God Bless that dear Mother of yours! If it had not been for her teachings after she came into the spirit world, I probably would be an easy going spirit, as I was a man, enjoying the happiness which my good nature and love of things generally gave me. But when your mother came over, and I saw that she had a Love which I had not, and which I must get in order to be with her, and when she told me how much she loved me, I sought for the same kind of Love which she had. And with her help and the help of the Father's Holy Spirit, I obtained this Love and am now very happy, for it is this love which alone may make it possible for me to be with her where she is. But I am not yet with her, as her soul condition is above mine for me to be able to share her home. She is so beautiful and good that I am not satisfied to live away from her and I am trying with all my soul's desire to be together with her, through prayer to the Father for this Divine Love, the one possession that can make me worthy of her.

So Leslie believe what we say to you and trust in God and you will be happy.

Your loving father,
William Stone[83]

The Master declares that he has selected Dr. Stone to do a work for the Kingdom, just as he selected Mr. Padgett. This work will be a labor of love, requiring much physical as well as spiritual exertion

December 15th, 1915

I am here, Jesus:

I have heard what you have said to your friend, Dr. Stone, and I must say that while you have some appreciation of the Great Love that came to you last night, yet you cannot fully understand, for no mortal can, although you did experience a wonderful feeling of its inflowing. But let me emphasize that if you continue to have the great longings and desires that you had last night, the Father's Love will come to you in increased abundance.

And I want further to say that the same Love that you received is waiting for Dr. Stone and will be his if he will only let his longings go out to the Father with all his soul's earnestness. While I have selected you to perform the great task of receiving my truths and spreading them to all mankind, I have also selected Dr. Stone to do a work which will be of great importance and will involve a labor of love on his part, and much physical as well as spiritual exertion. He must not only believe in me and

---

[83] This message is a composite of two, being published in Volume I and Volume IV. (G.J.C.)

trust in the Father, but let all his longings and prayers and desires go to obtain the great Love, and it will be his.

I am glad that you two men have come so closely together in your beliefs and in your faith in the Divine Love; and I will further tell you that you will both receive a happiness that can never be taken from you, even while you are on earth, and when you come to the spirit world this happiness will be increased beyond all human conception. I am also glad that you can exchange thoughts on these important subjects of my religious teachings, and feel that you both have a work to do, and, above all, am happy that you are willing and anxious to do it.

I am with you in all my love, and will make both of you the special objects of my care and keeping—and in the great hereafter when you shall end your work on earth, you will both receive a reward that angels would wish for and wonder that you two could receive it. So I will give you both my love tonight, and will also pray to the Father to bestow upon you His Great Love and blessings. So believe with all your hearts and His Love and blessings will be poured out upon you.

Your friend and brother,
Jesus

The publisher's mother is grateful that he has some of the Father's Love and wishes her other children would also seek His Love

May 13th, 1917

I am here, Priscilla Stone:

I want to say just one word before you stop writing, for I have been present all evening and have heard your conversation, and have seen the condition of the souls of both yourself and my dear boy, and to tell you that I am happy because of this hardly expresses my feelings. I am so thankful to the Father that He has in His great Love and mercy enabled my son to know and experience the presence of this great redeeming Love. When I think of the great number of human beings nearly all whom have no true knowledge of this Love and the Way to the great Celestial Kingdom of God where there is so much happiness and the assurance of Immortality, I am almost overcome and wonder that such a privilege should be bestowed on my son, who of course is no more deserving of this blessing than are thousands of others of mankind. God is good and I am so very thankful.

Tell my boy to remember what James the Apostle wrote him, and to believe and trust in what he said, as to what reward shall be his when he comes to the spirit world and realize the results of his efforts to help both mortals and spirits.

If my other children would only listen to him and turn their thoughts to these spiritual things, and to seek this Divine Love, I would be so happy that I would exclaim with David when he wrote in the 23d Psalm *"my cup of joy runneth over."* And I am praying and hoping that some little truth will find lodgment in their souls and germinate until at last they shall find the pearl of great price from the Father.

Tell my boy to believe that his mother loves him so much and is with him so very often and that she is now trying to unfold her love to him and convey her thanks to the Father of All.

His father is here too and sends his love and blessings and says that his son must pray and believe and work, for in these three things will be found a power that will overcome all obstacles and bring to him that Love and peace that only the redeemed children of the Father can possibly possess or understand.

I will not write more now and thank you for the privilege. God bless my boy and keep him in the way of Love that leads to the Celestial Heaven. And so I will say, good night. His mother—he knows that I am his mother without signing my name.

The skeptical writer of colonial days, called by contemporaries an infidel, admits he was mistaken in some of his beliefs

June 20th, 1915

I am here, Thomas Paine.

When I died, I did not believe in Jesus as the son of God or as his messenger sent to show the world that the Father had bestowed upon it His Divine Love and Immortality and the Way to obtain it. But now I believe to the fullest these truths and am a follower of Jesus and the possessor of the Divine Love.

How different would my condition now be if that erroneous and damning doctrine taught by the churches—that there is no redemption beyond the grave—were true. I never thought that there was any necessity for redemption either while on earth or after I should become a spirit, but thought that if there was a God, He would deal justly with me and bestow upon me happiness and enjoyment of the future life according to my idea of His love and mercy.

But I must tell you that I was mistaken in some particulars. God is Love and He is merciful, but His love and mercy are exercised only in accordance with His fixed and unchangeable laws—laws that apply impartially to all men, and which in their operation make no exceptions. What a man sows so shall he reap is as true as that the sun shines for you on earth.

I found the truth of this great law in my own experience and I paid the penalties of my sins. Jesus could not do this for me and he never pretended that he could. But he could and does show the Way by which the operations of the laws which produce these penalties may be superseded by the operation of other laws which, as it were, removes the penalties from the individual spirit. This does not change the law but changes the condition of the spirit which invokes these penalties; and if men would only learn this Way, they would not remain in darkness and sin, because they believe and assert that God's laws never change. If they would only understand that while the laws do not change, yet the condition of the spirit which calls for the operation of these laws does change, and new laws are brought into operation.

I have not time tonight to more fully explain these principles, but should I in the future have the opportunity, I will be glad to do so. Christ was and is the Way and the Truth and the Life.

I am in the first Celestial sphere and my name was Thomas Paine, the so called infidel. I believed in God, but only one God. Jesus was never God to me and is not now. And he does not claim to be God now. So you see even the so called infidel could come into the Truth and Love of the Father, even after he left the material plane and became an inhabitant of the spirit world.

So, my dear brother, I will say good night and God be with you,
Thomas Paine[84]

Kate Stone: Dr. Stone's sister tells him what her work is in spirit world, and informs him that his efforts to help the spirits turn to the Father for His Love are having positive results

June 19th, 1917

I am here, Kate Stone:

Tell my brother that what he heard a few nights ago in reference to me is true, and that I am engaged with my whole heart and soul in the work of helping the dark and suffering spirits, and when I succeed in turning some towards the light and the Father's Love, there comes to me a happiness I cannot describe. The fact of being an instrument in the redemption of one lost soul affords greater happiness than any mortal can dream of, and when I tell my brother that I have succeeded in showing the way to many of these spirits, he may perhaps, in a small way, realize what my happiness is.

To me the work is one of the greatest that we spirits can possibly

---

[84] This message is a composite of two, being published in Volume I and Volume III. (G.J.C.)

engage in, and I never get tired or disheartened, and even though sometimes I fail to convince a spirit as to the way to light and relief from his suffering, yet I never feel disappointed, for I know that sometime sooner or later that spirit will perceive the meaning of my words and they will have their effect.

But not only can I see the results of my own work, but also that of you three mortals, for you all help these dark spirits by your talks with them; and my brother must not think that just because he cannot write and thus be certain that the spirits are listening to him, that he cannot perform this task, for I must tell him that he does. When he talks to them, they give him their attention and believe him, and many take his advice and seek the Father's Love through the only way it can be obtained, through earnest prayer. He will know some day what the results of his efforts are, and when he does, he will thank the Father that he was given this gift. Tell him to continue, and even though he cannot hear their response, I will come at times to inform him of results: a soul in darkness and torment rescued by a mortal who knows the truth. A crown of one star representing salvation of a soul is a glorious possession, but a crown of many stars bestowed for the saving of many souls is a treasure beyond description. This crown will be his, but while it will not be one to be worn, yet it will be a crown set in the joyous countenances of spirits relieved of their sufferings and radiant in the glory of the Father's Love.

I will stop now, as Helen says you are tired and must not write more tonight. With my love, I will say good night to you and Leslie.

Your sister in Christ,
Kate

Made in the USA
Middletown, DE
17 August 2022

71595230R00246